Tourism Enterprise

Developments, Management and Sustainability

———————————

Tourism Enterprise

Developments, Management and Sustainability

David Leslie

www.cabi.org

CABI is a trading name of CAB International

CABI	CABI
Nosworthy Way	38 Chauncy Street
Wallingford	Suite 1002
Oxfordshire OX10 8DE	Boston, MA 02111
UK	USA
Tel: +44 (0)1491 832111	T: +1 800 552 3083 (toll free)
Fax: +44 (0)1491 833508	T: +1 617 395 4051
E-mail: info@cabi.org	E-mail: cabi-nao@cabi.org
Website: www.cabi.org	

A catalogue record for this book is available from the British Library, London, UK.

Library of Congress Cataloging-in-Publication Data

Leslie, David, 1951-
  Tourism enterprise : developments, management and sustainability / David Leslie.
     p. cm.
  Includes bibliographical references and index.
  ISBN 978-1-78064-356-4 (alk. paper)
  1. Tourism--Environmental aspects. 2. Environmental management. 3. Green movement. 4. Sustainable development. I. Title.

  G156.5.E58L47 2014
  910.68--dc23

2014006672

ISBN-13: 978 1 78064 356 4

Commissioning editor: Claire Parfitt
Editorial assistant: Alexandra Lainsbury
Production editor: Laura Tsitlidze

Typeset by Columns Design XML Ltd, Reading, UK.
Printed and bound in the UK by CPI Group (UK) Ltd, Croydon, CR0 4YY.

Contents

Acknowledgements

Any undertaking always involves the support of other people. In this instance given the timeframe of the research involved such support extends back into the early 1990s through to the present time. Throughout this period many persons in their different ways have contributed to the research that forms the basis of this book for which I am indeed grateful.

I would also like to thank those persons who have helped in the development of the book from the outset commencing with the team at CABI particularly Alex Lainsbury and Claire Parfitt, the reviewers for their insightful comments, and the production team. Most especially I would like to thank Patrick 'Paddy' Boyle, Carol Leslie, Russell Ecob, Jakki Holland and Debbie Hinds.

As has been the case in the past and similarly throughout this undertaking, there has been the ever present Susan, putting up with my distractions and pre-occupation, and without whose help this book would not have come to fruition.

David Leslie
Glasgow

1 Introduction

The emergent green agenda of the 1960s and its gradual morphological shift in the 1980s and early 1990s to sustainable development, now more generally termed sustainability, appears to have subtly changed in the 2000s to climate change. This shift in emphasis on the part of post-industrial nations to the more politically acceptable climate change (Leslie, 2009) has led to a loss of focus on the aims of sustainable development, i.e.

- to protect and improve the environment;
- to ensure economic security for everyone; and
- to create a more equitable and fairer society (Church and McHarry, 1999, p. 2).

Evidently far more attention is paid to greenhouse gases (GHG) with an accent on carbon emissions and carbon footprinting. This environmental agenda hardly needs rehearsing here given the breadth of discourse on such matters over the last 25 years, which has raised more questions than answers (see Ekins, 1986; WCED, 1987; Pearce, 1993; Jacobs, 1996; Johnson and Turner, 2003; Blowers and Hinchliffe, 2003; Connelly and Smith, 2003). As environmental concerns expanded then so pressure mounted

on industry to address the actual and potential contribution of their operations in contributing to environmental degradation and develop systems to assess the environmental performance of individual operations – enterprises (Welford and Starkey, 1996, p. xi).

Tourism has certainly not escaped such attention, particularly in the 1990s, leading to a plethora of conferences, myriad books and articles over the years (see Romeril and Hughes-Evans, 1979; Krippendorf, 1987; Harrison, 1992; Jenner and Smith, 1992; Smith and Eadington, 1992; Cater and Lowman, 1994; Hunter and Green, 1995; McCool and Moisey, 2001). Such an outcome was supported and furthered by the development of tourism as a field of study in its own right within academia since the 1980s. This largely coincided with the recognition of tourism as a tool for regional development in response to the decline of rural areas due to changing agricultural practices (Champion and Watkins, 1991) or the socio-economic problems arising from the decline of traditional industrial and manufacturing bases in urban areas, e.g. Glasgow (Leslie, 2001a). In many instances tourism was promoted and often grant funded by the government and notably so by the EU (Leslie et al., 1989; Leslie, 2011).

Sustainability, succinctly described as striving for social, environmental, economic and ethical responsibility (see Hall and Gossling, 2009), not surprisingly gained attention, albeit limited when considered in the overall context of such output. However, a key theme within such work was, and continues to be, that the development and impacts of tourism should not be detrimental to the physical environment and should be beneficial to the destination locality and communities involved. An agenda for tourism that first gained prominence in the 1980s; as Krippendorf (1987) argued, tourism enterprises should be more responsible – environmentally and also socially. A period during which we saw the rise of alternative tourism as tourism development and enterprises were slowly coming under more scrutiny. Furthermore that:

> ... the industry and tourists individually are being expected and required to shoulder more responsibility for the effects of travel and behaviour on host environments, both physical and human (Butler, 1995, p. 5).

This is well illustrated in the outcomes of the UK's Tourism and Environment Task Force – set-up post the Brundtland Report, the renowned outcome of the United Nations Environment Programme's (UNEP) Stockholm Congress of 1987. The report listed four key areas:

- tourism business to develop ways to support rather than detract from the quality of the environment;
- promote respect of the environment;
- ensure staff are trained to consider the environment; and
- promote environmentally positive tourism.

The quintessential point to be made here is that much that can be done in response to the issues of sustainability, that is by way of reducing consumption of non-renewable resources, reducing greenhouse gas (GHG) emissions, and promoting positive economic and social impacts has been advocated for over 20 years (as previously noted) and, though to a much lesser extent, with specific examples of practices that tourism businesses can adopt (for example, see Middleton and Hawkins, 1993, 1994), the most substantive without doubt is InterContinental Hotel's promotion of their environmental management system which subsequently became the International Hotels Environment Initiative (see Black, 1995). However, the wider dissemination of such advocacy by and large has been within the context of the greening of tourism policy (see Leslie, 2001a, 2002a) and conferences designed with the objective of promoting such policy, related initiatives and best practices, and within academia (for example, through

learned journals and books). This largely escapes the attention and/or interest of most practitioners. That is 'most' in terms of the vast majority of owners/managers involved directly in the supply of tourism provision. Obviously there are exceptions but mainly such exceptions are leading representatives of national and multi-national enterprises, leading stakeholders and players in the tourism sector such as hotel chains, airlines and major tour operators.

These leading players established the World Travel & Tourism Council (WTTC) in the early 1990s to represent their interests on the international stage, especially in the wake of the United Nations 'Earth Summit' in Rio de Janiero, 1992. As they have since argued, there is a:

> ... need, now more than ever, for travel and tourism to be recognised as a vital part of the global economy, a view that has yet to be fully acknowledged by governments. (WTTC et al., 2002, p. 7)

and to reinforce their own role and vested interests went on to say that:

> The inevitable transition to sustainable development gives the travel and tourism industry an opportunity to confirm itself as a solution, rather than a contributor to the economical, social and environmental challenges facing the future. (WTTC et al., 2002, p. 7)

Whilst many analysts would not support such high sentiments, there is some truth in such claims given that there is much tourism enterprises can do to reduce their environmental impacts. To some extent, and in its favour, the WTTC has been at the forefront of promoting 'Sustainable Tourism' and environmental management initiatives and practices; well illustrated by its 'Local Agenda 21 for the Travel & Tourism Industry' (WTTC et al., 1996). Professional associations in the sector have also advocated environmental management (EM) practices (see Bricker, 2009); for example, the HCIMA (now Institute of Hospitality (IH)) in 'Hospitality', the members' journal (see Leslie, 2001b). Without the specific context of the latter, much of what is written focuses on developing countries and involves, by way of illustration, national and international companies; yet whilst these enterprises predominate in financial terms and influence at international and national levels they are hardly representative of tourism supply in terms of the number of enterprises involved.

Overall, the recognition (albeit in hindsight) of first the negative impacts of tourism, attributed predominantly to mass tourism and second, the promotion of the greening of tourism which involves:

> ... much greater awareness of the interconnectedness of the economic, the physical and social dimensions of the environment rather than just the physical or natural e.g. pollution and damage. (Leslie, 2005, p. 251)

As Millman (1989) argued in the late 1980s, travel organizations should develop more 'sensitive forms of tourism' which rather catalysed the categorisation of different manifestations of tourism consumption e.g. sustainable-, alternative-, green-, eco-, nature- (see Leslie, 2012a). The problem with this development is as Jay Appleton (1991) wryly put it:

> Once we begin to categorise, we begin to moralize also, and before we know where we are we have set up a highly inflexible binary system of good and evil, right and wrong. There are no grey areas where there are green enthusiasts. (cited in Glyptis, 1995, p. 195)

In this instance it appears that 'mass' tourism was/is the 'evil' and the alternative categories the 'good'. But this is misleading in that the ills attributed to tourism are not necessarily confined to or absent from these other forms of tourism consumption. Certainly they will vary according to the type of touristic activity and destination environment. More importantly given the context here of tourism enterprises and sustainability they have responsibility irrespective of the type and scale of tourism development for their own operations. The interpretation therefore that these other forms of tourism, i.e. not considered mass, are more aligned with the concepts and more so the practices promoted under the umbrella of sustainability is very much open to question. Especially when one considers that those tourism enterprises involved in what are considered to be mass tourism destinations are potentially better placed to respond to the imperatives of 'greening tourism' supply due to the presence of the very infrastructure essential to facilitate their adoption in the first instance. But whether in the popular 'sand, sun and sea' destinations of the world or on eco-trips in Kenya, these enterprises still consume resources, and generate waste and pollution, which is rather contrary to the view of times past that tourism is a 'smokeless' sector.

Attention to environmental pollution has been generally limited to enterprises in traditional industries, e.g. oil and chemical sectors, coal and steel. Yet, small and medium size enterprises (SMEs) invariably dominate numerically in terms of the number of firms operating in most sectors. Thus, whilst their impacts on the environment expressed in terms of consumption per unit may be negligible compared with national and international business operations in such sectors, cumulatively they might be considered the biggest consumer and thus the biggest polluter! As Hillary (2000) argued, SMEs account for around 70% of all pollution. The tourism sector is no different. Through the processes involved in the provision of products and services, which are largely fossil fuel dependent (Kelly et al., 2007; Mintel, 2007), tourism enterprises generate pollution and waste thereby placing additional burdens on the locality, the infrastructure and wider environment to handle these by-products. Of further significance is that these SMEs have gained little attention in research; be it past or present (see Leslie, 1995; Geiser and Crul, 1996; Buckley, 2007; Blanco et al., 2009; Thomas et al., 2011). An explanation for this is that small enterprises (which predominate in tourism and hospitality) hardly meet the standard models of business promulgated in business schools and the ways of managing a business be that in finance and accounting, marketing or, perhaps most notably in what is inappropriately termed 'Human Resource Management' in the business schools of so many universities. Compensating for this in many ways has been the rise in attention, especially over the last decade, to entrepreneurship. The latter is of particular significance given the EU's initiative 'responsible entrepreneurship' (essentially Corporate Social Responsibility), which is seen as a way towards balancing the three pillars of sustainability which itself is considered by the EU to be a societal responsibility (EC, 2002). A further factor in the lack of attention to SMEs in tourism, especially in the UK, originally bespoke hospitality and tourism management degree programmes are now located in various guises of what in effect are general business management programmes. A shift away from vocational and operational knowledge and skills, especially in hospitality, is very much a function of 'academic drift' (Leslie, 1990) and maintaining student enrolments. A significant outcome of this is the lack of research into SMEs generally both past (Geiser and Crul, 1996) and present, especially in the context of the greening of small/micro tourism enterprises. In this context, 'greening' may well be interpreted as meaning at least 'good environmental housekeeping, reducing energy consumption, saving water and minimising waste' (Porritt, 1997, p. 32).

It is widely recognized that tourism supply overall comprises predominantly micro-businesses (defined as businesses employing ten or fewer persons), a low proportion of small enterprises (less than 50 employees) and, in comparative terms based on actual number of businesses, few enterprises which employ more than 50 persons. To illustrate, in the EU wherein tourism is considered to be the third largest economic sector, it is estimated to account for 40% of all international arrivals and has a total estimated tourism income of Ç266 billion approximately three quarters of which is attributed to EU residents (EC, 2010). Figures for the tourism enterprises in the EU show that there are 1.8m businesses employing a total of 9.7m people, which equates to 5.2% of the workforce. It is estimated to account for 5% GDP, which if linkages are included, rises to 10% of GDP and 12% of total employment. Over 90% of these enterprises, it is predominantly hotels and restaurants that are SME in size of which some 90% are micro-enterprises. Collectively, these tourism enterprises represent some 70–80% of the total number of SMEs in Europe and approximately 6.5% of attributed turnover (Leidner, 2004). Further, they have been considered to account

for 99% of European tourism supply (Vernon et al., 2003). These tourism enterprises are now very much a focus within the more general area of the Enterprise Directorate. Thus, they are subject to the influence of EU policy instruments promoting the greening of enterprise. Witness the 6th European Action Plan that called specifically for enterprises to 'go green' by way of becoming more efficient in the use of resources and reducing waste (EC, 2001), as well as those instruments aimed at the promotion and development of SMEs (Leslie, 2011, p. 45). This is further affirmed through their argument for '... increased energy efficiency, partly through the implement-ation of environmental management systems in SMEs.' (EC, 2008, p. 16). Interestingly, this greening has also been considered beneficial not only because of reducing GHG emissions but in generating jobs (Pratt, 2011). Furthermore, as Middleton argued:

> At their best micro-businesses deliver most of what is special and appealing about destinations – vibrancy, personality, product quality and leading edge excellence – at their worst they represent most of what is worst in modern tourism, dragging down the destination image (2000, p. 1).

They are a vital part of rural localities and in many instances to the national economy. Undoubtedly they are important at the destination level but also when considered more widely, be that at regional, national or international level, their significance becomes all the more important; witness the oft-cited claim that tourism is the biggest global industry! Individually these tourism SMEs may have little impact, but aggregated their energy consumption and waste becomes substantial and thus tourism per se is a major polluter, and largely unregulated (Leslie, 2007b). It is not difficult to concur with Blair and Hitchcock (2001) that in comparison with most other sectors of consumer services tourism overall has the most substantial negative impacts. Such argument also brings into contention the impacts of these enterprises in terms of their use and consumption of resources, and wider issues of sustainability. It has been argued that their: 'actions impact daily upon sustainability issues' (Becker et al., 1999, p. 1, cited in

Leslie, 2007b, p. 93). As the OECD (2009) argued, it is the responsibility of the tourism business to ensure that the products offered have as little impact on the environment as possible. Furthermore, it has been argued that:

> Conventional wisdom has it that small local business will have the greatest regard for the community environment but there is scant evidence to justify that. The opposite seems probable (EIU, 1993, p. 96).

It is a view which serves to reinforce the social dimension of sustainability and one which begs the question of whether such a critique is borne out by research into tourism SMEs. Essentially, tourism enterprises need to operate within the natural capacity of the destination. In other words there should be no diminution of the natural capital. The maintenance of this natural capital is not just a localized matter but global, for increasingly what happens 'there' affects 'here', and vice-versa, in what is now an increasingly globalized market. Addressing the overall impact of tourism therefore is more complex than, for example, simply considering the physical impact on the environment of a new hotel. At the same time they generate employment opportunities (Zientara, 2012), opportunities for entrepreneurs (Badulescu and Badulescu, 2012) and sociocultural benefits for many people within the host community (Scheyvens, 2002; Timothy, 2012) and support environmental initiatives (Leslie, 2009; Spenceley and Rylance, 2012). However, it also needs to be recognized that the potential pluses that can arise from tourism development and thus tourism enterprise are largely influenced by context and setting (for example, see Pleumarom, 2009, 2012).

What attention tourism enterprises have gained in the context of being 'responsible', thus to their environmental management systems (EMS), environmental performance (EP) and corporate social responsibility (CSR) in research papers, on close analysis often finds that they are based on national and/or multi-national corporations (N/MNCs), thus comparatively large hotels in the 3- to 5-star category. Rarely does such research evidence continuity over time by either the researchers involved and/or as regards the geographic area (for example, USA – Mensah 2004;

Scanlon, 2007; Vietnam – Trung and Kumar, 2005; Sweden and Poland – Bohdanowicz, 2006; Spain – Rodriguez and Cruz, 2007; China/Hong Kong – Chan et al., 2005; Turkey – Erdogan and Baris, 2006. Alternatively, when such research does involve SMEs the attention given to the greening of small tourism enterprises is limited (for example, see Robinson et al., 2000; Hall et al., 2005; Thomas and Augustyn, 2007; Blanco et al., 2009; Hall and Gossling, 2009). Overall, this limited attention in research and its contribution therefore to educational programmes may go some way to explain the lack of attention within tourism studies to SMEs and vice versa. Yet it has been well argued that education is the key to making real progress in addressing sustainability issues. Irrespective of this, examples of best practice, albeit invariably of national/international companies in the tourism sector are not hard to find but these tend to be in specific publications such as the 'Green Hotelier', though far wider in scope the United Nations Environmental Programme's (UNEP) publication 'Our Planet', and the Forum for the Future's 'Green Futures' or more localized, for example the publications of ATLAS and with emphasis on SMEs and culture, Tourism Concern's publication 'In Focus'. Thus the substantive contributions of Hall et al (2005), Herremans (2006), Thomas and Augustyn (2007), Buckley (2009) and with a specific focus on SMEs and greening Leslie (2009, 2012b) are all the more valuable. In effect, there is a lack of research into SMEs per se, and even less into the EP, EM and CSR related practices of SMEs in tourism. Witness Carter et al.'s (2004) study, which drew extensively on articles from the 1990s, into the EP of accommodation in Australia, few of which were actually based on empirical research; a situation which has hardly changed since (see Tzschentke et al., 2008; Hall and Gossling, 2009; Chan and Hawkins, 2010; Garay and Font, 2012). As Shaw and Williams (2010, p. 86) so cogently expressed it: 'despite considerable interest in issues of sustainable tourism there is limited information on the environmental practices of SMEs'. To which one may add, a lack of research into tourism SMEs more generally. It is undoubtedly recognition of such critique that lies at the heart of this text which is founded on extensive empirical research. This was initiated in the early 1990s, and although primarily focused on environmental performance, it provides substantive insights into the management and operational practices of these enterprises more generally.

Empirical Foundations

The paucity of research into SMEs in tourism, most especially in terms of their environment performance and related actions, became very much apparent from the tourism literature and at many a conference on tourism or involving sessions on tourism in the 1990s. An outcome which was all the more manifest whilst undertaking the requisite secondary research into the greening of tourism enterprises in preparation for a major study into the greening of tourism enterprises in the Lake District National Park (LDNP) in Cumbria (Leslie, 2001b), an area acclaimed for its physical attractiveness, a powerful constant of demand for tourists, and considered in the top 50 of worldwide destinations. The National Park itself is in the county of Cumbria, a rural area in north-west England, home to approximately 10% of Cumbria's population. Tourism is the major economic activity in the area and is estimated to support approximately 50% of employment (Leslie, 2005). Factor in the commitment of the Cumbria Tourist Board (CTB) to promoting the greening of tourism then the LDNP was a particularly appropriate area to investigate the environmental perform-ance of tourism enterprises especially given that it has been nationally recognized for promoting 'sustainable tourism' and its inter-national renown. Thus, the extent to which policies advocating 'the greening of tourism' and related initiatives have been realized was encompassed in the aims, i.e. to identify and evaluate the level of awareness, attitudes and perceptions of green issues, and associated practices, of owners/managers of tourism enterprises. In the process, to establish those factors influential to the adoption of such practices. In other words, their overall environ-mental performance thus EM practices and CSR activities.

Methodology

The extensive methodology formulated was designed primarily to investigate serviced accommodation (Leslie, 2001b). This, the initial and most substantive stage, was then expanded to encompass other categories of tourism enterprise, namely inns, restaurants, caravan and camping sites, attractions and given their increasing presence in tourism supply, self-catering operations were also brought into consideration. The latter have almost totally been ignored in myriad policies and initiatives aimed at promoting the 'greening' of tourism. This is perhaps sur-prising given the substantial growth in supply since the 1980s and today is substantially understated (Leslie, 2007a). Given that enterprises in the LDNP might be subject to factors particular to being in the Park, e.g. National Park Authority's regulations on planning and development, a sample of similar enterprises (serviced-accommodation, inns and attractions – 47 in total) located outside of the LDNP but within Cumbria was also researched by way of establishing a com-parative sample (the Fringe study). A key theme of CSR and thus in the research was the question of support for local produce and products. To further this area of enquiry, a sample of local food producers and cafes, were approached who, with very few exceptions, were very willing to participate and were particularly helpful in responding to the enquiries. A number of 'arts & crafts' producers and retail outlets were also investigated given their presence and visitor spending patterns.

The expansive set of indicators established for the study were derived specifically for hotels in the first instance in order to ensure comprehensive and detailed coverage of all aspects of an hotel's operations pertinent to its environmental performance. As such, it was recognized that the scope enquiry could be adjusted as necessary for any other category of tourism supply (excluding tour operators and travel agents) operating in a destination. These indicators were established through a diverse range of sources and set out in the following categories: business profile of the enterprise; staffing (including where from), training and development, recruitment, involvement in greening; perceptions and attitudes of the owners/managers; resource management and operations; purchasing, suppliers, local produce; guests and communications; factors discouraging progress and in the case of the audits profiles of the owner or manager of the enterprise. This was then translated first to formulate a broad, investigative general questionnaire designed for postal distribution, and then into a far more extensive and detailed format to serve as the basis for extended, personal interviews (akin to household surveys) involving a subset of those surveyed through the initial questionnaire.

The choice of indicators used has since been reflected in other studies (for example, Ceron and Dubois, 2003; Carter *et al.*, 2004; Mensah, 2009; Kucerova, 2012). Thus the appropriateness and quality of these indicators in terms of 'fit for purpose' is rather affirmed, which is especially important given that these same indicators were used in later research. This is not to suggest they are perfect but rather well-suited to the task, as Blackstock *et al.* (2008) noted, indicators tend to address what is desired. It is recognized that this is very much subject to the vested interests of the researcher or commissioning agent, which throughout this study was of no influential significance. Care was also exercised in communications throughout to avoid the terms 'sustainable development' and 'sustainability' as potentially this would lead to some degree of confusion over how such terms were interpreted by those involved in the study and, for example, create variability within the data itself. This was also why a focus group drawing on representatives of the sector was not initiated to establish the necessary criteria as potentially this would have also led to little more than fairly standard gross tourism data; as McCool *et al.* (2001) found in their study. The key point is the need to recognize and understand that in any one group of stakeholders there will be a mix of under-standing of the agenda and to echo Blackstock *et al.*, what is desired.

To potentially obtain a substantial sample of serviced-accommodation operations, it was decided that first a survey using the general questionnaire would be implemented by mail. By reference to a range of sources such as accommodation guides and promotional literature and business telephone lists a database of 853 serviced accommodation operations was established. The choice of enterprises was not based on any prior criteria other than the availability of accommodation. After the initial pilot stage and refinement of the questionnaire, the survey was then implemented by mail to all the listed enterprises along with a covering letter and to enhance the return rate, the offer of being entered into a free prize draw. On the basis that the study was about greening, thus in keeping with this theme, suitable paper and envelopes were reused as and when appropriate, throughout the research. This questionnaire was then tailored to meet the different and specific aspects of each of the other categories of tourism enterprise (349 in total) and implemented using the same process as for serviced accommodation. The survey into the self-catering operations (120) required the development of a different questionnaire. This process was then repeated for serviced accommodation, inns and attractions in the 'fringe area' (total 320), overall gaining a response of 336 from the LDNP and 47 for the fringe area. As previously noted, food producers and arts and/or craft producers were also surveyed, again using a similar method, though with a specifically designed questionnaire for the locally based food producers and also for the craft person's elements of the study. Additional research into arts and crafts involving direct personal inter-views of the managers/owners of retail outlets (42 outlets) to investigate the range of arts and craft products sold and their views on stocking local products was undertaken.

The initial survey into the environmental performance of serviced accommodation included an invitation to take part in more detailed investigations to explore in depth the approach and practices of owners/managers of these tourism enterprises, which gained 52 positive responses. These took the form of personal interviews, in effect extended environmental audits (the forms for these interviews consisting of 24 pages). Further enquiries involving additional research were also undertaken during the extensive field work to investigate matters arising from the surveys and the interviews. Following on from this

study, research into the environmental performance of enterprises in rural Scotland was
undertaken utilizing the same methodology,
with minor adjustments of the survey vehicle to
allow for geographic variances, but with no
follow-up interviews. A database of 1000
enterprises was established and questionnaires
specific to the category of enterprises were
then mailed gaining a response of 363; similar
in make up to that of the LDNP study. The
category with the lowest response rate was
that of the larger hotels, which might be
indicative that hotel managers were less
interested in the study. The location of these
enterprises in Scotland has added value given
the Scottish Government's proclaimed policies
on seeking to be *the* ecotourism destination
within the EU (Leslie, 2010) and more widely
their proclaimed objective of being the leader
in the field of green initiatives, promoting the
sustainability of the landscape and biodiversity
(Leslie, 2013). Scotland is also where the
Green Tourism Business Scheme (GTBS) was
launched in the late 1990s and since promoted
throughout the UK and potentially in other
European countries (Leslie, 2011).

The lack of resources to undertake the
audit interviews was disappointing. However
an opportunity did arise a little later and thus a
third stage to the overall study was initiated.
This third stage involved a majority of urban
enterprises and included a number of
comparatively larger enterprises and as per the
LDNP audits only involved serviced accommodation. Following established practice the
preliminary survey was undertaken and then
the owners/managers were invited to participate in the more in-depth audit and personal

interviews stage (78 enterprises). It should be
noted that there is a potentially significant
difference between this sample and that of the
LDNP in that the enterprises were each invited
to participate in the audit stage but they were
also encouraged to do so by asking each one
personally if they would support the project as
this would be beneficial to the student
interviewers as part of their final year studies in
Tourism Management. It is logical therefore
that the urban sample is less subject to the
possibility of bias towards the promotion of
greening than their counterparts in the LDNP
group, who volunteered. The focus in this
stage on urban tourism enterprises is
particularly notable given that they have
received even less attention in terms of their
environmental performance and similarly in
the context of 'sustainable tourism' than their
rural counterparts (Hinch, 1996). Whilst
Hinch's analysis is dated to nearly 20 years
ago, there is little evidence since to change
such perception. But then it is far easier for
policymakers to consider tourism in rural
settings when it comes to advocating greening,
where tourism supply may well dominate whilst
the same cannot be said for urban, especially
city, localities, wherein questions might well be
raised by the owners as to why tourism
enterprises are apparently being singled out to
address their environmental management
practices! In total, this research amounts in
effect to a longitudinal study into the greening
of tourism enterprises that commenced in the
1990s and concluded in terms of empirical
research in 2012. For clarity and reference,
the sample sets for the three stages are
presented in Table 1.1.

Table 1.1. Categorization of survey returns.

Category	LDNP (%)		SCOTLAND (%)	
	2001	2001 Audits	2006	2011 Audits
Serviced accommodation	230	52	224	72
e.g. Hotels including private Hotels; Inns with accommodation; Guests Houses; Bed & Breakfast				
Other sectors	106		139	
e.g. Restaurants; Inns; Attractions; Caravan & Camping Sites				
Total	336	52	363	72

The implementation of predominantly the same methodology, including only slightly modified questionnaires, e.g. VisitScotland or Area Tourist Board instead of Cumbria Tourist Board, means that these four data sets are directly comparable. Various areas encompassed within this research were found to be evident in similar studies and this contributes further to opportunities for comparison and the robustness of the study. Certainly there are some differences between the data sets. The first to note is the different time frames. It is argued this is of little significance between the 2006 set and that of 2001 though during this period utility costs increased, the infrastructure for recycling improved and the period witnessed further attention to promoting EMS practices and, more widely, CSR. These factors are equally pertinent to the 2011 data set. However, a further factor is that the empirical research was undertaken in the wake of the 2007–8 financial/economic crisis. This may well have influenced some of the data, especially any indicators that involved costs and also possibly the attitudes of the owners/managers to such matters. The possibility of such influences is considered, as and where appropriate, in the analysis of the data, which is presented in the following sequence of chapters. Findings from the studies into local food producers and arts and crafts, as and where appropriate, are included in these chapters.

The Findings and Structure

The basis of the second chapter, drawing primarily on the data from the LDNP, is the presentation of the findings on the enterprises themselves, for example, period of operation, length of ownership, turnover and the owners/ managers with attention to their memberships of trade associations, which may or may not be influential to their awareness of and attitudes towards EM practices. Employment, a key element in the rationale for supporting the development of tourism, is given particular attention and includes training and development, recruitment and influences on employment. Overall, the aim is to establish a general profile of the participating enterprises and their owners/managers. Although similar data

were gathered in both stages two and three, it is considered that given the similarities between these data and with consideration of the constraints of space within these pages that the presentation of similar data from 2006 and 2011 would add little value, especially as within Chapter 2 comparisons are drawn across all the categories and, as to be expected, marked differences in the findings according to the data from 2006 and 2011 are highlighted. Chapter 3 addresses the theme of 'Sustainable Supply Chain Management' (SSCM), which encompasses the 'purchasing patterns and practices' area of the surveys of the enterprises. However, SSCM is far wider in scope and application than this and draws attention to EMS and CSR. In tourism, SSCM is arguably most readily recognized and has gained prominence in relation to the tour operating sector. This led to some deliberation as to whether SSCM as a theme for discussion should be included given the comparatively limited data to present that would not fit well in the context of the other themes/chapters, resulting in the decision to include SSCM as a chapter focus given the following factors:

- Tour operators, as a category within tourism supply, were not included in the empirical research consideration of SSCM.
- Tour operators account for approximately 29% of tourist spending within the EU (Leidner, 2004).
- Tour operators are significant players in tourism:

> Although the tourism sector includes many actors, to date tour operators still have significant power in selecting and assembling suppliers in a holiday package, as well in influencing consumers' choices with respect to destinations, accommodations and additional services. (Mosselaer et al., 2012, p. 74).

- Tour operators are being encouraged to adopt EMS and to encourage their suppliers to adopt such practices.

Their inclusion draws attention to issues that do not arise so directly in the other areas and thus contributes to the scope and comprehensiveness of the discussion and overall value.

It is within this context that findings arising from the study into the purchasing practices of the enterprises are presented, though not all the data in this category as some of this fits better within other themes, e.g. Chapter 6. This theme of wider responsibility of enterprises is continued in Chapter 4, which introduces Corporate Social Responsibility (CSR). The primary focus herein is on the enterprises' wider contribution to the local economy and other aspects of CSR such as support for environmental initiatives and community activities. The focus then narrows in the following chapter to concentrate on environmental policy and EM practices. In simple terms this could be considered as what the enterprises are doing to address the three Rs: reduce, reuse and recycle.

Throughout these chapters a recurrent element is that of 'in what ways are tourism enterprises contributing to the local economy and local community?' This is a significant aspect of the social dimension of sustainability. To an extent, this is addressed in Chapter 6 'Local Produce, Local Products' which addresses the promotion of 'local food', 'slow food' and the utilization as well as promotion of local crafts, in encouraging customers to consume local produce and now actively encouraged along with increasing attention to promoting and developing the supply of local products. The findings relating to the promotion of local produce and local products across a range of activities and the interrelationships between the needs of an enterprise and the local community are discussed; in the process bringing into contention the environmental costs – the carbon footprint – of food imports. This is particularly significant as each enterprise has a role to play in developing links with other sectors of the local/regional economy thereby promoting more localized economic activity.

A key element in the sustainability of tourism enterprises is access. An enterprise may well be performing exceptionally well when judged on the basis of its environmental performance but rarely will this include how the customers travel to and within the destination. Thus although the travel element involved is not a direct aspect of most tourism enterprises, nevertheless it was a consideration in the research; for example, did the enterprises take any measures to encourage their customers to travel using alternative modes of transport to that of the car (Chapter 7)? However, this is very limited in the context of the travel element of tourism and all the more so when it comes to the enterprises in the study, especially given demand is predominantly domestic. Thus the scope of this chapter is broadened to bring into consideration wider issues and debate, for example the impact of different forms of transportation and consideration of alternative options and measures to promote reductions in fossil fuel consumption, thereby facilitating a more comprehensive discussion.

A recurrent theme throughout the preceding chapters is that of tourist demand. That tourists want, for example, tour operators to adopt environmentally responsible practices, destinations and their communities should benefit from tourism, local culture should be promoted and accommodation enterprises should have an accredited EMS eco-label. Furthermore, that tourists are willing to support some CSR actions, e.g. local community initiatives, conservation projects and carbon offsetting. It was also suggested, that tourism enterprises have a role to play in educating visitors in how to be more 'environmentally friendly' in their actions. The latter areas to some degree were investigated through the surveys and the findings are thus presented in Chapter 8. However, this does not address satisfactorily the former comments on tourists wanting such developments thus the scope of the chapter is broadened to bring into discussion what could be termed the greening of tourists. As Millman (1989) argued in the late 1980s, tourists are becoming 'green conscious' yet 10 years later, as Wright (1997) portrays, there was little evidence of this in the traditionally popular parts of the Mediterranean basins. Is the same true today? Chapter 9 serves to narrow the focus back on the enterprises and is based on the findings drawn from the explorations into the 'awareness, perceptions and attitudes' of the owners/managers of the enterprises. Their perceptions and attitudes, coupled with their level of awareness and knowledge, are a key factor to the introduction of EM and CSR practices and more widely the EP of the enterprise. As such, the attention here includes their awareness of environmental initiatives and potentially related, influential factors.

Within these chapters a range of factors influential to the adoption of many of the practices discussed emerge. This is recognized in Chapter 9 which seeks to draw out the main issues arising and identified as barriers to progress. Thus the chapter brings into contention policy and planning that directly relates to these issues; for example, as manifest in a plethora of international, intra- and national policy iterations relating to sustainability and climate change. Reflection on these barriers coupled with the fact that most enterprises involved in tourism supply are small/micro in size, under single ownership and invariably family businesses leads to substantive conclusions. The way they are managed and operated is largely based on the values and attitudes of the owners themselves, who are just as much a part of the local community as other people and families living in the same area. Equally, they are consumers and as such no doubt are similar in many ways in their general consumer behaviour, their purchasing and consumption patterns, and particularly applicable in this context, their environmental behaviour.

It is through discussion of this wider context of consumers and society that we seek to gain a better understanding of what progress may or may not have been made in regard to the environmental performance of these enterprises over the last 15 years. As the DETR (2000, p. 10, Para l. 41) opined some 10 years ago:

> A number of the pressing problems identified [earlier] including climate change, traffic patterns and waste, will require significant behavioural change by businesses and the general public as well as by government. There is still widespread ignorance about the nature of some of these problems and the need for more sustainable solutions.

Overall, and in seeking to bring together the key issues that emerge from the findings, and discussion on tourism enterprises and sustainability, it is clear that addressing the environmental performance and within this context issues of sustainability is not just a matter of assessing the EP of tourism enterprises to ascertain what, if any, progress has been made since the early advocacy of such matters in the early 1990s, but also that this involves the consumption of tourism; thus the motivations of tourists and more generally consumers are also significant factors. Therefore furthering the objectives of sustainability involves a more complex solution than deepening the greenness of these enterprises.

In total these chapters seek to present a comprehensive analysis of those tourism enterprises, and the ways in which they are addressing sustainability, which constitute in numerical terms most of the supply of tourism products and services and most especially so when considered in the context of domestic tourism. Based that is on the longitudinal study of these enterprises in the UK that investigated their environmental performance and thus EMS and CSR practices over a period spanning 15 years. An additional strength of the text is that given the time frame involved, the discussion draws on sources from over the past 20 years to establish those policies, initiatives and issues pertinent to tourism enterprise throughout the period of the study. Further adding to the comprehensive analysis is that in the process due attention is given to other categories of tourism supply not included in the study per se, thus attention not only to the responses of the enterprises involved but also to national/multinational companies in the hospitality sector and also tour operators. Therefore seeking overall to establish a broad review of the responses of tourism enterprises to sustainability issues and developments. In the process contributing in some small measure to the paucity of research in this area of enquiry and addressing Buckley's critique on the lack of research into the operations and practices of tourism SMEs with the accent on small/micro enterprises.

To what extent this has been achieved is very much for the reader to decide. There will no doubt be criticisms as to what should (or should not) have been included but such is the way with all academic texts to the well informed. Even allowing for the length available, constraints of space may still preclude further discussion of any one area.

The ultimate objective though is to stimulate thought on the many and diverse facets of tourism enterprise and environmental performance within the far broader framework of sustainability, thus not only potentially to establish a range of benchmarks and areas for future/further research but also to stimulate engagement with the issues arising and promote debate. To achieve such an outcome would indeed make this undertaking worthwhile.

Further Reading

For a very clear and comprehensive discussion on climate change see Giddens, A. (2009) *The politics of climate change*. Polity Press, London.

A comprehensive collection on the inter-relationships between tourism and different environments and in different contexts is presented in Gossling, S. and Hall, C.M. (2006) *Tourism & Global Environmental Change: Ecological, social, economic and political interrelationships*. Routledge, New York.

For a good overview on the theme of tourism development and sustainability see Sharpley, R. (2009) *Tourism Development and the Environment: Beyond Sustainability*. Earthscan, London.

References

Badulescu, A. and Badulescu, D. (2012) Entrepreneurship and local resources. In: Leslie, D. (ed.) *Tourism Enterprises and the Sustainability Agenda across Europe*. New Directions in Tourism Analysis. Ashgate, Farnham, UK, pp. 151–168

Black, C.W. (1995) The Inter-Continental Hotels Group and its Environmental Awareness Programme. In: Leslie, D. (ed.) *Promoting Environmental Awareness and Action in Hospitality, Tourism and Leisure*. Environment Papers Series No.1, Glasgow Caledonian University, Glasgow, UK, pp. 31–46.

Blackstock, K.L., White, V., McCrum, G., Scott, A. and Hunter, C. (2008) Measuring responsibility: an appraisal of a Scottish National Park's Sustainable Tourism Indicators. *Journal of Sustainable Tourism* 16 (3), 276–297.

Blair, A. and Hitchcock, D. (2001) *Environment and Business*. Routledge, New York.

Blanco, E., Rey-Maquieira, J. and Lozano, J. (2009) Economic incentives for tourism firms to undertake voluntary environmental management. *Tourism Management* 30 (1), 112–122.

Blowers, A. and Hinchliffe, S. (2003) *Environmental Response*. Wiley, Chichester, UK.

Bohdanowicz, P. (2006) European hoteliers' environmental attitudes: greening the business. *Cornell Hotel and Restaurant Administration Quarterly* 46, pp. 188–204.

Bricker, K.S. (2009) Sustainable tourism development in the United States of America: An intricate balance from policy to practice. In: Leslie, D. (ed.) (2009) *Tourism Enterprises and Sustainable Development - international perspectives on responses to the sustainability agenda*. Routledge, New York, pp. 64–89.

Buckley, R. (2007) Is mass tourism serious about sustainability? *Tourism Recreation Research* 32 (3), 70–72.

Buckley, R. (2009) *Ecotourism: Principles & Practices*. CAB International, Wallingford, UK.

Butler, R. (1995) Introduction. In: Butler, R. and Pearce, D. (eds) *Change in tourism: people, places and processes*. Routledge, New York, pp. 1–11.

Carter, R.W., Whiley, D. and Knight, C. (2004) Improving environmental performance in the tourism accommodation sector. *Ecotourism* 3 (1), 46–68.

Cater, E. and Lowman, G. (eds) (1994) *Ecotourism - a sustainable option*. Wiley, Chichester, UK.

Ceron, J.-P. and Dubois, G. (2003) Tourism and sustainable development indicators: the gap between theoretical demands and practical achievements. *Current Issues in Tourism* 6 (1), pp. 69–83.

Champion, T. and Watkins, C. (1991) *People in the Countryside – Studies of social change in rural Britain*. Paul Chapman, London.

Chan, E.S.W. and Hawkins, R. (2010) Attitude towards EMSs in an international hotel: an exploratory case study. *International Journal of Hospitality Management* 29 (4), 641–651.

Chan, W.W., Wong, K.K.F. and Lo, J.Y. (2005) Partial analysis of the environmental costs generated by hotels in Hong Kong. *International Journal of Hospitality Management* 24, pp. 517–531.

Church, C. and McHarry, J. (eds) (1999) *One small step … a guide to action on sustainable development in the UK*. Community Development Foundation, London.

Connelly, J. and Smith, G. (2003) *Politics and the Environment – from theory to practice*. Routledge, London.

DETR (2000) *Indicators of Sustainable Development*. UK Round Table on Sustainable Development, Department of the Environment, Transport and the Regions, London.

EC (2001) *Executive Summary from E.C. Environment 2010: Our Future, Our Choice*. 6th A.P. COM (2001) 31 Final, Commission of the European Communities, Brussels.

EC (2002) *Corporate Social Responsibility: A Business Contribution to Sustainable Development*. COM (2002) 347 Final, Commission of the European Union, 2 July, Brussels.

EC (2008) '*Think Small First*' *A* '*Small Business Act*' *for Europe*. COM (2008) 394 Final. Commission of the European Communities, 25 June, Brussels.

EC (2010) *Europe, the World's No.1 Tourist Destination – a New Political Framework for Tourism in Europe*. COM (2010) 352 Final European Commission, June, Brussels.

EIU (1993) Travel and Tourism Analyst. Economic Intelligence Unit, Number 1, London.

Ekins, P. (1986) *The Living Economy: a new economics in the making*. Routledge and Kegan Paul, London.

Erdogan, N. and Baris, E. (2006) Environmental protection programs and conservation practices of hotels in Ankara, Turkey. *Tourism Management* 28 (2), pp. 604–614.

Garay, L. and Font, X. (2012) Doing good to do well? Corporate social responsibility reasons, practices and impacts in small and medium accommodation enterprises. *Journal of Hospitality Management* 31, 329–337.

Geiser, K. and Crul, M. (1996) Greening of small and medium sized firms: government, industry and NGO initiatives. In: Groenewegen, P., Fischer, K., Jenkins, E.G. and Schor, J. (eds) *The Greening of Industry: resource guide and bibliography*. Island Press, Washington, D.C.

Glyptis, S. (1995) Recreation and the environment: challenging and changing relationships. In: *Leisure and Tourism: Towards the Millennium*. Leisure Studies Association, Brighton, UK.

Hall, C.M. and Gossling, S. (2009) Global Change and Tourism Enterprise. In: Leslie, D. (ed.) (2009) *Tourism Enterprises and Sustainable Development – international perspectives on responses to the sustainability agenda*. Routledge Advances in Tourism Series. Routledge, New York, pp. 17–35.

Hall, D., Kirkpatrick, I. and Mitchell, M. (eds) (2005) *Rural Tourism – Issues and Impacts*. Aspects of Tourism Series 26, Clevedon, Channel View, London.

Harrison, D. (ed.) (1992) *Tourism and the less Developed Countries*. Wiley, Chichester, UK.

Herremans, I.M. (ed.) (2006) *Cases in Sustainable Tourism: an experiential approach to making decisions*. Haworth Press, Binghamton, New York.

Hillary, R. (ed.) (2000) *Small and Medium-Sized Enterprises and the Environment*. Greenleaf, Sheffield, UK.

Hinch, D. (1996) Urban tourism: perspectives on sustainability. *Journal of Sustainable Tourism* 4 (2), pp. 95–110.

Hunter, C. and Green, H. (1995) *Tourism and the environment: a sustainable relationship?* Routledge, London.

Jacobs, M. (1996) *The Politics of the Real World: Meeting the new century*. Earthscan, London.

Jenner, P. and Smith, C. (1992) *The tourism industry and the environment*. The Economist Intelligence Unit, London.

Johnson, D. and Turner, C. (2003) *International Business – themes and issues in the modern global economy*. Routledge, London.

Kelly, J., Haider, W., Williams, P.W. and Englund, K. (2007) Stated preferences of tourists for eco-efficient destination planning options. *Tourism Management* 28, pp. 377–390.

Krippendorf, J. (1987) *The Holidaymakers*. Heinemann, Oxford, UK.

Kucerova, J. (2012) Environmental management and accommodation facilities in Slovakia. In: Leslie, D. (ed.) *Tourism enterprises and the sustainability agenda across Europe*. New Directions in Tourism Analysis. Ashgate, Farnham, UK, pp. 121–134.

Leidner, R. (2004) *The European Tourism Industry – a multi-sector with dynamic markets. Structures, developments and importance for Europe's economy*. EC, Enterprise Directorate General (Unit D.3) Publications, Brussels.

Leslie, D. (1990) The challenge of the 1990s. *International Journal of Hospitality Management*, 9 (2).

Leslie, D. (1995) Promoting environmentally friendly management and practices. In: D. Leslie (ed.) *Promoting Environmental Awareness and Action in Hospitality, Tourism and Leisure*. Glasgow Caledonian University, Glasgow, pp. 11–30.

Leslie, D. (2001a) Urban regeneration and Glasgow's galleries with particular reference to the Burrell Collection. In: Richards, G. (ed.) *Cultural Attractions and European Tourism*. CAB International, Wallingford, pp. 111–134.

Leslie, D. (2001b) Serviced accommodation, environmental performance and benchmarks. *Journal of Quality Assurance in Hospitality & Tourism* 2 (3), 127–147.

Leslie, D. (2002a) The influence of UK government agencies on the 'greening' of tourism. *Tourism Today*, No. 2, Summer, pp. 95–110.

Leslie, D. (2005) Rural tourism businesses and environmental management systems. In: Hall, D., Kirkpatrick, I. and Mitchell, M. (eds) *Rural Tourism – Issues and Impacts*. Aspects of Tourism Series 26, Clevedon, Channel View, London, Pp.228–249.

Leslie, D. (2007a) The missing component in the 'greening' of tourism: the environmental performance of the self-catering accommodation sector. Special Issue on Self-catering Accommodation. *International Journal of Hospitality Management* 26 (2), pp. 310–322.

Leslie, D. (2007b) Scottish rural tourism enterprises and the sustainability of their communities. In: Thomas, R. and Augustyn, M. (eds) (2007) *Tourism in the New Europe, Perspectives on SME policies and Practices*. Advances in Tourism Research Series. Elsevier, Oxford, UK, pp. 89–108.

Leslie, D. (ed.) (2009) *Tourism Enterprises and Sustainable Development – international perspectives on responses to the sustainability agenda*. Routledge Advances in Tourism Series, Routledge, New York.

Leslie, D. (2010) *Tourism, Bute and Inchmarnock Fish Farm Proposal. Precognition.* Interim scheme for the authorisation of Fish Farms Application by Offshore Farm development Ltd. Fish farm North of Inchmarnock, Isle of Bute. Public Enquiry. DPEA Reference IQC/35/24 March.

Leslie, D. (2011) The European Union, sustainable tourism policy and rural Europe. In: Macleod, D.V.L. and Gillespie, S.A. (eds) *Sustainable Tourism in Rural Europe: approaches to development*. Routledge, London, pp. 43–60.

Leslie, D. (2012a) The responsible tourism debate. In: Leslie, D. (ed.) *Responsible Tourism: Concepts, theory and practice*. CAB International, Wallingford, UK.

Leslie, D. (ed.) (2012b) *Tourism enterprises and the sustainability agenda across Europe*. New Directions in Tourism Analysis. Ashgate, Farnham, UK.

Leslie, D. (2013) Key players in the environmental performance of tourism enterprises. In: Reddy, M.V. and Wilkes, K. (eds) *Tourism, Climate Change and Sustainability*. Earthscan, London.

Leslie, D., McDowell, D.A. and McGurran, F. (1989) *European Regional Development Fund and Northern Ireland: the additionality issue*. Public Policy and Administration. Volume 4, Number 3, pp. 32–41.

McCool, S.F. and Moisey, R.N. (eds) (2001) *Tourism, Recreation and Sustainability – linking culture & the environment*, 2nd edn. CAB International, Oxford, UK.

McCool, S.F., Moisey, R.N. and Nickerson, N.P. (2001) What should tourism sustain? The disconnect with industry perceptions of useful indicators. *Journal of Travel Research* 40 (2), 124–131.

Mensah, I. (2004) *Environmental Management Practices in US Hotels*. Hotel Online: Special Report. Available at: www.hotel-online.com/News?PR2004_2nd/May04_EnvironmentalPractices.html (accessed 14 November 2006).

Mensah, I. (2009) Environmental performance of tourism enterprises in Ghana: A case study of hotels in the Greater Accra Region (GAR). In: Leslie, D. (ed.) *Tourism Enterprises and Sustainable Development – international perspectives on responses to the sustainability agenda*. Routledge Advances in Tourism Series, Routledge, New York, pp. 139–156.

Middleton, V.T.C. (2000) Image and reality: Tourism, environment and sustainability in the 21st century. Paper presented at Westlakes Conference, Whitehaven, UK.

Middleton, V.T.C. and Hawkins, R. (1993) Practical environmental policies in travel and tourism part 1: The hotel sector. *Travel and Tourism Analyst* 23 (3), pp. 63–76.

Middleton, V.T.C. and Hawkins, R. (1994) Practical environmental policies in travel and tourism part II: Airlines, tour operators and destinations. *Travel and Tourism Analyst* 24 (1), pp. 83–97.

Millman, R. (1989) Pleasure seeking v the 'greening' of world tourism. *Tourism Management* December, pp. 275–277.

Mintel (2007) *Holiday Lifestyles – Responsible Tourism – UK*. Available at: http://academic.mintel.com/sinatra/oxygen_academic/search_results/show&/display/id=221204/display/id=256074?select_section= 256076 (accessed 3 March 2011).

Mosselaer, F., Duim, R. and Wijk, J. (2012) Corporate social responsibility in tour operating: the case of Dutch outbound tour operators. In: Leslie, D. (ed.) *Tourism Enterprises and the Sustainability Agenda Across Europe*. New Directions in Tourism Analysis, Ashgate, Farnham, UK, pp. 71–92.

OECD (2009) *The Impact of Culture on Tourism*. Organisation for Economic and Cultural Development, Paris.

Pearce, D. (1993) *Blueprint 3; measuring sustainable development*. Earthscan, London.

Porritt, J. (1997) Green grows the marketing jargon. *Green Hotelier* January, pp. 32–33.

Pleumarom, A. (2009) Asian tourism: green and responsible? In: Leslie, D. (ed.) (2009) *Tourism Enterprises and Sustainable Development: international perspectives on responses to the sustainability agenda.* Routledge, New York, pp. 36–54.

Pleumarom, A (2012) The politics of tourism and poverty reduction. In: Leslie, D. (ed.) *Responsible Tourism: Concepts, Theory and Practice.* CAB International, Wallingford, pp. 90–106.

Pratt, L. (2011) *Tourism investing in energy and resources efficiency towards a green economy.* United Nation Environment Programme, Paris.

Robinson, M., Swarbrooke, J., Evans, N., Long, P. and Sharpley, R. (eds) (2000) *Environmental management and pathways to sustainable tourism.* Centre for Travel and Tourism and Business Education Publishers, Sunderland, UK.

Rodriguez, F.J.G. and Cruz, Y. del M.A. (2007) Relation between social-environmental responsibility performance in hotels. *International Journal of Hospitality Management* 26 (4), pp. 824–839.

Romeril, M. and Hughes-Evans, D. (1979). Tourism and the environment – an introduction. In: Romeril, M. and Hughes-Evans, D. (eds) *Tourism and the Environment. Proceedings of the First European Conference on Tourism and the Environment.* Jersey. Institute of Environmental Sciences, London, pp. 1–8.

Scanlon, N.L. (2007) An analysis and assessment of environmental operating practices in hotel and resort properties. *International Journal of Hospitality Management* 26 (3), pp. 711–723.

Scheyvens, R. (2002) *Tourism for development: empowering communities.* Pearson, Harlow, UK.

Shaw, G. and Williams, A.M. (2010) Tourism SMEs: changing research agendas and missed opportunities. In: Pearce, D.G. and Butler, R.W. (eds) *Tourism Research: 20-20 Vision.* Goodfellow, Oxford, UK, pp. 80–93.

Smith, V.L. and Eadington, W.R. (eds) (1992) *Tourism alternatives: potentials and problems in the development of tourism.* Wiley, Chichester, UK.

Spenceley, A. and Rylance, A. (2012) Responsible wildlife tourism in Africa. In: Leslie, D. (ed.) *Responsible Tourism: Concepts, Theory and Practice.* CAB International, Wallingford, UK, pp. 1301–1341.

Thomas, R. and Augustyn, M. (eds) (2007) *Tourism in the New Europe, Perspectives on SME policies and Practices.* Advances in Tourism Research Series. Elsevier, Oxford, UK.

Thomas, T., Shaw, G. and Page, S.J. (2011) Understanding small firms in tourism: A perspective on research trends and challenges. *Tourism Management* 32 (5), pp. 963–976.

Timothy, D.J. (2012) Destination communities and responsible tourism. In: Leslie, D. (ed.) *Responsible Tourism: Concepts, Theory and Practice.* CAB International, Wallingford, UK, pp. 72–81.

Trung, D.N. and Kumar, S. (2005) Resource use and waste management in Vietnam hotel industry. *Journal of Cleaner Production* 13, pp. 109–166.

Tzschentke, N., Kirk, D. and Lynch, P.A. (2008) Going green: decisional factors in small hospitality operations. *International Journal of Hospitality Management* 27, pp. 126–133.

Vernon, J., Essex, S., Pinder, D. and Curry, K. (2003) The 'greening' of tourism micro business: outcomes of group investigations in south-east Cornwall. *Business Strategy and Environment* 12 (1), 49–69.

WCED (1987) *Our Common Future.* World Commission on Environment and Development. Oxford University Press, Oxford, UK.

Welford, R. and Starkey, R. (eds) (1996) *The Earthscan Reader in Business and the Environment.* Earthscan, London.

Wright, G. (1997) Targeting Sustainable Tourism in the Mediterranean Basic. *EG* June, pp. 2–4.

WTTC (World Travel and Tourism Council), WTO (World Tourism Organisation) and Earth Council Report (1996) *Agenda 21 For the Travel and Tourism Industry: Towards Environmentally Sustainable Development.* WTTC, Madrid.

WTTC, IFTO, IH&RA, ICCL (2002) *Industry as a partner for sustainable Development.* World Travel and Tourism Council, International Federation of Tour Operators, International Hotel and Restaurant Association, International Council of Cruise Liners, London.

Zientara, P. (2012) Hospitality enterprise – a key influence. In: Leslie, D. (ed.) *Responsible Tourism: Concepts, Theory and Practice.* CAB International, Wallingford, UK, pp. 154–164.

2 The Tourism Enterprises

Introduction

This chapter serves two primary objectives. First to present a profile of the enterprises involved in the study. Second, to establish the foundation, essential context and parameters to further the analysis and interpretation of the extensive data obtained from this longitudinal study into the environmental performance (EP) of tourism enterprises. Thus, some of the data presented in this chapter may potentially appear on first sight to be of limited relevance. However, the significance lies not only in contributing to the overall profile but also, and more importantly, in terms of comparative analyses both within this study and also for future research. For example to establish a raft of benchmarks to assess to what extent progress has been achieved in the EP of tourism enterprises. Such progress could be expected, especially within the EU (see Leslie, 2011), given the ongoing attention to sustainability issues, ecological modernization of firms and carbon footprinting. Furthermore, as ECORYS' (2009) study into tourism supply within the EU argued, sustainability is a key to maintaining competitiveness in the world market.

These enterprises account for the major proportion of visitor spend in any destination within which spending on accommodation and hospitality operations accounts for over 50% (see Table 2.1).

The high proportion of spending attributed to food and beverage operations is reflected in the allocation of the EU's total tourist spending to the various categories of enterprise in tourism supply, as estimated by Leidner (2004):

- Restaurants (includes bars, canteens, catering): 49% of revenues; considered share of supply approximately 82%.
- Hotels (includes other accommodations): 22% of revenues; considered share of supply approximately 15%.
- Travel agents and tour operators: 29% of revenues; considered share of supply approximately 3%.

What is notable about these figures is the revenue share accorded to travel agents and tour operators (TOs) compared with their considered share of supply. TOs, in the form of local enterprises, were not present in the study though their presence was through, for example, coach tour operations. It is partly in recognition of this that they are the main focus in Chapter 3. The focus here on the other enterprises in supply (97%), commences with findings relating to the ownership of the enterprises, the type of business, current period of operation and includes insights on the properties involved. Following on from this, the annual turnover of the enterprises is considered prior to the findings and discussion

Table 2.1. General visitor spend by category (%).[a] (Adapted from Leslie, 2007a.)

Sector	Day visitors	Domestic tourists
Accommodation	–	37
Retail – leisure shopping, souvenirs	12	11
Food and beverage operations	60	26
Attractions	13	5
Travel	16	20
Total	100	100

[a]Minor differences in summation reflect rounding errors.

on employment and recruitment. The final area covered is based on the findings into the background of the owners/managers themselves. As and where appropriate, outcomes of the related enquiries into food producers (FP) and arts and crafts (A & C) are included. To aid clarity, the data are generally considered and referred to as follows:

• 2001, for the LDNP stage overall;
• 2001 audits for those enterprises that took part in the extensive interviews;
• 2006 for the rural enterprises in Scotland; and
• 2011 (audits) for the predominantly urban-based enterprises interviewed in Scotland.

Throughout the chapter, specific comments of participants are included both to highlight, as appropriate, their views and practice and to enliven the discourse. These comments are presented in quotes throughout the text. Before consideration of these areas, additional insights on these enterprises are provided by way of further background.

The spatial distribution of tourism enterprises in any popular destination invariably reflects the general distribution of visitors and the strength of tourism demand in 'honey pot' areas. Not surprisingly therefore the study found that the rural enterprises were predominantly located in and around the most popular towns (the majority) and villages. For example, in the LDNP in 2001, 93% were located in the most popular areas, namely Keswick, Ambleside, Windermere and Bowness.

In the LDNP sample, the proportion of serviced-accommodation (SA) operations with over ten, and more so those with over 30 (10%), rooms is above the UK's national average. This suggests that the LDNP has a higher proportion of larger enterprises compared with other popular rural destinations

and potentially that these enterprises are managing well, which reflects ongoing and robust visitor demand. However, the majority do have less than 15 rooms, which is similar to the EU statistic (69%) for rooms per accommodation operation (Leidner, 2004). Overall, these small enterprises account for by far the majority of total bed spaces in the area, which is not to be unexpected given that the 'large hotel chains and brands only represent between 10 and 20 percent of the total room capacity in Europe.' (Leidner, 2004, p. III). Over half of the guest houses (GH) in 2001, and most in 2006, were licensed to sell alcoholic beverages, which reflected the continuing upward trend in the UK to consume wine with meals. In some ways contrary to best EM practice, e.g. individual portions, another trend in the GH/Bed & Breakfast (BB) category was the increasing provision of tea/coffee making facilities (90%) and television (90%) in guest rooms and though to a lesser extent individual toiletries. As one owner remarked: 'I am not happy providing tea and coffee in the room, prefer to offer early morning tea and coffee. Would like to create a "social" room for guests but have to have facilities in rooms for RAC/AA grading.' The restaurant sector ranged from 'tea shops', and small cafes, in some instances with less than 16 covers, to comparatively large restaurant operations of more than 100 covers. Many of these enterprises produce their own products for service and also for retail hence these operations were also included in the study.

The diversity to be found amongst the visitor attractions serves to illustrate the historic and cultural heritage in the LDNP, which rather dominated the survey of attractions in that Historic buildings and museums accounted for some 50% whilst A & C Centres/Galleries accounted for approximately 27%. Visitor numbers range from less than 10,000 to over 300,000 (the UK norm for the time was approximately 100,000) with the majority experiencing increased numbers during the 1990s; an overall growth of 30%. A number of attractions have developed since, one most notably the World of Beatrix Potter. Also, two other major developments in the area, one in the 1990s and the other 2000s, are Hayes Garden World and Lakeland, a major retail outlet for all things in the kitchen. Both of these retail outlets draw 1000s of visitors and are popular stopping places for coach tour parties. Further evidencing the popularity of the area is that between 1992 and 1998 there was an 11% increase in the number of pitches for caravan and camping sites in Cumbria.

Ownership (see Table 2.2)

The majority of enterprises are owner managed, single businesses (83%) and in many cases the family home, which is similar to Carlsen *et al.* (2001) and Garay and Font's (2012) study into CSR and tourism enterprises in Catalonia (90%). This is a finding that is generally applicable to many of the food producers though they have a higher incidence of managers (12%). Further of note is a study into TOs based in Scotland, the majority of which were small operations and owner managed (84%) (Gaunt, 2004). The majority of the enterprises have Tourist Board grading (69%). In contrast, Garay and Font's study included 24% with grading reflecting the different system operating in Spain. Demonstrating the trial and tribulations of successfully managing inns in rural areas is the finding that the Fringe Inns (see p. 6) have the highest incidence of new owners, which also reflects the more general pattern in the UK of change in both ownership and management in this sector, especially in the inns category.

The 2006 sample evidences longer average ownership and lower turnover of ownership compared with the LDNP (which is at par with the average for hotels and inns in England (Leslie, 2001)). Also, it includes slightly more enterprises that are part of a company group. In comparison the attractions are less likely to be owner managed, more

probably part of a local or national group and have charitable status, e.g. National Trust, Historic Scotland. A marked contrast is to be found with the 2011 set, 26% of which are single businesses with a manager and 50% are part of a company group. Otherwise they are very similar to the Scottish sample of 2006. Findings that overall are similar to the Scottish TOs; 29% had been established within the previous 5 years and 25% between 5 and 10 years (Gaunt, 2004).

Factors identified as being influential as to why the owners were involved in the tourism/ hospitality sector generally revolved round aspects of quality of life and are very similar with the findings of other research studies (see Cawley *et al.*, 1999; Carlsen *et al.*, 2001; Vernon *et al.*, 2003; Garay and Font, 2012) namely:

- family home;
- attractiveness/quality of the physical environment of locality/wanted to live in this area. This factor would include 'sustainability entrepreneurs' whose values include being responsible for environmental and social aspects which are not seen as a cost or added extra (see Badulescu and Badulescu, 2012);
- manage own business; and
- took over family business.

Table 2.2. Category of ownership and duration.

Category	2001[a]	2006	2011
Ownership			
Owner managed	83	75	24
Manager	7	9	26
Local group	3	3	11
Regional group	1	3	5
National group	5[b]	8[b]	33
Length of time in current ownership (years)			
1–5	28	14	14
6–10	14	19	18
11–15	19	27	19
16–19	5	11	9
20–30	17	13	22
31+	19	16	18

[a]All the enterprises
[b]Includes attractions that are National Trust properties

As Clive Watson, Managing Director of Bowness Leisure plc (LDNP) said:

> ... huge demand for guesthouses by people who saw them as their only way of achieving their dream of moving into the lakes ... and .... These people were moving for quality of life rather than for business income ... (Leslie, 2001, p. 65)

Interestingly McGehee and Kim's (2004) research into small farm (less than 100 acres) farmers in Virginia found a similar range of motivations. Another motivation is a personal interest/activity which is the basis for many a small tourism enterprise (see Badulescu and Badulescu, 2012). This is especially found in the supply of nature-based or outdoor adventure pursuits (see Leslie, 2010; Spenceley and Rylance, 2012; Holland, 2012). These factors were further affirmed through the audit interviews; manifest in the LDNP by the number of owners who are from outside of the area and are comparatively recent entries to the sector.

A locality's attractiveness and 'escape from urbanity' are also motivations in the purchase of second homes or holiday homes in attractive locations. Opportunities have been encouraged by the potential to let as self-catering operations and by the prevailing upward trend in house prices for the better part of the last century i.e. secondary investment. Overall, these operations present a diverse variety of accommodations, e.g. new houses, flats, cottages, renovated/converted farm buildings. It is not surprising that the number of self-catering apartments in so many other rural locations in the UK, especially within a two hour drive of major conurbations, increased substantially during the 1980s and again by over a third in terms of supply in the 1990s (Leslie, 2007b). They are often managed for the owners by an agency. To illustrate: one agency in the LDNP has a portfolio comprising 50% of second/holiday homes and properties bought as a long-term investment. The management of these properties includes ensuring they are made ready for new guests and general housekeeping matters. Comparatively few of these properties are owned by people who live in the area and of these the majority are involved in farming or estate management. As such, much of the

letting cost is lost to the locality. However, there is visitor spend on food and beverage operations, purchases of supplies and a small element of employment generation through the development of letting agents and also their staffing teams to prepare the premises for new guests etc.

Duration of ownership (see Table 2.2)

The enquiries into how long the enterprise had been operating under the current ownership established that many of the 'younger' operations, particularly for 2001, involved a change in ownership. For example, of all the categories in 2001, BB enterprises are more likely to be a new/recent business based in a 'modern' house. This is reflected in the higher presence of cavity wall insulation and double glazing, which is indicative of a less traditional building design than that commonly found in the area; similarly self-catering premises. The following selections drawn from the 2001 data serve to highlight various differences between the categories of enterprise:

Duration	Category
1–5 years	serviced accommodation 28%; arts and crafts 20%
10–16 years	63% of the food producers
20+ years	serviced accommodation 30%; majority of inns, attractions and arts & crafts have been operating for over 25 years; a quarter of the food producers operational for over 80 years

Garay and Font's (2012) study found that 55% of the enterprises in their sample had been operational for 10 years or less, which is similar to the 62% of the 2001 audits. Restaurants, particularly cafes, attractions and the self-catering sector evidence the highest propensity for new developments in the last 5 years, reflecting the popularity of the area and the growth of the self-catering sector in the 1990s. In the self-catering sector approximately one in five properties (19%) had been built during the 1990s. In contrast, hotels and inns are far less likely to be in contemporary properties. An indicator as to the long-standing of these operations is demonstrated in the findings of the audits:

- 40% of the properties have 'always been' operating as designated; and
- 45% of the properties were previously homes.

As one local authority noted:

In many cases, hotels and guest houses are the result of conversions of large country houses and buildings of Special Architectural or Historic Interest which might otherwise have become redundant or been poorly maintained. (SLDC, 1997, para 4.7)

The age of many of these properties in rural locations holds an added 'benefit' in that repairs and renewals help to maintain and develop traditional skills of restoration of old buildings; this feeds into other areas of repairs, renewals, extensions and so forth. That such skills are largely available is partly due to the work of the National Trust, which has developed a set of principles for restoring or maintaining their buildings (see Jarman, 2000) and fostering the development of traditional building methods.

Maintenance and development of the property

A facet of the interrelationships of tourism enterprises with the local economy recognized and explored through the surveys is of building works, regular maintenance and repairs which generates demand for local tradesmen on a fairly consistent basis and thus contributes to the local economy and community more generally. Second, continued visitor demand and improved profitability encourages new works; witness the finding in 2001 from the accommodation category: one out of every five enterprises indicated that they had current plans for upgrading the operation in some way, e.g. redecoration, upgrade rooms, add rooms, develop catering operations, add a conservatory. In rural locations, the majority of the enterprises by far, including owners of self-catering properties, refer such work to local trade persons, who within the LDNP use local materials. This is partly due to their availability,

but also to maintain character and, as applicable, meet the Park Authority's planning regulations. This demand helps contribute to the maintenance of traditional skills and the presence of skilled tradesmen in the area.

One area not explored was whether the owner/manager had or was taking into consideration good environmental practice with regard to design or fixtures and fittings; for example, from amongst the many choices that are now available for introducing more environmentally friendly designs, building materials and products. However optional choice in such matters over the last decade due to new building regulations is more limited today. This does not apply to everything, for example one respondent noted: 'all redecorated rooms have hospital type taps as seemingly lots of people have problems with ordinary type taps' i.e. turn/screw style.

Annual Turnover

The first survey of serviced-accommodation in the LDNP did not invite respondents to indicate their turnover though this was addressed in the auditing stage. It was subsequently included in the surveys of the other categories in the LDNP and when researching the enterprises in Scotland. The findings for 2001 are presented in Table 2.3; each of the categories from 2001 is included to allow for cross-category comparisons (the equivalent data for 2006 are very similar). The majority of the enterprises have a turnover of less than £250,000. To place this in one perspective – it was estimated at the time that in general, tourism enterprises in the UK had a turnover of less that £250,000 (Bardgett, 2000). The comparatively higher revenues of the serviced accommodation operations in the Fringe are largely attributable to the much lower proportion of BBs in that data set. The inns in both the LDPN and the Fringe compare well with the SA (serviced accommodation) category in that the majority (70% and 65% respectively) also offered accommodation.

The data for 2006 are very similar allowing for price increases over the intervening period. However, where substantial differences arise is in the 2011 stage. The urban sample

Table 2.3. Indicative turnover.[a]

Turnover (£000s)	LDNP (%)					Fringe (%)		Arts & Crafts (%)
	SC	R	I	A	C	Af	If	
Less than 50	36	8	7	18	55	–	15	36
50–99	12	8	11	27	9	38	12	
100–149	4	8	15	9	9	13	15	18
150–249	8	16	11	14	18	13	12	6
250–349	8	–	7	9	–	–	12	
350–499	6	16	30	9	–	13	12	12
500+	18	–	–	–	–	13	15	
No response	8	42	19	14	9	10	7	29

[a]Food producers – 13% £350,000–400,000; 63% £400,000+

comprised comparatively a higher proportion of non-micro-enterprises and operations that were part of a national group. This is reflected in the revenue figures: 64% had a turnover in excess of £0.5m whilst 10% achieved less than £100k, a significantly lower proportion than either 2006 or 2001.

Influences on turnover

A major factor for many rural enterprises is that of seasonality. Across Europe this is traditionally the major holiday period of June to September, which coincides with school holidays and generally warmer weather. This is far less noticeable in urban settings given the shift from 'business' to leisure custom over this period. However, for rural and coastal locations this can be a problem outside of the high days of June through August, which was more noticeable for 2006. In the LDNP the highest occupancy was achieved in the September/October period – slightly better than for June/August. This was largely attributed to a combination of factors, as respondents commented:

- 'The season is now longer' (18%).
- 'More people are taking winter breaks' (16%).
- 'More day visitors in winter' (16%).
- 'Increase in numbers of visitors overall' (12%).

Further enquiries into the performance of the business over the previous 5 years found that the majority of enterprises reported an increase in profitability and an increase in staffing over the same period. Also more of the rural enterprises were achieving a consistent level of activity and profitability over the year (less markedly seasonal). Allowing for these factors, participants in the 2001 stage noted that this performance was also due to improvements in service offerings and especially promotion, development of internet usage and websites, etc. This is well illustrated by Country Lanes, the Windermere-based company that operates cycling day trips, short breaks and longer tours in the Lake District which gained a top E-commerce 2000 Award. To quote Country Lanes:

> The trick has been to transform our traditional niche travel business into a global e-commerce enterprise. And I'm happy to say that our web site now generates 90% of our business (Anon., 2000b, p. 5).

Employment

The figures on employment, as presented in Table 2.4, affirm that by far the large majority of the rural enterprises are micro-businesses. The employment figures for 2001 and 2006 evidence comparatively few in the small enterprise category let alone medium (similarly the attractions). Slightly more than 50% employ similar numbers of staff on a part-time basis. The findings for 2001 indicate higher than average per enterprise employment whilst 2006 closely correlates with Leidner's (2004) analysis of employment by tourism enterprises in the EU (i.e. 93% employ 1–9 persons; 6.5% 10–49; approx 1% over 50). They also compare favourably with Garay and Font (2012) who found that 77% employed five or fewer staff (rising to 87% for those employing ten or fewer). In the case of Gaunt's (2004) study, 71% of the Scottish TOs were identified as employing nine or fewer staff. Overall, the key difference between the data sets is with 2011, which included comparatively fewer in the BB and inns categories.

Overall, these enterprises individually generate limited employment opportunities but collectively the story is very different. In the case of the LDNP, the serviced accommodation operations in total employ approximately 1000 persons, when the sample is taken as a whole the average per enterprise is 9.9 staff, two thirds of whom are in full-time positions. This excludes owners, who gain their livelihood through the business and members of their family who may also work in the business.

The many part-time positions present opportunities for local people for whom full-time work might not be suitable, e.g. a parent with young children to look after, or teenagers and students seeking holiday jobs. Also, part-time positions may be available which involve working times that fit in with the public transport service. The availability of transportation to enable employees to get to and from their place of work is a key factor; all the more so in rural areas. If not able to walk to their work then in the absence of access to their own transportation

they will be dependent on public transport and at the times required to meet their working hours (e.g. early start: 0700 hours or late finish: 2300 hours) which is often unlikely. Thus having their own means of transport is very important as illustrated by the finding in 2001 that one in six staff resided outside the LDNP. In one particular case, a woman living some distance away from the enterprise applied successfully for a job but subsequently found that although the hours were between 1100 hours and 1700 hours, the available public transport made for a much longer day and substantial cost. After a short period she resigned. This is one of the factors that explain why so many of these enterprises provide accommodation for staff, which also enables persons from outside the area to be employed. This is well illustrated by Lake District Hotels Ltd, which in total employs 460 staff of whom 250 live in accommodation provided. A further influential factor on staffing is that demand for many of the rural enterprises is less markedly seasonal than it was in the early 1990s. Thus continuity of revenues throughout the year supports appointment of full-time permanent staff, which might well not suit persons already in part-time positions; a situation that also brings problems as regards recruitment (see page 23).

There is no doubting that sustainability includes the social welfare of staff and their development, hence the surveys and audits gave attention to staff training and personal development. By far, most of those enterprises that do employ staff provide in-house training (84%) and opportunities for staff development (72%) though, as a number of respondents noted, this was mainly to do with good practice in health and safety. Of all the categories, it is the inns that are most likely to provide staff training and opportunities for personal development. One reason accounting for this is that bar service staff, perhaps more than any other hospitality staff, require training to fulfil their duties from the moment they start their employment. Staff are also potentially significant role-players in the greening of any enterprise and thus communicating and explaining why actions are being introduced, encouraging to take on responsibility and to promote support and involvement for local

Table 2.4. Employment.[a]

	Full time (%)		
Number of staff	2001	2005	2011
None	46	31	3
1–2	16	28	6
3–5	13	22	30
6–9	6	10	8
10–18	8	5	23
19+	10	12	31

[a]Arts & Crafts producers – very few employees; Food Producers – 63% employ 10 or fewer, 25% more than 50 persons, on average they employ 2.2 part-time staff and are not markedly seasonal (three enterprises employ seasonal staff full-time).

community based and conservation initiatives is important (see Wisner *et al.*, 2010). There is little to doubt that gaining their support can have a substantial impact on the success of any initiative, for example whether saving water in the kitchen, reducing electricity consumption through turning off lights in accommodation or encouraging customers to donate to community initiatives when settling their accounts. Overall their recognized contribution to furthering an EMS and wider social activities of the enterprises rather brings into question a recent United Nations Environment Report that suggests that tourism jobs do not contribute to preserving or restoring environmental quality. However, this does depend on the stance on such matters taken by the owners/managers. In the light of which it is notable that 23% of them did not think that their staff were concerned over such matters and a further 37% indicated that they did not know.

Recruitment

The restaurant and inns sectors in particular continue to find difficulty recruiting not only unskilled or semi-skilled personnel but also staff with specific skills; for example good quality managers for inns are hard to find and will often be 'imported'. This situation is not solely a problem for the hospitality sector as, for example, in November 1999 the Windermere Steamboat Museum faced a shortage of skippers to operate its services after the winter lay-off and was seeking new captains and crew members for training in sufficient time for the forthcoming season.

A notable contrast is manifest between urban and rural operations when it comes to employment. In the case of the urban enterprises the majority of staff are recruited from within the area (including and perhaps surprisingly the managers). But this may often not be the case, especially with senior positions in tourist resort localities and emerging destinations. As Prosser (1992) argued, opportunities for personal development and senior jobs are invariably limited and cites the case of Club Mediterranean's resort in Turks and Caicos Islands where locals complained that the jobs open to them were the lowest

paid and menial. This is a recurrent argument and one which is by no means restricted to emerging destinations. This further illustrates 'leakages' through the import of more experienced staff, and flags up the influence of multinational companies and foreign investors.

Recruitment can also be difficult due to the level of demand overall as this can exceed local resources. In rural or coastal localities that develop as they become more popular tourist destinations, the generation of employment will inevitably outstrip local supply due to a combination of factors, including:

- declining number of potential employees in the locality;
- lack of desire on the part of some persons who are available; and
- lack of the necessary supporting infrastructure to attend the place of work.

Further exacerbating the situation in the UK is that these employment opportunities are predominantly in hospitality operations (estimated to account for some 93% of employees in tourism (Leidner, 2004)), which are not renowned for being attractive to young people in the UK. Additional to this is the oft cited denigration of tourism jobs (part-time, seasonal, low paid, female) invariably by commentators not involved in the business and as such are basing their opinions more on their own values in that such employment does not meet their perceptions of some ideal type of employment. This is certainly something of a myopic view; for example, Andriotis and Vaughan's (2004) study based on Crete reveals it is neither so simple nor necessarily problematic (see Zientara, 2012). Secondly, it is generally recognized as an opportunity for young people. Thirdly, given declining rural populations there are not that many younger persons (18–25 year olds) available. Staff are therefore imported leading to the need for staff accommodation, as in the LDNP and rural Scotland. This importation of staff is also a most likely occurrence in any developing tourist destination in undeveloped rural/coastal areas; witness Cancun in Mexico or the Galapagos Islands (see Chapter 3). Thus some of the acclaimed socio-economic benefits arising through local employment are lost to the community.

Profile of the Owners/Managers

The study encompassed a focus on the owners/managers and their background on the basis that the information so gained might illuminate the management of the enterprises as regards EP. Yet, such information can be invaluable in the context of seeking to explain/account for some of the key elements of the study; for example potentially influential factors on why an owner/manager may act in a particular way.

The policies and thus operational practices of any organization are a direct function of the governance, thus of the owners' values and attitudes whether a public limited company, partnership or sole trader. As such, if the chairman of the company, chief executive officer or the senior partner decides that the enterprise will in future ensure that all employees, irrespective of location will be treated equally as regards terms and conditions, and further that they will all be equitably paid at a higher rate than the average for the region, then every operation within that company follows suit. Equally so if a company decides that supplies of X will always be sourced locally whenever it is possible so to do. This is just as applicable to SMEs. In so far as national and multi-national companies (MNC) are influenced in their practices by the attitudes of their owners so too individual enterprises by their owners. Therefore the study sought to gain a profile of the owners (managers in comparatively few cases) of those enterprises that participated in the extended interviews of 2001 and 2011; an aspect that has hardly gained attention in the published research.

The areas covered not only contribute to the overall picture of the enterprises but also, and more usefully, serve to provide helpful criteria to subsequent analysis and interpretation, especially in the context of their awareness of, and attitudes towards, sustainability issues and EM practices (see Chapter 9). Insights into the background of the owners in the 2001 stage are presented in Table 2.5. Not surprisingly, given the motivational factors previously noted, one in four of these owners moved into the LDNP within the last 10 years. More surprisingly perhaps is the finding that close to one in

three owners are comparatively recent entrants into the tourism sector. This factor rather affirms the view that there are few barriers to entry into the business of tourism. Also and potentially evidencing that many persons are new to the tourism sector is the limited membership of professional associations (see Table 2.6). The significance of such memberships lies in the attention to environmental matters by such associations. For example, the Hotel, Catering and Institutional Management Association (HCIMA) (now the Institute of Hospitality, IH) produced a technical brief for their members on environmental issues in 1993 within which it was argued that all hospitality businesses should produce an Environmental Policy Statement as well as promoting EM practices, particularly energy conservation. In 2000, they launched a campaign to reduce energy consumption in hotels by a minimum of 15% over 3 years, which they argued would lead to reduced carbon dioxide emissions of some 40% based on consumption in 2000 (Forte, 2000, p. 18).

Whilst approximately one in four of the 2001 interviewees were members of the IH, this falls to one in ten across the whole sample for 2001 (8% for 2005; 4% in 2011). Conversely, in 2001 few interviewees were members of the Tourism Society compared with 5% overall (3% for 2005; 6% for 2011). Such low membership is understandable in that the owners perhaps do not see themselves as part of the oft cited 'tourism industry'. This speculation is not so readily argued in the case of managers with career aspirations who might be expected to demonstrate recognition of their commitment through membership of these associations. However, the findings for 2011 certainly indicate that this is not the case (see Table 2.6).

As the WTTC et al. (2002) argued, there is a need for multisector partnerships and effective involvement of all stakeholders in order to achieve sustainable, and economically successful tourism. This is well illustrated by the Lake District's Tourism & Conservation Partnership (TCP), which well exemplifies how environmental partnerships can be very successful in their aims (see Long and Arnold, 1995) and the benefits attributable to

Table 2.5. Profile of the LDNP interviewees (audits).

Category	Response (%)
Where is proprietor originally from: i.e. home	
Local	6
Not local but within Cumbria	8
NW England	36
NE England	6
Mid-England	12
SW England	12
SE England	10
If not originally from LDNP when did they move into LDNP?	
1970s	22
1980s	22
1990s	26
Period of time involved in the hospitality sector [years]	
5 or less	32
6–10	8
11–15	12
16–20	6
21 +	36
Period of time in current position [years]	
1–3	40
4–7	20
8–10	4
11–14	6
15–20	14
21+	10
Membership of professional bodies	
HCIMA (now Institute of Hospitality (IH))	28
British Hospitality Association	6
Licensed Victuallers Association	4
Tourism Society	2

collaboration and partnerships in the tourism sector (see Bramwell and Lane, 2000). Membership and participation in professional and community groups are all potential steps in initiating the development of partnerships of one form or another. Involvement in such groups and also membership of green organizations are also potential indicators of environmental behaviours as well as influences on the management practices of the enterprise. Thus membership of such organizations was investigated (see Table 2.6). All the categories of supply in the LDNP stage are included here, as well as the overall figures for 2006 and 2011. The reason for this is to provide for comparative analysis across the spectrum of enterprises. Though this is just the 2001 stage the data for the different categories of 2006 are similar. Reference to Table 2.6 draws attention to the fact that many of these owners, for whatever reason, recognize a benefit to being a member of their respective Tourist Board (TB). Largely, if not solely, this is accounted for by the fact that if they wish both to gain accredited grading status of their operation and be promoted by the TB they must take up membership.

Further analysis of the data across the categories opens up wide scope for discussion; too much for here given the constraints of

Table 2.6. Membership of a cross section of organizations.

Organization	LDNP (%)[a]						Fringe (%)[b]		All Enterprises		
	SA	R	I	A	C	S	A	I	2001	2005	2011
CTB/VisitScotland	72	33	52	60	44	61	38	27	65	84	44
Chamber of Commerce	40	33	22	5	0	0	0	4	32	15	4
The National Trust	34	17	33	14	22	39	0	8	31	15	26
RSPB/SRSPB	12	8	7	0	22	18	0	0	12	10	6
HCIMA/IH	13	0	22	0	0	0	0	12	11	8	4
World Wide Fund for Nature	7	8	0	5	11	18	0	0	7	2	4
Local Community Group	6	8	7	14	22	14	0	0	8	15	18
Friends of the Lake District	6	8	4	0	0	21	0	0		N/A	N/A
Friends of the Earth	1	8	0	0	0	14	25	0	2	1	1
Greenpeace	4	17	0	5	0	11	13	0	4	1	0
CPRE	1	8	0	0	0	11	0	0		0	0
A Tourism Forum	3	8	0	36	0	11	13	0	6	14	9
Local Agenda 21 Group	0	0	0	5	0	0	0	0	0	0	0

[a]SA= Serviced accommodation; R= Restaurants; I= Inns; A= Attractions; C= Caravan and camping sites; S= Self-catering.
[b]Fringe study – 46% of serviced accommodation enterprises were members of the CTB.

space. Even so, a number of such differences are highlighted as follows:

- Membership of green organizations is most apparent among the owners of self-catering operations.
- The urban enterprises are comparatively the least likely (except for restaurants) to be members of a TB and most likely (except for Caravan/Camping operations) to be involved in a local community group.
- Attractions are the most likely to be members of a Tourism Forum.
- Given the rural locality of 2001 and 2005 one might anticipate higher memberships of green organizations. However this clearly is not so and similar to Carlsen *et al.*'s (2001) study. This is perhaps especially notable given that within their sample there were a number of wildlife/nature-based enterprises and one might readily speculate that they would be members of green groups.

Overall, in general the owners/managers of these tourism enterprises are not members of professional associations (with the exception of a TB), and perhaps one in three is involved in a business forum. One might speculate with some confidence that the owners do not see themselves for the most part as being part of the 'tourism industry', and in many cases perhaps not really a part of the business community.

Further of note is the low membership of green organizations which might be considered surprising given that for many owners in rural areas the attractiveness of the location was identified as a primary reason for their enterprise. Thus one might expect higher involvement in such organizations. However, the low level of memberships was also identified by Gaunt (2004) in her study into Scottish based TOs, which found that 17% were members of a green organization (similarly Erdogan and Baris, 2006) though their study was wholly based on larger hotels i.e. 40 bedroom plus). Again perhaps such a low figure is surprising given that many of the operations of these TOs involve tours around Scotland and walking or cycling tours. In contrast Carlsen *et al.*'s (2001) study into family run tourism enterprises in Australia

found that 39% were members of a conservation organization and did identify a
correlation between such membership and the
introduction of EM practices.

Summary

In total these enterprises are predominantly
family owned and managed with low numbers
of employees; as such they are mainly micro-
enterprises. This is significant on two counts;
first it establishes that their profile correlates
with the wider statistics that tourism enterprises
are mainly small or micro-businesses, and
second, that the data gained through the
research is more widely applicable in that it is
far more representative of the tourism sector
than research findings based on international
and national businesses, predominantly in the
hotel sector. Even so, there is some variance
between the data sets. The audits of 2011
given the composition of the sample and
comparative size of the enterprises are not
that representative of the sector as a whole,
which does include a higher proportion of
medium sized enterprises, larger hotels based
on room numbers, and those that are part of a
company group. This sample is thus a little
more representative of the small share in total
tourism supply accorded to medium sized
enterprises, mainly the national and
international companies. The data on these
enterprises may therefore reveal comparable
differences with Stage 1 and Stage 2; such as
it is often found in studies and examples that it
is the major companies which are apparently
addressing their EP, adopting EM and more
broadly CSR related practices. If this is the
case such differences will become apparent in
the following chapters as quite possibly will
the validity of the argument propounded by
the WTTC et al. (2002) that a major barrier to
progress in sustainable development is the
multitude of SMEs that numerically dominate
supply and, this in part at least, accounts for
the lack of accountability of both the private
and the public sector for tourism development.

The diversity to be found in tourism
supply in any popular destination is well
represented by these enterprises, ranging
from a farmhouse BB operation of two rooms
to a 40-bedroom 5-star hotel to a small
attraction receiving less than 10,000 visitors
per annum. Further, within any one category
there is potential for segmentation based on
capacity or turnover or type of locality and
also reason for ownership. This in itself brings
into question the efficacy of policies and
initiatives directed at tourism enterprises per
se, policies which all too often appear to see
tourism as some form of homogenous activity.

Employment on the part of most
enterprises is clearly limited but when collated
for any popular tourist destination will be
substantial. This is invaluable to any locale
where there has been a continuing decline in
more traditional opportunities for work such
as in rural areas wherein the traditional
mainstays of the economy, such as farming,
have declined. However, continued tourism
development and expansion over time in rural
or coastal areas will lead to employment out-
stripping the area's labour supply and the
importation of labour. The danger here is the
impact if the area's popularity starts and
continues to decline. This can lead to substantial socio-economic problems as has and
continues to be evident in many of the cold-
water resorts of the past century. Thus it is all
the more important that these enterprises
seek to support and promote interrelationships
with other aspects of the local economy, local
enterprises and the community. Even so, in
such popular rural locations at some point the
continued promotion of tourism by local and/
or national government, Area Tourists Boards
and Destination Management Organizations
(invariably largely funded by the taxpayers) on
the basis that this will generate local
employment becomes highly questionable.
Conversely, if tourist demand begins to decline
and continues to do so then the impact on
employment will be dramatic.

A weakness of professional associations
involved in tourism is that these all too often
comprise the major players in the market – as
well illustrated by the comparatively recently
established government's Tourism Advisory
Group in the UK which comprises members
from Arora International Hotels, Eurostar,
Virgin Atlantic, Center Parcs, British Airways
and representatives from a range of national
tourist organizations. Such a grouping bears

little resemblance to the profile of enterprises involved in the supply of tourism. Further, the representatives involved may have no experience of working in those enterprises which constitute over 90% of tourism supply and thus have no real understanding of those operations at ground level. Therefore they have little place on such a group other than to foster their own vested interests, which predominantly will be of little relevance to the majority of owners and managers.

The fact that few of these enterprises, especially within the 2011 group, noted 'hard times' over the previous 5 years trading suggests a positive outlook, which it might be argued was a factor in their participation i.e.

poorly performing enterprises were not likely to participate in the study.

Further Reading

A substantive element of this study are tourism enterprises in the LDNP. The LDNP has witnessed substantial tourism development over the last two centuries, which has obviously had a large impact on this highly popular tourist destination. How it has changed is of interest in itself and thus readers' are referred to Davies, H. (1979) *A Walk Around the Lakes.* Weidenfield and Nicholson, London.

References

Andriotis, K. and Vaughan, D.R. (2004) The tourism workforce and policy: exploring the assumptions using Crete as the case study. *Current Issues in Tourism* 7 (1), 66–87

Anon. (2000b) Cycle hire earns e.com accolade. *Lakeland Echo,* 6 June, p. 5.

Badulescu, A. and Badulescu, D. (2012) Entrepreneurship and local resources. In: Leslie, D. (ed.) *Tourism Enterprises and the Sustainability Agenda Across Europe.* New Directions in Tourism Analysis, Ashgate, Farnham, UK, pp. 151–167.

Bardgett, L. (2000) *The Tourism Industry.* Research paper 00/66, June, House of Commons Library, London.

Bramwell, B. and Lane, B. (eds) (2000) *Tourism Collaboration and Partnerships: Politics, Practice and Sustainability.* Channel View, Clevedon, UK.

Carlsen, J., Getz, D. and Ali-Knight, J. (2001) The environmental attitudes and practices of family run businesses in the rural tourism and hospitality sectors. *Journal of Sustainable Tourism* 9 (4), 281–297.

Cawley, M.E., Gaffey, S.M. and Gillmor, D.A (1999) The role of quality tourism and craft SMEs in rural development: evidence from the Republic of Ireland. *Anatolia* 10 (1), pp. 45–60.

ECORYS (2009) *Study on the competitiveness of the EU tourism industry. - with specific focus on the accommodation and tour operators travel agent industries.* Final Report, Directorate-General Enterprise & Industry, European Commission, Brussels.

Erdogan, N. and Baris, E. (2006) Environmental protection programs and conservation practices of hotels in Ankara, Turkey. *Tourism Management* 28 (2), 604–614.

Forte, J. (2000) Energy: an issue we can no longer ignore. *Hospitality,* February, pp. 18–19.

Garay, L. and Font, X. (2012) Doing good to do well? Corporate social responsibility reasons, practices and impacts in small and medium accommodation enterprises. *Journal of Hospitality Management* 31, 329–337.

Gaunt, S. (2004) An analysis of environmental awareness among tour operators in Scotland. Unpublished dissertation, BA (Hons) International Travel with Information Systems. Glasgow Caledonian University, Glasgow, UK.

Holland, J. (2012) Adventure tours: Responsible tourism in practice? In: Leslie, D. (ed.) *Responsible Tourism: Concepts, Theory and Practice.* CAB International, Wallingford, UK, pp. 119–128.

Jarman, R. (2000) Presentation to 'Go for Green' Conference, Tourism and Conservation Partnership, Lake District, 22 March, Keswick, UK.

Leidner, R. (2004) *The European Tourism Industry – a Multi-sector with Dynamic Markets. Structures, Developments and Importance for Europe's Economy.* EC, Enterprise Directorate General (Unit D.3) Publications, Brussels.

Leslie, D. (2001) *An Environmental Audit of the Tourism Industry in the Lake District National Park.* Report for Friends of the Lake District and the Council for the Protection of Rural England, Murley Moss, Kendal. Glasgow, UK.

Leslie, D. (2007a) Scottish rural tourism enterprises and the sustainability of their communities: A Local Agenda 21 approach. In: Thomas, R. and Augustryn, M. (eds) *Tourism in the New Europe: Perspectives on SME Policies and Practices*. Advances in Tourism Research Series. Elsevier, Oxford, UK, pp. 89–108.

Leslie, D. (2007b) The missing component in the 'greening' of tourism: the environmental performance of the self-catering accommodation sector. Special Issue on Self-catering Accommodation. *International Journal of Hospitality Management* 26 (2), 310–322.

Leslie, D. (2010) *Tourism Bute and Inchmarnock Fish Farm Proposal. Precognition*. Interim scheme for the authorisation of Fish Farms Application by Offshore Farm Development Ltd. Fish farm North of Inchmarnock, Isle of Bute. Public Enquiry. DPEA Reference IQC/35/24, March.

Leslie, D. (2011) The European Union, sustainable tourism policy and rural Europe. In: Macleod, D.V.L. and Gillespie, S.A. (eds) *Sustainable Tourism in Rural Europe: Approaches to Development*. Routledge, London, pp. 43–60.

Long, F.J. and Arnold, M.B. (1995) *The Power of Environmental Partnerships*. Dryden Press, Fort Worth, Texas.

McGehee, N.C. and Kim, K. (2004) Motivation for agri-tourism entrepreneurship. *Journal of Travel Research* 43, pp. 161–170.

Prosser, R.F. (1992) The ethics of tourism. In: Cooper, D.E. and Palmer, J.A. (eds) *The Environment in Question: Ethics and Global Issues*. Routledge, New York, pp. 37–50.

SLDC (1997) *South Lakeland Local Plan 2006*. South Lakeland District Council, Kendal, UK.

Spencely, A. and Rylance, A. (2012) Responsible wildlife tourism in Africa. In: Leslie, D. (ed.) *Responsible Tourism: Concepts, Theory and Practice*. CAB International, Wallingford, UK, pp. 130–141.

Vernon, J., Essex, S., Pinder, D. and Curry, K. (2003) The 'greening' of tourism business: Outcomes of groups investigations in South-East Cornwall. *Business Strategy and Environment* 12 (1), 49–69.

Wisner, P.S., Epstein, M.J. and Bagozzi, R.P. (2010) Environmental proactivity and performance. In: Freedman, M. and Jaggi, B. (eds) *Sustainability, Environmental Performance and Disclosures*. Emerald, Bingley, UK.

WTTC, IFTO, IH&RA and ICCL (2002) *Industry as a Partner for Sustainable Development: Tourism Report*. Prepared by the World Travel and Tourism Council, International Federation of Tour Operators, International Hotels & Restaurateurs Association and the International Council for Cruise Lines Kenya, United Nations Environment Programme, London.

Zientara, P. (2012) Hospitality enterprises – a key influence. In: Leslie, D. (ed.) *Responsible Tourism: Concepts, Theory and Practice*. CAB International, Wallingford, UK, pp. 154–164.

3 Sustainable Supply Chain Management

Introduction

This chapter addresses sustainable supply chain management (SSCM), which encompasses all the elements involved in the delivery of tourism products and services. As Eastham et al. (2001, p. xviii) expressed, it involves the:

> co-ordination and integration of all activities in delivering a product from its initial primary source through to the consumer into a seamless process, thereby linking all partners in the chain internal and external to the organization.

More conceptually, supply-chain management can be defined as:

> a philosophy of management that involves the management and integration of a set of selected key business processes from end user through original suppliers, that provides products, services and information that add value for customer and other stakeholders through the collaborative efforts of supply chain members (Ho et al., 2002 as cited in Mosselaer et al., 2012, p. 74).

Therefore in order to develop sustainability in the supply chain, all involved need to address their EP and adopt EM practice. Thus, in the case of a TO, for example, it is implicit that each component supplier of a tour, e.g. transportation, accommodation, travel agent, should be selected on the basis of their environmental policy and accredited related practices. The choice here of a TO is significant given that:

> the supply chain approach offers a more clearly delineated context and framework for tour operators to pursue CSR policies and practices, implying that the degree of supply chain sustainability depends on the performance of all the components, the suppliers and their links with the supply chain (Mosselaer et al., 2012, p. 74).

Comprehensive guidelines on this have been promoted since the early 2000s, including not only who to choose but also how to develop better linkages with the local/regional economy and the community. The comprehensive scope of SSCM when interpreted and applied most positively in the context of tourism and sustainability reflects Eber's (1992, p. 2) statement that 'if tourism is to be truly beneficial to all concerned and sustainable in the long-term, it must be ensured that:

- resources are not over-consumed;
- natural and human environments are protected;
- tourism is integrated with other activities,
- it provides real benefits to the local communities;
- local people are involved and included in tourism planning and implementation; and
- cultures and people are respected.'

This view was echoed comparatively recently by Goeldner and Ritchie (2009). Furthermore, the 'Pro-Poor Tourism' lobby affirms the importance of SSCM, claiming that it played a key role in their efforts in the Gambia to alleviate poverty (see Goodwin and Bah, 2004); a counterpoint success to the all-inclusive resorts which developed, largely due to the influence of European Operators, as illustrated here by ACTSA:

> One British tour operator offers an all-inclusive beach holiday to the Seychelles. You fly with a British airline and stay in a British owned hotel. Within the hotel resort there is a range of restaurants, bars and leisure facilities, so you may not spend any money outside the resort. People on this kind of holiday contribute virtually nothing to the local economy. The only local people who benefit are those directly employed in the resort.
> (2002, p. 2)

Such examples encapsulate the problems arising from tourism and development that have long been recognized (see Leslie, 2012a). Amongst the many responses to such problems noted in the 1990s, one of the most comprehensive as regards different stakeholders – government, agencies, business and NGOs – and potential solutions is that of the UNCSD (1999), which presents a comprehensive range of negative impacts and potential solutions on the part of tourism enterprise with many examples of good practice. However, the arguments propounded in support of SSCM, which have arisen in the wake of the advocacy of sustainability and climate change, are mainly propounded against a backdrop of the perceived negatives of tourism resort development often attributed to mass (traditional) tourism and rather conveniently laid at the feet of TOs.

Undoubtedly, TOs are very influential in terms of range and choice of opportunities and destinations – witness the rise in popularity of Spain in the 1970s, East Africa and Nepal in the 1990s, so too Thailand and the expansion of Pattaya and Phuket (Prosser, 1992). They are also often major stakeholders in many destinations and hold substantial influence in their development and growth (see Briasspoulis, 2003) and therefore to support furthering the aims of initiatives designed to address sustainability issues (see Budeanu, 2005; Font et al., 2008). As Carey et al. (1997) noted, it is not just their influence on destinations but

also their ability to influence market trends and demand for new areas, arguing that they hold more influence than the marketing efforts of a destination. Allowing for scale, the scope of this influence is applicable to all TOs but may be far more manifest today in the niche markets of nature/eco/adventure tourism (NEAT), which increased by approximately 180% between 2006 and 2009 (Anon., 2011). As Leslie (2012b, p. 11) argued:

> TOs, more than any other tourism agent, through creating and delivering holiday packages, hold substantial potential to influence the other enterprises involved in their tours and thus the importance of promoting and developing sustainability in managing the supply chain is stressed.

Moreover, larger tour operators are also often owners of airlines and hotels, as for example TUI Travel PLC which owns some 150 aeroplanes, over 3500 retail shops and hotel chains like Grecotel, Iberotel and Rui-hotels (Mosselaer et al., 2012, p. 74). Thus, more perhaps than ever they are well positioned to shape the tourist destination environment rather in the manner of an 'eco-bubble', whether this be the Costa Brava of Spain or subsequent 'exotic' resorts such as the Nusa Dua resort on Bali (Prosser, 1992). The idea of the eco-bubble is also evident in package tours to Europe designed for Americans; often the TOs involved will select American owned hotels, e.g. Sheraton, failing which they will select accommodation on the basis of whether it is tuned to the American market (Ritzer, 2000). However, the exemplar today of the eco-bubble is that of cruises (see Jaakson, 2004). In emerging destinations, development may largely reflect the mores of the major source markets; thus, as tourism supply expands so too does the economic impact of tourism, leading to a gradual and growing dependency on tourism activity, which is not then in tune with the cultural norms and values of the host population. Further, to subsequently then influence its development through their ability to influence tourist demand and thus tourist numbers for any particular destination; as such they have a strong negotiating position and potential to play off one destination against another. A position which is certainly aided by their role as major players in destination access and thus transportation, whether through their own operations or secondary suppliers, which also involves issues of sustainability (see Chapter 8).

It is in recognition of the major initiative to promote SSCM, and specific to this chapter, that the focus on tourism enterprises rests largely on TOs. This is not to imply that the study's tourism enterprises are being ignored here or that SSCM is not applicable to them. But they are more in the background whilst they are also part of the supply chain in some cases, e.g. coach-based tours; and as a supplier of tourism products and services they should also be addressing SSCM. Second, and perhaps the more significant, is that comparatively few of the researched enterprises have the capacity to be considered as potential suppliers by most TOs. Furthermore, even when one considers the increasing number of people seeking to make their own travel and accommodation arrangements for their trips, TOs still 'play a key role in directing tourism flows and coordinating supply chains, especially in the mainstream market' (Mosselaer et al., 2012, p. 71). Yet in comparison with research involving hotels or transportation TOs have received little such attention (see Tepelus, 2005). This is perhaps surprising given their international scope and the fact that their products not only involve other major elements (e.g. transportation, hotels) but also that they are in *the* position to influence those suppliers as well as fitting the main dimensions of SSCM, which as presented by Manente et al. (1998) are:

- awareness of variety and complementarity of tourism attractions;
- creation of tourism products through integration/linkages;
- promotion of unique images; and
- strategies that are based on co-operation and synergy.

It is within this context that we can establish most pertinently the perceived ills attributed to tourism development, the negative impacts which are invariably noted in the context of destinations that are long haul flights from Europe/USA – the more exotic or romantic – that are far more likely to involve large enterprises. As such the enterprises portrayed in this study might well be considered as having very little to do with such problems. Even so, they are being encouraged to adopt 'best practice' as their national and international counterparts. The chapter thus brings to attention many of the aspects involved in addressing sustainability that were explored in the research and addressed in the following chapters. Thus the attention in these pages is on what SSCM involves, including consideration of potential influence on destinations and development, and its applicability/adoption primarily by TOs. Prior to this and by way of illustrating that SSCM is applicable to all tourism enterprises discussion first draws on those findings from the study to be most pertinent here, when considered in the context of other chapters (mainly Chapter 6), namely the purchasing patterns and practices of the enterprises in the study.

Overview of SSCM

SSCM is not a recent initiative, gaining considered attention in the 1990s though more in the context of general business, which led to recognition that much more could be done. As Welford et al. (1999) argued there is a need for closer links between supply and demand and integration in suppliers. Projects were designed to encourage and promote good environmental practice on the part of suppliers, for example, 'The Green Supply Chain Network' and 'Project Acorn' both of which included in their aims a focus on SMEs (EC, 2000). It was at this time that SSCM came to be recognized by the World Tourism Organization (WTO), who in partnership with other agencies such as the United Nations Environment Programme (UNEP) and UNESCO, led the establishment of the Tour Operators Initiative (TOI) in 2000 and the promotion of SSCM under the umbrella of CSR since 2001 (Gordon, 2002). By 2004 it had 23 members worldwide though the majority are based in Europe. The first iteration of this introduced SSCM and included indicators to facilitate reporting by TOs and comparability between TOs (it also advocated raising consumer awareness of sustainability) (see Tables 3.1 and 3.2). This is far more comprehensive than solely SSCM. Essentially it is a framework for all aspects of sustainability seen to be applicable to TOs and thus encompasses CSR (see Chapter 4) and EMS (see Chapter 5). This development coincides with the Association of Independent Tour Operators' 'Responsible Tourism Guidelines' established in 2001. As the then Chairman argued, the organization realises that members need to recognize and address their responsibilities and concern for the environment, thus the promotion of conservation, minimizing of pollution and respect for local culture (Miles, 2001). On such a basis one may well ask what have they been doing previously given this was first highlighted in the 1960s! It is also another ecolabel and, according to Goodwin, accredited members therefore are seen to be meeting 'globally recognized corporate sustainable development standards' (Goodwin, 2005, p. 1). That such promotion and guidance is seen to be necessary is well conveyed in Tearfund's (2002, p. 5) report:

> With few notable exceptions, tourism has been one of the slowest industries to adopt corporate social responsibility practices. Research in 2001 by Tearfund revealed that of 65 tour companies, only half has responsible tourism policies – many of these were so brief as to be virtually meaningless.

Table 3.1. Locating SSCM in the context of business operations. (Adapted from GRI, 2002, pp. 10–16.)

Business operations	Areas encompassed
Product management and development	Includes actions related to the choice of the destination as well as the type of services to be included (e.g. the use of train versus plane) (nine indicators)
Internal management	Labour practices; health and safety; training and education; materials; waste; reflects all the operations and activities that take place in the headquarters or country offices (e.g. use of office supplies, production brochures, direct employment) (nine indicators)
Sub-division of Internal management	*Criteria*
Internal operations management	*Building design and construction services; building materials, suppliers; real estate agents and rental services*
Obtaining office space	*Water supply and waste water disposal services; energy suppliers; waste disposal services;*
Daily business processes	*Telecommunication and IT services; suppliers of office equipment, furniture, paper and other supplies; cleaning services; catering services; gardening/landscape services; couriers; vehicle renting and parking services; management and financial consultants; PR and communication agencies; financial institutions*
Supply chain management	Addresses actions related to the selection and contracting of service providers (16 indicators)
Customer relations	Summarizes the actions taken to deal with customers, not only with regards to the responsibility to serve them and reply to their comments, but also the opportunity to provide information and raise consumer awareness regarding sustainability (seven indicators)
Co-operation with destinations	Partnerships; community development; philanthropy and charitable donations: includes all activities and decisions related to destinations that tour operators make beyond the production and delivery of their holiday packages. This mainly includes efforts made by tour operators to engage in dialogues with destination operators about the impacts of tour packages, and philanthropic activities (six indicators)

Table 3.2. Indicators for supply chain management. (Adapted from GRI, 2002, pp. 12–14.)

Indicator	Description
1	Describe the supply chain management policy, objectives and targets on environmental, social and economic performance. (State the use if supplier prioritization and screening criteria.)
2	Describe processes through which suppliers, by type, are consulted during development and implementation of the supply chain management policy, described in 1.
3	Describe issues identified through supplier consultation and actions to address them.
4	Describe processes through which suppliers, by type, are engaged in the implementation of the supply chain management policy, described in 1. (Processes include: one way (e.g. questionnaires), two-way communication (e.g. information exchange), active co-operation (e.g. supplier training), rewards and recognition for high performers.)
5	State joint actions taken with suppliers, by type, to support improvements in suppliers own environmental and social performance.
6	Describe progress in achieving objectives and targets related to supply chain policy.
7	Indicate percentage of suppliers, by type, subject to supply chain management policy.
8	Indicate percentages of suppliers, by type, subject to supply chain policy that have a published sustainability policy, implemented a sustainability management system and/or have a staff person with management responsibility for corporate sustainability.
9	State types of information requested from suppliers, by type, on their: • Environmental practices and performance. Include: materials, water, energy, purchasing, solid waste, hazardous waste, effluents, emissions, transport, land-use and biodiversity. • Social practices and performance. Include: community and staff development, indigenous and tribal people's rights, formal employment contracts, social security, working conditions according to ILO Convention 172, equal treatment, non-discrimination, recognition of independent trade unions and application of collective bargaining agreements, health and safety committees, policy excluding child labour as defined by ILO, programmes to combat commercial sexual exploitation of children, and to combat and mitigate the social impacts of HIV/AIDS.
10	Indicate percentage of suppliers, by type, subject to supply chain management policy that provided requested information.
11	Indicate percentage of suppliers, by type, subject to supply chain management policy whose environmental, social and economic performance has been reported. Through for example: • suppliers declaration; • spots checks by reporting organization; • environmental and social audits; • certification schemes (including eco labels); and • third party verification (state if verifier is accredited, and by whom).
12	State actions taken by the reporting organization in response to suppliers reported performance (as per 11), by type of suppliers. (Include incentives and rewards.)
13	State actions to inform suppliers of customers' requirements.
14	State contracting policy and how it is communicated to suppliers. (Include negotiating terms and conditions for payment, cancelation and compensation of contracts with suppliers.)
15	Describe joint initiatives with suppliers to improve environmental, social and economic conditions in destinations.
16	State benefits for the reporting organization from implementing the sustainable chain policy.

Their report also noted on the basis of their survey that holidaymakers would prefer a TO with an environmental policy and promoted responsible tourism guidelines, a finding that suggests a change in attitude to that of 2 years earlier when, as noted by Welford *et al.* (1999, p. 175), there was 'no great demand from the tourists themselves for the greening of the supply function.' Further to these initiatives, comprehensive and well-illustrated guidelines to aid TOs engage with and develop SSCM were introduced in 2004 (TOI and CELB, 2004). Here our primary concern is SSCM, which involves most aspects of the business and, as shown in Table 3.2, many aspects of a supplier's business practices and related areas such as destination development and the involvement of local communities.

It is no coincidence that the attention of the TOI to SSCM closely follows the establishment, with the support of the UNEP, of the Global Reporting Initiative (GRI) in 2002 as an independent non-profit organization. Their guidelines, first developed in 1999,

> set out the principles and indicators that organizations can use to measure and report (*including structure and contents thereof*) their economic, environmental and social performance (Visser, 2009, p. 172).

In effect, these reports are recognized as CSR/ sustainability reports. Amongst the sector-specific supplements are guidelines for TOs, including performance indicators, which were established in partnership with the TOI, UNEP and the World Tourism Organization (WTO); reputedly based on the life cycle of the holiday product. Early leaders to adopt these guidelines and who have been formally reporting on their sustainability practices since 2003 are TUI, which includes First Choice Holidays, and Kuoni Travel. These guidelines are certainly extensive as shown in Table 3.1, which draws attention to many of the elements involved in an EMS (*see* Chapter 5), and quite detailed as the sub-section detail on 'Internal Operations Management' in the main category Internal Management further illustrates. Further detail on SSCM is subsequently presented in Table 3.2.

The IH&RA also contributed to the development of these guidelines and whilst supporting they noted that it 'maintains the importance of establishing limits to which hospitality operators can be asked to report to tour operators.' (Anon., 2003, p. 48). It is not just 'how much to report' but also, as Charlton and Howell (1992) identified, there is the problem of establishing the boundary lines along the supply chain. If, for example, a coach tour is supplied, what is the starting point? Is this where the customer joins the coach or should it include the selection of the coach vehicle itself? If it is a package tour sold by a travel agent, does the supply chain include the possibility of the customer being transferred from home to the airport? Does it also mean that the contractor also considered the environmental credentials of any organization acting as a sub-agent within any element of their supply chain? To a degree this appears to be the case in that TOs are being encouraged, for example, by the WTO and ETOA, to adopt an EMS and also to encourage their suppliers to adopt such practices. Equally, the opposite is also true in that companies seeking to negotiate rates for their business and, to a lesser extent, individual customers may start asking about an enterprise's environmental policy.

As with most business systems there is not only a need for effective liaison with staff and suppliers but also the community who should be part and parcel of the procurement process; a key point to achieving success in SSCM as noted by the British Airport Authority (BAA), a relatively early leader in this field. BAA 'see SSCM as very much part of their aim to reduce the consumption and emissions which result from our business practices' (Howell, 2000, p. 10). They see it very much as a continuous process that includes a major element of trust and integrity on the part of suppliers and, as such, there are advantages to working with fewer rather than more suppliers.

Further recognition that SSCM is applicable to all tourism enterprises are the guidelines produced specifically for hotels that to varying degrees are applicable to all tourism and hospitality enterprise. These guidelines include the following advice and benefits:

Advice:

- 'sourcing more products and services locally to encourage local business, provide "authenticity" and cut down on transport costs;
- sourcing products with less environmental impact in their manufacture, use and disposal;
- buying products in bulk and reusing packaging;
- importing only "fair trade" products; and
- ensuring that suppliers adhere to safe and ethical working practices.' (Anon., 2006, p. 1).

This advice certainly appears appropriate on first consideration and all the more so for national and international hotel companies who will have procurement policies and quite probably departments with a specific remit for sourcing supplies. But this does include potential contradictions that become all the more apparent when considered in terms of application to small and micro tourism enterprises; for example between sourcing locally and bulk buying. Advice supported by Gossling *et al.* (2011) who argue in environmental impact terms that bulk production and distribution may be a better option than production, for example, of bread within a hospitality kitchen or, though to a lesser extent, a local bakery. There is also the matter of purchasing fair trade goods but what of availability and cost? These are issues that all relate to support for local suppliers and so forth, which are discussed in more detail in Chapter 6.

Benefits:

- 'a destination with more local colour and more to do – creating a market advantage for new and repeat business;
- the potential for lower operating costs through more efficient use of energy and water resources and reduced waste;
- risk reduction by avoiding suppliers with a doubtful track record on environmental and social issues;
- better relationships with suppliers giving improved loyalty and service;
- a better relationship with the community whose economy you are supporting;

- increased security of supply of the goods or service through long-term contracts and a better negotiating position (i.e. through increased purchasing power); and
- the ability to demonstrate to all your stakeholders the importance you place in sustainability issues' (Anon., 2006, p. 1).

These benefits are widely applicable and in some ways would be achievable at the expense of alternative suppliers such as those involved in local produce and products (see Chapter 6). On the plus side however, we can also add such potential benefits as fostering innovation, enhanced company profile and gaining a competitive advantage. They also echo the positives of relationship marketing, which is not just about relationships with customers but should include building good working relationships with suppliers, which should achieve many if not all of these benefits. In effect, irrespective of sustainability this is just good management practice and as such could be reasonably expected of all enterprises (see Budeanu, 2009). In part this is apparent in major influential factors in supply chain management drawn from general practice in the hospitality sector. Namely, that suppliers are generally not selected on a short-term basis but rather on value for money, continuity and general consistency and convenience. Managers do not wish to be changing suppliers often. A problem with such criteria for TOs is whether they will commit to longer-term relationships involving some degree of trust and loyalty. Furthermore, given the pressure on costs, a 'fair deal' may be less likely in those situations where there are other potential suppliers or a similar destination available. Also, should a TO or other enterprise in the tourism supply change a long-standing supplier who meets most SSCM criteria but lacks a formalized EP and an accredited EMS? As Mosselaer *et al.* (2012, p. 75) argue:

> The CSR performance of different suppliers poses several challenges. Many of the 'grassroots' suppliers in developing countries lack the capacity and ability to implement advanced techniques for waste management and pollution control. Dismissing them in favour of more environmentally friendly and often more wealthy suppliers would be unsustainable from a socio-economic perspective.

Such a situation is well exemplified by Jones (1999) who drew attention to the provision for hire by irresponsible operators of quad bikes and four-wheel driving which were damaging the local, relatively undisturbed fragile environment. Blame for this was largely attributed to local enterprises that were not controlling the users as to where they could go. Whilst there were a number of ways considered to resolve the problem, one solution proposed was to restrict supply to the large tour operators who were seen to control their customers much better. In general this is one of the major difficulties with SSCM and therefore it is all the more important that third-party suppliers are selected with due care and, as Holland (2012, p. 121–122) argues, with the potential for 'working closely with the suppliers to improve their input and performance in all the components of the holiday.'

The Study Enterprises

As the foregoing discussion implies, commitment to SSCM presents a conundrum for these small/micro tourism enterprises and thus it is not surprising to find that attention to the environmental policies of suppliers is still very much in its infancy outside of national and international hotel groups (see Bohdanowicz and Zientara, 2012). Though there are initiatives within the EU that specifically focus on SMEs (see Leslie, 2011) but with little sign of impact thus far (for example, see Kucerova, 2012; Lebe and Zupan, 2012). That none of the enterprises (with one exception) indicated that they had an SSCM policy is perhaps surprising given the number of enterprises who were members of the GTBS and others which were part of a national hotel group. This is not perhaps to be unexpected given Barrow and Burnett's (1990) study of many small companies that found few had such a policy. Albeit this was 10 years before the findings of 2001, there is little evidence to indicate there has been progress since. A number of respondents' comments from the 2011 population provide a sense of why this is the case:

- 'We send our laundry out to a laundry company and what they do with it I don't know. I suppose they will be environmentally friendly but I don't know.' (The supposition here might well be correct given that Fishers Services Ltd (includes a laundry service) claim they are amongst the most efficient and environmentally aware companies in their industry in the United Kingdom.)
- 'Our brochure print goes to an external contractor; how they source paper is not really our concern.'
- 'According to company policy we should check the environmental policy of suppliers right down the chain, make sure that their processes are not harmful, but at the end of the day there has to be a balance between economics, profitability and the environment.'

There was just one enterprise (a restaurant in the 2001 population) in the whole study that indicated that it did consider the environmental policies of its suppliers. Unfortunately perhaps it was not possible due to anonymity to check the accuracy of that detail. However, a similar study into SMEs on a smaller scale and involving a higher proportion of large enterprises, is that of Kucerova (2012). This research found just one hotel, notably ISO 14001 accredited, that sought to establish if a supplier had an environmental policy; favouring those who could demonstrate appropriate accreditation. This hotel, compared with the other operations in the study, was identified as providing the highest standard of services, a finding which rather supports the view that those owners who are most concerned about their operations and the environment/sustainability are also customer oriented. Even so, this outcome that few, if any of these tourism enterprises have adopted an SSCM is not unexpected given that Barrow and Burnett's (1990) study into SMEs in general business found that less than 10% had such a policy though it is recognized that such policies are far more likely to be found in N/MNCs in the hospitality sector and also tour operators (see page 44).

However, the sole criterion for suppliers in SSCM is not whether or not they have an EP. As noted earlier, it is more complex than this. An important factor is whether or not supplies can be sourced locally; generally the favoured sustainability option. As Hall *et al.* (2003, p. 26) argued:

> ... the development of strong local food identities and sustainable food systems has substantial potential to grow, with tourism playing a significant role in this process.

As Chapter 6 addresses local produce and local products, the focus here is on the more general purchasing practices of the study's enterprises, thereby providing insights into their typical supply chains. In general, the purchasing patterns of the rural enterprises tend to be from suppliers based within the area and predominantly from 'local' outlets. For example:

- Dry goods for catering operations are sourced from major catering supply companies which operate in the region.
- The majority of enterprises (excluding BBs and GHs) purchase prepacked portioned items such as butter, jams and sugar, as well as coffee sachets for guest accommodation. This is for convenience of service, especially in premises with busy food and beverage operations during the day.
- Comparatively few source local produce and local products from small producers in their locality.
- Restaurants and cafes in rural areas are more likely to purchase fresh produce from local stores and local producers, with many respondents noting that such suppliers will deliver to the enterprise contrary to the views of other respondents on this matter.
- The cleaning materials for the majority of self-catering operations not managed by an agency are purchased from local stores, usually a supermarket i.e. potentially lowest cost price.

In terms of the purchasing spend of these enterprises by far the majority is accounted for by major regional suppliers. However the majority of the enterprises did indicate that they favour and would prefer to purchase local produce and products. The key point here being 'prefer' rather than actually do. Yet, as Spenceley and Rylance (2012, p. 139) argue:

> ... supporting the community or society which the tourism businesses operate within is important for strengthening the efficiency of their supply chains for both employees and fresh produce, increasing the number of quality activities available to tourists enabling them to spend more locally, as well as improving the security of the tourism establishment.

Further supporting such argument, as noted in Table 2.1, is the significant proportion of visitor spend attributed to food and beverage services and shopping, e.g. souvenirs and gifts; for example purchases from A & C outlets which in the LDNP account for approximately 80% of the sales of the producers of A & C living in the area. These areas are also identified as a facet of tourism supply chains (see Tapper and Font, 2004). The research into this area found that many of the food producing enterprises showed an awareness of the sources of their purchases; as a number of interviewees said: 'ingredients are bought locally but not produced locally'. One in four of the cafe managers said they purchase their ingredients from local wholesalers but were vague as to the primary source. As regards arts and crafts artisans, it was interesting to identify that the majority considered their biggest competition was not from other producers but 'imported' similar, cheaper products, a view confirmed by two retail outlets who affirmed they stock very few (or no) local products due to the prices involved; as the managers noted: 'we buy in bulk to gain much lower prices; we do not favour local artists as it costs more to stock their products'. However, the majority of outlets offered a different perspective, as the following quotes from managers demonstrate:

- 'Local paintings sell better than others, a lot of the products are bought by locals.'
- 'Lots of local art exhibits sold, sales very good.'

In addition, as one retailer remarked: 'We do not buy locals' work; we display items and take some commission.' This is a practice that can also be adopted by tourism enterprises whereby in liaison with the artisans they offer to display appropriate items for sale in their own premises on a commission basis. A small number of the arts/crafts producers did work on this basis with some of the hotels and restaurants though again this was evidently practised far more by rural enterprises than their urban counterparts i.e.:

Data set	2001	2011
Arts displayed for sale	30%	15%
Local products in service	18%	10%

Tour Operations

Given the primary focus of the study was on the EP of tourism enterprises it is germane that SSCM is particularly pertinent to best practice by TOs (Leslie, 2012a). As noted, TOs have a major influence on the development of destinations, indeed the publication *Which*, produced a special edition titled 'The worst resorts in the world' (1992 cited in EIU, 1993) that highlighted problems arising from a lack of control on development and the multiplicity of players. Major factors which partly account for 'overdevelopment leading to environmental damage through tourism.' (EIU, 1993, p. 67). The extent to which such damage is attributable to TOs is a matter of debate but their adoption of SSCM might in some ways address some of the 'ills' which have and still do arise. But the ongoing popularity of many resorts brings into question whether the tourists themselves see such overdevelopment as a negative. Research into such perceptions is hard to find and thus Guley's study (1994) is all the more welcome. The research involved a survey of perceptions of tourists visiting a popular Mediterranean resort undertaken in 1977 and then repeated in 1989. A key finding was that the perceptions of the 1989 tourists with regard to the physical environment found one significant difference which was a drop by 5% of visitors who considered the nature of the area to be unspoiled. However, expansion of popular coastal resorts invariably brings with it problems; for example Mallorca, notably popular with UK residents, went from an agricultural based economy in the 1960s to become dependent on tourism by the 1980s, which was greatly facilitated by TOs (Sykes, 1995). Major problems identified included the drinking water supply, waste disposal and

limited attention to conservation. Similarly, Dodds (2007) argues that the popularity of Malta and the Balearics rather led to ad hoc tourism development throughout the 1960s and 1970s but began to decline in the 1980s due to degradation of the environment by unplanned, uncontrolled expansion of the tourism supply. TOs promoted the destination and may be considered to some degree, certainly not totally, to be responsible though they were a major influence. But, as Dodds argues, government policies were less than effective due to prioritizing economic factors whilst primary failings included a lack of accountability in regard to implementing tourism policy, poor co-ordination and integration and a lack of involvement on the part of the local community in the process.

Whilst such traditional resorts in and around the Mediterranean are decried as evidencing the ills of mass tourism this has not appeared to influence or stop such problems arising, e.g. touristic development of Turkey's western Mediterranean coastline (see Erdogan, 2009). Nor are they by any means limited to traditional or latter day resorts of Europe; witness the Canary Isles, Belize (see Holden, 2005) or the increasing number of resorts in Eastern Asia (see Pleumarom, 2009). As Bianchi (2004) argued, in the case of the Canary Islands, there is a clear need for the active involvement of all stakeholders, their participation and ownership of policy and actions and that implementation is subsequently monitored, reviewed and adapted to changing circumstances if problems and negative impacts are to be ameliorated if not avoided. Though these factors are largely outside the scope of SSCM, one can see how full commitment to such a system can certainly make a positive contribution. In popular destinations where a national policy promoting 'sustainable tourism' has been developed, for example Malta and Calvia (Mallorca) in the early–mid 2000s, questions arise as to whether there was real commitment to sustainability or rather more a strategy designed for repackaging a destination experiencing declining demand (see Dodds, 2007). As Farsari *et al.* (2007) argue, sustainable tourism is quintessentially the ongoing promotion of tourism and that such policies, in the case of the Mediterranean at least, are more a response to saturation or decline in markets and an re-orientation to what is perceived as quality in tourism i.e. prices up/demand down. Further to this, going up-market through renovation and market repositioning may well be less sustainable given the tourists' expectations and demands of higher standards and better services (Butler, 2007). The counterpoint to such critiques are the potential benefits, which over time can be substantial. As the WTTC *et al.* (2002) argue; for example:

- The Balearic Islands were the poorest province in Spain in the early 1950s but due to tourism development and package holidays, by 2000 they were one of the richest (for a more recent appraisal see Dodds, 2007).
- Due to tourism development the Maldives is no longer classified as a 'lesser developed country' and is essentially now totally dependent on tourism (29% direct GDP). This is a particularly interesting example, as Moosa's (2009) study of the Maldives demonstrates. A new policy on tourism was introduced in 2009 which encouraged greater inward investment (including 100% ownership) whilst also seeking to become carbon neutral by 2020, including no use of fossil fuel and environmental impact assessments for all development. However, how can it be carbon neutral given the access factor for tourists? Furthermore, little attention appears given to the issue of waste and, more importantly from a community perspective, what of attention to a community integrated approach to tourism? Factors which all bring into question the claim to be aiming to be a totally 'sustainable tourism' destination and what is meant by this term.
- Turkey's growing popularity in the 1990s and beyond is credited as accounting for 30% of the country's commodity revenues.
- Cancun, Mexico, was a poor area of perhaps 600 people but by 2000, again due to tourism, had substantially changed, with a population of some 600,000.

    Other examples include:

- The Galapagos Islands, which by 2000 were considered to be the most affluent

part of Ecuador due to the influx of tourism (Vidal, 2001). But as Vidal argues, the islands are overexploited leading to damage to this acclaimed environment and conflicts between those earning a living from tourism and conservationists.
- Further to these cases is the finding from Holzner's (2007) study that countries with a comparatively high percentage of tourism in GDP terms evidenced higher economic growth and higher investment and also higher secondary school enrolments, but a common factor to all was that they were small island economies. Basically the development and expansion of many emerging tourist destinations is driven by TOs. It is therefore not surprising that 'tour operators are increasingly expected to take their social responsibility within their daily operations, in managing their supply chain and in operating in holiday destinations' (Mosselaer *et al.*, 2012, p. 73). As noted, this will not change the situation overnight but could herald greater commitment towards the objectives of sustainability within tourist resorts and in this, as Pearce (1995; see also Laisch (2002)) argued, transnational companies may be more influential than local organizations. The caveat here is – but whose interests are being served?

Issues in SSCM

For much of this discussion on TOs so far the orientation has been to major TOs, but what of the comparatively small operators in niche markets, are they that different in their impact? For example, adventure tour companies are not without detractors as Seabrook (2007, p. 14) argued:

> Adventure tourism scatters debris and waste in formerly inaccessible places on the earth; pristine mountain slopes, ice-floes and high plateau receive their quota of mementos from the unquiet visitations of people avid for sensation and novelty.

A point that might be equally applied to those enterprises promoting scuba diving on coral reefs, or cetacean watching or safari tours, for example, in Kenya or Natal. The latter may well bring into question the reality of SSCM on the part of the TOs involved:

> Witness the safari camps provided in Africa to higher paying guests, where rates run upwards of 400 Euros a night and fine wines and gourmet meals are provided to ensure a comfortable eco/sustainable visit. (Butler, 2007, p. 21)

Two specific examples from Jackman and Rodgers (2005) of this are first a packaged safari in the Serengeti, Tanzania involving a mobile camping safari which is comparatively basic but even so the food is of high quality (£300 per night; package based on four people for eight nights from London all inclusive is approx. £2600). The other involves the Lebombo Lodge, Singita on the very edge of Kruger National Park and costs £600 per night. This is a boutique lodge offering luxury (including power shower) in each of the six rooms; as one customer said, 'We were in a bubble of First World designer comfort surrounded by bush.' (p. 3).

This raises issues of the operators involved regarding their supply chain and sustainability. Further, and perhaps implicit in SSCM, are the issues that arise in opening up new destinations in hitherto remote places of the globe, for example cruise ships now arriving in previously little known areas, e.g. Tasiilaq and 'polar tourism' in general (see Nuttall, 1997; Luck et al., 2010). As Hall and Johnston (1995) in their text on this subject identified, there is a clear need for enforceable codes of conduct which reach across the whole area and are applicable to all enterprises. During the 1990s certainly many codes/guides, whilst supporting tourism development, focused more on the physical environment with little attention to either enterprises or social responsibility. An approach that is based on the principle that by and large stakeholders adopt an ethic of conservation (Holden, 2003; see also Prosser, 1992; Bansal and Howard, 1997). In the case of TOs this may have been overly expectant given that 'TOs are generally reluctant to accept responsibility for the environments their operations are based in' (Hudson and Miller, 2005, p. 139) and as Blackstock et al. (2008) affirm, codes of conduct are predicated on the assumption that informing people (that is all those involved) will encourage responsible behaviour. Parsons and Woods-Ballard (2003) in their study into tourism enterprises involving cetacean watching found limited evidence that codes provide enough protection for the cetaceans amongst operators and argue that specific legislation such as that found in New Zealand to protect whales will be required. But as Font and Carey (2005) note, the implementation of such schemes is very limited, which as Cole (2006) argues, the difficulties are not only in implementing but also in the evaluation of the effectiveness of codes and notes the lack of research into their effectiveness. Despite or perhaps because of this, by the late 2000s environmental and social codes of conduct were widespread (Lawton and Weaver, 2009).

The need for such codes undoubtedly arises due to increasing visitor demand and thus opportunities for TOs and local tourism enterprises to capitalize. In the absence of government control and monitoring what control there is may often take the form of a code of practice or guidelines. For example, guidelines for enterprises in the NEAT category, such as Australia's 'Tread Lightly' for off-road vehicles or 'Leave-no-Trace' in the USA, were considered to be most advanced in terms of best environmental practices (Buckley, 2000).

Codes of Conduct

It is inescapable that such codes of conduct are encompassed within SSCM. This is well illustrated in demand for hiking along the Inca Trail to Machu Picchu. The government introduced guidelines and a code of conduct for tour guides which included restricting visitor numbers, increasing visitor charges and that tourists should be gathered into groups, each with their own guide. But issues still arose, on the one hand concerns were raised over who was actually checking the numbers of visitors and also that some local TOs were more interested in making money than concern for the environment (Bedding, 2000). An alternative example, where tourism development has been managed and controlled with the assistance of a local supporting network is that of the Noel Kempff Mercado National Park (Holden, 2005). But what is it like today? Similarly ecotourism packages which were mostly to be found in less developed countries (Wight, 2002) but latterly there has been a growing number in the 'western' world (as Destination Management Organizations *et al* jump on the bandwagon), which partly accounts for Pratt's (2011) analysis that ecotourism is growing six times faster than the sector (e.g. NEAT) average. But what has happened since to those small tourism enterprises which were developed in the early days of ecotourism destinations? For example, Belize was once renowned for ecotourism but has since developed more into mass tourism and Cancun arguably even more so. An outcome that is certainly raising concerns over the application of the basic principles on which ecotourism is based, namely 'a natural setting, ecological sustainability and an environmentally educative or interpretative element' (Page and Dowling, 2002, p. 58). To which one should also add, shows consideration for and, as appropriate to the setting; supports the community. Aspects which may also gain little recognition as Stern *et al.*'s (2003) study based on four communities living on the periphery of two National Parks – the Corcovado and Piedras Balancas in the Osa Conservation Area in the southeast of Costa Rica – found that the ecotourism developments involved actually achieved very little in regard to these four communities. Overall it is very unsafe to assume that ecotourism developments, and thus the enterprises involved, fit well with sustainability particularly in terms of sustainable consumption, as Redclift (2001) argues, when meaning and use are context dependent.

Such cases bring into question whether TOs and tourism enterprises in the early stages of destination development consider that they have some responsibility for the outcomes of their operations and certainly brings into contention SSCM in such instances. Partly in their defence is that planning and control are primarily the domain of government, though such a defence might well be considered no excuse, especially when considered in terms of sustainability and social responsibility. But it should also be recognized that negative impacts can equally arise in apparently planned and controlled destination developments. As Li's (2004) research based on ecotourism projects in nature reserves found, negative consequences arising from 'unexpected negative influences' (2004, p. 559) identified as partly due to too many visitors and also limitations on the water supply, which raises substantive questions over the initial planning and more importantly control procedures.

A Question of Control?

The rarely articulated problem of these small scale tours, albeit apparently considered as low-impact tourism, is that they attract the attention of the major TOs; well illustrated by Whinner (1996). His discourse is based on the Alternative Travel Group (ATG), founded in 1979, on principles now articulated as the basis of sustainable tourism, and draws on their early experience of two early tours to parts of Turkey that had hardly seen a tourist before. They were very successful and as word spread so too others followed 'Tourism began to grow insidiously' (Whinner, 1996, p. 223). Conflict arose between locals and tourist companies and the ATG pulled out completely and learnt well from the experience, subsequently improving staff training and establishing standards; all with the aim of managing their customers in these 'foreign' environments. Such 'insidious growth' is equally applicable to many popular destinations whether discussing the cold-water seaside resorts of the 19–20th centuries of northern Europe or the USA, or their equivalents in Cuba, the Caribbean or the Mediterranean of the 1950s. As Holzner well identified, 'Even monster resorts like Benidorm and Ibiza were once sleepy villages, frequented by a privileged few who thought they were in on a secret.' (Holzner, 2011, p. 13), a secret that is never kept, as so well conveyed in Alex Garland's novel *The Beach*. In most cases such expansion is incremental and subtle, well exemplified in the case of Ayia Napa in southern Cyprus, a process Prosser (1992, p. 45) rather aptly termed 'penetrative tourism', or Kuta on Bali which morphed from a 1960s backpackers' stopover to mass tourism by the 1990s, so too Goa, now a popular resort, with

Europeans greatly facilitated by TOs though also by hotel companies in the region. Local communities may well object to such encroachment (see Pleumarom, 2012) and as more tourists seek to escape from the crowds and penetrate what could be considered the private areas 'behind the scenes', which brings its own concomitant impacts and in turn coping measures by locals (see Boissevain, 1995).

The foregoing examples might suggest these problems arise today in those destinations which are long haul from their traditional main markets, e.g. Europe and the Americas, but this is not so, as Atkins (2010, p. 3) argued that 'Trinis and Bahamians do things very differently but they certainly feel more in control of their tourism industry than the Cornish.' (See also Pleumarom, 2012). Whilst these examples are comparatively new there is no doubting that the equivalent situation arose in many of the destinations of the past, whether the spa resorts of the 18th century, seaside resorts of northern Europe from the mid-19th century or, as previously noted, the popular resorts of southern Europe or south-east America. The major difference between all these is more the fact of just how quickly emerging destinations can become substantial. This is equally applicable to the drawing power of renowned environments. This is well illustrated in Liggett et al.'s (2010) research, a rare longitudinal study in the tourism field, based on the Antarctic, and tourism demand and development. They identified a substantial increase in visitor activity over the last three decades with increased air links, a developing tourism infrastructure and substantial growth in visitation by cruise liners which has given rise to concerns amongst stakeholders leading to clearer calls for a stronger conservation ethic to prevail. Their study captures well how incremental growth goes largely unnoticed and even more so unreported until it is potentially too late to address the resultant negative impacts, by which time tourism development has become substantial; and this in spite of calls for limiting numbers and an effective management plan for the area in the early 1990s and curbs planned on limiting tourists to Antarctica in the late 2000s (Gray, 2009).

These findings further indicate the ineffectiveness of policy and codes of conduct, and beg the question of whether the adoption of SSCM would make a real difference. The guidelines for SSCM and attention to social responsibility raises an interesting conundrum in that should TOs and national/international tourism companies invest in new developments that demonstrate inequity in the planning process, for example the Kalpitiya Tourism project in Sri Lanka. According to Noble (2011), Kalpitiya, a coastal area in the western province known for its diversity of marine habitats and which encompasses 14 islands, is the location for a major tourism development which lacks community participation, involves the displacement of local people and appears to show little consideration for opportunity costs of land use and impact on traditional economic activities. To be successful requires substantial investment, the achievement of which rather indicates, once again, a government's prioritizing of the economic at the cost to the social and environmental dimensions of sustainability. Thus decisions of potential external stakeholders to invest also raises ethical questions. By way of contrast there is the sustainable tourism development project at Mata de Sesimbra, southern Portugal, that is spread over 5200 hectares and involves a combination of conservation, cork oak forest restoration and a 500-hectare tourism development. This is a joint initiative between the WWF and BioRegional (see www.bioregional.com) at a cost of Ç1billion.

The Matter of Influence

The foregoing discussion, whilst establishing that TOs are indeed major role-players in destination development, rather casts them in a poor light. Yet many examples of good practice by various and varied TOs are readily found, as previously noted and also in a range of research papers and publications (see Tepelus, 2005; also the *Green Hotelier* journal). We should also not lose sight of the fact that through their operations they are providing direct and indirect employment opportunities and generating revenues for other tourism enterprises. Furthermore, their operations and influence in the main require the development of supporting facilities, infrastructure and other suppliers, this could not happen without the support of government. However, they do have direct control over their own business enterprise(s) and some degree of influence over those enterprises with which they work. It is within this context that SSCM comes to the fore. Certainly there are examples of good SSCM practice from research (albeit limited) into this area in the early 2000s but they were limited to a minority of operators (Tapper and Font, 2004). Hence it is not surprising to find Scheyvens (2002, p. 231) arguing that 'Tour companies will need more encouragement to implement socially and environmentally responsible initiatives.' To what extent TOs were encouraged in these early years of the 2000s is debatable, though the advocacy of SSCM and CSR will certainly have helped as later research by Wijk and Persoon (2006) into the environmental performance of TOs demonstrates. They established that, in contrast to hotels, there was no evident bias in the EP of TOs to the larger enterprises and more significant to this context they did perform better on SSCM issues.

Early leaders in SSCM were identified to be TOs based in Germany and the UK whilst Dutch firms were considered 'laggards'. Since then there has been substantial progress in the Dutch based companies (Mosselaer *et al.*, 2012). But the latter are comparatively significantly smaller companies and whilst the smaller operators may well perform better based on sustainability criteria, it is the big firms that have the substantial influence on development and supply issues; without them on board little wider effect can be achieved. Whilst their study affirms that the larger companies are more likely to be more attentive to social responsibility, this is partly, if not wholly, attributable to the fact that 'firms remain tuned to their home country in terms of business and social mores' (Leslie, 2012a, p. 30). What is particularly notable from Mosselaer *et al.*'s findings is that overall TOs performed generally weakly, including the top companies (based on turnover) but there were marked variances between them across all areas of EP except for SSCM. Secondly, in comparison with other research in this area, mainly international/national hotel companies

in the hotel sector, it was not the case that it was predominantly the larger enterprises which performed better; albeit TUI was identified as achieving the highest performance but even then little above average. Even so this is progress, albeit:

> the principal driver behind broad-scale acknowledgement and action towards chain responsibility – the business case at *firm level* for 'going sustainable' – has not yet been clearly defined or made accessible for the majority of tour operators. (Mosselaer *et al.*, 2012, p. 86)

The opposite argument might be used for N/ MNC companies in the hotel sector as demonstrated by Blanco *et al.*'s (2009) discussion of the case of Scandic Hotels. This company was in financial difficulties in the early 1990s but managed to overcome the problems and subsequently prosper, which is largely attributed to a substantive change in orientation involving the greening of the business and the development of an environmental programme including substantial attention to SSCM involving the imposition of environmental conditions on suppliers. But whilst evidently a very positive outcome for Scandic, their major suppliers gained a competitive advantage to the disadvantage of other potential suppliers. The company launched their acclaimed 'Suppliers Declaration' which aimed to progress sustainable production and sourcing involving 30 of its largest suppliers in 2003 (Anon., 2006). Also in the hotel category Hilton International have introduced a global supply monitoring system. One conclusion to be drawn from these and similar steps in SSCM is to what extent such a process is actually counter to localized suppliers both in terms of selection of accommodation on the part of TOs and in the suppliers to those operations.

As regards the major TOs, a leading example is TUI, arguably the largest TO in the EU, which since 2010 has been working towards having all of its suppliers accredited with its Travelife award through due auditing procedures. This initiative includes promoting the introduction of an EMS in its partner hotels, relationships with the local community and ensuring good working conditions for their employees (TUI, 2010, p. 2). That they can pursue such a policy is testament to their size and extensive operations, also in terms of the numbers of bedspaces required for their tours but also the importance of continuity of demand. To some extent, the initiative is also driven by arguments that their customers increasingly appear to expect their tour operator not only to provide quality and value-for-money but also seek to safeguard the environment and maintain social sustainability. In part, such argument is supported by Choat's (2004) study reporting on a survey of tourists, which found that 60% think big tour operators produce superficial holidays and 80% stated that tour operators have a responsibility for the local environment and culture (also see Leslie, 2012c). Conversely major TOs in Europe have argued that there is little actual consumer demand for them to be more proactive (Budeanu, 2005). At the other end of the TO enterprise spectrum are the small TOs, some of which are undoubtedly sensitive to potential negative impacts arising from their operations and not just recently (see Whinner, 1996). In the case of adventure tours for example, problems that have arisen include the negative impacts of accommodation operations, which is particularly problematic in rural areas, such as deforestation, as well as litter and sanitation, exacerbated by increasing pressures to accommodate more tourists, and effects on flora and fauna (see Nepal, 2000; Bedding, 2000). Such problems have not gone unnoticed by various TOs in the adventure tour market as Holland (2012, p. 124) attests, for example:

> Explore Worldwide are encouraging teahouse owners to use paraffin stoves and not to provide hot water showers for guests. Attention is also given to the potential for alternative energy sources such as the use of solar panels but they are expensive to introduce and very unlikely to be found in accommodation in remote towns and villages in response to which a number of operators have provided financial support to enable changes in operations such as popular African lodges in Botswana and Namibia, which now utilise solar power for provision of electricity and low energy bulbs.

Such actions might well be attributed to SSCM but it may also be, and probably all the more so, driven by the values and attitudes of the owners/managers of these small enterprises which is well demonstrated by Spenceley and Rylance (2012) in their discussion of wildlife-based tourism in Africa. A potential problem though is that a buoyant market will attract other operators, albeit small, leading to many enterprises in the locality which might just be more damaging than if but a few larger operators were managing supply. However the development of nature tourism in many areas of Africa has been acclaimed; for example, in Kenya in the 1990s/early 2000s due to the revival of game reserves and improved provision for tourists and quality of offering. In various cases this did involve local communities and their participation, e.g. Meru National Park, Masai Mara or Amboseli, a safari camp in Tsavo, also the Sarara Lodge run by the Namunyak Wildlife Conservation Trust. The local community has a 50% stake in the business in Namunyak (see Jackman, 1999 and 2000; also Spenceley, 2008 and Spenceley and Rylance, 2012). Such examples illustrate that participation of the local community in tourism development needs to be integrated in the process rather than just consultative, and in that process 'stressing the use of more empowering participatory measures that give factual evidence to the communities' (Zimmermann, 2006, p. 121–122, cited in Schiler, 2008). The involvement of TOs in funding conservation projects in lesser-developed localities has been noted but due to their significance as major role players in destinations they also can have substantial influence on government to address threats to flora and fauna, as Psarikidou (2008) discussed in the case of the sea turtles of Crete and their beach nesting sites. TUI is largely credited as a major influence in persuading the government to take the necessary actions to protect the species and the quality of the environment; albeit their actions held valuable PR opportunities.

Conclusion

SSCM potentially is very wide in its scope and clearly incorporates elements of CSR and EMS (whilst being very much a part of both of these). It is not surprising therefore that some degree of confusion arises in its application and just what it does or does not entail. In effect, there are no clear boundaries between SSCM, CSR and EMS. But what is clear is that it is the mainstream of the TOI under which umbrella it has been advocated for adoption by TOs since the early 2000s. As discussed it is also applicable to all tourism enterprises and thus an area covered in the research into tourism enterprises. The reporting herein of the data relating to this further illustrates the blurring of boundaries between what is advocated under SSCM, CSR and EMS given that anything to do with an enterprise's supply chain is potentially applicable to all these facets of business and sustainability depending on how they are interpreted and applied. In this instance, under SSCM, findings from the study are limited to general purchasing which found that in general those enterprises with substantial food and beverage operations did not consider the EP of suppliers and bought dry goods from major suppliers in the region. Comparatively small operations, mainly BBs and GHs, obtained their supplies from local supermarkets. Quite possibly and by chance they were thus supplied by a company whose environmental performance is highly rated, as in the case of the supermarket company Booths, based in the north-west of England, which has outlets in the LDNP.

Also, and in some ways stepping away from tourism enterprises, the research brought into consideration two other areas of what could be termed the tourist's supply chain, namely local food producers and A & C producers. In general, food producers were found to be more supportive of local suppliers though they recognized that the sources of the latter were not necessarily local. A key finding from the A & C producers was that they could be supported better by retailers in their area, some of whom do not sell their products, instead importing cheaper though similar items. It was also found that the tourism enterprises could be more supportive. As noted, discussion of such support and interrelationships with the local economy and community is discussed in the following chapters. In recognition of the fact that there were no TOs in the study's overall research population nor were TOs mentioned by any

enterprise involved and the importance of TOs both as key role-players and stakeholders in tourism, the discussion was expanded to consider TOs, in the process thereby to highlight some of the major problems which have and do arise as a result of tourist destination development. In this, drawing on other research, it was established that these enterprises are making progress in addressing sustainability in the context of SSCM.

Thus, it was identified that smaller companies in the TO sector may well perform better across the whole spectrum of sustainability criteria but it is the large TOs that have the substantial influence on destination development and SSCM issues. Without them on board little wider effect can be achieved. Whilst the larger TOs are more likely to be more attentive to social responsibility as advocated by international agencies, this is partly if not wholly attributable to the fact that firms are tuned to the business practices and social mores of their home base. However it is also evident that the way many a small TO operates is very much influenced by the owner/managers' pro-environmental attitudes and values, especially in the niche markets of soft adventure tours and wildlife tourism.

However, there is little doubt that TOs in general could do more to address sustainability issues not only in their own business practices but also by way of informing/educating tourists and also for destinations through exercising their influence on third-party suppliers. Furthermore, TOs often have to work with a range of suppliers providing diverse services, which in the short term at least militates progress in developing sustainability in the supply chain. A further factor working against such considerations in the short term is the competition between TOs which engenders attention on cost/price at the expense of responsibility-orientated initiatives; this though need not necessarily be the case as suggested by the success of, for example, TUI (see Mosselaer et al., 2012). But such success rather masks the complexity of the issues involved. For example, large TOs require major companies capable of providing the products and services to meet their needs. Such companies are better placed to develop and formalize the requisite credentials. In effect, this reduces the potential choice of suppliers. Thus the situation arises which leaves small enterprises, more likely to be locally based, at even more of a competitive disadvantage. An outcome that is not surprising as the larger the enterprise the more will it seek to work with fewer main suppliers. This general business practice, especially on the part of national and MNCs will inevitably happen in developing destinations and regions as tourism demand grows. It is no coincidence that it is in the major urban conurbations where economies of scale can be realized that the hotels of national companies are predominantly located, to be then followed by MNC operations, a process of development which could initially create opportunities for entre-preneurs on the supply side who might then develop into major suppliers, again at a cost to other small-scale enterprises.

Overall, progress on the part of TOs in developing sustainability in their SSCM is limited and unlikely to be helped by the outcome of a survey, which found '… that only around one-third of travel agents and tour operators believe that "the travel industry has a role to play in limiting global warming"' (Taylor, 2008; cited in Sharpley, 2009, p.xiv). Even so, progress is hindered by an array of factors; witness Mosselaer *et al.* (2012, p. 75):

> The brokering role of inbound tour operators and local agents provides a great opportunity to pursue social and environmental responsibility along the chain. However, these local agents and inbound tour operators often lack the urge or capacity for taking on this role. More generally, local knowledge concerning sustainable development is often absent or minimal. In sum, although the concept of sustainable supply chain management has received increasing recognition and few doubt the importance of sustainable supply chain management for supporting CSR in the tour operating industry, for many companies pursuing genuine sustainable supply chain management is still a bridge too far.

A further factor, potentially of increasing significance, is the growing practice of consumers making their own, direct holiday arrangements, for whom responsible practice on the part of TOs may be of little concern or even interest (see Chapter 7). This is partly counter to SSCM initiatives, for example as promoted by the TOI, and further encourages price-based competition, which is also counter-productive to SSCM and more widely CSR actions. But, and the key point, SSCM is no panacea for the negatives associated with inconsiderate development of tourism and negative environmental impacts well noted in the 1980–1990s and not dissimilar to today (see Pleumarom, 2009 and 2012). The reality is that it only, if at all, becomes perceived as negative after the fact – with hindsight. Furthermore, as well articulated by Saarinen *et al.* (2009), there is a failing to recognize and appreciate that tourism takes place and develops in destinations within the context of prevailing government policy and thus whichever which way a destination develops largely rests in the purvey of the government of any destination area. In the case of destinations that are not in the post-industrialized nations it might be argued that tourism development legitimizes prevailing power relations – that inequality is masked in terms of tourists wishing to experience other cultures. As Crick argued:

> For all the talk about sacred journeys, cultural understanding, freedom, play and so on, we must not forget the fundamental truth that international tourism feeds off gross political and economic inequalities (Crick, 1991, p. 9; cited in Hutnyk, 1996, p. 218).

Further Reading

On sustainable supply chains: TOI (2004) *Supply Chain Engagement: Three Steps Toward Sustainability.* Tour Operators Initiative and the Center for Environmental Leadership in Business, United Nations Environment Programme (also see_www.sscf. info).

For a range of articles on the theme of supply chain management and issues in the food sector see Eastham, J.F., Sharples, L. and Ball, S.D. (eds) (2001) *Food Supply Chain Management: Issues for the Hospitality and Retail Sectors.* Butterworth-Heinemann, Oxford, UK.

For discussion on tourism development and impacts see Mowforth, M. and Munt, I. (2008) *Tourism and Sustainability: Development and New Tourism in the Third World.* 3rd edn. Routledge, New York.

On local communities: supporting local communities and their involvement in tourism development is a facet of SSCM but there is only so much that an external agency such as a TO can achieve (see Scheyvens, 2002, p. 189) thus potentially far more beneficial to local communities would be the establishment of community partnerships or tours created by the local community (see Mann and Ibrahim, 2002); also see on indigenous peoples – Tribes Travel (www.tribestravel. com).

As regards national and international tourism companies the *Green Hotelier* provides many examples whilst for a comprehensive discussion on this see Bohdanowicz and Zientara (2012) and Mosselaer *et al.* (2012).

For a different perspective on 'Pro-Poor Tourism' see Pleumarom, A. (2012) *The Politics of Tourism, Poverty Reduction and Sustainable Development.* Environment & Development Series 17, Third World Network, Penang, Malaysia.

References

ACTSA (2002) *People-first Tourism.* Action for Southern Africa, London.

Anon. (2003) 'Social responsibility' new industry buzzword. *Hotels* March, IH&RA, p. 4.

Anon. (2006) Sustainable supply chains. Know-How Section. *Green Hotelier,* January.

Anon. (2011) Pollution in aquifers threaten Mexico's Riviera Maya. Available at: http://www.business-review. com/polluted-riviera-may-mexico-news2630 (accessed 1 March 2011).

Atkins, R. (2010) *What's it like to live with tourists?* Available at: http://www.guardian.co.uk/travel/blog/2010/ apr/07/living-with-tourists-tourism (accessed 6 April 2012).

Bansal, P. and Howard, E. (eds) (1997) *Business and the Natural Environment.* Butterworth-Heinemann, Oxford, UK.

Barrow, C. and Burnett, A. (1990) *How Green are Small Companies?* October, Cranfield, Cranfield School of Management, UK.

Bedding, J. (2000) Trouble on the Inca trail. Travel Section, *The Daily Telegraph,* pp. 1–2.

Bianchi, R.V. (2004) Tourism restructuring and the politics of sustainability: a critical view from the European periphery: The Canary islands. *Journal of Sustainable Tourism* 2 12 (6), 495–525.

Blackstock, K.L., White, V., McCrum, G., Scott, A. and Hunter, C. (2008) Measuring responsibility: an appraisal of a Scottish National Park's sustainable tourism indicators. *Journal of Sustainable Tourism* 16 (3), 276–297.

Blanco, E., Rey-Maquieira, J. and Lozano, J. (2009) Economic incentives for tourism firms to undertake voluntary environmental management. *Tourism Management* 30 (1), pp 112–122.

Bohdanowicz, P. and Zientara, P. (2012) CSR-inspired Environmental Initiatives in Top Hotel Chains. In: Leslie, D. (ed.) *Tourism Enterprises and the Sustainability Agenda Across Europe.* New Directions in Tourism Analysis, Ashgate Farnham, UK, pp. 93–121.

Boissevain, J. (ed.) (1995) *Coping with Tourists: Europeans Reactions to Mass Tourism.* Berghahn, Oxford, UK.

Briasspoulis, H. (2003) Crete: endowed by nature, privileged by geography, threatened by tourism? *Journal of Sustainable Tourism* 11, 97–115.

Buckley, R. (2000) Neat trends: current issues in nature, eco- and adventure tourism. *International Journal of Tourism Research* 2, pp. 437–444.

Budeanu, A. (2005) Impacts and responsibilities for sustainable tourism: a tour operator's perspective. *Journal of Cleaner Production* 13, pp. 89–97.

Budeanu, A. (2009) Environmental supply chain management in tourism. *Journal of Cleaner Production* 17 (16), pp. 1385–1392.

Butler, R. (2007) Destinations – development and redevelopment or visioning and revisioning? In: Smith, M and Onderwater, L. (eds) *Destinations Revisited: Perspectives on Development and Managing Tourist Areas.* ATLAS, Arnhem, the Netherlands, pp. 17–24.

Carey, S., Gountas, Y. and Gilbert, D. (1997) Tour operators and destination sustainability. *Tourism Management* 18 (7), 425–431.

Charlton, C. and Howell, B. (1992) Life cycle assessment – a tool for solving environmental problems. *European Environment*, pp. 1–6.

Choat, I. (2004) Package firms urged to be responsible. *The Guardian*, March 13, p. 16.

Cole, S. (2006) Implementing and evaluating a code of conduct for visitors. *Tourism Management* 28 (2), 443–452.

Dodds, R. (2007) Sustainable tourism policy: rejuvenation or a critical strategic initiative. *Anatolia* 18 (2), 277–298.

Eastham, J.F., Sharples, L. and Ball, S.D. (eds) (2001) *Food Supply Chain Management: Issues for the Hospitality and Retail Sectors*. Butterworth-Heinemann, Oxford, UK. (See this book for further reading on range of issues, etc.)

Eber, S. (ed.) (1992) *Beyond the Green Horizon: A Discussion Paper on Principles for Sustainable Tourism*. Worldwide Fund for Nature, Godalming, UK.

EIU (1993) *Travel and Tourism Analyst*. Economic Intelligence Unit, London No 6.

Erdogan, N. (2009) Turkey's tourism policy and environmental performance of tourism enterprises. In: Leslie, D. (ed.) *Tourism Enterprises and Sustainable Development: International Perspectives on Responses to the Sustainability Agenda*. Routledge, New York, pp. 194–208.

Farsari, Y., Butler, R. and Prastacos, P. (2007) Sustainable tourism policy for Mediterranean destination: issues and interrelationships. *International Journal of Tourism Policy* 1 (1), pp. 58–78.

Font, X. and Carey, B. (2005) *Marketing Sustainable Tourism Products*. United Nations Environment Programme, Kenya.

Font, X., Tapper, R., Schwartz, K. and Kornilaki, M. (2008) Sustainable supply chain management in tourism. *Business Strategy and the Environment* 17, pp. 260–271.

Global Reporting Initiative GRI (2002) *Tour Operators' Sector Supplement: for use with the GRI 2002, Sustainability Reporting Guidelines*. Global Reporting Initiative, Amsterdam, the Netherlands, November. Available from: www.globalreporting.org.

Goeldner, C.R. and Ritchie, J.R.B. (2009) *Tourism: Principles, Practices, Philosophies* 2nd edn. Wiley, New York.

Goodwin, H. (2005) *Responsible Tourism and the Market*. Occasional Paper No.4, Int. Centre for Responsible Tourism, University of Greenwich, UK.

Goodwin, H. and Bah, A. (2004) The Gambia: paradise or purgatory? *Developments* 27, 3rd Quarter, pp. 4–7.

Gordon, G. (2002) *Improving Tour Operator Performance – The Role of Corporate Social Responsibility and Reporting*. Tearfund, ABTA and Tour Operators Initiative, London.

Gossling, S., Garrod, B., Aall, C., Hille, J. and Peeters, P. (2011) Food management in tourism: reducing tourism's carbon 'footprint'. *Tourism Management* 32 (3), pp. 534–543.

Gray, R. (2009) Curbs planned on Antarctica tourism. *The Sunday Telegraph*, 12 April, p. 7.

Guley, S. (1994) Green tourism: a case study. *Annals of Tourism Research* 21 (2).

Hall, C.M. and Johnston, M.E. (eds) (1995) *Polar Tourism – Tourism in the Arctic and Antarctic Regions*. Wiley, Chichester, UK.

Hall, C.M., Mitchell, R. and Sharples, L. (2003) Consuming places: the role of food, wine and tourism in regional development. In: Hall, C.M., Sharples, L., Mitchell, R., Macionis, N. and Cambourse, B. (eds) (2003) *Food Tourism Around the World: Development, Management and Markets*. Butterworth-Heinemann, Oxford, UK, pp. 26–59.

Holden, A. (2003) In need of new environmental ethics for tourism? *Annals of Tourism Research* 30 (1), 94–108.

Holden, A. (2005) *Tourism Studies and the Social Sciences*. Routledge, Oxford, UK.

Holland, J. (2012) Adventure tours: responsible tourism in practice? In: Leslie, D. (ed.) *Responsible Tourism: Concepts, Theory and Practice*. CAB International, Wallingford, UK, pp. 119–129.

Holzner, M. (2007) Tourism and economic development: The beach disease. *Tourism Management* 32, 922–933.

Howell, D. (2000) Working with suppliers towards environmental improvement. Paper presented at 'Greening the supply chain: the route to environmental improvement?' The Environment Council, London, 11 May.

Hudson, S. and Miller, C.A. (2005) The responsible marketing of tourism: the case of Canadian Mountain Holidays. *Tourism Management* 26(2), 133–142.

Hutnyk, J. (1996) *The Rumour of Calcutta: Tourism, Charity and the Poverty of Representation*. Zed, London.

Jaakson, R. (2004) Beyond the tourist bubble? Cruiseship passengers in port. *Annals of Tourism Research* 31 (1), 44–60.

Jackman, B. (1999) Reinventing Kenya. *Telegraph Travel, The Daily Telegraph*, 13 November, p. T5–T6.

Jackman, B. (2000) Infinity and beyond. *Travel Africa, The Daily Telegraph*, 16 September, p. 7–9.

Jackman, B. and Rodgers, D. (2005) The perfect African safari: bare bones or luxury. *Travel Section, The Daily Telegraph*, pp. 1–3, 6th August.

Jones, L. (1999) Tourists ruin oldest desert. *Telegraph Travel, The Daily Telegraph* 20 February, T2.

Kucerova, J. (2012) Environmental management and accommodation facilities in Slovakia. In: Leslie, D. (ed.) *Tourism Enterprises and the Sustainability Agenda Across Europe*. New Directions in Tourism Analysis, Ashgate, Farnham, UK, pp. 121–134.

Laisch, A. (2002) *Corporate Futures: Social Responsibility in the Tourism Industry*. Tourism Concern, London.

Lawton, L.J. and Weaver, D.B. (2009) Normative and innovative resources management at birding festivals. *Tourism Management* 31 (3), 527–536.

Lebe, S.S. and Zupan, S. (2012) From eco-ignorance to eco-certificates: Environmental management in Slovene hotels. In: Leslie, D. (ed.) *Tourism Enterprises and the Sustainability Agenda Across Europe*. Ashgate, Farnham, UK, pp. 135–150.

Leslie, D. (2011) The European Union, sustainable tourism policy and rural Europe. In: Macleod, D. and Gillespie, S.A. (eds) *Sustainable Tourism in Rural Europe: Approaches to Development*. Routledge, New York. Chapter 5, pp. 43–60.

Leslie, D. (2012a) The responsible tourism debate. In: Leslie, D. (ed.) *Responsible Tourism: Concepts, Theory and Practice*. CAB International, Wallingford, UK, pp. 17–42.

Leslie, D. (2012b) Introduction. In: Leslie, D. (ed.) *Responsible Tourism: Concepts, Theory and Practice*. CAB International, Wallingford, UK, pp. 1–16.

Leslie, D. (2012c) The consumers of tourism. In: Leslie, D. (ed.) *Responsible Tourism: Concepts, Theory and Practice*. CAB International, Wallingford, UK, pp. 54–71.

Li, W. (2004) Environmental management indicators for ecotourism in China's nature reserves: a case study in Tianmushan Nature Reserve. *Tourism Management* 25, 559–564.

Liggett, D., McIntoch, A., Thompson, A., Gilbert, N. and Storey, B. (2010) From frozen continent to tourism hotspot: Five decades of Antarctic tourism development and management, and a glimpse into the future. *Tourism Management* 32 (2), pp. 357–366.

Luck, M., Maher, P.T. and Stewart, E.J. (eds) (2010) *Cruise tourism in polar regions: Promoting environmental and social sustainability?* Earthscan, London.

Manente, M., Furlan, M.C. and Scaramuzzi, I. (1998) *Training strategies and new business ideas for the development of a local system of tourism supply. The role of partnerships*. Tourist Research Centre, 21/98 Leeuwarden, the Netherlands, May.

Mann, M. And Ibrahim, Z. (2002) *The Good Alternative Travel Guide: Exciting Holidays for Responsible Travellers*, 2nd edn. Earthscan, London.

Miles, P. (2001) Green holidays given a boost. *Telegraph Travel, The Daily Telegraph* 12 January, p. 4.

Moosa, A.S. (2009) Case study: Maldives, *Tourism* Issue 142, Winter.

Mosselaer, F., Duim, R. and Wijk, J. (2012) Corporate social responsibility in tour operating: the case of Dutch outbound tour operators. In: Leslie, D. (ed.) *Tourism enterprises and the sustainability agenda across Europe*. New Directions in Tourism Analysis, Ashgate, Farnham, UK, pp. 71–92.

Nepal, S.K. (2000) Tourism in protected areas: the Nepalese Himalaya. *Annals of Tourism Research* 27 (3), 661–681.

Noble, R. (2011) *International calls grow for end to tourism land grabs in Sri Lanka*. Press Release, Tourism Concern, 25 July.

Nuttall, M. (1997) Packaging the wild: Tourism development in Alaska. In: Abram, S., Waldren, L. and MacLeod, D.V.L. (eds) *Tourists and Tourism: Identifying with People and Places*. Berg, Oxford, UK, pp. 223–238.

Page, J.S. and Dowling, K.R. (2002) *Ecotourism*. Pearson Education Limited, Harlow, UK.

Parsons, E.C.M and Woods-Ballard, A. (2003) Acceptance of voluntary whale watching codes of conduct in west Scotland: the effectiveness of governmental versus industry-led guidelines. *Current Issues in Tourism* 6 (2), pp. 172–182.

Pearce, D.W. (1995) *Blueprint 4. Capturing global environmental value*. Earthscan, London, UK.

Pleumarom, A. (2009) Asian tourism: Green and responsible? In: Leslie, D. (ed.) *Tourism Enterprises, Environmental Performance and Sustainable Development*. Perspectives on Progress from across the Globe. Advances in Tourism Research Series. Routledge, New York, pp. 36–54.

Pleumarom, A. (2012) The politics of tourism and poverty reduction. In: Leslie, D. (ed.) *Responsible Tourism: Concepts, Theories, Practices*. CAB International, Wallingford, UK, pp. 90–106.

Pratt, L. (2011) *Tourism investing in energy and resources efficiency towards a green economy*. United Nations Environment Programme, Paris.

Prosser, R.F. (1992) The ethics of tourism. In: Cooper, D.E. and Palmer, J.A. (eds) *The Environment in Question: Ethics and Global Issues*. Routledge, New York, pp. 37–50.

Psarikidou, K. (2008) Environmental ethics and biodiversity policy in tourism: The Caretta-Caretta case in Greece. *Tourismos* 3 (1), pp. 153–168.

Redclift, M. (2001) Changing nature: the consumption of space and the construction of nature on 'the Mayan Riviera'. In: Cohen, M.J. and Murphy, J. (eds) *Exploring Sustainable Consumption: Environmental policy and the social sciences*. Pergamom, Amsterdam, pp. 121–136.

Ritzer, G. (2000) *The Macdonaldization of Society*. SAGE publications, London.

Saarinen, J., Becker, F., Manwa, H. and Wilson, D. (eds) (2009) *Sustainable Tourism in Southern Africa: Local Communities and Natural Resources in Transition*. Channel View, Clevedon, UK.

Scheyvens, R. (2002) *Tourism for development: empowering communities*. Prentice Hall, Harlow, UK.

Schiler, D. (2008) A review of community destination management in developing economies. *Journal of Sustainable Tourism* 16 (3), 365–368.

Seabrook, J. (2007) Tourism, predatory and omnivorous? Rethinking Tourism – an engine for Third World development? *Third World 'Resurgence'* 207–208, 13-14.

Sharpley, R. (2009) *Tourism, Development and the Environment: Beyond Sustainability*. Earthscan, London.

Spenceley, A. (2008) Impacts of wildlife tourism on rural livelihoods in South Africa. In: Spenceley, A. (ed.) *Responsible Tourism: Critical issues for Conservation and Development*. Earthscan, London, pp. 159–186.

Spenceley, A. and Rylance, A. (2012) Responsible wildlife tourism in Africa. In: Leslie, D. (ed.) *Responsible Tourism: Concepts, Theory and Practice*. CAB International, Wallingford, UK, pp. 130–141.

Stern, C.J., Lassole, J.P., Lee, D.R. and Deshlet, D.J. (2003) How 'eco' is ecotourism? A comparative case study of ecotourism in Costa Rica. *Journal of Sustainable Tourism* 11 (4), pp. 322–347.

Sykes, L. (1995) The holiday crowd. *Geographical* February, pp. 14–15.

Tapper, R. and Font, X. (2004) *Tourism Supply Chains*. Report for the Travel Foundation. Environment Business & Development Group. Leeds Metropolitan University. January.

Tearfund (2002) *Worlds Apart: A call to responsible global tourism*. Tearfund, London.

Tepelus, C.M. (2005) Aiming for sustainability in the tour operating business. *Journal of Cleaner Production* 13, pp. 99–107.

TOI and CELB (2004) *Supply chain engagement: Three steps toward sustainability*. Tour Operators Initiative and the Center for Environmental Leadership in Business, United Nations Environment Programme, Paris.

TUI (2010) *New Holidays Forever brand outlines Thomson and First Choice's five year sustainable tourism commitments*. Press Release, 29th June.

UNCSD (1999) *Tourism and Sustainable Development – Sustainable tourism: a non-governmental organisation perspective*. Background Paper 4. Prepared for the Commission on Sustainable Development, Seventh Session, 19-30 April, New York Department of Economic and Social Affairs, NGO Steering Group. United Nations Commission on Sustainable Development.

Vidal, J. (2001) Oil in troubled waters. *The Guardian* 24 January, p. 19.

Visser, W. (2009) *Landmarks for Sustainability: Events and Initiatives that have Changed our World*. Greenleaf Publishing, Sheffield, UK.

Welford, R., Ytterhus, B. and Eilgh, J. (1999) Tourism and sustainable development: an analysis of policy and guidelines for managing provision and consumption. *Sustainable Development* 7, 165–177.

Whinner, C. (1996) Good intentions in a competitive market: training for people and tourism in fragile environments. In: Price, M.F. (ed.) *People and Tourism in Fragile Environments*. Wiley, Chichester, UK, pp. 221–230.

Wight, P.A. (2002) *Supporting the Principles of Sustainable Development in Tourism and Ecotourism: Government's potential role*. Pam Wight Associates, Alberta, Canada.

Wijk, J.V. and Persoon, W. (2006) A long-haul destination: sustainability reporting among tour operators. *European Management Journal* 24, 381–396.

WTTC, IFTO, IH&RA, ICCL (2002) *Industry as a Partner for Sustainable Development: Tourism report.* Prepared by the World Travel and Tourism Council, International Federation of Tour Operators, International Hotels & Restaurateurs Association and the International Council for Cruise Lines Kenya, United Nations Environment Programme.

4 Corporate Social Responsibility – The Wider Context in Environmental Performance

Introduction

Within the spectrum of research into tourism enterprises and environmental performance (EP) (albeit limited), Corporate Social Responsibility (CSR) is an area which gains little explicit attention in most research studies based on tourism enterprises. That is outside of major companies in the hospitality sector but also, though to a lesser extent, tour operators (TOs) (see Laisch, 2002; Holland, 2012). This is hardly representative of the majority of tourism enterprises per se. The focus here on CSR is all the more germane and provides the context within which to consider wider concerns than those encompassed in environmental management systems (EMS) (see Chapter 5). CSR therefore is seen as being more about the interface with the external environment and external relations of an enterprise and thus involvement with the local community and interrelationships with the local/regional economy. However, there is certainly some blurring of the boundaries between these two and in terms of what CSR entails vis-à-vis sustainability; for example, with some hotel chains 'CSR and sustainability constitute separate domains' (Bohdanowicz and Zientara, 2012, p. 94). Thus some confusion may arise though this may largely be more a function of the size of the enterprise, i.e. for small/micro-enterprises there is little to be gained by disaggregating the activities involved; as implied by the Institute for Hospitality which appears to amalgamate CSR activity with EM actions (Anon., 2008). For example, certainly one might argue that reducing energy consumption has a social dimension but treating CSR activity within the context of EMS loses the key focus of the former, namely social responsibility. Conversely, in response to enquiries about CSR owners/managers may think they are doing little, if anything, but actually are when considered in a different context. Hence there can be some confusion and furthermore a failing to recognize such involvement. To clarify, CSR complements the internal focus of an EMS; in combination these are the key elements of the EP of these enterprises. But whilst environmental responsibility in the consumption of resources is implicit in EMS, such responsibility is explicit in CSR. The accent is very much on being 'responsible' and that, irrespective of category or size, tourism enterprises and each and every component of supply should accept this. As the UK government argued:

> Responsibility for our environment is shared by all of us: it is not a duty for the Government alone. Businesses, central and local government, schools, voluntary bodies and individuals must all work together to take good care of our common inheritance (the environment) (DoE, 1990, p. 3).

A view shared by some of the leading players in the tourism sector; witness the Director for Environment with British Airways:

It is only through collective ownership of the issues and their management that this great industry will achieve true environmental responsibility. Without acceptance of shared responsibility we cannot begin to talk seriously of sustainable development. (Somerville, 1993, p. 3)

A view echoed some 15 years later by Richard Branson of the Virgin Group, who stated that he wanted all his operations to be environmental leaders in their fields and, speaking more generally, argued:

We need to address the environmental issues, both those created by travel and those generated at the destinations themselves, before others do it for us. (Branson, 2006, p. 3)

This shared responsibility includes contributing to the environmental management of a destination, in which these enterprises very much have a role. This can also be beneficial through encouraging demand whilst potential additional costs incurred by the enterprises as a result of this are offset by the increase in demand (see Huybers and Bennett, 2003). Branson's prescient observation reflects the status accorded to such responsibility at the World Economic Forum of 2005 in Davos, which confirmed that major environmental issues are now high on the agenda and that there has been an increase in CSR activity and reporting on the part of business (Elkington, 2005). This increase is attributed to an array of factors, most notably 'Globalization, UN guidelines and compacts, organized activism, socially responsible investment growth, and threats of regulation' (Wight, 2007, p. 3).

The attention to employment within CSR incorporates 'international labour and human rights, anti-corruption, and the global poverty reduction agenda' (Utting, 2005, p. 1, cited in Wight, 2007). This is particularly pertinent to tourism development given that an invariably cited major factor in the rationale for supporting its development is the potential to generate employment. Whilst this is well recognized, what is much less so is whether such employment is equitable in society – especially with regard to the local community. All tourism enterprises therefore, irrespective

of location should provide quality terms and conditions on employment and more widely support local communities and promote sustainability (Bohdanowicz and Zientara, 2008). In other words to adopt a broader approach with the accent on promotion of social equity and economic opportunity for indigenous peoples. Currently this is readily recognized in the promotion of the 'Pro-Poor Tourism' lobby. Their aim is to make tourism in developing countries more sustainable by enhancing the linkages between tourism businesses and the local people, to ensure that the tourism contribution to the area is increased and local people benefit from tourism to the area (Pro-Poor Tourism Partnership, 2011). This might well be considered somewhat idealistic and especially if taken in the context of a debate about the primary purpose of business, as Morris (1998, p. 2) argued, the idea 'That tourism is all to the benefit of the indigenes is, of course, pure baloney.' Counterarguments may well be limited in substance given the past focus of research studies. Invariably then 'social context' asks about the poor and/or the disenfranchised, yet what research in this context is there to find on the influence of power on the form and outcomes of development? (Hutnyk, 1996). This is a question which 18 years on appears to still not have been adequately addressed. Overall, this brings into consideration ethics and that CSR does have an ethical dimension; one that perhaps should be explicit and added to the 'Triple Bottom Line'.

The concept of the Triple Bottom Line (TBL) coined in relation to company environmental reporting (SustainAbility, 1996; Elkington, 1997) may today be considered as now the quadruple bottom line, the added factor being that of climate change (see Johnstone, 2007). An alternative view is that the quadruple bottom line means explicitly incorporating the ethical dimension, which as Wight (2007) argued, not only holds implications for responsibilities involving stakeholders and in partnerships but also SSCM (see Chapter 3). Certainly in the 1990s many codes of practice developed in response to the intrusion of tourism SMEs and tourists included a conservation ethic (see Chapter 3). But the more substantial is the World Tourism

Organization's 'Global Code of Ethics for Tourism' in 1999. This is very much part of 'responsible tourism' by which is meant that all actors in tourism have a responsibility for the impacts arising from their participation – whether a tourism enterprise or a visitor or agencies involved – and implicitly includes moral and ethical considerations (Leslie, 2012a). This is a stance that is manifest in the outcomes of debate on tourism, which was part of the United Nations Commission on Sustainable Development Congress in Johannesburg 'Rio+10' in 2002 (see Blackstock, et al., 2008; Spenceley, 2010). CSR was further promoted at 'Rio + 20' and the criteria of environmental quality and social equity were notably emphasized (UNEP, 2013); to an extent masking the tensions that exist in tourism between sustainability and environmental ethics, which do not readily coincide though they are closely connected (Saarinen et al., 2009).

Leading international agencies involved in tourism have been advocating CSR since the late 1990s, though the actions identified have certainly been promoted for much longer (witness Bowen, 1953) but not articulated under the umbrella of CSR; for example aspects of CSR were promoted in the International Hotels Environment Initiative of the early 1990s and similarly through accommodation eco-labels of that time. However, what is both different and significant is the use of the term 'social responsibility'. This social dimension has gained substantial influence on business thinking since the 1990s (WBCSD, 2000; Elkington, 2005) and became manifest in the tourism sector at the turn of the century (see Gordon and Richards, 2002; WTTC et al., 2002). Indeed, such was the acclaim that: '68 percent of CEOs agree that the proper exercise of corporate social responsibility is vital to companies' profitability.' (WTTC et al., 2002, p. 2). The IH&RA was similarly promoting 'social responsibility' and produced an environment teaching pack 'Sowing the Seeds of Change'. But the WTTC et al. evidently expect government support, arguing that it is the responsibility of companies to place sustainable development issues at the core of their management structure and encourage corporate citizenship, whereas it is

the responsibility of governments to develop mechanisms to support SMEs in the adoption of sustainable good practice, and policies to create incentives for CSR in tourism (WTTC et al., 2002). This could be taken to imply that in the absence of the latter further progress might be limited! There are though clear indications of support. The EU, for example, has been explicitly supporting CSR since the turn of the century (EC, 2001, 2006). As they argued at the time, CSR is relevant to all: '... its wider application in SMEs including micro-businesses is of central importance given that they are the greatest contributors to the economy and employment' (EC, 2001, p. 8). This was reinforced almost a decade later in the Madrid Declaration, which included the objective: 'to promote responsible and ethical tourism and especially – social, environmental, cultural and economic sustainability of tourism' (EU, 2010, p. 2).

To explore CSR on the part of tourism enterprises it is first appropriate that we briefly consider what CSR involves. Discussion can then move on to drawing out those findings of the study most pertinent when considered in the context of the areas covered in the following chapters. Following on from this, the attention turns to national/MNCs in tourism, which are recognized as the main players as regards recognition of CSR as a business model and reporting framework.

Overview of Corporate Social Responsibility

Whilst CSR may have come to prominence in tourism in the early 2000s it is not new either in concept or practice. For example according to Chan (2005), accounting for environmental aspects, as promoted under CSR, was considered in some quarters in the early 1970s in China and affirmed in the 1990s. At its altruistic best CSR is 'basically about companies moving beyond a base of legal compliance to integrating socially responsible behaviour into their core values, in recognition of the business benefits in doing so.' (Oliver, 2007, p. 1). The key phrase here is 'social responsibility'; defined by the International Standards Agency as:

The responsibility of an organization for the impacts of its decisions and activities on society and the environment, through transparent and ethical behaviour that contributes to sustainable development, health and the welfare of society; takes into account the expectations of stakeholders; is in compliance with applicable law and consistent with international norms of behaviour; and is integrated throughout the organization and practiced in its relationships (cited in Mosselaer *et al.*, 2012, p. 73).

On such basis it becomes clear why the objectives of CSR are generally articulated in societal terms, which is well illustrated by Zollinger (2004, p. 95):

- economic prosperity through, for example, employment creation and distribution of wealth;
- social responsibility reflects in, for example, commitment to using skills, power and influence to make a positive contribution to society; and
- environmental protection, by preventing any further damage to society, and where possible, reversing past damage.

These objectives can be expanded into further detail to demonstrate just how extensive CSR is as regards social and ethical dimensions (see Table 4.1). Within all of these areas, the interests of the enterprise's stakeholders need to be considered (Wight, 2007), which may be considered to comprise two categories – namely those for whom CSR activity impacts on individual experiences or alternatively 'other-related' stakeholders (see Hillenbrand *et al.*, 2013). Thus the view that irrespective of how CSR is defined 'the only conclusion to be made … is that the optimal performance depends on the stakeholders of the business.' (Dahlsrud, 2008, p. 6). Though realistic it rather flies in the face of the oft-cited iteration that the local community needs to be involved in the development of tourism.

Irrespective of such realism (or cynicism depending on one's perspective) there is no doubt that CSR has gained considerable attention by business in general over the last decade (see Wight, 2007) and all the more so in the latter part of the 2000s – a time of global economic recession. Witness Hanson of Acre Resources, a sustainability recruitment consultancy, who argued that whilst in recession the evidence is that more attention is being given to CSR:

> CSR has gone from something that was a bit fashionable to something that is much more broadly accepted. Some companies have whole teams doing this now – we have just been working with SKY, which has a team of 20 to 30 people dedicated to it. (2008, p. 66)

Table 4.1. Overview of the main elements of CSR. (Adapted from TOI, 2002, p. 3.)

Area	Indicative operationalization
Mission/vision/values	Reflecting CSR in the company's underlying principles.
Business ethics	The integration of a company's core values into its policies, practices and decision-making, e.g. policies in covering corruption and bribery.
Governance/accountability	How the Board of Directors operates, how the company engages stakeholders and how it measures, reports and verifies its impacts.
Community involvement	The company's donated resources to the communities where it operates, e.g. donations of goods and money, staff volunteering time.
Community economic development	Increasing economic benefits to local communities, e.g. favouring excluded business, supporting activities that simulate wealth creation, and community participation in decision-making.
Human rights	The basic standards of treatment to which all people are entitled, e.g. avoiding forced and child labour, protecting indigenous rights.
Environment	Increasing efficiency and minimizing pollution and physical degradation, e.g. energy efficient, waste reduction and recycling, reducing resource use.
Workplace	The human resource policies that directly affect employees, e.g. paying fair wages, training and education, non-discrimination.
Marketplace/consumers	The activities involved in marketing, production and distribution, e.g. accurate marketing, consumer privacy, product safety and disposal.

Furthermore: 'The most sustainability focused companies may well emerge from the current crisis stronger than ever.' (Anon., 2009, p. 1). Such views are well illustrated by developments in CSR activity amongst low fare airlines such as Flybe (see Coles, 2011, 2012). In effect, the argument is that there is a large degree of ambiguity in the application of CSR in that it can be seen to be either a PR exercise (in other words a greenwash), an influential factor in attracting external investment or based on a sincere conviction that such activity is for the good (see Hillenbrand et al., 2013). However, the key point identified is that those companies which are really committed are focused on the long-term, have strong corporate governance and a history of investing in environmental initiatives. This advocacy of CSR would not have gained such acclaim if there were not potentially substantive benefits. In rather general terms, such benefits attributed to CSR are as follows:

- *Positive investment* – for example, in a strategic asset or distinctive capability and as such not seen as expense; potential also lies with those investment companies with concern over green/ethical investments.
- *Cost savings* – well illustrated in the following quote: 'can have significant business advantages for a company, in terms of its cost savings, market share, reputation and preservation of its main business assets - the places and cultures their clients are willing to pay to visit' (UNEP, 2005, p. 8).
- *More efficient* – as Simm (2006, p. 24) says: 'in the longer term organisations might find that scrutinizing their operations through a green lens makes them more efficient, productive and sustainable.'
- *Brand image* – as Graeme Crossley of Brand Reputation (cited in Anon., 2010b, p. 5) argued: 'Building a reputation as a responsible business can set you apart from the competition as more and more customers look to do business with more ethical companies'
- *PR value* –contributes to positive image; to attracting new customers, customer retention (see Nicolau, 2008; Tsai et al., 2009; Kang et al., 2010).

- *Staff* – positive influence of staff recruitment and retention (Bohdanowicz and Zientara, 2008).
- *Consumers/new markets* – tourists respond well to clear messages relating to such activity (Nicolau, 2008); a point well exemplified by Ballantyne et al. (2010).
- *Competitiveness* – all these benefits will contribute to being more competitive (see also Burgos-Jimenez et al., 2002; Wight, 2007).

In the light of these benefits it is understandable why Franklin (2008) argued that it is almost inconceivable today for a large international company to be without a CSR policy (Franklin, 2008; Bohdanowicz and Zientara, 2008).

Reference to any of these areas of benefit, and notably so in the case of financial performance, brings into contention the reporting of CSR not only in terms of judging a particular enterprise but also for comparative analyses between enterprises. Albeit not explicitly based on CSR this need was recognized in Chapter 30 of Agenda 21 (a major outcome of 'The Earth Summit' in Rio de Janeiro, 1992) which includes that businesses should 'report annually on their environmental records as well as on their use of energy and natural resources' (UNEP, 1994). To be effective this requires a well-defined procedure so that companies can communicate accurately with stakeholders about economic prosperity, environmental quality and social justice (Wheeler and Elkington, 2001). Such reporting was initially to be found in the financial sector from which the basis and format of such reports has gradually developed. It is thus not surprising, for example, to identify that Deloitte introduced a Sustainability Reporting Scorecard in 1997 (see Lehni, 2004). Closely following on from this was the development of the GRI guidelines on sustainability reporting, which then led to the production of guidelines specific to different business sectors, including tourism (see Chapter 3). As the 2000s unfolded, there was a major increase in the number of companies reporting on social and environmental issues. Equally so in the case of tourism as Wight (2007) noted and in the process that such reporting holds potentially further benefits through serving two functions, namely as a planning and external reporting framework and internally an aid to decision making (Wight, 2007). However, it is also evident that some companies have been exploiting CSR as a way of promoting brand image and/or PR (Oliver, 2007). Hence the view that in some cases such reports may be seen more as greenwashing propaganda. To varying degrees this is also true of major enterprises in tourism as Bohdanowicz and Zientara (2008) established through their study into CSR in the hotel sector. Whilst there are companies doing little more than an initiative designed to show some intent and perhaps as a PR exercise, more and more companies are giving CSR substantial attention and responsive action; in some cases to the extent of being embedded, e.g. Scandic Hotels. However, they also found that it is the major hotel companies who are incorporating CSR (see also Hawkins and Bohdanowicz, 2011; and Bohdanowicz and Zientara, 2012).

The Study Enterprises

As Table 4.1 demonstrated, the scope of CSR is extensive and in one way or another seeks to address all aspects of an enterprise's internal and external activity. However the focus here is primarily on 'community involvement' and therefore community projects. The findings presented are based on those data drawn from the study relating to the enterprises and their support for 'green' initiatives and/or participation in locally based environmental projects. This was explored through the questionnaires that invited respondents to indicate whether they were involved in a pre-coded list of 'projects' of which they could be expected to be aware. From a research perspective the consistency of, and correlations between, the data gained through these questions affirms the care with which most, if not all, of the questionnaires and interviews were completed. This was further confirmed through open-ended questions and invitations to comment on the possibility that they were involved in other environmental actions not noted in the questionnaire. A number of other initiatives were identified in this way by respondents but rarely were any of these mentioned by more than one or two respondents. The findings, based on those initiatives gaining some level of participation are presented in Table 4.2 followed by mainly brief comments on the noted initiatives. However, the TCP and participation in a conservation scheme are given more consideration as these two more closely meet the criteria noted for 'community involvement'.

Further analysis of the data on the basis of the category of the enterprise found few discernible differences other than those noted, apart from the findings that hoteliers were more likely and GHs and BBs the least likely to be involved in any scheme.

International Hotels Environmental Initiative (IHEI)

The IHEI was included originally because of the extent of its promotion in the 1990s; it is

Table 4.2. Involvement in selected 'green' initiatives.[a] (Adapted from Leslie, 2013.)

Initiative	Yes (%)		
	2001	2006	2011
Made in Cumbria/Made in Scotland or in local region	7	4	1
Participate in a conservation scheme (excludes TCP)	15	16	6
The Green Tourism Business Scheme (GTBS)	n/a	11	16
Tourism and Conservation Partnership (TCP)	12	n/a	n/a
A Tourism Forum	4	14	10
Business Environment Network	2	2	6
International Hotels Environmental Initiative	1	2	1

[a]GTBS not operational in the LDNP; 2001 audits 18% for TCP.

now better known as the International Tourism Partnership (ITP). However, as the findings evidence, it hardly gains a mention, which is not surprising in the cases of 2001 and 2006 given their generally small inclusion of large enterprises and hotels that are part of a group. The opposite was the case in 2011 and thus a higher representation might have been expected. One reason countering such an expectation is the comparatively high participation in the GTBS (comparative that is when considered in the context of membership of other, similar schemes).

Business Environment Network

The very low involvement for 2001 and 2006 and showing higher participation on the part of the urban data set potentially suggests that managers of the larger company enterprises have more time and/or more interest (opportunity for networking) to participate in business fora.

A Tourism Forum

The higher participation amongst the 2006 population is largely explained by a combination of factors, though mainly due to the spatial diversity of the enterprises and thus the number of area Tourist Boards and local authority tourism committees potentially involved.

Made in Cumbria/Scotland or local region

The findings here bring into question support for local produce/products (see Chapter 6). But it may partly be accounted for by the respondents not considering that they were involved although they did purchase such branded goods. Restaurants and attractions were identified as far more likely comparative to the other categories to be involved in these initiatives. The Made in Cumbria scheme serves to bring to the attention another dimension of the potential problems that can arise through such well-intended initiatives. In this case conflicts of interest based on unfair competition as illustrated by the following extract:

Small business owners to lose vital source of income following the decision of SLDC to ban Made in Cumbria members from trading on the Glebe at Bowness. Decision defended by SLDC saying Windermere Parish Council objected to the fairs on the basis that the events are in direct competition with established businesses and other shops in Windermere (Westmoreland Gazette, 4 February, 2000).

The Green Tourism Business Scheme (www.green-business.co.uk)

This was established in Scotland in the 1990s and is basically an accredited EMS for tourism enterprises promoted by VisitScotland and has since developed into the national tourism certification scheme for the whole of the UK. This eco-label is considered to be one of the most successful schemes of its kind on the basis of membership level and it has been adopted by other countries (Leslie, 2012b). In terms of participation in such schemes the comparatively high proportion of the 2011 enterprises can be explained by a number of factors. First, overall membership increased during the 2000s and thus it would be expected that compared with 2006, the number involved would be higher. Secondly, the higher proportion of large company hotels in the 2011 data set. Third, membership of VisitScotland is higher, which was a requisite for membership of the GTBS and finally, the promotion of the scheme as a marketing tool.

Tourism & Conservation Partnership (www.nuturelakeland.org)

This project was established in the 1990s and has since been critically acclaimed and promoted as an exemplar of a 'visitor payback scheme'. Witness the UK government promotion of such schemes:

… the development and uptake of visitor payback schemes to encourage tourists or businesses to contribute (financially or in kind) to local environmental protection and enhancement programmes (DCMS, 1999, p. 53).

Basically every member of the Partnership presents all customers with the opportunity to add a donation (originally £1) to their bill to go to the TCP. The funds so raised are used for conservation projects within the LDNP. An enterprise may also identify a specific conservation project which they wish to directly support and in this instance the funds raised by that enterprise are solely used for the said project. Essential to the success of the scheme is that it is well presented and explained to customers with the accent on promoting the conservation message. This holds potentially wider benefits in that it can help engender a sense of place and more specifically attachment with that place, which then has positive impacts on their appreciation of and support for such practices (see Hwang et al., 2005; Ballantyne et al., 2010). This initiative, and in some ways similarly the GTBS, are also seen as aspects of social marketing in that there is potential to attract tourists more likely to be environmentally oriented, with concerns over social obligations and appreciative of the physical landscape (see Dinan and Sargeant, 2000). The TCP later developed and became known as 'Nuture Lakeland' with a current (2013) membership of some 400 individual businesses and it now also promotes the GTBS and the more localized initiative 'Green at Heart'.

Whilst this has been particularly successful, questions arise on two counts. First, why do relatively few enterprises participate? A lack of interest or perhaps they 'could not be bothered'? They may see the action of requesting the donations and explanation as 'bothering' their customers. Possibly they see it in some way as a form of 'visitor tax' and oppose it just as seen in the outcry on the part of local businesses and TOs in the UK against the proposal (and implementation – albeit short-lived) of a tourist tax in the Balearic Islands. The second question is why many visitors opt not to contribute. For example, a number of the agencies managing self-catering units in the LDNP adopted the practice of applying a voluntary levy of £1 to all guests' accounts. Enquiries regarding whether or not customers pay the levy found that in the case of one agency, approximately 50% of customers did not pay the levy. If one

considers the customers accounts, especially for accommodation, then the addition of a relatively very small charge by way of a donation to this scheme hardly appears to justify cost sensitivity on the part of the enterprise. As Kelly et al. (2007) found, visitors will accept such an extra when the fee (donation) is such a low sum. The TCP more than the other initiatives illustrates the importance of local networks and how these can greatly facilitate participation of small stakeholders (see Erkust-Ozturk and Eraydin, 2009). They argue that irrespective of global/national partnerships and associations it is still the local context that is primary in environmental governance. However, their study also found that networks are more likely to form for economic reasons.

Participation in a conservation scheme

The data from 2001 and 2006 is very similar and notably significantly higher than that of 2011, which is largely attributed to their rural locations where such schemes are prevalent. However, in the case of national/MNCs such opportunities do not need to be local/regionally based (see Chapter 3); for example, they could promote Conservation International or the WWF, as per Novotel and Hotel Ibis, or Homebush in Australia, who donated $1 per overnight guest to the WWF (Mensah, 2004). Thus they, as with all other respondents/interviewees, could have cited these if applicable in response to the invitation to indicate whether they participated in any conservation schemes. A minority responded positively to this, leading to a diverse range of examples:

- promoting activities under the David Bellamy Awards (caravan and camping sites);
- maintaining the grounds, adding bird boxes, wild flowers, and removing rhododendrons and sycamores;
- looking after nearby water fowl;
- supporting the red squirrel campaign;
- maintaining stone walls and countryside stewardship;

- re-using materials instead of purchasing new when undertaking conversion work; and
- external features are made by local craftsmen.

Overall, the findings indicate that the owners/managers of these enterprises are not necessarily any more concerned about their local environment or participate in a 'green' business forum of one type or another or support locally based green initiatives. Perhaps it is surprising that the levels of involvement on the part of the rural enterprises are not higher given the importance of the quality of the physical environment to their businesses. This is an outcome which does little to counteract the perception that:

> Conventional wisdom has it that small local business will have the greatest regard for the community environment but there is scant evidence to justify that. The opposite seems probable (EIU, 1993, p. 96).

However, these findings are not to be unexpected and are similar to other studies such as Hobson and Essex (2001), Jorge (2004), Erkust-Ozturk and Eraydin (2009) and Erdogan (2009). As the latter found in rural locations there was limited environmental awareness and a lack of interest in environmental protection and environmental policy. However, that is but one perspective and whilst it does account in some ways for a lack of participation, reasons as to why some owners/managers do participate implies other factors may be more important; as illustrated by the following reasons given by respondents as to why they were involved in these schemes: 'living here'; 'want to give to the community'; 'suitable organization to serve community'; and 'put something into community'. Such comments are more in tune with the findings of Garay and Font's (2012) study, which found that 68% of the participants were involved in local initiatives and conservation schemes.

Involvement in Local Community Projects

How a question within a survey is understood and/or interpreted obviously influences the response. Thus it was found through open questions and the interviews that many participants did not consider local projects necessarily the same as 'Green Initiatives' and established that some enterprises were involved in other 'social responsibility' related activities. The exemplars in this context are the village-based inns that often play a significant part in their communities as a place to meet, support local sports teams and events, and were identified through the data as more likely to be involved in local initiatives. One reason to account for the latter is their comparatively higher level of direct, personal involvement with the local community, for example:

- 'We support and sponsor local sports teams.'
- 'We support, and encourage guests to support, the Mountain Rescue Service.'

Of special significance here is that very few participants considered mentioning such involvement, which was largely established during the extensive fieldwork. As Nicolau (2008) argued, CSR activity in the community promotes trust and value with consequent ongoing positive benefits to the enterprise both in social terms and financial performance. Secondly, and arguably the more substantial in terms of tourism and sustainability is the involvement of the enterprise in directly supporting the local economy and community, and thus fostering and developing the interrelationships that exist between the tourism enterprise, the economy and the community. This is most readily illustrated by reference to the purchase of local produce and products (see Chapter 6), which has added value in that buying local, seasonal produce and so forth can reduce the environmental costs involved in food purchasing and processing and so contribute to reducing an enterprise's carbon footprint (see Gossling et al., 2010). A view which is also affirmed by the launch (2010) of the Sustainable Restaurant Association in the UK.

To investigate further the involvement of these enterprises in support for the local economy in other areas, respondents were asked a number of questions regarding local arts and crafts (see Table 4.3). As the results convey, the 2011 enterprises demonstrate far

Table 4.3. Use of arts and crafts in premises

	Crafts	Paintings	General
Area of enquiry	Yes (%)	Yes (%)	Yes (%)
Are arts and crafts by producers living within the NP used for decoration?	33	26	–
Are local products used in delivering the service in some way(s), e.g. cruets, ashtrays, coasters?[a]	18	–	–
Are arts and crafts by producers living within the NP displayed for sale?	–	–	30

[a]The crafts identified specifically were: local slate; ceramics; honey and mustard pots.

less involvement in this practice. Partly accounting for this would be the comparatively fewer opportunities (i.e. outlets) available in their locality to find such products and also the generally lower profile of A & Cs producers in their area. Of all the enterprises, a major market is the self-catering category with 15% of owners saying that they do buy locally made A & C for their properties; one owner rather contradictorily said that very few items made locally were suitable. Attractions were also found to support local A & Cs artisans, notably so in the Fringe area. However, a noted constraint was that of price and display space. As the findings indicate, there is support for local craft producers though this could be much higher. For example, many craft producers are prepared to have their work displayed on a sale or return basis and pay commission on sales (see p. 37–38). Enterprises could adopt this practice more and thus not only support local craft persons, but would also have an opportunity at no expense to introduce/change decorative features. Evidently this is an area that could be supported by more enterprises. That more do not is a matter of individual choice. However, other factors have an influence such as a lack of awareness that this could be done and a lack of promotion of such ideas on the part of the producers.

National/International Enterprises

Earlier discussion identified that in general it is mainly the national/MNC in tourism that are engaged in CSR. Therefore the aim here is to bring into this context of tourism enterprise

and sustainability these larger enterprises, in the process drawing on a range of examples (including TOs) of community involvement selected to help form a representative cross-section. Thus and although in the preceding chapter, discussion predominantly was based on TOs and incorporated aspects of CSR, the attention here seeks to highlight different facets of TOs and their involvement in local communities. It is not though the intention to go into detail on CSR and related practices as these are well covered elsewhere (see Bohdanowicz and Zientara, 2012). As is often the case, there are invariably early leaders in any 'new' business model. An early exemplar of a tourism enterprise demonstrating CSR activity is that of Abercrombie and Kent International in the 1980s, which involved tours that today would be considered as ecotourism, e.g. camps in the Masai Mara (EIU, 1993). Also in the 1980s, British Airways were developing their environmental policy and related initiatives; for example they developed an 'Assisting Nature Conservation' programme and forged partnerships with such organizations as the Dian Fossey Gorilla Fund and the Smithsonian Museum (Somerville, 1993). Similarly, McDonald's developed its first environmental programme and related initiatives in the late 1980s (Cairncross, 1995). The exemplar in the hotel category is InterContinental Hotels and Resorts, which was one of the first companies to practise and widely promote the incorporation of environmental issues in general practice. They further introduced and promoted the practice of reporting on environmental performance with their first review published in 1996

(Hawkins, 1996). More recently, Whitbread plc, which currently owns the Costa Coffee brand, has gained the Carbon Trust status award for steps taken to reduce carbon emissions. In 2010, they launched the 'Good Together' programme of targets as part of their environmental policy introducing such initiatives as all Costa Coffee production to be Rainforest Alliance certified and also raises funds for the WaterAid Charity. Such examples appear to bear witness to Holden (2009, p. 380) that adopting CSR 'seems to represent a combination of environmental altruism, a need for market competitiveness and a medium to long term business strategy.'

These MNCs are by no means alone in addressing some aspects or other of CSR. For instance and well illustrating Holden's observation is Euro-Camp, which took an early initiative with guidance from Green Flag, on greening their operations. They introduced environmental audits and then developed their CSR activity to include SSCM. Further, they considered it important to educate their customers to awareness of conservation and their own actions (Atkinson, 1993). There is though a downside to this which is that too much/many environmental initiatives promoted to customers will act as a 'turn-off'. Comprehensive promotion of steps taken as regards the environment and being responsible can draw the attention of conservationists, etc. who seek to challenge such messages, as Hudson and Miller (2005) found through their study into the approach of Canadian Mountain Holidays to environmental issues and their responsibility. In the wider context of sustainability, concerns do arise over such enterprises that seek to develop opportunities for tourists such as skiing in remote areas, especially where access may only be gained at times through the use of helicopters. Is this being responsible? It certainly appears that environmental concerns tend to dominate, though not exclusively, as the following two examples illustrate more comprehensively CSR. The CSR programme of the Taj Group of Hotels shows that they are extensively involved in supporting local communities where, for example, staff have direct involvement in a variety of ways to help the underprivileged (Tapper and Font, 2004). The

significant factor here is that the hotels are owned by the Tata Group, a substantial private conglomerate that has established a charitable trust fund to aid community development. Each company within the group has a mandate to develop community development programmes. Second, Serena Hotels launched through the support of the Aga Khan Fund for Economic Development, which aims to improve living conditions and opportunities for the poor. The company had 26 properties in 2007 of which 19 were in Africa (Howells, 2007). CSR extends to designing accommodation based on outstanding ethnic design and staffed almost totally by locals. For example, the Mara Serena Safari Lodge in Kenya 'blends' into its hillside location. The company appear to be aware that their developments whilst promoting tourism should not on balance generate negative impacts on the local environment. The hotels all have clearly defined environmental policies and management programmes. Even so questions remain as to the longer term impacts, for example arising from the domino effect.

Away from such major operations there are many examples of local community successes in developing low-scale, low-key tourism operations. Often these are manifest in the NEAT category of tourism supply (see Wheat, 2004; Leslie, 2012b). Given that CSR includes the rights of indigenous peoples, a good example in this case is that of 'conservancies' in Namibia and specifically the Torra Conservancy in the Gergsig area where local residents developed a camp style operation rather than the more lucrative lodge-based operation based on a consensus that the latter would have greater and potentially unwelcome impact (Wood, 2002; also see Spenceley and Rylance, 2012). As the latter writers attest, such projects are not just about the local environment, but very much about communities, small tourism enterprise and economic opportunities. In part this is exemplified by a situation which arose at Victoria Falls. A decline in visitor numbers coincided with a significant increase in poaching. This led to the establishment of the Victoria Falls Anti-Poaching Unit, supported by the Lokuthula Lodges Company, with some degree of success (Bennett, 2006).

Conclusion

Evidently CSR in any formal sense, such as portrayed in the reporting guidelines, is not a business model suited to the majority of tourism enterprises given their small or micro SME status. Even so this does not mean that they are not engaging in CSR activities as both the findings presented in the previous section and those of subsequent chapters confirm. Rather in design, it is largely taken on board by N/MNCs in the tourism sector that appear to realize the potential value of instituting procedures for CSR; as well illustrated here by the TUI's Director of Group Sustainable Development, who said:

> Driving sustainability supports the long term success of our tourism business – it's as simple as that. Whilst we have made progress we certainly recognise that we still have a long way to go and that there are challenges involved. But the potential benefits are significant – for our business, destinations, customers, colleagues and the environment. (TUI, 2011, p. 2)

Such an approach might well be considered essential if they seek on-going success in the longer term. As Elkington and Burke (1987) in their book, *The Green Capitalists: Industry's search for environmental excellence,* make the point that by and large all the examples in Peters and Waterman's 'In search of excellence – lessons from America's best run companies' whilst they all manage well the key aspects of business, they all most notably 'help build bridges between various interests'. Today CSR is seen as very much part of such a function. As Peter Lacy, Executive Director of the European Academy of Business in Society is quoted as saying 'Even if you don't care about the environment CSR simply makes good business sense.' (Lacy, 2011, cited in *The Director*). Even so, the adoption of CSR is only prevalent in larger firms (Pratt, 2011). Considering the number of large enterprises involved in tourism, the adoption of CSR in the tourism sector has been (Wight, 2007) and still is limited (Anon., 2010b). Partly accounting for this is that:

> many companies still focus too much on product and price to compete. Too little attention appears to be focused on the creation of added value for customers. Moreover 'eco-innovation' – which is high on the research agenda in many other industries – has hardly entered the tourism industry. (ECORYS, 2009, p. v)

On such a basis, it is arguable that the large companies such as airlines and international tour operators may balk at the costs of CSR unless business activity (and thus so too profitability) justifies it. In other words having a responsibility for a destination is a function of dollars! A view that overriding profit motive counteracts other concerns of businesses such as social bonds and contributing to the local economy (Borgstom and Wackernael, 1999).

Is adopting CSR therefore more political in the sense of the enterprise's reputation and market positioning rather than ethical concerns? In the absence of in-depth, internal analysis this could be difficult to ascertain. But what is undoubtedly influential in such an outcome is the leadership and thus the attitudes (morals) of the key internal role-player(s) in the enterprise. A view that is supported by the fact that it is voluntary, which suggests that formal adoption and reporting is either a function of the attitude of top management or perceived financial benefit or a combination of the two. Particularly when considered in the context of tourism that without concerned shareholders one questions whether there is a significant demand for such reports. In effect, there is a clear need for a 'champion' to promote CSR (Lawton and Weaver, 2009). Such a champion needs to be well placed within the company, ideally the Chief Executive Officer. But what happens if they leave the company? This is why it is so important that such policy and attitudes are pervasive within the company and in terms of employees all-inclusive. It goes almost without saying that successful development of CSR demands personal involvement and the encouragement of employees and their involvement. Furthermore, as Paget-Brown (2007, p. 59) opined, 'Without this top-level leadership we are more likely to see PR puffery as opposed to new, dynamic business models fit for a more sustainable world'. This top-level leadership is equally applicable in all tourism enterprises be it in the person who is the CEO of the company or the owner of the enterprise. As Carter *et al.* (2004, p. 46) stated 'commitment to continual improvement in environmental performance is attributable to individual and corporate ethics'.

But achieving progress in sustainability is not just a matter of addressing EP and more broadly perhaps CSR, it requires change and international and national government support, including regulations (Welford *et al.*, 1999). Undoubtedly it is complex and all the more so given that tourism is based on heritage resources and impacts are a function of interaction with diverse resources. Furthermore, as Wight (2007) opines, CSR is not an answer to key development issues and the realities in developing countries. Also, raising social and environmental standards implies costs that may constrain enterprise development and employment generation. In effect for greater sustainability in tourism this is a need that CSR does not address.

Further Reading

A very interesting critique of CSR and tourism businesses is presented by Anson Wong (2006) CSR in the Guangdong hotel industry. *CSR Asia Weekly* 2, Week 30, 26 July available at http://www.csr-asia.com. Following on from this readers are directed to Corporate Watch (2006) *What's wrong with Corporate Social Responsibility?* Available at http://www. corporatewatch.org.uk.

Wood, M.E. (2002) *Ecotourism: principles, practices & policies for sustainability.* Division of Technology, Industry and Economic, UNEP Paris.

On communities and tourism see Singh, S., Timothy, D.J. and Dowling, R.K. (eds) (2003) *Tourism in Destination Communities.* CAB International, Wallingford, UK; for examples of best practice involving local people and communities see: Draper and Murray (2008) Special Issue. *Forum for the Future,* London; and Timothy, D.J. (2012) Destination Communities and Responsible Tourism. In: Leslie, D. (ed.) *Responsible Tourism: Concepts, Theory and Practices.* CAB International, Wallingford, UK.

References

Anon. (2008) Members News. *Hospitality,* Issue 11, p. 9.

Anon. (2009) Green companies do better during downturn. *Greenbiz* 11 February. Available at http://www.greenbiz.com/news/2009/02/10/green-companies-do-better-during-downturn-study (accessed 12 February 2009).

Anon. (2010b) Social and economic impacts: measurement, evaluation and reporting. *Ethical Corporation.* September.

Atkinson, R. (1993) Tour operators' contribution to sustainable tourism. Paper presented to Developing Sustainable Tourism, Conference, London Marriott Hotel, May.

Ballantyne, R., Packer, J. and Falk, J. (2010) Visitors' learning for environmental sustainability: testing short- and long-term impacts of wildlife tourism experiences using structural equation modelling. *Tourism Management* 32, 1243–1252.

Bennett, L. (2006) Duty Free? *Resource* 20, pp. 20–22. July/August Resource Media Bristol.

Blackstock, K.L., White, V., McCrum, G., Scott, A. and Hunter, C. (2008) Measuring responsibility: an appraisal of a Scottish National Park's Sustainable Tourism Indicators. *Journal of Sustainable Tourism* 16 (3), 276–297.

Bohdanowicz, P. and Zientara, P. (2008) Hotel companies' contribution to improving the quality of life of local communities and the well-being of their employees. *Tourism and Hospitality Research* 9 (2), 147–158.

Bohdanowicz, P. and Zientara, P. (2012) CSR-inspired environmental initiatives in top hotel chains. In: Leslie, D. (ed.) *Tourism Enterprises and the Sustainability Agenda across Europe.* New Directions in Tourism Analysis. Ashgate, Farnham, UK, pp. 93–120.

Borgstrom, H.B. and Wackernael, M. (1999) Rediscovering place and accounting space: how to re-embed the human economy. *Ecological Economics* 29 (2), 203–213.

Bowen, H.R. (1953) *Social Responsibilities of the Business*. Harper & Row, New York.

Branson, R. (2006) The environment. *Tourism*, Quarter IV Issue 130, p. 3.

Burgos-Jimenez, J., Cano-Guillen, C.J. and Cespedes-Lorente, J.J. (2002) Planning and control of environmental performance on hotels. *Journal of Sustainable Tourism* 10 (3), 207–217.

Cairncross, F. (1995) *Green, Inc.: a guide to business and the environment*. Earthscan, London.

Carter, R.W., Whiley, D. and Knight, C. (2004) Improving environmental performance in the tourism accommodation sector. *Journal of Ecotourism* 3 (1), 46–68.

Chan, W.W. (2005) Partial analysis of the environmental costs generated by hotels in Hong Kong. *Hospitality Management* 24, pp. 517–531.

Coles, T. (2011) *CSR: Issues for the Future Development in the Low Fares Airline Sector*. University of Exeter, Exeter, UK, 31 March.

Coles, T. (2012) *Flybe: Working with Business*. University of Exeter, Exeter, UK, 13 November.

Dahlsrud, A. (2008) How corporate social responsibility is defined: An analysis of 37 definitions. *Corporate Social Responsibility and Environmental Management*. 15, 1–13.

DCMS (1999) *Tomorrow's tourism: a growth industry for the new millennium*. Department of Culture, Media and Sport, London.

Dinan, C. and Sargeant, A. (2000) Social marketing and sustainable tourism – is there a match. *International Journal of Tourism Research* 2(1), 1–14.

DoE (1990) *This Common Inheritance*. Department of Environment, HMSO, London.

EC (2001) *Promoting a European framework for corporate social responsibility: Green Paper*. Directorate-General for Employment and Social Affairs. European Commission, Luxembourg. July.

EC (2006) *Implementing the Partnership for Growth and Jobs: Making Europe a Pole of Excellence on Corporate Social Responsibility*. Available at: http://ec.europa.eu/enterprise/csr/policy.htm (accessed 20 February 2011).

ECORYS (2009) *Study on the competitiveness of the EU tourism industry. – with specific focus on the accommodation and tour operators travel agent industries*. Final Report Directorate-General Enterprise & Industry, European Commission, Brussels.

EIU (1993) Travel and Tourism Analyst. Economic Intelligence Unit, London, No 1.

Elkington, J. (1997) *Cannibals with Forks: The Triple Bottom Line of 21st Century Business*. Capstone Publishing, Oxford, UK.

Elkington, J. (2005) Sea change – Letter from Davos. *The Director* March, pp. 29.

Elkington, J. and Burke, T. (1987) *The Green Capitalists: Industry's search for environmental excellence*. Victor Gollancz, London.

Erdogan, N. (2009) Turkey's tourism policy and environmental performance of tourism enterprises. In: Leslie, D. (ed.) *Tourism Enterprises, Environmental Performance and Sustainable Development*. Perspectives on Progress from across the Globe. Advances in Tourism Research Series. Routledge, New York, pp. 194–208.

Erkust-Ozturk, H. and Eraydin, A. (2009) Environmental governance for sustainable tourism development collaborative networks and organisation building in the Antalya tourism region. *Tourism Management* 31 (1), 113–124.

EU (2010) *Declaration of Madrid*, European Commission, Brussels, April.

Franklin, D. (2008) Just Good Business *Economist* 8563, 3–22.

Garay, L. and Font, X. (2012) Doing good to do well? Corporate social responsibility reasons, practices and impacts in small and medium accommodation enterprises. *Journal of Hospitality Management* 31, 329–337.

Gordon, G. and Richards, K. (2002) *Improving tour operator performance – the role of corporate social responsibility and reporting*. Tearfund, ABTA and Tour Operators Initiative, London.

Gossling, S., Garrod, B., Aall, C., Hille, J. and Peeters, P. (2010) Food management in tourism: reducing tourism's carbon 'footprint'. *Tourism Management* 31 (3), 534–543.

Hanson, S. (2008) Make room for CSR. *The Director* June, pp. 65–67.

Hawkins, R. (1996) *Environmental reviewing for the hotel sector: the experience of Inter-Continental Hotels and Resorts. Tourism Focus* United Nations Environment Programme, Industry and Environment April–June, Number 5.

Hawkins, R. and Bohdanowicz, P. (2011) *Responsible Hospitality: Theory and Practice*. Goodfellow Publishers Ltd, Oxford, UK.

Hillenbrand, C., Money, K. and Ghobadian, A. (2013) Unpack amend the mechanism by which corporate responsibility impacts stakeholder relationships. *British Journal of Management* 24 (1), pp. 127–146.

Hobson, K. and Essex, S. (2001) Sustainable tourism: a view from accommodation businesses. *Service Industries Journal* 21 (4), 133–146.

Holden, A. (2009) The environment–tourism nexus – influence of market ethics. *Annals of Tourism* 36 (3), 373–389.

Holland, J. (2012) Adventure tours: responsible tourism in practice? In: Leslie, D. (ed.) *Responsible Tourism: Concepts, Theories, Practices*. CAB International, Wallingford, UK, pp. 119–129.

Howells, R. (2007) Another way. *Leisure Management* July/August, pp. 44–46.

Hudson, S. and Miller, C.A. (2005) The responsible marketing of tourism: the case of Canadian Mountain Holidays. *Tourism Management* 26(2), 133–142.

Hutnyk, J. (1996) *The Rumour of Calcutta: Tourism, Charity and the Poverty of Representation*. Zed, London.

Huybers, T. and Bennett, J. (2003) Environmental management and the competitiveness of nature-based tourism destinations. *Environmental and Resource Economics* 24, 213–233.

Hwang, S-N., Lee, C. and Chen, M.C. (2005) The relationship among tourists' involvement, place attachment and interpretation satisfaction in Taiwan's national parks. *Tourism Management* 26 (2), 143–156.

Johnstone, K. (2007) Accommodating climate change. *Hospitality* Issue 8, pp. 50–57.

Jorge, R. (2004) Institutional pressures and voluntary environmental behaviour in developing countries: evidence from the Costa Rican hotel industry. *Society and Natural Resources* 17, 779–797.

Kang, K.H., Lee, S. and Huh, C. (2010) Impacts of positive and negative corporate social responsibility activities on company performance in the hospitality sector. *International Journal of Hospitality Management* 29, pp. 72–82.

Kelly, J., Haider, W., Williams, P.W. and Englund, K. (2007) Stated preferences of tourists for eco-efficient destination planning options. *Tourism Management* 28, pp. 377–390.

Lacy, P. (2011) Social responsibility and business. *The Director* p. 3–4.

Laisch, A. (2002) Corporate futures: social responsibility in the tourism industry. *Tourism Concern*, London.

Lawton, L.J. and Weaver, D.B. (2009) Normative and innovative resources management at birding festivals. Tourism Management 31 (4), 527–536.

Lehni, M. (2004) Deloitte Sustainability Reporting Scorecard. In: Seiler-Hausmann, J-D., Liedtke, C. and von Weizsacker, E.L. (eds) *Eco-efficiency and Beyond: Towards the Sustainable Enterprise*. Greenleaf Publishing, Sheffield, UK, pp. 73–92.

Leslie, D. (2012a) The responsible tourism debate. In: Leslie, D. (ed.) *Responsible Tourism: Concepts, Theories, Practices*. CAB International, Wallingford, UK, pp. 17–42.

Leslie, D. (ed.) (2012b) *Responsible Tourism: Concepts, Theories, Practices*. CAB International, Wallingford, UK.

Leslie, D. (2013) Key players in the environmental performance of tourism enterprises. In: Reddy, M.V. and Wilkes, K. (eds) *Tourism, Climate Change and Sustainability*. Routledge, Oxford, pp. 134–152.

Mensah, I. (2004) *Environmental Management Practices in US hotels*. Hotel Online: Special Report available at www.hotel-online.com/News?PR2004_2nd/May04_EnvironmentalPractices.html (accessed 14 November 2006).

Morris, J. (1998) Tourism is destructive, in anybody's language. *The Independent* Saturday 11 July, pp. 5–6.

Mosselaer, F., Duim, R. and Wijk, J. (2012) Corporate social responsibility in tour operating: the case of Dutch outbound tour operators. In: Leslie, D. (ed.) *Tourism Enterprises and the Sustainability Agenda across Europe*. New Directions in Tourism Analysis. Ashgate, Farnham, UK, pp. 71–92.

Nicolau, J.L. (2008) Corporate social responsibility: worth-creating activities. *Annals of Tourism* 35 (4), pp. 990–1006.

Oliver, J. (2007) Wake-up call for firms doing the right thing. Jobs.telegraph. *The Daily Telegraph*. September 27, p. 1.

Paget-Brown, N. (2007) The burning issue. *The Director* December, pp. 56–59.

Pratt, L. (2011) *Tourism investing in energy and resources efficiency towards a green economy*. United Nations Environment Programme, Paris.

Pro-Poor Tourism Partnership (2011) Available at http://www.propoortourism.org.uk/index.html (accessed 9 February 2011).

Saarinen, L., Becker, F., Manwa, H. and Wilson, D. (eds) (2009) *Sustainable Tourism in Southern Africa: Local Communities and Natural Resources in Transition*. Channel View, Clevedon, UK.

Simm, J. (2006) A green light for change. *The Director* November, p. 24.

Somerville, H. (1993) How the airline industry can manage its environmental impacts. Paper presented at Conference on Sustainable Tourism, Marriott Hotel, London, May 11–12.

Spenceley, A. (ed.) (2010) *Responsible Tourism: Critical Issues for Conservation and Development*. Earthscan, London.

Spenceley, A. and Rylance, A. (2012) Responsible wildlife tourism in Africa. In: Leslie, D. (ed.) *Responsible Tourism: Concepts, Theory and Practice*. CAB International, Wallingford, UK, pp. 1301–1341.

SustainAbility (1996) *Engaging Stakeholders: the 1996 Benchmark Survey. The Third International progress report on company environmental reporting*. United Nations Environment Programme.

Tapper, R. and Font, X. (2004) *Tourism Supply Chains*. Report for the Travel Foundation. Environment Business & Development Group, Leeds Metropolitan University, Leeds, UK. January.

TOI (Tour Operators Initiative) (2002) *Improving Tour Operator Performance: the Role of Corporate Social Responsibility and Reporting*. TOI, Association of British Travel Agents, Tearfund. Available at: http://www.abtamembers.org/responsibletourism/csr_guide.pdf (accessed 28 March 2011).

Tsai, H., Song, H. and Wong, K. (2009) Tourism and Hotel Competitiveness Research. *Journal of Travel and Tourism Marketing* 26 (5–6), pp. 522–546.

TUI (2011) *The Sustainable Development Report*. (Available at http://www.tuitravelplc.com in the 'latest news' section.)

UNEP (1994) *Company environmental reporting: a measure of the progress of business and industry towards sustainable development*. Technical Report No 24, United Nations Environment Programme – Industry and Environment Office.

UNEP (2005) *Integrating Sustainability into Business: a Management Guide for Responsible Tour Operations*. United Nations Environment Programme, Paris.

UNEP (2013) Rio + 20: From outcome to implementation. *Our Planet* February.

Utting, P. and Marques, J.C. (2009) *Corporate Social Responsibility and Regulatory Governance: Towards Inclusive Development?* Volume 1. Palgrave Macmillan, Basingstoke, UK.

WBCSD (2000) *Corporate Social Responsibility: Making Good Business Sense*. World Business Council for Sustainable Development, January.

Welford, R., Ytterhus, B. and Eiligh, J. (1999) Tourism and sustainable development: an analysis of policy and guidelines for managing provision and consumption. *Sustainable Development* 7, 165–177.

Wheat, S. (2004) Back to nature. *Leisure Management* February, pp. 76–79.

Wheeler, D. and Elkington, J. (2001) The end of the corporate environmental report? Or the advent of cybernetic sustainability reporting and communication. *Business Strategy and the Environment* 10 (1), 1–14.

Wight, P. (2007) Ecotourism, CSR, and the fourth dimension of sustainability. In: Higham, J. (ed.) *Critical Issues in Ecotourism*. Butterworth Heinemann, Oxford, UK, pp. 214–240.

Wood, M.E. (2002) *Ecotourism: principles, practices &policies for sustainability*. Division of Technology, Industry and Economic, United Nations Environment Programme, Paris.

WTO (1999) *Global Code of Ethics for Tourism*. World Tourism Organisation, Madrid.

WTTC, IFTO, IH&RA, ICCL (2002) *Industry as a partner for sustainable Development*. World Travel and Tourism Council, International Federation of Tour Operators, International Hotel and Restaurant Association, International Council of Cruise Liners, London.

Zollinger, P. (2004) Sustainability management? Don't bother! Practical steps in bringing sustainability in core management practice. In: Seiler-Hausmann, J-D., Liedtke, C. and von Weizsacker, E.L. (eds) *Eco-efficiency and Beyond: Towards the Sustainable Enterprise*. Greenleaf Publishing, Sheffield, UK, pp. 93–99.

5 Resource Management and Operational Practices – Environmental Management Systems

Introduction

Tourism, unlike perhaps other more traditional sectors of the economy, does not and cannot operate in isolation but rather is inextricably entwined with all the facets of a locality. Tourism enterprises draw on local resources and through the production and delivery of services returns pollution and waste back into the locality. As demand and supply expand, so does the consumption of resources and production of waste. It is therefore essential for all enterprises and those organizations involved in tourism – as well as the visitors themselves – to address these issues of resource usage, consumption and waste that are so quintessential to sustainability.

The main approach towards increased sustainability on the part of tourism enterprises in the management of resources may be simply expressed as the application of the three Rs: reduce, reuse, recycle; all of which are often described as environmentally friendly practices. In business terminology such practices are encompassed within what is formally termed an environmental management system (EMS). Basically, an EMS is all about: 'managing an organization's activities that give rise to impacts upon the environment …' and essentially therefore:

> … the interaction between the organization and the environment. It is the environmental aspects (as opposed to the financial or quality aspects) of an organization's activities, products and services that are subject to management. (Sheldon and Toxon, 1999, p. 2).

Such systems came to the fore in the early 1990s and in various forms have been promoted in the wider context as 'the greening of tourism', similar to the 'greening of industry'. A premise in the promotion of EMS is that, as Russo and Fouts (1997) demonstrated, it pays to go green based on their finding that growth industries evidence a stronger relationship with improved environmental performance and increased profits. Furthermore, as the UNEP (1998, p. 6) so eloquently, and in regard to climate change (CC), expressed:

> you will be harmonizing your own activities with what is best for the environment while at the same time building a solid basis for long term growth; you will be offering your visitors a better product and projecting a responsible and credible image; you could also be saving money and attracting new visitors, guests, passengers or customers.

This shift in the focus on environmental management in businesses generally is considered as 'ecological modernization'; the new name for environmental politics in the EU (Revell, 2003). The concept recognizes that economic growth and environmental quality are mutually dependent, which is certainly manifest in the development of tourism – at least in the initial stages of development (see

Jackson and Roberts, 1999). EMS can be considered as being within this context, especially if considered as a tool promoting 'eco-efficiency' in the management and operational practices of an enterprise, which:

> prescribes reducing the amount of energy and natural resources used, as well as wastes and pollutants discharged in the production of goods and services (Kelly et al., 2007, p. 377)

Engaging SMEs in this is considered a key element of the EU's drive towards greater sustainability (see Hillary, 2004). However, a key weakness in terms of sustainability is that it hardly addresses wider concerns (see Welford et al., 1999). In investigating the EP of enterprises it is necessary, as noted in Chapter 4, to include CSR and related activities in order to assess the enterprises' environmental performance. In combination these two areas serve as the basis for an enterprise's environmental policy. Thus the focus in this chapter is on the environmental practices of the study's tourism enterprises and the adoption of an EMS system, which can be furthered through the development of an environmental policy and the undertaking of an environmental audit of the business.

As noted, environmental management practices and the adoption of an EMS has been promoted extensively in the tourism sector. Advice and guidelines have been readily available for a long time, promoted through government policy, National Tourist Organizations (NTOs) and related agencies involved in tourism (Leslie, 2002); all advocating the greening of the tourism sector and:

> to promote better understanding among operators of the business benefits available from programmes to reduce energy consumption, waste production and water use (DCMS, 1999, p. 59)

This was also manifest in EU policy for tourism; for example, encouraging tourism enterprises to adopt 'responsible behaviour' and address their environmental performance (see EC, 2000). Further, that enterprises:

> must operate in a more eco-efficient way, in other words producing the same or more products with less input and less waste, and consumption patterns have to become more sustainable. (EC, 2001, p. 3)

'... and promoting sustainability in the tourism value chain and destinations.' (EC, 2003, p. 3). To further this approach, they were and still are: '... increasingly seeking to use policy instruments that tap into market dynamics such as taxation, eco-labelling ...' (Johnson and Turner, 2003, p. 289).

This is well illustrated in the launch of the Green Audit Kit in 1996 (RDC, 1996) and the GTBS in Scotland. But of special significance in this context is that such promotion was extensive throughout the 1990s hence the potential that the tourism enterprises in the 2001 population would be aware of and influenced in the adoption of such practices and systems. The professional organizations in the sector were also advocating EM practices and an EMS with the main impetus being in the 1990s. Furthermore, environmental auditing was also advocated. Witness the WTTC which stated in 1991 that:

> Annual environmental audits of all ongoing tourism activities are an integral management tool of a tourism firm with a proactive commitment to environmentally responsible tourism (Goodall, 1995, p. 658).

They also produced their 'Agenda 21 for the Travel & Tourism Industry' (WTTC et al., 1996) that conveyed, in a very comprehensive style with a raft of examples, both EM and CSR practices that could be adopted. As noted in Chapter 2, the IH has been promoting energy efficiency since the beginning of the 1990s. They also produced a technical brief for their members on environmental issues in 1993 within which it was argued that all hospitality businesses should produce an 'Environmental Policy Statement' as well as advocating environmental auditing, which as Simpson (1999) opined is not rocket science. Leading players in the market were also active in promoting EM. Early leaders in this field were Canadian Pacific Hotel and Resorts and the InterContinental Hotels (Black, 1995; also see Diamantis, 1999); also the Grecotel Hotel Group which introduced an environmental policy, an EMS and SSCM in 1992 (Diamantis, 2000). The InterContinental Hotels and Resorts Group merits particular attention. They have been promoting their EM programme since 1990 which was taken up through the IHEI, established in 1996 and the launch of the 'Environmental Action Pack for Hotels' (IHEI *et al.*, 1996); as noted in Chapter 3 the IHEI is now known as the International Tourism Partnership (ITP).

The significance of introducing an EMS is that, initially at least, it can lead to substantial savings as well as potential marketing benefits. As studies of the environmental performance of the accommodation sector (albeit based mainly on large hotels) in the 1990s found, those companies with an environmental policy rated the marketing advantages and/or increased profits more highly than other advantages such as public relations (Brown, 1994; Kirk, 1996; Middleton and Hawkins, 1998; Slee *et al.*, 1999). Such benefits though are debatable and may be seen to be not worth pursuing (see Revell, 2003; Hillary, 2004) and perhaps especially so the view that they hold of competitive advantage (see Blanco *et al.*, 2008; Baird, 2010; Preigo *et al.*, 2011). Even so, the potential of actual cost savings and perceived benefits gained more significance as the early years of the 21st century unfolded as international acceptance of, and responses to, GHG emissions and CC increased along with concerns over energy supplies and debate on perceptions of a decline in oil reserves (see Becken, 2010; Becken and Lennox, 2011). Additional to such considerations another factor supporting the introduction of an EMS and promoting this in the enterprise's market profile is the manifest presence in the general market of green consumers and demand for green produce/products. The extent to which green consumers translate their environmental concerns into their tourists' demands though is a matter of debate (see Chapter 9). However, there was certainly some evidence of market demand for 'green' hotels in the 1990s. Gustin and Weaver (1996) identified a correlation between pro-environmental consumers and the market for 'green' hotels though, as they acknowledge, limitations of the research meant they could not establish the strength of this correlation. This is supported by the experience of Marriott Hotels in the late 1990s, which introduced 'green rooms' let at an added premium, the number of which was subsequently increased due to demand. Further, Masau and Prideaux's (2003) research into

hotels and environmental performance in Kenya found some evidence of a willingness on the part of the tourists to pay a premium for accredited green accommodation. The meetings and conference market is also significant business for many larger hotels and conference organizers could potentially be influenced by an hotel's environmental policy; for example the Saunders Hotel Group gained new conference business in 1992 which they attributed to their environmental programme (Mensah, 2004).

Whilst EMS has clearly been promoted and well exemplified, two key points merit consideration when it comes to the findings of the study. First, that most of the examples used advocating 'Go Green' to tourism enterprises are invariably drawn from N/MNC with which few small/micro enterprises can readily relate. Second, and coupled with a plethora of non-sectoral specific guidance, and thus of general application, promotions and initiatives as well as media coverage of such over the years not only reinforces the advocacy of EMS but pre-empts the potential argument that the owners/managers of these enterprises may be unaware of the promotion of EM practices if it were solely in the tourism domain of government tourism policy and NTOs. The question therefore arises as to what extent is the management of these enterprises addressing their environmental performance and therefore able to establish some insight as to the current position regarding progress towards greater sustainability in their operational practices. The notification here of adopting an EMS and environmental auditing invites discussion on what an EMS entails and the associated auditing before consideration of the findings. This brings to attention the formulization of EM practices through an accredited system, which in tourism has led to the emergence of many variants which merit further discussion and in the process provides the appropriate opportunity to highlight actions of N/MNCs with regard to their adoption of EMSs. The findings of those aspects of the surveys and interviews designed to identify the extent to which the enterprises have introduced EM practices and whether they have introduced an EMS and correlating environmental policy are then presented. These findings are considered in the four main areas of policy, energy, water and waste. Comparative analyses between the samples are limited to those more general factors considered equally applicable to all and thus primarily involving serviced-accommodation. Thus detail on the actions of enterprises in the different sub-group categories between and within the sample populations are largely avoided except where specifically merited. In the process of discussion of these findings comparatives are drawn with other related studies though not always in a tourism context, thereby seeking to highlight that these enterprises are not necessarily that different in their practices from other SMEs in general. Further, as noted in Chapter 1, these related studies are drawn from across the time spectrum of the study. This is particularly pertinent in that, for example, by establishing what was manifest in the 1990s, and 2000s, it might be anticipated that by 2011 progression in response to the advocacy of EM practice would be evident.

Overview of EMS

Attention to the consumption of resources on the part of tourism enterprises can be traced to the Bruntdland Report and more specifically in the UK to 'This Common Inheritance' (DoE, 1990) in the wake of which the Government set up a task force with the remit of identifying ways through which the negative impacts of visitors could be minimized. The terms of reference for the Task Force are notable, in particular:

> to draw up guidance on how the tourism industry and other agencies might ensure that their present activities and policies as well as future tourism developments are in harmony with the need to conserve and preserve the environment, and to serve the wellbeing of host communities (ETB, 1991, p. 5).

This initiative was furthered by a major outcome of the 'Earth Summit' namely Agenda 21. Chapter 30 of Agenda 21 – 'Strengthening the Role of Business and Industry' – aims to promote increasing the efficiency of resource utilization and reducing the waste generated, and argued that businesses should as a matter

of course report on their consumption of resources and thus their environmental management practices (UNEP, 1994). Clearly to achieve this in any meaningful way necessitated the development of an appropriate system suited to that purpose and hence the development of EMSs. An EMS, as explained by Visser (2009, p. 155), is:

> that part of the overall management system of an organisation that includes organisational structu..e, planning activities, responsibility, practices, procedures, processes and resources for developing, implementing, achieving, reviewing and maintaining an environmental policy.

A major step in this was taken by the EU in 1993 with the launch of the Community Eco-management and Audit Scheme (CEMAS) and in the UK, the BS 7750. This was shortly followed by the establishment in 1996 of ISO 14001, all of which had variable degrees of success in terms of the number of accredited businesses. For example, by 2006 little more than 5000 businesses were registered under ISO 14001 in the UK, Germany or the USA. In contrast the world leaders had similar numbers of accredited businesses, the world leaders at that time were Japan and China with approximately 23,000 and 18,000 respectively (Visser, 2009). Why the registrations in China and neighbouring Hong Kong are comparatively higher is partly an outcome of early environmental policy initiatives by the government and leadership from within the hotel sector, notably by Hotel Nikko and also the Hong Kong Hotels Association scheme for Hotel Building Environmental Assessment, as well as the launch of the ECOTEL certification scheme, which is exclusive to international hotels, inns and resorts, launched in 1994 in America (Anon., 2002). As with any formal system, an EMS is based on various standards, which in this case is generally seen to require the following:

- a sound understanding of environmental effects or impacts;
- an environmental policy stating the intention and principles of the organization in relation to its overall environmental performance;

- objectives and targets which define environmental goals and more detailed performance requirements;
- an environmental programme for the objectives and targets;
- appropriate control procedures for activities; and
- internal audits of the EMS. (DNV Quality Assurance, 1996, p. 5).

The starting point is the recognition that the organization does have environmental impacts and that, for example, energy consumption and waste could be reduced. A preliminary review of the operation and identification of ways through which the consumption of resources could be reduced is the first step in the formulation of an environmental policy, which is:

> the company's [or enterprise's] overall aims and principles of action with respect to the environment including compliance with all relevant regulatory requirements regarding the environment. (Hillary, 1994, p. 18);

for example, BS7750, EMAS or ISO 14001 (see Barrow, 1999). To illustrate: BS 7750 basically is a formalized method of demonstrating how an enterprise complies with environmental legislation and regulations; for example: '... that their products or services are produced, delivered and disposed of in an environmentally friendly manner, minimizing any adverse effects on the environment ...' but also that '... planning for future investment and growth reflects market needs and the environment' (PRC (Jersey), 1998, p. 03). Although the standard does not dictate performance benchmarks its adoption does require external verification. Potentially, the most appealing aspect to management adopting such auditing practice is that an independently certified EMS potentially holds competive advantages. Whilst this sounds more applicable to industrial processing operations it is equally valid to tourism enterprises (see Pratt, 2011) and, as viewed by the EU, engaging SMEs in environmental improvements is a necessity to sustainability (Leslie, 2011). In this as Scanlon (2007) argued, education of the enterprises' owners/managers is the key to adoption.

On the plus side, introducing some form of EMS holds benefits, which as previously noted and as discussed by Hillary (2004), include not only for the environment but also communication and the enterprise overall; added to which Pratt (2011) argues that there are benefits for the local economy through, for example, the attention given to local employment and local products. The system itself holds benefits when integrated into general management and especially when, as per best practice, staff are totally involved; from attention to small measures such as turning off water taps and lighting when not necessary and encouraging participation in CSR activity such as local community projects. In this, good communication within the enterprise is very important in order to:

- bring consistency to environmental aspects;
- help to focus everyone's attention on targets; and
- foster feedback on performance against targets.

However, as prescribed, the requisite is to undertake an environmental audit. In the case, for example, of a hotel this is most neatly expressed as giving attention first to operational procedures. As Simpson (1999, p. 29) advises:

> This should be broken down by department: front of house, housekeeping, food preparation, building maintenance, etc. Every aspect of the business should be examined, their environmental impact assessed and a simple action plan drawn up. This will require some initial thought, as each hospitality business is different. However, no rocket science is required. In fact, one of the most quoted acronyms in the environmental field is 'KISS' or 'Keep It Simple, Stupid'

A sentiment that was well conveyed in the words of one hotelier in the study who said, 'It is just good housekeeping.' Even then, it may still be a function of the size of the operation and thus substantial costs of utility supplies and a decision by head office. For example, Chan and Wong's (2006) findings of research into hoteliers and their attitudes towards incorporation of ISO 14001 not surprisingly found that the majority (67%) who had introduced this were large 4–5 star operations and a third were foreign owned. The key point of their findings is that predicting factors of adoption are corporate governance and legislation. Similarly Chan and Hawkins (2011), whose study, albeit based on one hotel (not surprisingly, not only a major international hotel but also the flagship and founding member of the Asian Pacific Hotels Environment Initiative), found that key influences in gaining ISO 14001 accreditation were reduced costs, image and PR. In similar ways to national/MNCs, major tour operators and airlines also seek ISO 14001 accreditation; for example Thomson and First Choice have reduced their brochures by some 300 million pages, have increased recycling, reduced energy and water waste by implementing new water saving taps, new automatic PC shutdown software and infra-red motion sensors to help stop lights being left on unnecessarily and their airline operation has gained ISO 14001 accreditation (TUI, 2011). Thomas Cook's UK airline has also achieved ISO 14001 and in the process reduced its carbon footprint through, for example, increased recycling and improved energy efficiency. Improving energy efficiency is further recognized, as illustrated here by Hilton Hotels, which gained the Carbon Trust award in 2010 in recognition of cuts achieved to carbon emission. As the company's Vice President for Europe said, 'It's essential that we remain competitive and cater for customers who are becoming increasingly environmentally conscious – the Standard will help communicate our sustainability credentials to those that matter' (Anon., 2010).

However with regard to the majority of tourism enterprises these systems are not suitable given their potential complexity in what they involve, the associated costs, particularly in gaining the requisite external verification. As Welford and Starkey (1996, p. xi) confirmed, there was a clear need 'to develop systems to assess the environmental performance of individual operations – enterprises.' Recognition of this led to the development of various eco-labelled EMS schemes. Eco-labels are perhaps most readily associated with popular household and consumer goods first introduced as an official label in the EU in 1992 and involves a 'Life Cycle Analysis' of the product (Fouhy, 1993; see also Wisner et al., 2010).

EMS and Eco-labels

The need for tourism enterprises to have an EMS that is both fit for purpose and reflects the size and scale of the operations of small/micro enterprises led to the development of various accredited EMS eco-labels post the mid-1990s. By and large in the UK these were all based on the Green Audit Kit such as the New Forest's Little Acorns or Lancashire's Blue Lantern. However the most successful of these is the GTBS, which as 'a simple environmental auditing process can achieve worthwhile results with clear economic gains.' (PRC (Jersey), 1998) and acclaimed as the world's leading scheme (by Visit Scotland) and now includes Ireland and has been trialled in Sweden (Leslie, 2012a). By 2000 the scheme had 231 accredited members and 842 by 2007 (a figure which includes National Trust for Scotland and Historic Scotland properties) (see Blackstock et al., 2008; Baird, 2010). However, the numbers dipped in 2009 to 746, which is probably due to a combination of costs and the owners' perceptions that the scheme was not actually influencing demand (Baird, 2010). The noted decrease has also been found in other studies; for example a recent survey found that the number of enterprises with a formalized EMS has decreased and the main reason cited for this was that such systems are of no use to their business (Anon., 2009), which is contrary to the oft-cited point that these systems are beneficial in terms of marketing and promotion. Yet major national and international companies do consider the adoption of EMS and social responsibility as 'good for business' (see Tari et al., 2010). Additional to such schemes one might add the relatively recently established 'own brand' eco-labels such as 'Travel Life' (see Chapter 2) and Whitbread Plc's (includes Costa Coffee and Premier Inns) 'Good Together'; the first hospitality company to gain the Carbon Trust Award. Tourism enterprises can also seek the international Green Globe accreditation, which was launched in 1994 by the WTTC (though has been the subject of much criticism) (Buckley, 2002), or Greenleaf and Ecotel. A number of schemes have also developed in most countries of Europe albeit the EU established the European Flower eco-label, which encompasses accommodation operations (Kucerova, 2012). However, major schemes in the EU have been brought under the umbrella of the Voluntary Initiative for Sustainability in Tourism (VISIT), which includes an alliance of 12 accommodation eco-labels operating in different countries of Europe (see Lebe and Zupan, 2012).

States in the USA also have their own certification programmes (Pizam, 2008; Bicker, 2009) and so too specific areas and categories of enterprise; for example there is the Green Hotels Association, Green Seal, Green Hotel in the Mountain State, Greenpath (see Mensah, 2004). By the turn of the century there were over 100 such green labels (Miles, 2001) and even more so today (Lawton and Weaver, 2009). The actual success of these schemes measured in terms of the number of accredited enterprises proportional to the total number of such enterprises in any one area or region is limited. All the more so when examined in further detail, which reveals that a substantial number of accredited enterprises are part of a national or international company. Evidently, rather than establishing an ISO for each of the different categories of tourism enterprise Tourist Boards, professional organ-izations representing specific sectors of interest or indeed individual companies prefer to develop their own eco-label. In other words government agencies involved seek to establish an outcome for which they can take credit and thereby justify in some way their role and funding; which is all rather counterproductive! Not surprisingly there is confusion in the marketplace. More importantly, though, the problem with these various eco-labels is a lack of uniformity and comparability.

From a company perspective, the larger organizations arguably recognize the sub-stantive savings in costs they can achieve through environmental management (EM) practices; and the potential value in the marketplace of promoting a 'green image' (Chan and Wong, 2006; Chan, 2009; Preigo et al., 2011; Leslie, 2011). Thus, all operations within the same company adopt, as appropriate, the same environmental measures (though there are exceptions, see Anon., 2009). In contrast the majority of small, individual, often owner-managed enterprises

do not adopt such measures. Yet, in percentage terms at least, it is arguable that the cost savings on reducing resource consumption would not be proportionally dissimilar. Why is this? That it is voluntary and may be taken up on the basis of cost savings:

> does not necessarily invalidate eco-efficiency activities. Indeed, many more environmental activities could be undertaken in the interests of increased profitability, or at least with additional cost savings as an ancillary benefit. But while it is beneficial to see corporations consuming less and reducing waste and pollution, it is equally important to note that such eco-efficiencies alone do not address the deeper and wider issues related to sustainability. (Wight, 2007, p. x)

It has also been argued that EMS accreditation to some extent may influence consumer choice of enterprise. Han et al.'s (2010) research into accredited green hotels in Africa supports the potential demand for green hotels but notes that such accreditation needs more effective marketing. In contrast Rodriguez et al. (2007) from their study into environmental responsibility in hotels drawn from a wide geographical range found that an EMS does not lead necessarily to increased profitability, noting that, in contrast, CSR activity did. Blanco et al. (2008) drawing on their study found it difficult to argue that EMS directly leads to marketing advantages, which is supported by findings that indicate the influence on customer choice is limited (Mintel, 2007; and in the following text). However, in recognizing that there are benefits to be gained through promotion, enterprises may seek such an EMS label whilst not actually being that committed. As Buckley (2002) notes, the key point that entry for many eco-labels is relatively easy thereby encouraging take up; in part this can be overcome by the eco-label offering a ranking according to action criteria such as the GTBS. Even so and as Tzschentke et al.'s (2008) research found, accreditation by programmes such as the GTBS is seen primarily as a promotional tool. But, as Miles (2001) argued, people do not necessarily believe in these eco-labels. Second, there are difficulties in ensuring that the promises are actually met. Hence it is not surprising to identify that the value of eco-labels has been questioned for a long time. Witness Sasidharan *et al.* (2002, p. 171) who note that 'no conclusive evidence exists to support their (the eco-labelling agencies) assertive claims that eco-labels improve the environment' nor that they are influential to choice of enterprise on the part of potential customers. In effect, in some cases they may be little more than a 'greenwash'. Hence questions over authenticity of green claims have been regularly raised. Witness DEFRA's (2009) initiative in 2009 to establish a committee for the purpose of addressing and revising, as necessary, their Code of Practice on Green Claims with the aim of providing improved assurance to consumers that such claims are accurate and meaningful. This problem is more widely recognized and has led to the establishment of a new website – The Global Eco-label Monitor – that aims to monitor eco-labels (www.wri.org). The site provides information on the eco-label, criteria involved, enforcement and was primarily initiated to address the lack of transparency and accountability. The UK has also introduced new guidance on green claims for products, which must be clear and more robust (DEFRA, 2011).

Environmental Policy

The establishment of an environmental policy is a key signifier of an enterprise's commitment to the environmental agenda and requisite for EMS accreditation allied with an environmental audit. As such this was a primary line of questioning in the surveys leading to the findings presented in Table 5.1.

Those enterprises in the 2011 sample with a written environmental policy, with one exception, were all involved in the GTBS, which also largely accounts for the 2006 figure being higher than 2001. Further accounting for the larger proportion compared with 2001 is the presence of a higher number of large hotel operations. Comparatively few enterprises in 2001 had developed an environmental policy or introduced an EMS; similar to the findings of other studies of the time. For example, Berry and Ladkin (1997) researched small accommodation operations and found that 7% had environmental programmes and 6% had undertaken an environmental audit (see also Carlsen *et al.*, 2001; Vernon *et al.*, 2003). But a little at variance with the outcomes of Gaunt's (2004) study into Scottish-based TOs which found that 38% had a policy (though how formal was not identified) and 4% had undertaken an environmental audit. The findings for 2006 are notably higher than in Erdogan and Baris's (2006) study into independent hotels, which found that 10% had a policy and 5% had some form of environment programme. Partly accounting for the significant difference between 2001 and 2006 and 2011 is that VisitScotland has been promoting the GTBS to some degree of success whilst there was no equivalent scheme being promoted throughout England, though there was something of a similar localized initiative called 'Solway Green' in Cumbria. However, more recently the Cumbria Tourist Board introduced and actively promoted the Responsible Business Scheme, which is not that dissimilar (Leslie, 2007). The findings do indicate some degree of progress in addressing environmental performance since the 1990s, notably so when compared with the manufacturing and service sector as Barrow and Burnett (1990, p. 3) found: 'most small companies have no policies or procedures on green issues and

Table 5.1. Environmental policy and auditing.

Question	Yes (%)			
	2001	2001 Audits	2006	2011
Does the business have a written environmental policy?	7	15	25	16
Has an environmental performance audit been undertaken?	10	20	20	28

only 10% carry out environmental audits.' However, a survey in the late 2000s similarly involving general businesses found that 40% of respondents indicated they had an environmental policy (Greenbiz, 2007).

This on first glance at least indicates some progress but also represents a substantially higher proportion than might be expected given for example, Freezer and Font's (2010) research, which found that some 3000 leisure and tourism companies in the UK participate in some form of EMS-based eco-label scheme. To put this 3000 in perspective, the database for the LDNP stage alone comprised 1600 enterprises. Even so the findings indicate that tourism enterprises are giving more attention to EM practices than, for example, by Erdogan's (2009) study that found few (4%) of the enterprises had a written environmental policy, though similarly identified that some 50% of the enterprises lacked any form of environmental programme. Further analysis of the data found few correlations of note except, that is, for those with GTBS status. What can be established through analysis of the data is that individual size, scale and type of operation is likely to have a significant influence on whether an enterprise has a formal environmental policy adhering to the principles and practices of resource management. However, the absence of a written policy does not mean that the owners/managers were not practising various environmental management practices but rather that this has not been formalized into a written policy or developed, and given their closeness to the operation then the need for a formal or written policy is seen to be unnecessary. This is further supported by the high percentage of enterprises undertaking an environmental audit albeit that the actual format of such was not actually defined and certainly it would be erroneous to suggest that these were formalized undertakings in many cases. As Tzschentke et al. (2008) said, the presence of ad hoc measures reflecting a lack of formal planning and the absence of an environmental policy are factors often found in such research involving small and micro enterprises and reflects Preigo et al.'s (2011) study that found a lack of integration of EM into mainstream strategic management. The following comments from interviewees provide further insight into why an operation may not have a defined policy:

- 'Smaller businesses do not put "policies" into writing.'
- 'We do things that are effective and efficient.'
- 'Looking into it in business plan.'
- 'Should be developed as business develops – as staff are developed this will be done also. Still a young business. Environmental practice may place extra burden on staff workload.'

Monitoring environmental performance

From one in four in 2001 to a little more than one in three in 2011 the audited enterprises indicated that they monitor aspects of environmental performance of the business, therefore demonstrating that although relatively few enterprises have a formalized policy this does not mean that they do not attend to some areas, such as monitoring consumption, which was most often found to be on energy consumption, e.g. electricity and/or gas. The absence of formal procedures once again evidences the small scale operations of many of the enterprises and the fact that in the majority of cases the owners are very much 'hands on', directly in contact with the operations and the costs. For example, witness the responses of some of the interviewees:

- 'There is a regard for environmental performance, particularly waste.'
- 'There is no rigid environmental plan, part of financial plan.'
- 'We are aware and careful of issues within hotel.'

Communicating environmental performance

Obviously to gain any marketing advantage, the green credentials of the operation need to be promoted externally. It is also important that this is promoted internally and thus to guests. Overall 30% of the LDNP enterprises, rising to 44% in 2011, did seek to promote related practices, e.g. not changing towels daily, encouraging recycling and the use of public transport to guests. Further enquiry established that in one case, the policy is included in the hotel's brochures and literature, in another case it is included in the organization's literature and in one operation displayed in every bedroom and details on this included in the staff handbook; not surprisingly this was one of the comparatively large hotel enterprises, which also had GTBS accreditation. An 'environmental policy' in itself is meaningless – a greenwash – unless this is translated into actions, which requires the support and contribution of all staff. It has also been noted that such responsible actions are 'good for morale, performance, and reputation and marketing' (Pratt, 2011, p. 436). Therefore to improve the environmental performance of the business, it is essential for this to be communicated to the staff and their involvement encouraged whether this is simply giving due attention to saving costs, reducing waste to promoting CSR activities and participating in and promoting such to customers. This was found to be the practice in 38% of the operations which employ full-time staff. As one interviewee remarked:

> We encourage the staff to participate wholeheartedly in improving and promoting the environmental performance of our business.

In terms of the wider applicability of such action it is noteworthy that the cultural norms relating to staff behaviours are taken into account; as exemplified by Chan and Hawkins (2011) in their case study based on a major hotel into the implementation of an EMS system and their impact on employees, which identified that the culture of employees is an influence in terms of outcomes, i.e. in this case with Chinese staff and, given their cultural norms, a top-down approach works better than the more westernized approach of encouragement.

Energy Management

GHG emissions are largely attributed to the consumption of energy, which in general is mainly accounted for by three main areas, namely housing, transport and food (Maguire et al., 2008), all of which are manifest in tourism, which is considered to account for 5% of global GHGs (Pratt, 2011). Thus for tourism enterprises to reduce the consumption of energy is not only a cost saving but also will be a potentially substantial contribution to reducing GHG emissions. Given the importance of energy supplies to and the extent of consumption of non-renewable resources by enterprises, it is surprising that this has gained such limited in-depth attention, especially outside of transportation. Shiming and Burnett's (2002) study is one of very few to research into the energy use of tourism enterprises. In this case and albeit one 'quality' hotel, the most notable outcome is to highlight the substantial energy consumption of air-conditioning (see also Becken and Simmons, 2002; Nepal, 2008). Allowing for air-conditioning, across the range of categories it is hotels which generally consume the most energy whilst caravan and camping sites consume comparatively the least. The major factor accounting for the difference between the various categories is the provision of catering services and not surprisingly therefore hotels offering extensive food and beverage services are the highest energy consumers.

Across the three research populations no more than 50%, and in some of the categories far less, of the enterprises have introduced measures to reduce energy consumption. Few enterprises and only in the 2011 set have an integrated system and use 'key cards' for guest rooms. These systems are very much a function of cost, building design (new) and the number of rooms (economies of scale) and thus not practical for most accommodation enterprises. The significant increases in energy costs witnessed since the mid-2000s suggests increased attention would be given to such costs. However this was not found to be the case in general. Three quarters of the 2011 population did not have any form of energy policy, which is actually lower than for the 2001 audited enterprises at 62%. This is all the more surprising given the higher proportion of large operations in the 2011 population, which will have substantially higher energy bills. However this finding is not dissimilar to

SMEs in general, for a study by the Federation of Small Businesses found that 25% of the businesses surveyed were undertaking some action, predominantly in energy consumption (Russell-Wallings, 2008). Thus very similar to the 2011 data and largely attributed to seeking to reduce costs; as the Director of one company hotel said: 'Monitoring energy usage is more driven by money than by the environment.' For most of the enterprises, the majority being accommodation operations, indications that they did take some action is well portrayed in the following respondents' comments:

- 'We strive for greater energy efficiency.'
- 'Encourage guests to re-use towels when staying for more than one overnight.'
- 'We always switch off bathroom towel rails when guests leave and there is a message in the bathroom to this effect so that we can conserve energy.'
- 'We opted not to equip the restaurant toilets with hot air hand dryers as they waste energy.'

Lighting is also a significant consumer of energy; whilst this may vary between 7% and 20% it can be possibly as high as 40% (Bohdanowicz, 2006). Measures to reduce energy used by lighting were found to have gained limited attention and mainly involved increasing the use of low energy light bulbs internally. A finding which compares unfavourably with Lebe and Zupan's (2012) study of accommodation operations in Slovenia, also those of Mensah (2009) and Erdogan (2009), though the latter studies predominantly involved hotels and a higher proportion of 4 star and 5 star operations; and also Bohdanowicz (2006) who found 75% of the hotels in her study (Sweden and Poland) have introduced measures to reduce energy consumption though they were all large hotels. However, the findings are generally similar to those of like studies in Australia (Buckley, 2009). Other measures on lighting were explored, such as the use of timer switches and movement sensitive lighting, but were all found to be minimal and elicited a range of comments from participants of which the following serve well to illustrate the potential complexities involved:

- 'Sensor lights are only used in staff areas due to safety, low energy lighting is used everywhere else.'
- 'A problem with installing high cost low energy lighting is what happens if we leave?'
- 'Movement sensitive lights are fine in many situations but not where small children are about; they can be very sensitive and as such almost any movement [e.g. a small animal] could set them off and thus hardly beneficial.'

As noted in Chapter 2, many of the accommodation operations are accredited by their respective Tourist Board's national grading scheme. This is of particular significance in that the criteria involved can be counterproductive to the introduction of some environmental management practices, for example to quote respondents:

- 'Guest corridors should be well lit at all times.'
- 'Car parks should be well lit.'
- 'Energy saving light bulbs may be considered unsightly.'

Whilst monitoring and taking easy steps potentially to reduce energy costs are an obvious first stage there are opportunities to reduce energy consumption through, for example, the use of SavaPlugs which reduce energy consumption of electric appliances, e.g. fridges (see Toke and Taylor, 2007) though on the basis of the findings not one participant indicated such use. Also, due attention should be given to electrical appliances and their energy efficiency rating. This rather demands review of such equipment; a practice that was investigated through the audits and found that no more than 50% actually considered reviewing their electrical operational equipment. To illustrate, if an enterprise is using an 'old' washing machine for in-house laundry (approx 67% of accommodation operations) then it is quite possible that in terms of energy consumption the latest model would relatively quickly pay for the replacement cost through energy savings. Laundering linen brings into contention the issue of which is the more environmentally friendly between laundering table linen and using paper napkins, etc. – in other words which is the best environmental option? Addressing such a question is complex, for instance:

- in-house laundry – may be seen to be lower cost as such costs are subsumed within the general energy bill;
- contract out – the cost is explicit but from the perspective of the supplier there are potential benefits given the economies of scale; and
- cleaning agent(s) used – are they considered to be 'environmentally friendly', e.g. Ecover products. The cost of such detergents is invariably higher than the standard prod-ucts and most enterprises do not have the purchasing power due to the limited quan-tity required as that of N/MNCs to counter such costs, e.g. Wyndham Hotels world-wide is supplied with the same environmen-tally friendly detergents (Bohdanowicz and Zientara, 2012).

A line of discourse which brings into contention is the use of linen versus disposable alternatives. For many enterprises this was identified as mostly being just a matter of convenience but for others the difference is very much based on quality of presentation and service. Thus a combination may be used, disposable in the bar and linen in the restaurant. In terms of equipment and energy consumption this equally applies to food production and thus ideally the use of energy efficient equipment and methods of use (see Hill, 2009; Gossling et al., 2012). An aspect of food production and service to consider in the context of reducing food waste is that of the service offering of 'all inclusive' resorts and also buffet style self-service provision, which further contributes to GHGs (see Maguire et al., 2008). Another factor of note is that many of the enterprises involved are old buildings, whether in rural or urban locations, and thus the property's age, structure and building materials were not designed to be energy efficient, e.g. central heating and insulation. The latter were most likely to be found in self-catering units. However, such properties may well score poorly based on sustainability indicators if such involved architecture and design criteria based on the use of local materials and design in tune with the physical environment (see Erdogan and Tosun, 2009).

Further, in the context of National Parks and conservation areas, planning regulations may counter opportunities for wind or solar power installations though no enterprises in the study indicated they had installed either of these systems, but one respondent did mention she had considered this but was dissuaded on the basis of cost. Given the increasing promotion of renewable energy supplied it is notable that the case of renewables is not that clear cut as to benefits compared with fossil fuels and more so atomic energy supplies; and in the case of wind farms not that clear at all (see Booker, 2009). Furthermore, Levett's examination into the externalities of eight different energy supply options concluded that there was 'no unequivocal basis for the ordinal ranking of electricity supply options' (Levett, 2001, p. 143). However, in lesser developed areas alternatives to traditional fuel supplies can be very beneficial; for example alternatives to the use of wood as a fuel in the Annapurna region of Nepal (see Nepal, 2008)

Overall, the findings on energy con-sumption and management show little evidence of progress being similar across the surveys and are comparable with Slee et al. (1999), Masau and Prideaux (2003) whose study involved hotels in Kenya, Warnken et al. (2005), Erdogan (2009), Rainford and Wight (2009) and Chan (2011), but less favourably with Garay and Font (2012) and Kucerova (2012) and very much so with Mensah's (2009) study of hotels in Ghana; and all the more so when compared with N/MNCs (e.g. Bohdanowicz, 2006; see Bohdanowicz and Zientara, 2012). Such comparisons certainly indicate that in terms of environmental performance these tourism enterprises perform poorly compared with other European countries in the area of seeking to reduce energy consumption. It rather seems that the cost of energy supplies is taken as given – if like 'death and taxes' they are a certainty about which little can be done.

Water Management

Water consumption is another area explored in the study. This might be considered a little strange given that for the most part the UK is not known for water shortages or lack of available clean water. It is though a valuable resource and whilst perhaps not in short supply, in the study areas it is nevertheless a resource that should not be treated lightly. It is essential to tourism. Yet this is an area that has gained remarkably little consideration in tourism research (Gossling, et al., 2012; Leslie, 2012b). A point on attention to water consumption is that in terms of general use this can be monitored directly and reported more easily where supplies are metered. This is also an area that in accommodation operations very clearly includes customers and in turn their consumption and related impact on the environment (Burgos-Jimenez et al., 2002). This is often higher when on holiday compared with their domestic consumption (see Gossling et al., 2012) and in terms of up-market hotels consumption attributed to tourists is even higher, as noted in the case of Malta (Ioannides, 2008).

The availability of clean, non-salt water throughout the world is raising serious concerns. Whilst UNESCO argued in 2009 that there is no water crisis per se they did note that there are areas suffering from water shortages which are predominantly localized. Nevertheless this does present an increasingly global problem (Dekker, 2009) and an increasing issue in many areas; witness the following factors:

- Availability of clean, fresh water is declining (Le Quesne et al., 2010).
- Increasing human demand i.e. ecological footprint is considered a factor in the decline of the Earth's biodiversity (WWF, 2010).
- Increasing trend in number of areas experiencing water shortages (WWF, 2010).
- Underground aquifers increasingly are being used to supplement water supplies not only for households etc. but also arable farming and are being consumed at a faster rate than natural replenishment (Lean, 2010).
- Water scarcity is seen as a bigger risk to global companies than access to energy in emerging economies (SustainAbility, 2011).

- The EU through the Water Framework Directive (2010) has been promoting the more efficient use of water. This is likely to gain momentum in the light of the European Environment Agency's (2013) recent report which argues that 'water is under stress in many parts of Europe' (EEA, 2013, p. 1).

In total this holds a potentially greater challenge to tourism activity than perceptions of declining fossil fuel reserves (see Pleumarom, 2013). Evident problems in both supply and usage are not difficult to find as the following examples serve to illustrate by way of exemplifying the situation in different parts of the world. Chan's (2005) research into environmental costs of one hotel in Hong Kong, where water pollution is a major consideration, also noted that this area has gained little attention in the context of hotels. He argues that '... hotel operators should place a greater focus on mitigating the pressure on the environment from the consumption of water.' Such consumption can be disadvantageous to local people; witness the case of Goa where supplies have been taken by hotels (Wilson, 1996) or that of tourists at the five star Umaid Bhawan Palace Hotel in Jodhpur enjoying apparently a plentiful supply of water whilst some 15 miles away villagers are desperate for water due to a prevailing drought. Similarly the 300 roomed Old Etonian Maharaja Gaj Singh Hotel that consumes 150,000 gallons of water per day, a not insignificant proportion of which is used to maintain the luscious gardens. The water supply comes via the Indira Gandhi canal but not so for the outlying lands (Bedi, 2000). However, the consumption of water and potential problems is not restricted to such localities. Scanlon's study into major hotel and resort companies in America, e.g. Hyatt and Fairmont, found that overall no more than on average 60% of these operations were addressing water conservation and re-use measures; noting the influence of the type of property but did identify a high correlation between adopted practices and cost saving measures instigated to address their situation of 'experiencing rising costs and limited resources challenges.' (Scanlon, 2007, p. 721). Water pollution arising from tourism developments is also a concern; for example, the pollution (and energy consumption) generated by ski resorts and by cruise liners (Bennett, 2006). Though it is not only the latter but also hotels offering all inclusive packages to business travellers and the meetings market, including Starwood Hotels and Resorts, notably in Cancun, Mexico and also around the Riviera Maya (south Cancun) which is experiencing significant water pollution from resorts and golf courses (Anon., 2011a). The latter have gained some degree of opprobrium, e.g. in Cyprus (Ioannides, 2008), south East Asia (Pleumarom, 2009; see also Gossling et al., 2012). Gossling et al. also note the major water usage by golf courses and ski-fields (due to the increasing availability of snow machines) but also the high consumption by luxury hotels, especially those with spas and pools; further adding to such consumption is that of kitchen use and laundry. Of particular significance in their research is that of the seasonality of major tourist flows leading to high consumption in the main tourist period which often coincides with a time of lowest water availability due to the climatic conditions, albeit that in such consumption there is a trade off with reduced consumption at their home bases. But, as Gossling et al. note, the travel direction is often from water rich areas.

In some ways, as with the findings on energy consumption and steps to reduce costs, so too the majority of the enterprises in the study did little to monitor and reduce water consumption including in some cases those enterprises with water meters. Few have installed automated taps or pressure taps in public rooms. However the cost of such replacements is a factor; for example, in the 1990s fitting 'press tex' taps would have cost about £50 each but, as Chief Engineer of the Hilton in Glasgow said, the cost can be recouped in a year. Many of the enterprises have not reduced the capacity of the older style, large capacity water cisterns (private hotels were the most likely to do this, e.g. 'We have placed "hippos" in the water cisterns. This has not affected efficiency and does reduce our water usage.'); though it is to be noted that the latter is very much a feature of older properties and thus in the longer term this will be addressed as and when refitting occurs. In rural and suburban areas re-using

water, e.g. water from bathing, washing machines, and so on, i.e. 'brown water', for the garden is one way of reducing water consumption. A number of operations (12%) do practice this to some extent. Also, 34% of the 2001 audits and comparatively very few of the 2011 data set commented that they catch rainwater (brown water) for use in the garden and in some cases for watering indoor plants. From these findings it would appear there is far more scope for encouraging enterprises to introduce such measures as the systems cost little and are relatively easy to install. It is noted though that for many urban premises this may not be possible given the structure of the building and/or in situations where there is no subsequent use.

Overall these findings are similar to Warnken et al. (2005). But again these enterprises are found to perform poorly compared with Mensah (2009), and especially with Carlsen et al. (2001), Spenceley (2009) and Garay and Font (2012), who identified that 77% of the tourism enterprises in Catalonia have adopted water saving measures. However, in contrast, enterprises in Turkey evidenced very little activity (Erdogan, 2009), whilst Kucerova (2012) notes little attention to conserving water despite high water costs; similarly Lebe and Zupan (2012).

Waste Management

In the delivery of their services tourism enterprises, as a matter of course, generate waste. This waste can be reduced through a range of methods, using less, reducing packaging (better still seeking suppliers using re-usable packaging which in the long run reduces costs, e.g. returnable bottles in re-usable crates [see www.StopWaste.org]), re-using and recycling. An interesting alternative is to instigate a ban on purchasing a product with a particular type of waste albeit such a measure is rare; for example Lean (2010) identified that no plastics are purchased by Soneva Fushi Resort, Maldives, which is acclaimed as one of the most expensive resorts in the world, and waste is recycled at the resort's own plant. Even allowing for such measures waste management is a major concern due to the ever-increasing volume of waste produced, and the amount of energy consumed and lost in the generation of waste and disposal; for example according to the Open University, in 2000 the waste bill for business in the UK was equivalent to £650 per employee. Whilst these small/micro enterprises individually may produce little waste, in some cases no more than a large family home especially when an EMS approach has been adopted, nevertheless in total at local or regional and certainly national level they account for a tremendous volume of waste matter. Also, irrespective of size, they are subject to business rates for waste collection and thus it is all the more pertinent that they seek to reduce these costs. Overall, it was found that waste is monitored by approximately 50% of the enterprises with little variance across the data sets. One in six of the participants said that there is not much to monitor, even though as one interviewee said: 'only two bags per week are provided for rubbish yet charged twice for removal (business and resident)'. Comparatively few undertake any analysis of this and do not know if it is decreasing; a finding similar to Warnken *et al.*'s (2005).

Of the areas of waste management investigated the one which gained most consideration was that of recycling. In response to the question as to whether waste is separated for recycling, 56% indicated 'yes'. In the case of the audited enterprises this was further affirmed by the interviewers who were required to observe and note the external appearance of the enterprises regarding presentation, general upkeep of facades and grounds and also to note waste collection points. Apart from other considerations, these are good indicators of the owners' attention to maintaining their main asset. The general finding was that in almost all instances where recycling storage facilities could be seen these were neat and tidy; not only is such presentation important but also, as three interviewees pointed out, they are sited for guests' use as well. The level of engagement with recycling was primarily predicated on the facilities provided by the municipal authority. These authorities throughout the EU have been encouraged through EU Directives (e.g.

Landfill and WEEE Directives) to increase their levels of recycling waste material and largely because of this the range and quantity of such material collected has risen remarkably over the last 15 years (LGA, 2010). In part this explains why there was little activity in composting food waste and recycling toner cartridges, plastic or aluminium cans amongst the 2001 population; the main recycling activity being paper and glass. Also the re-use of soap (from guest rooms), cooking oil and waste food was much lower in the accommodation operations than it was many years ago when such materials were often collected by small businesses specializing in recycling such materials. These are practices that have largely ceased due to a combination of environmental health legislation/regulations. The recycling of soap raised an interesting contrast in 2001 in that 14% of the operations did this in some way but as one interviewee said: 'Very interested in soap recycling but have found it very difficult to get information.' Conversely three ways were cited by other interviewees: tablet soap recycled and re-used, for example, in toilet facilities for restaurant guests, local schools and through an initiative established by the local Hotels and Caterers Association. However, more recently there has been resurgence in recycling cooking oil and initiatives to recycle printer cartridges. Factors identified as militating against recycling were:

- 'We would separate glass, plastic and paper if the Council provided bins for free.'
- 'Lack a suitable storage area.'
- 'It causes major headaches.'
- 'Cost and availability', i.e. hotel soap was recycled but the company concerned stopped due to cost.
- 'Tried to recycle newspapers but too much hard work; I work a 16 hour day and don't have time to deliver these articles to appropriate centres'; 'Transportation to recycling sites is time consuming and uses fuel.'

And conversely:

- 'What we cannot re-use in some way or other, we recycle.'
- 'Would like there to be much more recycling opportunities available.'
- 'We recycle everything, guests love it!'

- 'We provide a can bank'/'We provide bottle banks and paper recycling facilities'.
- 'Information is placed in each [of our] holiday flats regarding [our] recycling policy. Guests are invited to leave any waste in the flat in separate bags. Once each week, the waste is collected and taken in bulk to one of the sites at Windermere, Kendal or Ambleside.'

For the large operations with private contracts for waste removal it is comparatively only recently that contractors have introduced waste separation procedures thus facilitating enterprises to recycle more materials, though the use of a compactor for waste (one in ten of 2011 population) may be seen to be counter-productive. However, and further affirming the presence of suitable infrastructure is that enterprises in the more 'urbanized' rural areas of the 2006 population and in 2011 all demonstrated comparatively higher levels of recycling activity and notably of cans, cooking oil and printer cartridges. The former perhaps because of the comparative density of enterprises in urban settings and thus easier to collect large volumes and second, due to the potential to convert such oil waste to a bio-fuel, whilst the latter is probably due to a combination of charities which accept used cartridges and suppliers taking back used cartridges.

There are, though, various caveats to recycling being seen as always the best environmental option (see Harrison, 2003). For example, paper may be made from Forestry Sustainable Certificated sources, thus in the first instance choice is a factor and second, paper waste could be used in an energy recovery/generation process, such as incineration and the capturing of heat to generate electricity. Whilst incinerators today are far cleaner than ever, invariably communities will be up in arms against one being located in their area. However, before recycling paper it could be re-used in some way(s), which many enterprises did though far more so in 2001 and 2006 than 2011, perhaps because of increased recycling facilities. Recycling materials requires consumer demand for recycled products, e.g.

kitchen roll and toilet rolls. This was found to be at its highest amongst the 2001 population, with approximately half purchasing some type of recycled product (mainly paper products), dropping to 12% in the case of 2011. Whilst attitudes to such matters vary, the difference is largely accounted for by the managed operations and those that are part of a larger organization and the actual cost of the products. Of special note here is that the findings for 2011 mirror Barrow and Burnett's (1990) survey over twenty years ago, which found that some 10% of the businesses surveyed use recycled materials.

These findings are very similar to the previous studies and indicate little progress despite the pressures on local government to increase recycling arising from EU regulations and encouragement of households to recycle waste materials. Albeit an apparent general consensus in society that recycling is good for the environment, yet evidently not so readily practiced in the home nor does it seem in the workplace (Leslie, 2009). However, the data from the enterprises for 2011 finds clear progress in levels of recycling. Indeed, recycling of paper, glass and cans has increased over the period; a finding that mirrors other studies (IH, 2007; Anon., 2009). This is largely due to increased provision of recycling facilities, including recent requirements on private companies collecting waste to provide for waste segregation, which is attributed to further development of the supporting infrastructure for this purpose on the part of municipal authorities (as also manifest in the studies of Kucerova (2012) and Lebe and Zupan (2012) and conversely illustrated by Rainford and Wight (2009) and Mensah (2009)), demonstrating all too clearly that regulation will prompt the targeted actions. These authorities can also be proactive in encouraging visitors to recycle. For example, Cornwall, an area with a population of approximately 1m people, receives 5m visitors per annum thus generating a substantial increase in waste materials. A local government initiative – the Coastal Project – was introduced to encourage visitors to recycle as much as possible (Bennett, 2006).

Overall, and with attention to reduce and re-use, the findings suggest progress since the 1990s (Slee et al., 1999) and 2001 though similar to Vernon et al. (2003), Masau and Prideaux (2003), Erdogan (2009), Rainford and Wight (2009) and Radwan et al. (2010). Again the performance in this area compared with other EU countries is poor (Garay and Font, 2012; Kucerova, 2012) and also Carlsen et al. (2001) and Spenceley's (2009) study, based on enterprises in Southern Africa; and the N/MNCs more generally.

Conclusion

For a tourism enterprise to have a written environmental policy and monitoring system shows a commitment to EM but the absence of either does not necessarily represent a lack of EM practices, a negative attitude or ignorance of sustainability on the part of the owner/manager. The size and scale of the operation appears to be a more influential factor; the smaller the enterprise, the more likely there is to be no formal procedures regarding these areas. These small/micro enterprises have their own ways of operating. As one owner described:

> We do not have a rigid environmental plan, as this needs to be flexible and demonstrate our awareness and responsiveness to the concerns involved and issues that may arise.

Whilst larger companies consume substantially more resources per operation; for example consider a 40-bedroomed hotel, which is equivalent in scale to four guest houses or 10 B & Bs in a popular tourist destination, the collated consumption may be higher given the economies of scale achieved by the large hotel. Thus the view that these enterprises should also be reducing their consumption and waste. Both to promote and support such action EMSs designed for tourism enterprises were developed and have been implemented by many enterprises. However, this is more reflective of the finding that EMS and CSR are to be found in the major players in the marketplace rather than amongst the myriad small and micro-businesses that dominate tourism supply.

In general, and across the study's data spectrum, the findings do indicate there is an awareness of energy efficiency measures and that those enterprises which do monitor their environmental performance primarily focus on energy consumption. But, as Cooper et al. (2010) argued, consumption patterns are more a function of convention and infrastructure than choice per se. To an extent this explains why less than a quarter of the enterprises have adopted measures to reduce energy consumption, such as the use of more energy efficient light fittings, which has increased over the period of the study; and the use of more energy efficient equipment, e.g. eco-labelled fridges, dishwashers, which is increasing as older equipment is replaced. However, reducing consumption is an area where there is considerable scope for improvement. As regards water consumption, there is little evidence to suggest a significant number of enterprises have adopted measures to conserve water, other than the general trend in accommodation operations of encouraging guests not to change towels daily on the basis that this is more environmentally friendly, which was very much in evidence. It is in the area of recycling which is showing most progress. This has been greatly facilitated by the municipal authorities, leading to increased participation. Overall, these outcomes in general are evident in similar studies involving small/micro tourism enterprises in the UK but are generally poor in terms of environmental performance when compared with other EU countries and more widely. Overall, the indications are that little progress has been made despite the promotion of such activities, especially in the 1990s, in adoption of environmental/sustainable friendly practices. The findings though from the 2011 audited enterprises certainly suggest there has been progress. But this merits caution given the different locations and inclusion of a higher proportion of large hotels and companies involved in 2011. Even so, such progress is evident in the findings of recent studies (Pratt, 2011) and also in more general studies, though again, somewhat limited (see Goethe Institute, 2008; Ethical Corporation, 2010).

Yes, companies may introduce innovations and management initiatives which reduce energy consumption or water consumption but all too often such companies are international and national and their operations are large scale (see *Green Hotelier*; Robaththan, 2007). However, whilst seeking to 'minimize' their consumption on the one hand and through the provision of more expansive services and facilities their overall consumption increases; and rather reflects the principle that the more efficiently a resource may be used then the more consumption increases. In combination this is illustrated by TUI (2011) which has been very active in seeking to increase recycling, and reduce energy and water waste by implementing new water saving taps, new automatic PC shutdown software and infra-red motion sensors for lighting. But this is a major MNC with the resources to implement such measures and in the process gain the not insubstantial cost savings as a result. But in terms of scale and contribution to reducing resource consumption and waste, far more will be gained if many, many more of these small/micro tourism enterprises adopt an EMS than is currently being achieved through the N/MNCs (see Buckley, 2009). As regards the latter, their actions in adopting EMSs, and their CSR activities, may well be more driven by external factors and influence than costs savings; for example perceptions of the PR benefits of gaining environmental awards (see Buckley, 2007).

A survey by the EA (2009) also identified further progress in that some 50% of the SMEs involved had adopted EM practices. But 80% of these businesses indicated that they were very unlikely to invest in improving their environmental performance. Furthermore over 50% said an EMS is no use to them in the current climate (i.e. 2009) though on the positive side more companies indicated they were introducing environmental criteria into their supply chain management. Such findings rather re-affirm the lack of evidence to support that it does influence consumers rather more than the usual factors, i.e. price, location, quality and facilities (see Chapter 7); and may partly explain the decline in membership of the GTBS in the late 2000s. This extensively promoted scheme, as with other such EMS programmes, is voluntary which is fine for the more enlightened owners/managers but has

little impact on others, which goes a long way to account for the projection that the uptake of an EMS by SMEs was less than 1% by the mid-2000s (Hillary, 2004). Furthermore and based on the interviews and during fieldwork, those enterprises in the study which demonstrate extensive application of EM practices, joining for example the GTBS, would require little more to do beyond completing the requisite forms, a visit to verify and pay the appropriate fees (another cost). In effect, the motivation for the introduction of EM practices is either self-motivated or a function of corporate policy. Further and in the wider perspective of international tourism, the parochialism manifest in tourism, whether from the perspective of the tourist or enterprises in other regions, in the development of national and regional EMS eco-labels has certainly not helped. Why this has arisen merits in-depth research, especially as business in general across the globe apparently accepts far more readily national and more so international standards accredited systems without regional variations.

For all the 'do gooders', government rhetoric and subsidies it is inescapable that it is the owners/managers who must accept responsibility and take the action – it is not someone else's problem or for some other organization to address and tell them what to do – even so the presence of a 'champion' in an influential position in the locality could certainly advance progress. As Simms (2006, p. 24) argued 'Every business will have to clean up its act to stay successful, not just the traditional polluters such as oil companies and power generators.' An argument reinforced by Cooper *et al.* (2010, p. 7) 'Global sustainability problems cannot be addressed without a myriad of pro-environmental changes at local community level.' Essentially there is a need for tourism businesses not to be treated solely in terms of their products/ services but in the wider context of their external environment; an approach which reflects much greater awareness of the interconnectedness of the economic, physical and social dimensions of the environment rather than just the physical or natural, e.g. pollution and damage. Thus tourism enterprises should be encouraged and, for this to be effective; facilitated – for example to introduce 'smart meters' on energy and water supplies; as in some ways now happens with recycling.

> The bottom line is that hotels need to make sure they are not just paying lip service to sustainability but applying a sustainable approach across the business (Cushing, 2004, p. 9).

In the meantime it is worth revisiting the comments of the Chief Executive of Sustainability North West who said:

> … that he looked forward to a time when more than just a handful of well-meaning companies would assess their success with a three line bottom line – that is not just using economic profit as the criteria for success, but also taking into account the social and economic impact of their business and the power of the consumer in pushing companies down that road. (SLCCT, 2000).

Over a decade later that time has yet to arrive.

Further Reading

For a comprehensive, well illustrated discussion on EMS, including attention to employees see Sweeting, E.N. and Sweeting, A.R. (2004) *A practical guide to good practice: managing environmental and social issues in the accommodations sector.* The Center for Environmental Leadership in Business and the Tour Operators' Initiative for Sustainable Tourism Development. UNEP Paris, France.

On business initiatives in general – see Green Futures (www.greenfutures.com).

On energy savings measures visit the Carbon Trust – www.carbontrust.co.uk and the Energy Saving Trust at http://www.energy savingtrust.org.uk.

ISO 14001 can be reviewed at www. iso14000-iso14001-environmental-manage ment.com/iso14001.htm and BS7750 at www.quality.co.uk/bs7750.htm.

References

Anon. (2002) Environmental labels and certification schemes. *Green Hotelier*, Issues 25 and 26, May, pp. 12–19.

Anon. (2003) 'Social Responsibility' new industry buzzword. *Hotels* March, IH&RA, p. 4.

Anon. (2009) Green companies do better during the downturn. Greenbiz. 11 February. Available at: http://www.greenbiz/com.news/2009/02/11 (accessed 12 February 2009).

Anon. (2010) *Hotel companies vie for carbon emissions reductions.* Tourism Innovation Group, Edinburgh, UK.

Anon. (2011a) *All-inclusive packages at business hotels.* Available at http.//www.business-review.com/business-hotels-offer-all-inclusive-stays-news2631 (accessed 1 March 2011).

Anon. (2011b) Available at http.//www.business-review.com/polluted-riviera-maya-mexico-news2630 (accessed 1 March 2011).

Baird, J.H. (2010) Green Tourism Accreditation: the impacts of the Green Tourism Business Scheme (GTBS) on Scotland's Tourism Sector. Unpublished BA (Hons) Dissertation, Tourism and International Management, Glasgow Caledonian University, Glasgow, UK.

Barrow, C.J. (1999) *Environmental Management: Principles and Practice.* Routledge, Abingdon, UK.

Barrow, C. and Burnett, A. (1990) *How green are small companies?* Cranfield School of Management, Cranfield Institute of Technology, Cranfield, UK.

Becken, S. (2010) A critical review of tourism and oil. *Annals of Tourism Research* 38 (2), pp. 359–379.

Becken, S. and Lennox, J. (2011) Implications of a long-term increase in oil process for tourism. *Tourism Management* 33 (1), pp. 133–142.

Becken, S. and Simmons, D.G. (2002) Understanding energy consumption patterns of tourist attractions and activities in New Zealand. *Tourism Management* 23, pp. 343–354.

Bedi, R. (2000) Tourist oasis in land of famine. *The Daily Telegraph*, 29 April, p. 14.

Bennett, L. (2006) Duty Free? *Resource* No 20 (July/August 2006), pp. 20–22 Resource Media, Bristol, UK.

Berry, S. and Ladkin, A. (1997) Sustainable tourism: A regional perspective. *Tourism Management* 18 (7), pp. 433–440.

Bicker, K.S. (2009) Sustainable tourism development in the United States of America: An intricate balance from policy to practice. In: Leslie, D. (ed.) (2009) *Tourism Enterprises and Sustainable Development – International Perspectives on Responses to the Sustainability Agenda*. Routledge Advances in Tourism Series, Routledge, New York, pp. 64–89.

Black, C. (1995) The Inter-Continental Hotels Group and its environmental awareness programme. In: Leslie, D. (ed.) *Promoting Environmental Awareness and Action in Hospitality, Tourism and Leisure*. Environment Papers Series 1, pp. 31–46.

Blackstock, K.L., White, V., McCrum, G., Scott, A. and Hunter, C. (2008) Measuring responsibility: an appraisal of a Scottish National Park's Sustainable Tourism Indicators. *Journal of Sustainable Tourism* 16 (3), 276–297.

Blanco, E., Rey-Maquieira, J. and Lozano, J. (2008) Economic incentives for tourism firms to undertake voluntary environmental management. *Tourism Management* 30 (1), pp. 112–122.

Bohdanowicz, P. (2006) European hoteliers' environmental attitudes: greening the business. *Cornell Hotel and Restaurant Administration Quarterly* 46, pp. 188–204.

Bohdanowicz, P. and Zientara, P. (2012) CSR-inspired environmental initiatives in top hotel chains. In: Leslie, D. (ed.) *Tourism Enterprises and the Sustainability Agenda across Europe*. New Directions in Tourism Analysis, Ashgate, Farnham, UK, pp. 93–120.

Booker, C. (2009) The world faces its biggest ever bill. *The Sunday Telegraph* 24 May, p. 25.

Brown, M. (1994) Environmental auditing and the hotel industry: an accountant's perspective. In: Seaton, A.V. (ed.) *Tourism: the State of the Art*. Wiley, London, pp. 674–681.

Buckley, R. (2002) Tourism ecolabels. *Annals of Tourism Research*. 29 (1), 183–208.

Buckley, R. (2007) Is mass tourism serious about sustainability? *Tourism Recreation Research* 32 (3), 70–72.

Buckley, R. (2009) Large-scale links between tourism enterprises and sustainable development. In: Leslie, D. (ed.) *Tourism Enterprises and Sustainable Development: International Perspectives on Responses to the Sustainability Agenda*. Routledge, New York.

Burgos-Jimenez, J., Cano-Guillen, C.J. and Cespedes-Lorente, J.J. (2002) Planing and control of environmental performance on hotels. *Journal of Sustainable Tourism* 10(3), pp. 207–217.

Carlsen, J., Getz, D. and Ali-Knight, J. (2001) The environmental attitudes and practices of family business in the rural tourism and hospitality sectors. *Journal of Sustainable Tourism* 9 (4), 281–297.

Chan, E.S.W. (2011) Implementing environmental management systems in small and medium sized hotels. *Journal of Hospitality and Tourism Research* 35 (1), pp. 3–23.

Chan, E.S.W. and Wong, S.C.K. (2006) Motivations for ISO 14001 in the hotel industry. *Tourism Management* 27, pp. 481–492.

Chan, E.S.W. and Hawkins, R. (2011) Application of EMSs in a hotel context: a case study. *Tourism Management* 31 (2), pp. 405–418.

Chan, W.W. (2005) Partial analysis of the environmental costs generated by hotels in Hong Kong. *Hospitality Management* 24, pp. 517–531.

Chan, W.W. (2009) Environmental measures for hotel's environmental management systems ISO 140001. *International Journal of Contemporary Hospitality Management* 21 (5), 542–560.

Cooper, C., Muhern, G. and Colley, A. (2010) *Sustainability, the Environment and Climate Change*. Academy of Social Sciences and The British Psychological Society. No 3, London/Leicester, UK.

Cushing, K. (2004) Greener Growth *Caterer & Hotelkeeper* 19 February, pp. 7–9.

DCMS (1999) *Tomorrow's Tourism: a Growth Industry for the New Millennium*. Department of Culture, media and Sport, London.

DEFRA (2009) *Green Claims Code for Industry*. Press Release Department of Environment, Food and Rural Affairs, London, 18 February.

DEFRA (2011) *New Guidance on Green Claims for Products*. Department of Environment, Food and Rural Affairs, London, February.

Dekker, R. (2009) Troubled Water. *Courier* 3, UNESCO.

Diamantis, D. (1999) The importance of environmental auditing and environmental indicators in islands. *Eco-management and Auditing* 6 (1), 18–253; also 1998 Environmental auditing: a tool in ecotourism development. *Eco-management and Auditing* 5 (1), 15–21.

Diamantis, D. (2000) Ecotourism and sustainability in Mediterranean Islands. *International Business Review* July/August 42 (4), pp. 427–443.

DoE (1990) *This Common Inheritance*. Department of the Environment, HMSO, London.

DNV Quality Assurance (1996) *Environmental management Systems: BS7750, EMAS, ISO14001 – an independent guide*. DNV Quality Assurance Ltd, London.

EA (2009) *Small business stops its green practice.* Environment Agency, London, September.

EC (2000) *Towards Quality Rural Tourism: Integrated Quality Management (IQM) of Rural Destinations.* Brussels DG XXIII Tourism Directorate, Commission of the European Communities, Brussels.

EC (2001) *Executive Summary from E.C. Environment 2010. Our Future, Our Choice.* 6th A.P.COM (2001) 31 Final. Commission of the European Communities, Brussels.

EC (2003) *Using Natural and Cultural Heritage to Develop Sustainable Tourism.* Director-General Enterprise – Tourism Unit, Commission of the European Communities, Brussels.

EEA (2013) *Assessment of Cost Recovery through Water Pricing.* European Environment Agency, Copenhagen, Denmark.

Erdogan, N. (2009) Turkey's tourism policy and environmental performance of tourism enterprises. In: Leslie, D. (ed.) *Tourism Enterprises and Sustainable Development: International Perspectives on Responses to the Sustainability Agenda.* Routledge, New York, pp. 194–208.

Erdogan, N. and Baris, E. (2006) Environmental protection programs and conservation practices of hotels in Ankara, Turkey. *Tourism Management* 28 (2), pp. 604–614.

Erdogan, N. and Tosun, C. (2009) Environmental performance of tourism accommodations in the protected areas: case of Goreme Historical National Park. *Tourism Management* 28, pp. 406–414.

ETB (1991) *Tourism and the Environment: Maintaining the Balance.* English Tourist Board, London.

Ethical Corporation (2010) Social and economic impacts: measurement, evaluation and reporting. *Ethical Corporation.* September.

Freezer, J and Font, X. (2010) Marketing sustainability for small leisure and tourism firms. *Countryside Recreation* 18(1), 9–11.

Fouhy, K. (1993) Life Cycle Analysis. *Chemical Engineering* July, pp. 30–34.

Garay, L. and Font, X. (2012) Doing good to do well? Corporate social responsibility reasons, practices and impacts in small and medium accommodation enterprises. *Journal of Hospitality Management* 31, 329–337.

Gaunt, S. (2004) An analysis of environmental awareness among tour operators in Scotland. Unpublished dissertation, BA (Hons) International Travel with Information Systems. Glasgow Caledonian University, Glasgow, UK.

Goethe Institute (2008) *Sustainability – from Principle to Practise* (Translation Mary-Lane Eisberger). Goethe Institute.e.v.

Goodall, B. (1995) Environmental auditing: a tool for assessing the environmental performance of tourism firms. *The Geographical Journal* 161 (1), March, pp. 29–37.

Gossling, S., Peeters, P., Hall, C.M., Ceron, J-P., Dubois, G., Lehmann, La V. and Scott, D. (2012) Tourism and water use: Supply, demand, and security. An international review. *Tourism Management* 33 (1), pp. 1–15.

Greenbiz (2007) *Survey: U.K. Government not helping businesses turn green.* Available at http://www.greenbiz.com/news/printer.cfm?NewsID=36304 (accessed 30 November).

Gustin, M.E. and Weaver, P.A. (1996) Are hotels prepared for the environmental consumer? *Hospitality Research Journal* 20 (2), pp. 1–14.

Han, H., Hsu, L.-T.J., Lee, J.-S. and Sheu, C. (2010) Are lodging customers ready to go green? An examination of attitudes, demographics, and eco-friendly intentions. *International Journal of Hospitality Management.* 30 (2), pp. 345–355.

Harrison, D. (2003) Swedes trash the myth of refuse recycling. *The Daily Telegraph* 2 March, p. 17.

Hill, J. (2009) *Greener products: mapping the environmental policy drivers on products and production processes.* Green Alliance, London, September (www.green-alliance.org.uk).

Hillary, R. (1994) *The Eco-management and Audit Scheme: A Practical Guides.* Technical Communications (Publishing) Ltd, Letchworth, UK.

Hillary, R. (2004) Environmental management systems and the smaller enterprise. *Cleaner Production* 12, pp. 561–569.

IH (2007) *Envirowise and the Institute of Hospitality 'green' survey.* Institute of Hospitality, London.

IHEI, IHA, UNEP (1996) *Environmental Action Pack for Hotels.* International Hotels Environmental Initiative, International Hotel Association, United Nations Environment Programme Industry and Environment, London.

Ioannides, D. (2008) Hypothesising the shifting mosaic of attitudes through time: a dynamic framework for sustainable tourism development on a 'Mediterranean island'. In: McCool, S.F. and Moisey, R.N. (eds) *Tourism, Recreation and Sustainability – Linking Culture & the Environment.* 2nd edn. CAB International, Wallingford, UK, pp. 51–75.

Jackson, T. and Roberts, P. (1999) Ecological modernisation as a model for regional development: the changing nature and context of the Eastern Scotland Structural Fund programme. *Environmental Policy and Planning* 1 (1), 61–76.

Johnson, D. and Turner, C. (2003) *International Business – Themes and Issues in the Modern Global Economy.* Routledge, London.

Kelly, J., Haider, W., Williams, P.W. and Englund, K. (2007) Stated preferences of tourists for eco-efficient destination planning options. *Tourism Management* 28, pp. 377–390.

Kirk, D. (1996) *Environmental Management for Hotels.* Butterworth-Heinemann, London.

Kucerova, J. (2012) Environmental management and accommodation facilities in Slovakia. In: Leslie, D. (ed.) *Tourism Enterprises and the Sustainability Agenda across Europe.* Ashgate, Farnham, UK, pp. 121–134.

Lawton, L.J. and Weaver, D.B. (2009) Normative and innovative resources management at birding festivals. *Tourism Management* 31 (4), 527–536.

Lean, G. (2010) Luxury with a conscience – at a price. *The Daily Telegraph* October 9, p. 27.

Lebe, S.S. and Zupan, S. (2012) From eco-ignorance to eco-certificates: Environmental management in Slovene hotels. In: Leslie, D. (ed.) *Tourism Enterprises and the Sustainability Agenda across Europe.* Ashgate, Farnham, UK, pp. 135–150.

Le Quesne, T., Kendy, E. and Weston, D. (2010) *The Implementation Challenge: taking stock of government policies to protect and restore environmental flows.* World Wide Fund for Nature, Switzerland.

Leslie, D. (2002) The influence of UK government agencies on the 'greening' of tourism. *Tourism Today* 2, Summer, pp. 95–110.

Leslie, D. (2007) Scottish rural tourism enterprises and the sustainability of their communities: A Local Agenda 21 approach. In: Thomas, R. and Augustyn, M. (eds) *Tourism in the New Europe: Perspectives on SME policies and Practices.* Elsevier, Oxford, UK, pp. 89–108.

Leslie, D. (ed.) (2009) *Tourism Enterprises and Sustainable Development – International Perspectives on Responses to the Sustainability Agenda.* Routledge Advances in Tourism Series, Routledge, New York.

Leslie, D. (2011) The European Union, sustainable tourism policy and rural Europe. In: Macleod, D.V.L. and Gillespie, S.A. (eds) *Sustainable Tourism in Rural Europe: Approaches to Development.* Routledge, London, pp. 43–60.

Leslie, D. (ed.) (2012a) *Tourism Enterprises and the Sustainability Agenda across Europe. New Directions in Tourism Analysis.* Ashgate, Farnham, UK.

Leslie, D. (2012b) The responsible tourism debate. In: Leslie, D. (ed.) *Responsible Tourism: Concepts, Theory and Practice.* CAB International, Wallingford, UK.

Levett, R. (2001) Sustainable development and capitalism. *Renewal* 9 (2/3), 1–9.

LGA (2010) *Knowing me, knowing EU.* Local Government Association, London.

Maguire, C., Curry, R and McClenaghan, A. (2008) *Northern Ireland Visions – Footpaths to Sustainability.* Sustainability Resources Institute, Department of the Environment, London.

Masau, P. and Prideaux, B. (2003) Sustainable tourism: a role for Kenya's hotel industry. *Current Issues in Tourism* 6 (3), pp. 197–208.

Mensah, I. (2004) *Environmental Management Practices in US Hotels.* Hotel Online: Special Report. Available at www.hotel-online.com/News?PR2004_2nd/May04_EnvironmentalPractices.html (accessed 14 November 2006).

Mensah, I. (2009) Environmental performance of tourism enterprises in Ghana: A case study of hotels in the Greater Accra Region (GAR). In: Leslie, D. (ed.) *Tourism Enterprises and Sustainable Development: International Perspectives on Responses to the Sustainability Agenda.* Advances in tourism series. Routledge, New York, pp. 139–156.

Middleton, V.T.C and Hawkins, R. (1998) *Sustainable Tourism: a Marketing Perspective.* Butterworth-Heinemann, Oxford, UK.

Miles, P. (2001) Green holidays given a boost. *Telegraph Travel* 12 January, p. 4.

Mintel (2007) Holiday Lifestyles – Responsible Tourism – UK – January. Available at: http://academic.mintel.com/sinatra/oxygen_academic/search_results/show&/display/id=221204/display/id=256088#hit1 (accessed 2 February 2011).

Nepal, S.K. (2008) Tourism-induced rural energy consumption in the Annapurna region of Nepal. *Tourism Management* 29, pp. 89–100.

Pizam, A. (2008) Green hotels: a fad, ploy or fact of life. Editorial. *International Journal of Hospitality Management* 28, p. 1.

Pleumarom, A. (2009) Asian tourism: green and responsible? In: Leslie, D. (ed.) (2009) *Tourism Enterprises and Sustainable Development – International Perspectives on Responses to the Sustainability Agenda.* Advances in Tourism Series, Routledge, New York, pp. 36–54.

Pleumarom, A. (2013) *Tourism and Water – Make the Human Right to Water a Reality!* Tourism Investigation & Monitoring Team, Bangkok, Thailand.

Pratt, L. (2011) *Tourism: investing in energy and resources efficiency*. United Nations Environment Programme, Nairobi, Kenya.

PRC (Jersey) (1998) *Jersey in the New Millennium: a sustainable future*. Policy and Resources Committee, St. Helier, Jersey.

Preigo, M.J.B., Najera, J.J. and Font, X. (2011) Environmental management decision-making in certified hotels. *Journal of Sustainable Tourism* 19 (3), 361–381.

Radwan, H.R.I., Jones, E. and Minoli, D. (2010) Managing waste in small hotels. *Journal of Sustainable Tourism* 18 (2), pp. 175–190.

Rainford, S. and Wight, C. (2009) Owner-manager perspectives on environmental management in micro and small tourism enterprises in the Bay of Plenty, New Zealand. In: Leslie, D. (ed.) *Tourism Enterprises and Sustainable Development: International Perspectives on Responses to the Sustainability Agenda*. Advances in Tourism Series. Routledge, New York, pp. 139–156.

RDC (1996) *Green Audit Kit: The DIY guide to greening your tourism business*. Rural Development Commission, London.

Revell, A. (2003) The ecological modernisation of small firms in the UK. Paper presented to the Business Strategy and Environment Conference, Leicester, UK, September 16.

Robaththan, M. (2007) A better future. *Leisure Management* November/December, pp. 58–60.

Rodriguez, F.J.G., Cruz, Y. and Del, M.A. (2007) Relation between social-environmental responsibility and performance in hotels. *International Journal of Hospitality Management* 26 (4), pp. 824–839.

Russell-Wallings, E. (2008) Blue chips turn green. *Director* November, pp. 39–40.

Russo, M.V. and Fouts, P.A. (1997) A resources-based perspective on corporate environmental performance and profitability. *The Academy of Management Journal* 40 (3), pp. 534–559.

Sasidharan, V., Sirakaya, E. and Kerstetter, D. (2002) Developing countries and tourism ecolabels. *Tourism Management* 23, pp. 161–174.

Scanlon, N.L. (2007) An analysis and assessment of environmental operating practices in hotel and resort properties. *International Journal of Hospitality Management* 26 (3), pp. 711–723.

Sheldon, C. and Toxon, M. (1999) *Installing Environmental Management Systems – a Step-by-Step Guide*. Earthscan, London.

Shiming, D. and Burnett, J. (2002) Energy use and management in hotels in Hong Kong. *Hospitality Management* 21, pp. 371–380.

Simms, J. (2006) A green light for change. *Director* November, p. 24.

Simpson, J. (1999) How green is your business? *Hospitality* September, p. 19.

SLDC (2000) *South Lakeland District Council Sustainable Development in Southlakeland: Where are we at the start of a new millennium*. Report on 1st Annual Event, Kendal, Cumbria.

Slee, B., Hunter, C. and Liversedge, A. (1999) Tourism and sustainability in Ross and Cromarty. *The Environment Papers Series Journal* 2 (1), pp. 15–28.

Spenceley, A. (2009) Southern Africa, policy initiatives and environmental performance. In: Leslie, D. (ed.) *Tourism Enterprises and Sustainable Development: International Perspectives on Responses to the Sustainability Agenda*. Advances in Tourism, Routledge, New York, pp. 176–193.

SustainAbility (2011) *Survey on Urbanisation and Megacities: Emerging Economies*. Globescan, Toronto.

Tari, J.J., Claver-Cortes, E., Periera-Moliner, J. and Molina-Azorin, J.F. (2010) Levels of quality and environmental management in the hotel industry: their joint influence on firm performance. *International Journal of Hospitality Management* 28 (3), 500–510.

Toke, D. and Taylor, S. (2007) Green Land. *Caterer&Hotelkeeper* 127 (4463), pp. 2131–2140, February 15.

TUI (2011) *The Sustainable Development Report*. Available at http://www.tuitravelplc.com

Tzschentke, N., Kirk, D. and Lynch, P.A. (2008) Going green: decisional factors in small hospitality operations. *International Journal of Hospitality Management* 27, pp. 126–133.

UNEP (1994) *Company environmental reporting: a measure of the progress of business and industry towards sustainable development*. Technical Report No 24 United Nations Environment Programme – Industry and Environment Office, Nairobi, Kenya.

UNEP (1998) *How the hotel and tourism industry can protect the ozone layer*. United Nations Environment Programme – Industry and Environment Office, Nairobi, Kenya.

Vernon, J., Essex, S., Pinder, D. and Curry, K. (2003) Collaborative policymaking: local sustainable projects. *Annals of Tourism Research* 32 (2), 325–345.

Visser, W. (2009) *Landmarks for sustainability: events and initiatives that have changed the world.* Programme for Sustainability Leadership, University of Cambridge, Cambridge, UK.

Warnken, J., Bradley, M. and Guilding, C. (2005) Eco-resorts vs. mainstream accommodation providers: an investigation of the viability of benchmarking environmental performance. *Tourism Management* 26, pp. 367–379

Welford, R. and Starkey, R. (eds) (1996) *Business and the Environment. The Earthscan Reader.* Earthscan, London.

Welford, R., Ytterhus, B. and Eiligh, J. (1999) Tourism and sustainable development: an analysis of policy and guidelines for managing provision and consumption. *Sustainable Development* 7, 165–177.

Wight, P. (2007) Ecotourism, CSR, and the fourth dimension of sustainability. In: Higham, J. (ed.) *Critical Issues in Ecotourism.* Butterworth Heinemann, Oxford, UK, pp. 214–240.

Wilson, D. (1996) Paradoxes of tourism in Goa. *Annals of Tourism Research* 24 (1), 52–75.

Wisner, P.S., Epstein, M.J. and Bagozzie, R.P. (2010) Environmental proactivity and performance. In: Freedman, M. and Jaggi, B. (eds) *Sustainability, Environmental Performance and Disclosures.* Volume 4, Emerald, Bingley, UK.

WWF (2010) *Living Planet Report.* World Wide Fund for Nature, London

WTTC, WTO and Earth Council (1996) *Agenda 21 for the travel and tourism industry: towards environmentally sustainable tourism.* World Travel and Tourism Council, World Tourism Organisation and the Earth Council, Oxford, UK.

6 Local Produce, Local Products

Introduction

This chapter addresses the promotion of local produce across a range of activities relating primarily to food service and local products and the interrelationships between the needs of an enterprise and the local community. This is particularly significant as each enterprise has a role to play in developing links with other sectors of the local/regional economy thereby promoting further, and more localized, economic activity; as well as through supporting other local enterprises involved in the production of local produce and products. The promotion and development of this is often by local government (Leslie, 2001). Early recognition of this role was manifest in Chapter 28 of Agenda 21 and seen to be a part of every local authority's development of a 'Local Agenda 21' plan (Leslie and Hughes, 1997). Therefore the encouragement of building on and developing the connections between tourism enterprise and the local economy and community is very much a part of the sustainability agenda. Further to the employment of local people, enterprises can seek to support diversity in the economy through their purchasing practices and thus locally made produce and products.

These wider actions on the part of tourism enterprises, encompassed within SSCM, CSR and EMS schemes, have been promoted at least since the early 1990s, subsequently gaining considerably more attention by the end of the 1990s by government and encapsulated in government tourism policy:

> to encourage tourism businesses to source and promote the use of local goods (e.g. regional beers and specialty foods) and services, employ local people and offer discounts to encourage residents to use facilities provided for tourists (DCMS, 1999, p. 53);

and notably so by the National Trust (Leslie, 2001) and by the Countryside Agency (CA) (Leslie, 2002).

> The new agency will do more to show how the buying power of consumers can be harnessed to encourage markets in food products which reinforce the character of the countryside and strengthen rural enterprises (CA, 2000, p. 11)

The CA launched the 'Eat the View' campaign in 2000, designed not only to promote local produce but also encompassed local products and local production. This was subsequently followed by the Government's 'Sustainable Farming and Food' initiative (DEFRA, 2002) which includes attention to encouraging the production of produce for local markets. Furthermore, local produce and products have been recognized by the EU as part of a region's 'local distinctiveness', and encouraged and promoted under the EU's RECTE II programme since the early 2000s. Supporting the promotion of 'buying local' thereby to localize production and consumption are a range of benefits, which as identified by the English

Tourism Council and the CA (2000) are as follows:

- reduction in freight transport thereby reducing pollution and environmental damage;
- the creation of and/or support for employment and wealth in the region;
- redistribution of visitor spend within the area (multiplier effect);
- make better use of local resources and reduce waste;
- reduce imports into the area and also, potentially, imports produced in socially and/or environmentally unacceptable ways (see Hopkins, 2006; SDC, 2009);
- promotion of regional food and drink, which is a tourism asset promoted by many organizations; and
- promotion of the local area/region.

Overall, 'buying local' contributes to the economic and environmental sustainability of both tourism and the host community (Kim *et al.*, 2009; Schnell, 2013). A simple example of this in the UK is to encourage visitors and locals to drink tap water instead of bottled water, thereby reducing packaging (plastic bottles) and food miles; for example water from Fiji is transported over 10,000 miles to the UK and major brands such as Evian and Vittel on average travel 430 miles from France (Derbyshire, 2004). An alternative approach is not to allow bottled water to be brought into the locality though clearly this could only be applied effectively in island locations; for example the Maldives where the Soneva Fushi resort bans imported bottled water and produces its own through desalination with the profits from subsequent sales going to local charities (Lean, 2010). This promotion of 'local food' that is more localized and less processed prior to purchase is recognized in the concept of 'Slow Food'. This concept started in America and:

> envisions a future food system that is based on the principles of high quality and taste, environmental sustainability, and social justice – in essence, a food system that is good, clean and fair (Slow Food USA, 2008 cited in Sims, 2009, p. 323).

When applied to tourism this means tourism enterprises using local produce and locally produced foods. In effect, it is the complete opposite of fast food.

The promotion of local supplies is also of significance in the wider context of energy consumption, with the whole process of food production through to consumption accounting for a major share of energy consumption and contributing to GHGs (see SCRT, 2006; Maguire *et al.*, 2008; Gossling *et al.*, 2010). As Gyimothy and Mykletun (2009) say, the UK is a major source of research into food production, and consumption, food networks and GHG emissions; and a recognized leader in this field (see Hird *et al.*, 2010). Food and beverage services are estimated as being within the range of 31% of contribution to climate change and 20–30% of total environmental impacts of European consumption (ADAS, 2007). Thus, the closer and the more natural production is to the point of consumption, the greater the energy saving and the more sustainable. As J.M. Keynes is quoted as saying 'let goods be homespun whenever it is reasonable and conveniently possible' (Porritt, 1991, p. III). However, and particularly over the last ten years, initiatives promoting the purchase of local products and produce have significantly increased their availability in many areas including urban centres (see DEFRA, 2007), the latter most visibly through the presence of farmers' markets (see Hall *et al.*, 2003).

Since the early 2000s there has also been a substantial increase in attention to food, whether in the context of agriculture or tourism (see Leslie and Black, 2006; Sims, 2009), and especially so in terms of local produce (see Gossling *et al.*, 2010). A notable exception is that of Telfer and Wall's (1996) study, arguably the first substantive article on food and tourism. Even so, for the most part it has gained limited attention in research into the EP of tourism enterprises. It should though be noted that due care needs to be exercised in the use and interpretation of 'local' as this is a matter of perception and especially so when it comes to local produce and local products, which raises a number of issues not the least of which is the way local is defined/interpreted and with attention to spatial considerations as to what is local. For example, one interviewee considered the supply of eggs and fish to be local yet the eggs came from a major supermarket in the locality and the fish was from the West Coast. Basically, 'there is no single universally agreed definition of local foods.' (Enteleca, 2002); they tend to be based either on a specific geographic area or socio-culturally, e.g. a local recipe, or a combination of both, as for example, used by the EU for their Protection of Food Names Scheme. Thus, what was meant by local within the study was generally defined and more often explored through establishing who the suppliers were and by way of guidance, within five miles of the enterprise. But this can also be problematic as one respondent noted:

> Regarding the purchase of local supplies, the location of the inn is a key factor in the expense of obtaining local produce. All meat and vegetables are purchased from a local grocery store.

Furthermore, is local automatically the better environmental option and what of production, seasonality, availability and variability in supply and indeed food miles? All of these have an influence on demand for local produce and products. What is local and what is authentic in this context can be problematic. In an attempt to resolve such problems, Sims (2009, p. 329) offers three factors influential in how a visitor socially constructs authenticity in the consumption of local food and place:

- If it corresponds with our preconceptions about what a typical food experience for that place will look like.
- Can seem more authentic if it takes place in a sympathetic surrounding environment.
- Authentic experiences tend to emphasize some element of tradition or naturalness.

In the context of this study, examples illustrating these factors could be either sitting in an old fashioned inn ordering a dish of fell-bred lamb whilst gazing on the fells or at a picturesque loch-side hotel awaiting a dish of highland beef stew with locally sourced vegetables. Perhaps more specifically, the LDNP enterprises could source local food produce through Cumbria Food Specialities or Food from Fells, whilst those enterprises in the north-west of Scotland could source produce from the Skye and Lochalsh Food Futures

network. This neatly introduces the first area of discussion in the chapter which aims to establish the significance of local produce and products to the visitor experience. This is complementary to the rationale in support of the arguments favouring the environmental promotion of increasing the use of local produce and products on the part of tourism enterprises. The outcomes of the study into the tourism enterprises are then presented and discussed with consideration first to general purchasing practice, followed by demand for local produce and subsequently consideration of those factors identified as discouraging local purchasing. This is then further explored through the findings arising from the investigations into local food producers, before moving on to highlight a number of wider environmental issues in the food sector which are influential to the availability, purchase and/ or consumption of local produce.

Local Produce and the Visitor Experience

Food as in 'eating out' is all part of the visitor experience: visiting restaurants and cafes is seen as part of the local culture experience, and in many situations a necessity. For many visitors this activity will be limited – often to little more than a stroll and hospitality in the form of food and beverage (DCMS, 2011). Even so, with the exception of accommodation expenses it will account for a substantial proportion of visitor spend in any destination and may well be their largest out of pocket expense during their trip. As Enteleca (2002) noted, the role of food in the visitor experience can range widely from 'gastro-tourism' to a simple cup of tea.

Over the last decade there has been growing interest in and demand for quality food and distinctiveness on the part of visitors (Yeoman and Greenwood, 2006). 'Surveys have shown that tourists know locally produced foods are of high quality, but what they really value and appreciate is the opportunity to enjoy meals and snacks freshly prepared using local produce ...' and are a '... reason why someone makes return visits to an area or particular accommodation' (Anon., 2000). Indeed, findings of studies in the early 2000s identified that two thirds of holiday makers in the UK say they are prepared to pay more for quality food and beverage (Enteleca, 2002) and similarly in other European countries (CA, 2003). In a way this attraction of local food and beverage products serves to reconnect the consumer with the production processes and the location in question. Further to which it has been argued that local tradition on food is perceived to influence perceptions of quality (e.g. fresh, not mass produced), which itself is a factor in 'eating out' (see Hjalager and Corigliano, 2000). Certainly it holds a 'feel good' factor for many visitors and is seen to be a good thing to opt for local, to buy local products. This may be seen as behaving in a more responsible way, to be more supportive of 'the place'.

> In short, it is the meaning behind the food that many tourists are seeking and, by harnessing this meaning through the foods and drinks on offer at particular destinations, sustainable initiatives can have a better chance of success. (Sims, 2009, p. 334).

In this, as Francis (2008, p. 4) well argued, the key word to use is: 'local not, for example, sustainable tourism which many customers do not understand.'

Whilst this may be regarded as perhaps a little romantic, local food and beverages offer the tourist a 'feel good' factor, their popularity considered to be due to being 'Associated with a host of values, such as being better for the environment, conserving "traditional" rural landscapes and supporting the local economy' (Sims, 2009). Added to which 'Visitors can experience the moral satisfaction of choosing what they consider to be a more ethical form of consumption *and* the personal pleasures of eating and shopping differently' (Soper, 2007 cited in Sims 2009, p. 328). In effect, food, or rather the consumption of it, is very much a part of the tourists' experience and a major contributory factor to their overall satisfaction of the whole experience (Enteleca, 2002; Quan and Wang, 2004). As Gossling *et al.* (2010) identified, through an array of articles based on the consumption of food as part of the visitor experience, it can contribute to the image of the destination and also be an attraction in itself, which some commentators have called 'culinary

tourism' (Anon., 2010; see also see Hall *et al.*, 2003). Food becomes a pull factor, such as a visit to an internationally renowned restaurant, and a contributor to local/regional economies. Therefore local food and local products in themselves can become the basis of the branding of a destination or a tourist trail, e.g. FABulous Galloway (FAB as in Food – Attractions – Books); and by way of exemplifying such promotions as found across the globe – The Green Chile Cheeseburger Trail in New Mexico, which identifies 48 specialist providers. An apparently successful initiative to promote the consumption of local produce is 'The Real Bath Breakfast', which was launched in the late 1990s and developed by Envolve Partnerships for Sustainability – a real Bath breakfast requires that all ingredients are produced from within a 40 mile radius of Bath Abbey. Where ingredients are not produced within this area then they must be Fairtrade products, e.g. tea, coffee, fruit juice (for a critique of Fair trade see Mvula, 2001; Bohdanowicz and Zientara, 2012).

In such ways food is very much a contributor to and reflective of the local identity and culture of a place (Sims, 2009). As Cook and Chang (1996 cited in Hall and Mitchell, 2000, p. 35) argued, the promotion of 'local' foods is designed to 'differentiate them from the devalued functionality and homogeneity of standardized products, tastes and places'. As well illustrated by Reynolds (1993, p. 53) who found that visitors in Bali considered there to be '... less indigenous foods on offer than in other countries in South East Asia', which was considered to be due to developing dishes orientated to Western palates. Reynolds also identified that this degrading of local foods and dishes also applied more widely to their culture and traditions, a situation that appears not to have changed some ten years later as Wright (2003, p. 3) noted:

> Destinations as culturally distinct as Banjul and Bali fall over themselves to look and sound reassuringly, blandly, familiar. Such local 'culture' as there is on offer is reduced to a few decorative details – a different coloured icing on the cake.

This echoes Goodwin and Francis's (2003) point that tourism development leads to a loss of local cultural distinctiveness (see also Chapter 3). As Cotterill *et al.*'s (2002) study into tourists' perceptions found, whilst the quality of the ecological/environmental dimensions of a destination were considered to be the most important by visitors in their survey, 'local products and local culture' was ranked second as aspects influential to their overall satisfaction of a trip. Overall therefore there is no doubt that 'the idea of a link between food and place remains a powerful one ...' (Sims, 2009, p. 333). This is well illustrated by Sims who notes a bakery in the Lake District which produced Devon Fruit Cake which did not sell well. However the bakery changed the name to Cumbrian Fruit Cake and it became a best seller; similarly their Dundee Cake was renamed Westmorland Cake and again sales improved. As Sims (2009, p. 323) notes, visitors seek foods 'that they may consider to be related to the landscape, culture and heritage of their destination'. Such practice highlights the importance of provenance (confirmation of authenticity) to ensure that food and beverages seen to be specialties of particular locales may not be imitated elsewhere under the same name.

Visitors like to taste a region's local food dishes irrespective of where in the world they may be. As Bradley (2010) found in a survey of tourists in Scotland, 71% of the participants indicated that they choose locally produced food and traditional Scottish crafts during their holiday in Scotland. Also they will often purchase food and beverage products to take home as gifts or as reminders of their visit. This point serves to bring to the attention that there are two other aspects of 'local produce'. The first is that local food is generally taken as food produce of that area and thus should include food products produced within the area and also include any ingredients that may have been imported into the area for the purpose of production of a specialty of the locality (Kim *et al.*, 2009). Secondly that of arts and crafts, which have also been recognized in initiatives promoting local produce and products, as previously noted and by Cawlet *et al.* (1999) who discuss the connection between promotion of handicrafts and rural tourism services, noting that the tourists' experience of local

culture is not only about local foods but also arts and crafts (see also Richards, 1999; Lara and Gemelli, 2012). Furthermore, this has and continues to be supported by the EU, notably in the Leader programme as a way of encouraging diversification in rural areas (see Martinos, 2002). The promotion of crafts can also lead to significant economic activity. As argued by Clover (2004) local crafts, including traditional skills in the countryside, hold significant economic development potential. As Gyimothy and Mykletun (2009) affirm, crafts and local products all contribute to the tourist experience and encouraging visitors to consume local products is now actively encouraged along with growing attention to promoting and developing the supply of local products (see Timothy, 2012). This is also a facet of SSCM (see Chapter 3).

Local Foods and Local Products

Before discussing the purchase or otherwise of local produce and products, a number of general perspectives on the purchasing practices of the enterprises are presented by way of establishing the broader context within which such purchasing takes place.

General purchase practice

As regards general purchasing, management practices tended to be the same with limited indications of a bias to supporting local enterprises and local produce (see Chapter 3). The convenience of the buyer is often the main consideration and as such, local suppliers are often overlooked due to competition from, for example, supermarkets and wholesalers where the costs and thus cost savings may be more apparent; as participants noted:

- 'No storage space for bulk buying.'
- 'Want to start buying from a wholesaler – in the past we have not because the minimum order is £200 but now have the need so we will start as it is cheaper.'
- 'Supermarkets are often cheaper than cash and carry stores.'
- 'It is cheaper to buy from supermarkets.'

As regards the latter, supermarkets are increasingly sourcing more UK-based produce but are far less active in promoting local produce and products. The exemplar on local produce is Booths Supermarkets, which has two outlets in the LDNP, but it is comparatively more expensive than its competitors.

In general, the tourism enterprises appear to be less inclined to look at the longer-term value and benefit of buying locally as a way of supporting the community but rather favour short-term gain. Another influencing factor is that of whether an enterprise is part of a larger organization involving other operations. In such cases the organization can seek to establish preferential suppliers for each enterprise on the basis of cost savings; for example, attractions that are part of the National Trust or Historic Scotland or a national company. As such seeking local suppliers would not be appropriate irrespective of the managers' views. Even so, and with few exceptions all owners/managers of the enterprises indicated that they would prefer to 'buy local'; noting in some cases that this was not possible given their company policy. Further evidencing the small scale of many of these enterprises is that approximately one in four of the 2001 and the 2005 populations 'shop' for most of their needs. This was also manifest in the level of consistency throughout the data in that the majority of operations (60%) providing food services do not have one major supplier, which is partly a function of the scale of operation and demand, but also that they tend to 'shop around'; to seek value for money. This reinforces the perspective that the purchasing patterns of most of these tourism enterprises are subject to the same influences as general householders, e.g. shop for convenience at major supermarkets (see Weatherell et al., 2003). A key factor acting against the purchase of local produce/products is that supermarkets may account for some 80% of general demand (Dee, 2000). This is accounted for by a number of factors, the most significant of which are perceptions as to price and value for money, convenience (purchase most requirements in one place) and ease of parking. Thus, the owner of a small business is potentially already 'conditioned' to shopping at the nearest major supermarket.

Local produce

The purchase of local produce and products potentially offers a number of benefits; in particular the opportunity for a tourism enterprise to offer more locally distinctive products, whilst at the same time supporting other locally based enterprises. The most consistently popular area as regards buying local was found to be that of the supply of fresh meat on the part of those enterprises with restaurant operations. The selection of meat is often a discerning choice and this is reflected in the finding that approximately 50% of the rural enterprises use a local butcher who may also be more accessible than the nearest supermarket. A further point on local butchers is that in some small villages the local butcher would not survive in the absence of support from second homeowners and self-catering lets. That said, for some enterprises the quality and/or the quantity may not be considered as the best for their operation, e.g. 'sometimes local cannot supply due to quantity needed' and 'good quality is hard to find, our meat comes from Morecambe'. This supplier from Morecambe, branded as a 'British Beef' supplier, is noteworthy in that the meat supplied may well have come from beef cattle in Cumbria. As stated by one innkeeper: 'A high level of use of local produce brings extra trade; locals come for their own produce'. In this example, farmers in the area can dine at his inn on beef from cattle raised on their own farms that have been processed in an abattoir over 50 miles away.

Customer demand is also an influential factor, well illustrated in the case of one very popular inn located close to a major hotel and timeshare operation in the LDNP – one of their dishes involving lamb shanks was so popular as to exceed local supply of the meat cut involved and thus had to source from New Zealand – even though the operation prided itself on the use of local produce. As they noted, more shoulders of lamb could be obtained locally but that would mean buying whole carcasses leaving them with a major problem of surplus lamb. Reflecting the demand from visitors, the following comments from respondents offer valuable insights into the attitudes and practices of a number of the enterprises that are particularly supportive of using local produce:

- 'People visiting the area like to sample local produce.'
- 'We cook everything on the premises; we do not use prepared food from large companies.'
- 'We specialise in using as much local produce as possible.'
- 'Moving towards a more consistent "buy local" policy.'
- 'We make our own jams and chutney: cost and ease of obtaining products.'
- 'We use local jams because guests want particular products not a lot of specialised products.'
- 'Our local shop not only stocks local produce for our visitors but also is the "local store" for people living in the area.'

Conversely:

- 'Local produce/products are too expensive.'
- 'Cost of some items, both food and non-food is prohibitive and it is not always feasible to pass the increase onto a guest.'
- 'Guests are not interested in special jams.'

Interestingly further analysis of these findings identified a variance in that B & B and guest houses are less likely to use locally produced produce such as jams. When one considers that for most of them the revenues from guests are close to actual net operating profits, this begs the question as to the small cost savings gained by buying from supermarkets. It is not just accommodation operations and those enterprises providing a food service that are being encouraged to promote/support local produce but also the owners of self-catering properties. Their survey enquired if they encourage guests to purchase locally, and found that 52% advertised local shops in their apartments and 22% provided information to customers when they book and/or on arrival. The following comments, one by the owner of self-catering properties and, further to illustrate such support, one from the owner of a caravan/camping site provide further insights:

Guests are advised of local food suppliers and their opening times on arrival. Furthermore, having liaised with the suppliers, the goods are delivered to the accommodation at no extra cost. However, the first question that some guests still ask is 'Where is the nearest supermarket?'

However, as encapsulated in the following comment, their influence is limited:

Although guests are given extensive information and printed materials on purchasing goods locally, many people, particularly families, do their bulk shopping in supermarkets. Some people do take advantage of local suppliers.

Overall, the purchase of local products may have more to do with a 'feel good' factor rather than environmental concerns. Thus, the attitude of buyers is important (see Chapter 9). Their attitudes appear more influenced by saving costs where possible than the more altruistic influence of 'feeling good'. This arguably accounts for why over 90% throughout the study indicated that they 'prefer' to use local products in food production though by no means did they all do so; a finding similar to Barnett (2004) and Revell and Blackburn (2004). This is rather akin to the finding that a third of UK shoppers say they buy local food yet at best this accounts for 0.5% of food sales (Fitzpatrick and MacMillan, 2010). Basically the majority of these tourism enterprises make little effort to seek to purchase local products and produce. As Weatherell *et al.* (2003) argued, for many enterprises local foods and availability needs to fit with their usual purchasing practice. The operations of the Youth Hostel Association exemplify this very well and in marked contrast to these tourism enterprises are notably committed to supporting and buying local produce and products as much as possible.

Factors Discouraging Local Produce/ Products Purchasing

In the first survey, participants were invited through open-ended questions to indicate any reasons as to why they might not purchase local produce. Analysis of the responses established a range of reasons that gained some substantive level of consensus (see Table 6.1). These reasons were subsequently included in the audit interviews of 2001 and continued through the 2006 and 2011 stages. In each stage, the respondents were invited to indicate their perceptions as to the influential significance of those factors based on a Likert scale of 1 being 'not significant' to 5, 'very significant'. The findings based on the mean figures are presented in Table 6.1, which includes a range of respondents' comments by way of enlivening the data. Other points noted by interviewees as to why they might not make such purchases were delivery, service, limited choice and not convenient, which reflect earlier findings and also those of Torres (2003), Weatherell et al. (2003), Revell and Blackburn (2004) and Frey and George (2010).

As Table 6.1 shows, the data sets evidence little difference with the exception of cost. Ranking the data on the basis of what is considered most significant to least significant also shows little difference between the two sets. The main barriers are:

- Quality control: by which some respondents meant consistency of presentation.
- Hygiene/environmental health regulations: understandably caterers are not prepared to take risks on food safety (see Wade, 2001).

However, the fact that owners/managers of other enterprises do buy local produce/ products leads to speculation that this is something of a convenient excuse.

- Availability: this can be considered in three ways. First, availability as in continuity of supply. Second, as in not being available per se. But this may be more perception than an actual lack of availability. For instance, outcome of the response to questions as to the availability of a predefined range of popular foods, which has achieved some degree of consensus amongst the participants in the very first survey, indicated that those foods were available. This lack of awareness of what is or is not available within one's own locality is manifest amongst consumers in general (see Weatherell et al., 2003; Torres, 2003). The third consideration is that of the seasonality of local produce and both the range and quantities of produce available. Maintaining the availability of products throughout the year can become particularly difficult for small suppliers with a localized market. Issues that arise therefore involve how to manage such fluctuations whether supplying tourism enterprises or on the part of the enterprise itself in managing food service operations. As Telfer and Wall (1996) noted, the food production cycle at

Table 6.1. Factors discouraging local produce purchasing.

Factor	2001 mean[a]	2011 mean[a]	Indicative comments from interviewees
Cost, i.e. too expensive	3.26	4.00	'Sometimes'; 'will pay extra'; 'local better quality'; 'would buy local goods if available at a good price'
Portion control, e.g. not preportioned	2.35	2.67	'Do not buy local jams due to portion control and hygiene'
Quality control	4.22	4.50	'No problem with local suppliers'
Availability	3.91	4.11	'Christmas can be a bit difficult'; 'bit of a problem'; 'sometimes need to pre-order'; 'lack of variety'
Time, i.e. as in time to go and purchase	3.20	3.29	'Local delivery is possible'; 'can be delivered'
Hygiene/Environmental health regulations	4.07	4.16	'Shelf-life'
Lack of awareness, i.e. of what is available	2.89	2.80	'Local jam is available but hard to access, no promotion'

[a]Mean based on scale of 1 = not significant to 5 = very significant.

times might be compatible, e.g. low season demand ties in with low production periods. However, it has been noted that 'Environmentalists concede it will be impossible to persuade people to eschew out-of-season imported produce.' (Planet Ark, 2002, p. 3).

- Cost: the comments on costs rather reflect the view of the Marketing Director of Booth Supermarkets that whilst local suppliers may be passionate about their products they may not get the pricing right. Comparatively this reason evidences the most difference between 2001 and 2011. Possibly for these enterprises in 2011 this is influenced by the prevailing downturn in the general economy and/or perhaps because they can buy from major suppliers and are more attuned to the costs of those supplies.

By their very locality urban enterprises are possibly less likely to have available within their area a range of local products and produce which they could readily access. An important factor in this is that large enterprises with managers generally operate a departmental structure. As such the catering operations are the purvey of the Head Chef: thus on the one hand it is generally not the case that they will be going out to purchase local produce (furthermore they are more likely to want the more 'exotic' produce); equally the manager is highly unlikely to do so. Additionally and the more influential factor is that larger hotels invariably buy through major suppliers and thus import foods into the locality (Torres, 2003); a finding which is often the case with the larger, foreign-owned island-based hotels. Further analysis of the data found no appreciable differences in views between interviewees with or without restaurant operations.

It was also established that actual purchasing of locally produced products and produce was, at best, limited. A further factor that also has a major influence on buying local is a combination of the standardization of food service and the standardization of products through the use of convenience foods, condiments in pre-packed individual portions and pre-packed portioned menu items; a practice that is now standard across the globe. One in

five of the enterprises indicated that they buy in ready-made food dishes (not locally made). Inns were the more likely to purchase pre-packed portioned products and GHs and BBs were the least likely to use prepackaged products. All of which reduces the need for skilled staff and, as many an operator will argue, saves wastage. In total this lessens the use of locally produced goods and local distinctiveness. It has also been argued that in urban locations people in general are less interested in local produce compared with their rural counterparts (Weatherell et al., 2003), which may also be a factor in explaining the lack of interest in general on the part of the urban enterprises. More generally, the findings correlate with those of the Enteleca study in that enterprises are rather supply led and 'focus on selling produce and "adding value" rather than investigating and meeting consumer needs.' (2002, p. 3).

What would the enterprises like to be available and would buy?

Further reflecting interest (or otherwise) in the availability of local products, respondents were asked to identify produce/products that they would like to be available. This gained a limited response, with 30% of the enterprises indicating that there is nothing they would like to be available. A factor to such responses is that the question rather invited respondents to 'think of something' which partly explains why the responses encompassed a very diverse range of suggestions though few achieved any degree of consensus and some were just not accurate as regards availability. Items most mentioned gaining some degree of consensus were organic foods; vegetables, jams, bacon, sausages and fresh fish. However the majority of interviewees in the LDNP study disagreed that these items were not available ranging from 56% for jams to 90% for sausages. This suggests that these interviewees were better informed than many of their counterparts. However, the data indicate many enterprises have limited awareness of what local products/produce is available within their area, whilst speculation leads to the perception that many owners/managers are just not that interested.

Even so, the outcome does suggest a latent and potentially substantial market.

Local products – Arts and crafts

Another way through which enterprises can contribute to the local area is through the purchase of local crafts and products which might be suitable for daily use in the operation or for decoration and to display for sale (see Chapter 3; see Richards, 1999; Timothy, 2012). In this way they can encourage production, promote sales and help diversification in the local economy. The urban enterprises were found to be less supportive of this than their rural counterparts. This may be partly accounted for by the comparatively higher profile in rural communities of locally based arts and crafts artisans. As noted in Chapter 3, rural attractions with retail operations were likely to sell local pottery, paintings and wooden crafts; one participant noted that price and restricted display space limited the sale of local products.

Food producers

The purchase of local products and produce has been an area addressed in all the surveys and further explored in the audits. But to buy locally does not necessarily mean that the products purchased are themselves indigenous to the locality. Furthermore, when a product is considered to be locally produced, does the production process involve locally sourced ingredients? This was an area investigated in the primary study (Stage 1) where research was undertaken not only of food producers within the LDNP but also of the adjacent geographic area in order to establish a reasonable sample. The database of producers was derived from the British Specialty Food & Drink Directory 1999–2000 with a total of 25 producers being identified.

The majority of their sales (80% plus) were generated in the LDNP within their own operations and to some extent through supplies to hotels, restaurants, specialty food shops and in a few cases, to supermarkets. These producers were invited to comment on the basis of the scale of 1 being 'totally disagree' to 5, 'totally agree', on those influential factors on demand noted in Table 6.1. The findings, again based on mean figures, are presented in Table 6.2.

The high rating of quality control as being important was further evident in their responses to the question as to what factors they considered were most helpful to promoting sales of their products within the LDNP and are presented in Table 6.3.

Evidently producers are well aware of the importance placed on availability and quality by the enterprises. But they also showed some lack of thought as regards the other factors considered important by the enterprises, e.g. awareness, which producers did not consider a problem. This finding was also a factor identified by Enteleca (2002) in their study into local foods and tourism. Perhaps surprisingly no one mentioned the work of Voluntary Action Cumbria (VAC) or 'Made in Cumbria' both of which aimed to promote local enterprise; particularly when a number of the producers were promoted in the 'North West Fine Foods – Fine Food Trail' pamphlet, a combined initiative of VAC and Made in Cumbria. On the subject of products identified

Table 6.2. Influential factors on demand.

Factor	Response – mean
Availability	4.13
Quality control, e.g. consistency	4.13
Concern over hygiene regulations	2.87
Cost, i.e. too expensive	2.50
Time – to go and purchase	2.00
Portion control – not pre-portioned	1.88
Lack of awareness	1.75

Table 6.3. Factors influential in promoting products.

Factor	Responses (%)
Quality and regionality	25
Word of mouth in Cumbria	13
Able to site promotional literature in Tourist Information Centres	13
The area benefits from high visitor numbers	13

by the enterprises as not being available, it was found that as regards organic foods, the majority of producers agreed that there was limited availability whilst for jams the majority were not sure. However, they did predominantly indicate that fish, sausages and bacon were all available from local suppliers in contrast to the comments on the availability of such items from many of the enterprises.

Organic foods

In the light of rising concerns over the quality of foodstuffs in the late 1990s, the audits investigated specifically the purchase of organic vegetables (for a critique of organic produce see Bohdanowicz and Zientara, 2012). Approximately half of those interviewed in the LDNP study said that they did purchase some organic vegetables thereby also affirming that such produce was available from suppliers within the area. A few participants did consider it was not available though they would like it to be. Other comments were: 'hardly any organic products available'; 'only one thing available but too expensive'; 'organic foods are too expensive for business use'; 'organic foods are expensive though I would prefer to buy them'; 'more waste in organic food too, i.e. pest damage but I don't mind if the price was at least comparable'. The audits in 2011 found a substantial comparative difference, with far fewer enterprises indicating they purchased organic produce even though availability had increased.

Wider Considerations

The aim here is to highlight a number of the major issues that in some ways are addressed in the promotion of local produce, production and also to the concept of slow food applicable to tourism enterprises with the accent on sustainability.

Building bridges – between supply and demand

Tourism enterprises should not be passive when it comes to the availability (or lack of) local produce. As Telfer and Wall (1996) found, enterprises can seek to develop backward linkages between the enterprise and local food production. They make reference to the Caribbean islands and also the Sheraton Hotel on Lombok, near Bali in Indonesia. They discuss two initiatives, one involving the supply of fresh fish daily and the other for local herbs and vegetables. The former was very successful but the latter eventually failed due to various complications. The key point here is that whilst the local people involved supported these initiatives they were both catalysed by the Executive Chef of the hotel. They also cite the example of the Hotel Ucliva in Switzerland, a local co-operative venture with a major drive for sourcing as much as possible from within the local area, which was successful. Such actions bear witness to Vernon et al.'s (2005) study into collaborative partnerships and that for these to be successful requires the commitment of the private sector. Further, such success in building connections and networks, as Hall et al. (2003) note, can also attract external resources, e.g. expertise on marketing and promotion, and also help to build on the relationship between consumers and producers; factors which are very much in evidence in local product networks as promoted and supported under the umbrella of the EU's Leader + programme (see Martinos, 2002). In some ways this is illustrated by O'Neill and Whatmore's (2000) case study of the Hunter Valley in Australia. One entrepreneur's business initiative generated further economic activity based around the production of local produce. The key point is that entrepreneurs from outside the area started the initiative. Leading on from this, a second point is that this example illustrates that local networks are more likely to form for economic reasons, with aspects of sustainability being of lesser importance. Even so, as Erkust-Ozturk and Eraydin (2009) argue, such networks and collaborations are far more important than national/international initiatives and partnerships when it comes to local environmental governance.

Sage (2003) makes the point on heterogeneous networks that where these are successful it was found that the participants share similar attitudes including commitment to the locality, favour sustainability and are committed to the integrity in the system – that is from production to consumption. A key problem identified was that of scale – how to maintain the integrity of the localized system in the face of increased demand that encourages expansion – or due to external market pressures, of competing against bland mass production processes. As Sage (2003, p. 59) argued:

> It may yet prove decisive that the relations of regard founded on mutual appreciation of the socially embedded character of much of its food can bring together producers and consumers within the region to sustain a distinctive and flourishing alternative to culinary uniformity and tastelessness.

Healthy eating

The production of food and associated agricultural practice undoubtedly became a major issue in the 1960s, heralded by Carson's (1962) *Silent Spring*, leading to much attention to the use of pesticides and fertilizers. Since then there have been a series of food-related scares such that food in one way or another has rarely been out of the eye of the media for long, with notable coverage on threats to the populace from 'bird flu', SARS and, in the UK, salmonella and eggs, and problems with beef (Leslie and Black, 2006). It is not just production methods but also processing; witness the recent outcry over the inclusion of horse meat in processed meat-based products (e.g. beef burgers, lasagne) in Europe in February 2013 leading to a loss of confidence in the food industry. Thus it is not surprising to find suggestions that 'the whole food system is under widespread pressure to become more sustainable' (Sharpe, 2010, p. 4), meaning that it needs to be more ethical, of better quality, using fewer resources, of less negative impact and more equitable in terms of access (Sharpe, 2010). The overriding per-ception that food production and processing evidences a lack of sustainability is all the more manifest in the form of convenience eating out, which accounts for approximately 38% of the 'eating out market', and where there is

evidence that customers are not interested in the provenance of food or staff terms/conditions but only convenience and price (Sharpe, 2010). A counterpoint to this is the promotion of local supply networks and the slowing down of food production/service ('slow food'). A further factor supporting local food is that of healthy eating given the potential nutrient loss, notably vitamins and oxidants, arising due to storage – hence the promotion of seasonal produce (see SDC, 2009). But a problem lies herein with the promotion of such positive steps forward in that 'Local cafes and takeaways would go out of business if they were obliged to serve food that was healthy, fair and green' (Sharpe, 2010, p. 3). Food also concerns diet and arguments over what we eat and the related GHGs, for example the advocacy of reducing red meat consumption, which is seen to be a major contributor to GHG emissions (see Jackson et al., 2009, also Wahhab, 2013). Indeed and further illustrating that people in general at best adopt those environmentally behaviours which are easily adopted, a survey of UK residents on environ-mental actions found that the least likely of 12 options that they would adopt was a low-climate diet, i.e. reduced consumption of red meat and dairy products (Jackson et al., 2009).

The promotion of local foods is a counterpoint to mass produced goods and alternatives to the 'burger and a coke' – the production of which can have substantial negative impacts which are contrary to objectives of sustainability (see Sager, 1995; Hird et al., 2010). But, whilst there apparently is support for positive action amongst consumers (and thus tourists) this does not necessarily materialize in terms of demand for local produce. Weatherell et al. (2003) confirm this point through their survey which identifies that there is increasing concern amongst the general public over food issues. Approximately 25% of the respondents indicated that they prefer to buy local food as long as at no more than 10% extra cost compared with similar products in a supermarket for example. Overall the respondents rated taste, availability and convenience more important than social factors (sustainability) (see also SDC, 2009).

Basically:

> local foods are expected to accord with normal shopping habits, retail outlets and end-product formats, at least if they are to play a regular part in the food choice repertoire. (Weatherell et al., 2003, p. 241)

The key point here is that local food products are fundamentally food products and as such the choice of buying them in preference to other equivalent food products is subject to the same factors influencing their purchase; thus to encourage more local purchasing there is a need to address such factors as convenience to buy and presentation.

Farming

During the early part of the study, in 2001 there was an outbreak of foot and mouth disease amongst cattle. The actions taken to control the spread of this disease led to a 'crisis for the countryside' which was certainly in part due to a failing by the agencies involved to realize the impact of their actions on rural businesses in the areas affected and rather by default reinforced the interconnections between farming and related activities, the rural economy and especially tourism (Leslie and Black, 2006). In effect, a failing on the part of government to recognize the significance of the positive links between tourism and agriculture was all too well demonstrated by the foot and mouth outbreak in the UK (Leslie and Black, 2006). This crisis furthered the promotion of sustainable agriculture which encompasses:

> the role of farming in rural communities; the need for greater protection of the environment; concerns about rural land use; animal welfare; reducing 'food miles'; and the need for farming to support other sectors of the economy, such as tourism (SDC, 2002, p. 5).

Another aspect of sustainable agriculture is that of food security, the ability of a country to meet the population's food needs and the quality of food produce (Maynard, 2000). These are issues which further support the advocacy of promoting local produce and products and diversity on the basis that where

there is more control on production and less processing then it is less likely in some way to be mishandled and potentially reduce externalities and food scares. This partly explains why UK supermarkets have been increasing their attention to production and promotion of UK-sourced produce but then this raises issues over the range of produce, availability and storage costs. Even so there is little doubt that encouraging local production and processing can and does encourage farms to diversify and, where appropriate, to supply local tourism enterprises (Fleischer and Tchetchik, 2005), albeit that until relatively recently, at best, 'tourism typically failed to stimulate local agriculture' (Torres, 2003, p. 547). In essence, the authors of the Curry Report (2002) encapsulated this when they said:

> We believe that one of the greatest opportunities for farmers to add value and retain a bigger slice of retail price is to build on the public's enthusiasm for locally produced food, or food with a clear regional provenance. Increasing the market share of such food would have benefits for farmer and consumer alike (cited in CPRE, 2002, p. 2).

Food miles

Major external costs involved in food sourcing are transport (including that involved in domestic shopping) with the major comparative cost being that of road transport (Pretty et al., 2005). The distance food travels from source to a region is rather loosely termed 'food miles'; for example major food imports to the UK include lettuce from Spain (900 miles), mangetouts from Kenya (4200 miles), sugar snap peas from Guatemala (5400 miles) and prawns from Indonesia (7000 miles) (Derbyshire, 2004 and 2005). The levels of pollution generated from transporting foods across the globe will vary according to the transportation method; one suggestion is that goods moved by air generate 100 times more pollution than by rail and 200 times more than if shipped (Anon., 2007). But food miles are just one facet of food supply – the whole process from production to the point of consumption needs to be analysed in order for meaningful comparisons to be made. It is not a given that domestic production will always have a lower environmental impact; for example, according to Chi *et al.* (2010) British strawberries and tomatoes have a higher impact than imported Spanish ones due to the production processes involved in extending the UK growing season. Furthermore, to develop production in the UK of many imported foods may well be viable but the cost of production, e.g. need for controlled conditions given the energy consumption involved when considered on the basis of life-cycle analysis, may well be less sustainable then the equivalent imports, depending on how the latter are transported, e.g. via scheduled flights or shipped. Shipping accounts for much of the food imported by the industrialized world and has comparatively lower emissions (Chi *et al.*, 2010). Again, in comparative terms it is not just emissions per se but rather the content of those emissions and their effects also differ, e.g. aircraft emission at altitude, sulphur emissions from ships. In the context of sustainability there is also the matter of equity and the potential impact of benefits involved in production. For example, 'An estimated 1 to 1.5 million livelihoods in sub-Saharan Africa depend directly and indirectly on UK-based supply chains.' (Chi *et al.*, 2010, p. 10), involving approx. £1m per day on fresh fruit and vegetables. The UK is one of the biggest importers of fresh produce from there, much of which may be transported on regular air passenger flights. More specifically, UK food imports from Kenya have been estimated to have a value of £100m and direct jobs from this number 135,000 (Walker, 2010). A small farmer in Kenya involved in this supply can use the profits from ongoing sales, for example, to better his home and family and access education.

Clearly to establish accurately the externalities involved in food production, sourcing through to consumption, is a complex matter and includes emissions from soil producing crops, water usage, fertilizers and how processed and stored, and additional energy consumption involved, all of which are now accepted as part of the equation (see SDC, 2003). This is increasingly recognized and steps required to be taken to address the issues

of resources needed in production to make for more efficient operations identified (see Forum for the Future, 2011). To further such progress perhaps a tax on food miles should be introduced and the revenues so gained invested in supporting local farmers and farmers markets (Anon., 2012), though a carbon tax might be more appropriate and funding also used to support local food networks.

Conclusion

There is an inherent sense in the use of what is produced and available within a locality. Further, in past times, when produce was in abundance, creative recipes were developed and thrift prevailed and methods of preserving utilized in order to maximize such bounty beyond its natural shelf life. However, such good housekeeping in post-industrial societies for the most part has long gone, usurped by comparatively modern methods of storage, ways of extending shelf life and international food markets. Thus the situation that in an up-market restaurant a bowl of morning porridge adorned with fresh raspberries and mint arrives at the breakfast table in early February. Evidently much food produce available today in major supermarkets bears little relation to the seasons in the UK and even less it appears to agriculture. But this has come at a cost – from rising costs of production and environmental impacts to food scares and a dislocation in many societies between consumption and production. In combination this is recognized in the mantra 'Think global – act local', which came to the fore following the Earth Summit of 1992 and Agenda 21, leading to the advocacy of buying local that is manifestly part of the greening of tourism enterprise and thus the environmental performance of tourism enterprises. Hence the extent of the attention given to buying local within the study.

Basically the investigations into this have established that the convenience of the purchaser is often the main consideration in purchasing decisions, and, as such, local suppliers are often overlooked due to competition from, for example, supermarkets, and wholesalers where the actual cost of purchases is clear. The owners/managers are less inclined to consider the longer-term value and benefit of buying locally in terms of supporting the local community and favour short-term gain. Instead, the bias is towards direct, measurable gain, i.e. cost savings. This is particularly evident in the variances in the purchasing patterns of enterprises, which are largely a function of individual size and scale, i.e. many shop for convenience as and when required. The smaller the enterprise the more likely their supplies will be sourced through supermarkets whilst at the other end of the spectrum the majority of supplies are purchased through regional/national suppliers. An outcome similar to other studies with attention to local produce purchasing (Torres, 2003; Weatherell et al., 2003; Erdogan, 2009) but contrasts with Spenceley (2009) who identified a comparatively high level of support for both local produce and local products, which in part at least is attributable to the promotion of 'responsible tourism'.

One of the factors to emerge from the self-catering and caravan sites sectors is that tourists tend to conform to their normal behaviours (whether environmentally friendly or not) while on holiday. In effect, being in a different environment tends to have little effect on changing behavioural patterns. As such it is arguable that support for 'slow food' or fair trade is not a manifestation of changing consumer behaviour and counter to the view that all individuals are self-centred but rather they are also looking out for themselves. To go one step further and argue, as various authors have (see Sims, 2009), that this illustrates behavioural change based on more ethical choices is wide open to debate. All of which is pertinent to and helps explain why 'buying local' is not greater. However, on the basis of the findings, factors primarily given as militating against the purchase of locally produced produce and products are:

- *Cost* – If the cost of locally produced or supplied food or non-food items is considered to be significantly more than the similar 'imported' product then it is very likely in most cases that the purchaser will favour alternative, non-local suppliers. Any such decision is understandable in part in that there may be a reluctance to pass on

greater costs to the buyer due to a fear of reducing competitiveness. However in the case of BBs and GHs this is hardly a justifiable argument given the relative slightly higher cost of the supplies when considered against the income from a guest's accommodation.

- *Quality* – Yet quality and regional distinctiveness were cited by the producers of food products as being the most important factor in promoting products. This suggests something of a gap between the perceptions of the owners/managers and those of the producers. However, it might also be that some of the owners/managers are using 'quality' as a convenience to account for why they might not purchase local produce/products.

- *Health and safety regulations* – In the light of the regulations governing food processing, whether a food producer or in a restaurant kitchen, introduced over the last ten years and measures taken to ensure compliance. This brings into question the actual validity of this reason and leads to the conclusion that it is rather more of a convenient response.

- *Availability* – Awareness of what is available is also a factor. It was identified that awareness of what is/is not available is limited and as such that there is a latent demand for a range of local produce and food products. There is a wider range of local produce and products available than is generally known.

It is clear that opportunities exist for the development and promotion of existing and new produce and products. The findings also indicate there is substantial potential for the promotion of 'Made in X' branding for local produce and local products. The responsiveness of the operators of the cafes and food producers and their evident interest in the enquiries made leads to speculation that there is latent demand for more locally sourced ingredients. Furthermore, there was support for developing networks between these small, local enterprises, as also identified by Gyimothy and Mykletun (2009). Success in such matters will bring other issues to the fore such as how to manage the local context whilst potentially expanding the operation. Producers can develop and expand their operations to include selling in other areas whilst still maintaining their 'regionality' brand, but then if supplying through an outlet in another tourist destination in another part of the country this increases competition there. They could also seek to promote sales via their website (see Timothy, 2012) – perhaps then for some tourists a visit would become unnecessary! In both cases an issue would be how then are the purchases 'local'. A further consideration is what happens if due to success and good financially operating practices, a company becomes attractive to an external buyer? However, on the demand side, there is little argument that where possible, uniqueness of locally produced products should be promoted rather than serving products which can be purchased virtually anywhere; as well illustrated by one hotelier who commented:

> … put imported parrot fish on the menu and you lose the individuality and distinctiveness of the region. We use as much wild food from the area as we can get.

From a catering operations perspective this requires more skill both in production in the kitchen and in the service, which raises the potential wage costs of the enterprise that might also have difficulty in recruiting suitably qualified staff. Counter to this is that creating menu dishes from raw ingredients generates higher net profits than pre-prepared food dishes but then this all depends on the quality of staff, management practices and so forth. Hence, not surprisingly, many owners/ managers opt for the more convenient path in their food operations.

As the findings here attest, more effort needs to be made to contribute to the local community – to encourage local enterprise;

> … promoting the development of other sectors for example, greater production and utilization of local produce and products, thereby contributing to a stronger economy with more diverse opportunities for employment. (Leslie, 2002, p. 9)

and to a more sustainable society. There needs to be greater recognition on the part of the owners/managers that they are part of their wider environment which fundamentally is

what draws custom to their doors and to maximize the cross-sectoral economic links that can be achieved in the development of tourism (see preceding chapters). This requires the adoption of a more comprehensive, integrated approach, which has been largely missing, arguably not only due to a failing to recognize the linkages between the economic, social and environmental but also between these and wider issues of sustainability. A key facet of this is that tourism is not treated in isolation from the rest of the local economy and particularly of the community who are the oft-cited key beneficiaries of tourism. Tourism, unlike perhaps other more traditional sectors of the economy, does not and cannot operate in isolation but rather is inextricably entwined with all the dimensions of a locality. However, this is not only a matter for local enterprise, other stakeholders, and agencies are also required to address and promote integrated development including food networks (see Sims, 2009), particularly in rural areas. This should help tourist destinations cope with a sudden decrease in demand and more significantly a long-term shift in demand as the local economy will be more robust and less reliant on a major single economic activity such as tourism.

But, and on a note of caution, the local produce market is often highly fragmented. Therefore appropriate support is required with regards to infrastructure and marketing activity and hence the suggestion of the need for establishing networks and building partnerships between the tourism enterprises, suppliers and producers. Collectively such networks can bring the following benefits:

- greater access to fresh, seasonal produce;
- increased employment and reduced leakages;
- closer links between produce and consumer;
- great self-sufficiency;
- reduced pollution and congestion;
- encourages sustainable land management systems; and
- reduced risk of food contamination or 'bad' practice, e.g. BSE (Sage, 2003).

Additional to the foregoing factors there is also the fact that because these networks are localized the produce/products will involve less packaging, less wrapping and overall less waste, especially in comparison with casual/convenience eating 'out on the street' and encourages a more leisurely seated experience at the point of consumption. It is also widely argued that the flavour of seasonal, fresh food on the table is comparably better invariably than foods which have been stored for any period of time. Essentially this is what 'slow food' is primarily about.

In combination the needs of everyone are taken into consideration: effective measures continue to operate and develop, as necessary, to protect the environment whilst initiatives are promoted and due action taken to encourage the prudent use of natural resources. As such there is a demand for not treating enterprises and operations in terms of their products/services alone but in the wider context of their external environment; an approach which reflects much greater awareness of the interconnectedness of the economic, physical and social dimensions of the environment rather than just the physical or natural, e.g. pollution and damage. Given the need for all sectors of the community to become involved there is a substantial potential to address these linkages and seek ways to regenerate them. Linkages which can serve to accentuate the importance of the environment to the community and encourage more responsive action on the part of the community towards conservation. This will require the development of supportive networks, co-operation and communication.

All of which in terms of being effective requires that the local strategy needs to seek to maximize the benefits and reduce leakages; increase the multiplier effect of visitor spending within the local economy; and add value to local produce and products. In the final analysis it may not be so much environmental attitude, a value that is part of the nature of the owner/manager, but a deliberate decision taken in the interests of promoting the business that counts. In the short term, whichever of these is the driving force is perhaps not that important, what is – is that, to quote one interviewee:

> … the interest is there. A sustainable local economy requires it.

Further Reading

For an interesting range of articles on the theme of food and tourism see Hall, C.M., Sharples, L., Mitchell, R., Macionis, N. and Cambourse, B. (eds) (2003) *Food Tourism Around the World: Development, Management and Markets*. Butterworth-Heinemann, Oxford, UK; Croce, E. and Peri, G. (2010) *Food and Wine Tourism*. CAB International, Wallingford, UK.

The cultural dimension of heritage and particularly the natural heritage may be missing in some dialogues on the heritage and environment, and thus connections with agriculture and the locality, therefore readers are referred to Keitumetse, S.O. (2009) The Eco-tourism of Cultural Heritage Management (ECT-CHM): Linking heritage and 'Environment' in the Okavango Delta Regions of Botswana. *International Journal of Heritage Studies* 15 (2–3), March–May, pp. 223–244.

For a comprehensive discussion on the complexities of carbon footprinting food produce see RELU (2009) *Comparative merits of consuming vegetables produced locally and overseas: Fair and evidence based carbon labelling*. Note 11, Rural Economy and Land Use Programme, University of Newcastle, Newcastle, UK.

Overall, for a comprehensive discussion on local food and communities see SERIO (2012) *Making local food work: Understanding the impact*. Report for the Plunkett Foundation, SERIO, University of Plymouth, Plymouth, UK.

References

ADAS (2007) *The £100 barrel of oil: impacts on the sustainability of food supply in the UK.* ADAS, Leeds, UK, July.

Anon. (2000) B&Bs urged to use local produce. *Glasgow Evening Times* 26 January, p. 3.

Anon. (2007) How to pick a supermarket. News Special *The Daily Telegraph* 16 May, pp. 14–15.

Anon. (2010) *Hotel companies vie for carbon emission reductions.* Tourism Innovation Group, Edinburgh, UK.

Anon. (2012) Ban ugly bolt on solar panels in sustainable cities. Special Edition, *Business Reported* September, p. 16.

Barnett, S. (2004) Perceptions, understandings and awareness of Green Globe 21: the New Zealand Experience. Paper presented at the State of the Art Conference II, Glasgow, UK, July.

Bohdanowicz, P. and Zientara, P. (2012) CRS-inspired environmental initiatives in top hotel chains. In: Leslie, D. (ed.) *Tourism Enterprises and the Sustainability Agenda across Europe. New Directions in Tourism Analysis.* Ashgate, Farnham, UK, pp. 93–120.

Bradley, A. (2010) *Food and Tourism.* Tourism Innovation Group, Edinburgh, UK.

CA (2000) *Tomorrow's countryside – 2020 vision.* The Countryside Agency, London.

CA (2003) *Tourism and sustainable land management knowledge assessment.* Research Notes CRN 57. The Countryside Agency, London, March.

Cawlet, M.E., Gaffet, S.M. and Gillmor, D.A. (1999) The role of quality tourism and craft SMEs in rural development: evidence from the republic of Ireland. *Anatolia* 10(1), pp. 45–60.

Chi, K.R., MacGregor, J. and King, R. (2010) *Big ideas in development: Fair miles – recharting the food miles map.* International Institute for Environment and Development.

Clover, C. (2004) Rural crafts 'will earn more than farming'. *The Daily Telegraph* 17 November, p. 11.

Cotterill, S., Van der Duim, R., Ankersind, P. and Kelder, L. (2002) Measuring Sustainability of Tourism in M. Antonio Quepos and Texel: A Tourist Perspective. Paper presented at ATLAS Conference, Estoril, November.

CPRE (2002) *Local action for local foods.* Council for the Protection of Rural England, London.

DCMS (1999) *Tomorrow's Tourism: A Growth Industry for the New Millennium.* Department of Culture, Media and Sport, London.

DCMS (2011) *Government Tourism Policy.* Department of Culture, Media and Sport, London.

Dee, C. (2000) *Regional Sourcing and Food Mileage.* Presentation by the Marketing Director, Booths Supermarkets, to the Go for Green Conference, Keswick, UK, March 22.

DEFRA (2002) *Review of the Rural White Paper: Our Countryside: the future.* Department of Environment, Food and Rural Affairs, London.

DEFRA (2007) *Parents and retired more likely to adopt pro-environmental behaviours.* Press Release. Department of Environment, Food and Rural Affairs, London, 23 November.

Derbyshire, D. (2004) Source of latest fashion in drinks is Fiji in the Pacific. *The Daily Telegraph* November 3, p. 3.

Derbyshire, D. (2005) First UK tomatoes come in from the cold. *The Daily Telegraph* January 29, p. 9.

Enteleca (2002) *Tourist attitudes towards regional local foods.* Report for the Ministry of Agriculture Fisheries and Food and the Countryside Agency. Enteleca Research and Consultancy.

Erdogan, N. (2009) Turkey's tourism policy and environmental performance of tourism enterprises. In: Leslie, D. (2009) *Tourism Enterprises and Sustainable Development: International Perspectives on Responses to the Sustainability Agenda.* Advances in Tourism Series. Routledge, New York, pp. 194–208.

Erkust-Ozturk, H. and Eraydin, A. (2009) Environmental governance for sustainable tourism development collaborative networks and organisation building in the Antalya tourism region. *Tourism Management* 31 (1), 113–124.

Fitzpatrick, I. and MacMillan, T. (2010) *Making local food work: Influencing consumer buyer behavior.* Plunkett Foundation, Woodstock, UK, December.

Fleischer, A. and Tchetchik, A. (2005) Does rural tourism benefit from agriculture? *Tourism Management* 26, 493–501.

Forum for the Future (2011) Tomorrow's food, tomorrow's farms. Special Edition, *Green Futures*, March.

Francis, J. (2008) Comment. *Telegraph Travel. The Daily Telegraph* 14 June, T4.

Frey, N. and George, R. (2010) Responsible tourism management: the missing link between business owners' attitudes and behaviour in the Cape Town tourism industry. *Tourism Management* 31 (5), pp. 621–628.

Goodwin, H. and Francis, J. (2003) Ethical and responsible tourism – consumer trends in the UK. *Journal of Vacation Marketing* 9 (3), 271–284.

Gossling, S., Garrod, B., Aall, C., Hille, J. and Peeters, P. (2010) Food management in tourism: reducing tourism's carbon 'footprint'. *Tourism Management* 31 (3), 534–543.

Gyimothy, S. and Mykletun, R.J. (2009) Scary food: commodifying culinary heritage as meal adventures in tourism. *Journal of Vacation Marketing* 15 (3), 259–273.

Hall, C.M. and Mitchell, R. (2000) 'We are what we eat': Food, tourism, and globalisation. *Tourism, Culture & Communication* 2, pp. 29–37.

Hall, C.M., Sharples, L., Mitchell, R., Macionis, N. and Cambourse, B. (eds) (2003) *Food Tourism Around the World: Development, Management and Markets.* Butterworth-Heinemann, Oxford, UK.

Hird, V., Webster, R. and MacMillan, T. (2010) *Local food and climate change: the role of community food enterprises. Making Local Food Work,* Plunkett Foundation, Woodstock, UK, April.

Hjalager, A.-M. and Corigliano, M.A. (2000) Food for tourists – determinants of an image. *International Journal of Tourism Research* 2 (4), 281–293.

Hopkins, R. (2006) Energy scarcity is an opportunity for a better world. *Living Earth* Issue 228, Soil Association, Bristol, Winter, pp. 12–114.

Jackson, B., Lee-Woolf, C., Higginson, F., Wallace, J. and Agathou, N. (2009) *Strategies for reducing the climate impacts of red meat/dairy consumption in the UK.* Report for the Worldwide Fund for Nature, Imperial College, London, March.

Kim,. Y.G., Eves, A. and Scarles, C. (2009) Building a model of local food consumption on trips and holidays: a grounded theory approach. *Tourism Management* 28 (3), pp. 423–431.

Lara, A.L. and Gemelli, A. (2012) Cultural Heritage: World Heritage Sites and responsible tourism. In: Leslie, D. (ed.) *Responsible Tourism: Concepts, Theories and Practice.* CAB International, Wallingford, UK, pp. 142–153.

Lean, G. (2010) Luxury with a conscience – at a price. *The Daily Telegraph* October 9, p. 27.

Leslie, D. (2001) *An Environmental Audit of the Tourism Industry in the Lake District National Park.* Report for Friends of the Lake District and Council for the Protection of Rural England, Murley Moss, Kendal, UK.

Leslie, D. (2002) The influence of UK government agencies on the 'greening' of tourism. *Tourism Today* 2, pp. 95–110.

Leslie, D. and Black, L. (2006) Tourism and the impact of Foot and Mouth Epidemic in the UK: reactions, responses and realities with particular reference to Scotland. *Journal of Travel and Tourism Marketing* 19 (2/3), pp. 35–46.

Leslie, D. and Hughes, G. (1997) Agenda 21, local authorities and tourism in the UK. *International Journal of Managing Leisure* 2 (3), pp. 143–154.

Maguire, C., Curry, R. and McClenaghan, A. (2008) *Northern Ireland Visions – Footpaths to Sustainability.* Sustainability Resources Institute, Department of the Environment, London.

Martinos, H. (2002) *Adding value to local products. UK Leader+ Network Overview and Info-sheets* No. 1.2. Department of Environment, Food and Rural Affairs, London, November.

Maynard, R. (2000) *An inconvenient truth about food – neither secure not resilient.* Soil Association, Bristol, UK.

Mvula, C.D. (2001) Fair trade in tourism to protected areas – a micro case study of wildlife tourism to South Luangwa National Park, Zambia International. *Journal of Tourism Research* 3, pp. 393–405.

O'Neill, P. and Whatmore, S. (2000) The business of place: networks of property, partnership and produce. *Geoforum* 31, pp. 121–136.

Planet Ark (2002) Organic food-hungry Britons pile on the air miles. Available at http://.planetark. org'dailynewsstory.cfm?newsid=18176&newsdate=15-)ct-2002 (accessed 18 March, 2003).

Porritt, J. (1991) Sustainable Tourism? *Weekend Telegraph. The Daily Telegraph* September 28, p. III.

Pretty, J.N., Ball, A.S., Lang, T. and Morison, J.I.L. (2005) Farm costs and food miles: an assessment of the full cost of the UK weekly food basket. *Food Policy* 30, pp. 1–19.

Quan, S. and Wang, N. (2004) Towards a structural model of the tourist experience: an illustration from food experiences in tourism. *Tourism Management* 25, pp. 297–305.

Revell, A. and Blackburn, R. (2004) *UK SMEs and their response to environmental issues.* Small Business Research Centre, Kingston University, London, March.

Reynolds, P.C. (1993) Food and tourism: towards an understanding of sustainable culture. *Journal of Sustainable Tourism* 1, pp. 48–54.

Richards, G. (ed.) (1999) *Developing and Marketing Crafts Tourism.* ATLAS, Tilburg, the Netherlands, May

Sage, C. (2003) Social embeddedness and relations of regard: alternative 'good food' networks in south-west Ireland. *Journal of Rural Studies* 19, pp. 47–60.

Sager, G. (1995) 'Burger and a coke' and other environmental problems: reflections on the diet and the environmental crisis. *Sustainable Development* 3 (3), pp. 149–157.

Schnell, S.M. (2013) Food miles, local eating and community supported agriculture: putting local food in its place. *Agriculture and Human Values* 30, 615–628.

SCRT (2006) *I will if you will: Towards sustainable consumption.* Sustainable Consumption Roundtable, London, May.

SDC (2002) *From Vision to Action: SDC's perspective on the work of the Curry Commission.* Sustainable Development Commission, London, March.

SDC (2003) *Sustainability of sugar supply chains.* Sustainable Development Commission, London, April.

SDC (2009) *Setting the table: advice to Government on priority elements of sustainable diets.* Sustainable Development Commission, London, December.

Sharpe, R. (2010) *An Inconvenient Sandwich – the throwaway economics of take away food.* New Economics Foundation, London, June.

Sims, R. (2009) Food, place and authenticity: local food and the sustainable tourism experience. *Journal of Sustainable Tourism* 17 (3), 321–336.

Spenceley, A. (2009) Southern Africa, policy initiatives and environmental performance. In: Leslie, D. (2009) *Tourism Enterprises and Sustainable Development: International Perspectives on Responses to the Sustainability Agenda.* Advances in Tourism Series. Routledge, New York, pp. 176–193.

Telfer, D.J. and Wall, G. (1996) Linkages between tourism and food production. *Annals of Tourism Research* 23 (3), pp. 635–653.

Timothy, D.J. (2012) Destination communities and responsible tourism. In: Leslie, D. (ed.) *Responsible Tourism: Concepts, Theory and Practice.* CAB International, Wallingford, UK, pp. 72–81.

Torres, R. (2003) Linkages between tourism and agriculture in Mexico. *Annals of Tourism Research* 30 (3), pp. 546–566.

Vernon, J., Essex, S., Pinder. D. and Curry, K. (2005) Collaborative policymaking: local sustainable projects. *Annals of Tourism Research* 32 (2), 325–345

Wade, J. (2001) Stakeholders, ethics and social responsibility in the food supply chain. In: Eastham, J.F., Sharples, L. and Ball, S.D. (eds) *Food supply chain management: issues for the hospitality and retail sectors.* Butterworth-Heinemann, Oxford, UK, pp. 111–124.

Wahhab, I. (2013) Red alert on meat habit. *Director* April, p. 27.

Walker, B. (2010) Where does it come from? *Hospitality* 20, pp. 26–28.

Weatherell, C., Tregear, T. and Allinson, J. (2003) In search of the concerned consumer: UK public perceptions of food, farming and buying local. *Journal of Rural Studies* 19, pp. 233–244.

Wright, M. (2003) Travelling hopefully. *Green Futures* Jan/Feb, p. 3.

Yeoman, I. and Greenwood, C. (2006) *From fast food to slow food: the prospects for Scotland's cuisine to 2015. Tomorrow's World.* Edinburgh VisitScotland. Vol 2 (3), November.

7   Guests, Tourists, Visitors

_____

Introduction

The environmental concerns of the 1960s and societal and political reactions since gave rise to the emergence of the so called 'green consumer' in the 1980s, along with a shift in consumer values which shaped new consumption patterns and purchasing motives (Paavola, 2001). By the end of the 1980s, consumer surveys identified demand for green products and also, though to a lesser extent, organic produce and biodegradable products (Anon., 1989). Furthermore, surveys suggested that 21% of consumers were prepared to pay 5% to 10% more for environmentally friendly products (Elkington, 1989). As environmental awareness and concerns increased then green consumerism gathered momentum markedly in the late 1990s and notably so in the USA and has continued to expand through the 2000s; witness a survey of 22,000 shoppers in the USA that found that:

> ... consumers are focused more and more on the social and environmental impact of their consumer packaged goods purchases. [This has led] to a viable and growing US market for sustainable products and packaging. (Infor, 2008, p. 3)

Aligned with this was the promotion of environmentally friendly activities through information campaigns, media comment and the facilitation of activities such as waste separation for recycling (Cummings, 1997).

Overall, as Cole (1999) argued, 'There is increasing societal (and therefore market) pressure for higher environmental standards.' Though the evidence of surveys tends more often than not to be on what consumers said they will do rather than what they actually do, there can be little doubt that consumers and visitors are becoming more concerned about the environment and can influence operational practices by demanding more sustainable products. For example, as a result of consumer pressure, the fast food chain McDonald's introduced changes in packaging products and subsequently greater attention to waste management.

The rise of environmental concerns and demand for green products arguably catalysed developments in business practice and the emergence of corporate environmentalism (Cairncross, 1995) and, as noted in Chapters 3 to 5, advocacy for the greening of tourism on the part of many agencies. Not surprisingly the demand side also gained attention (e.g. see Leslie, 1991; Watkins, 1994; Scottish Office, 1995; Martin, 1998). Further supporting tourism 'going green' were suggestions that a green tourist was emerging (Millman, 1989), which was taken much further by Poon (1994), who argued of a 'new tourism' and the rise of the 'new tourist', who wants something different from the traditional tourism package holiday, a more discerning and environmentally concerned tourist. Although in the 1990s and since the reality of there being 'green tourists' has been questioned and considered to be more a matter of environmental awareness and concern rather than actual positive action by tourists (Lim, 1996; Leslie, 2012). Even so, just as the evidence presented to support the rise of green consumerism was used to influence the availability of green products, so too arguments were advanced that these green tourists provided a rationale for enterprises to go green and thereby gain additional custom (Gustin and Weaver, 1996; Silano and Meredith, 1997; Leidner, 2004). Further, that enterprises could seek to influence their customers through promoting their environmental credentials and practices. The information presented to guests can serve as opportunities with customers and host communities to pass on the messages and practices of sustainable development (WTTC et al., 1996, p. 36). In effect, tourism enterprises have and are being encouraged to communicate environmental issues to guests via their promotional material, and the availability of such information can serve as an indicator of an enterprise's promotion of/ orientation to environmental matters which may then be conveyed through the availability of such information to their guests.

The introduction and development of environmentally friendly practices can serve as a promotional tool to attract customers concerned about environmental issues (see McBoyle, 1996); as exemplified by the hotel chain in America which introduced a number of 'green' rooms at an additional charge of $50. Furthermore, such promotion can increase consumer awareness in general, as well as contributing to resource conservation. It is arguable tourists often take things for granted, not realizing the negative impacts of their actions or how they could enhance the benefits of their spending to the local economy. Therefore, if they are more aware through 'environmental messages' then greater local benefit may be achieved. This has been recognized as another dimension of the EP of operations (Environment Council, 2000; see Chapter 3). It was with cognisance of the advocacy that these enterprises should be promoting their EM and CSR practices and in the process enhance their customers'

awareness of sustainability issues that due attention was given to this area in the study. The outcomes of this facet of the investigation are presented in this chapter commencing with the enterprise's promotion of environmentally friendly actions, including whether they encourage their guests in such practices and the type of information made available to customers. This leads to questioning whether tourists are really interested, which is then discussed in the following section. But first, this is an appropriate point to draw attention that it is not just the environmental dimensions of sustainability that are of concern but also consideration for social dimensions. In this instance the provision of access and facilities for less able persons was also an aspect of the study gaining due attention in the surveys. That the needs of less able visitors should be given full consideration in the social context of inclusion is without question. They are also a valuable market. In terms of the less able this is all the more important given the ageing profile of the populations of post-industrial nations, and significantly the age profile of visitors now and especially looking to the future. The less able, in particular those with disabilities, have been largely excluded in the past as '… the special needs of visitors with disabilities have not been sufficiently considered in the provision of accommodation, attractions and facilities' (CTB, 1998, p. 25). As is invariably the case in such matters there are exceptions and exemplars as the following quotes from the 2001 stage illustrate:

- 'We have converted two of our ground floor rooms for use by disabled persons.'
- 'We have converted a studio bedroom designed entirely to suit the needs of disabled persons.'

Further, Cottage Life, an agency for self-catering accommodation in the LDNP, through the T&CP scheme raised substantial funding to further disabled access to White Moss Common in Rydal.

Provision in general since the 1990s has improved dramatically, largely due to the Disability Discrimination Act (1995). Compared with the other categories, attractions and restaurants are far more likely to be accessible to less able persons than the other sectors; particularly inns and caravan sites, the former invariably due to the age and physical structure of the building and the latter to physical typology of the sites in some cases. The specific point to be gained from these findings is the remarkable increase in attention to the provision of facilities for the less able and is almost entirely due to the legislation involved.

The Promotion of Environmentally Friendly Practices

As noted earlier, promotion of an enterprise's EM and CSR activity is considered to hold benefits: one in attracting custom and two, by way of increasing the awareness of customers of issues of sustainability and potentially influencing their environmental behaviour. The findings of the study into this aspect from across all three populations was that very little is actually done by way of such promotion with 60% taking few steps, if any, to communicate to customers what the enterprise may be doing regarding EM; an outcome that to a large extent reflects the findings presented in the preceding chapters. This apparent lack of responsiveness to the purported trend in 'green consumerism' is also evident from the responses to the attitudinal questions and further enquiries in the auditing stage (see Chapter 9). Few contributors were as sure as the respondent who, in response to the question on whether they seek to attract 'green' guests, said: 'Yes, people are very sensitive here.' One respondent indicated that he had sought the advice of the Cumbria Tourist Board regarding

where best to advertise for green tourists and was disappointed by the absence of any advice.

The participants were invited through an open question to indicate the way(s) in which they promoted their EM practices to their customers. The responses from the three stages were collated and analysed to establish potential areas of consensus (see Table 7.1). Interestingly a few participants from both the 2001 and 2011 audits did mention that they include information on an 'environmental message' in their promotional material and in some few cases that they promote 'fair trading', e.g. Cafe Direct, Body Shop toiletries, whilst one of the larger enterprises said they promoted environmental awareness and related initiatives through their newsletter. However, the number involved was less than the actual number of enterprises holding GTBS accreditation. Furthermore, none of the 2001 enterprises mentioned the TCP (see Chapter 5). Also of note is that within the 2001 and 2006 populations a number of the enterprises evidenced recognition that there are some tourists who are more concerned about the environment than others (see Wurzinger and Johansson, 2006; OECD, 2011; Leslie, 2012). This is well illustrated in a positive way by the family of Germans who asked the owner of the enterprise they were staying in where they could place their used batteries for recycling.

Overall, the findings presented in Table 7.1 rather indicate that these enterprises are not proactive in promoting environmental awareness or positive action. On the whole their responses serve to convey what they consider they do which is largely encompassed in general practice. This is best illustrated by

Table 7.1. Environmentally friendly practices promoted.

Response	Enterprises (%)
Encourage attention to environmental issues, e.g. wise use of energy and water	18
Promote walking and/or cycling	14
Encourage use of public transport	10
Promote appreciation and care of the countryside	6
Information is provided in guest rooms	4
Encourage guests to bring back their rubbish for recycling	2

their comments relating to environmental issues which were predominantly all related to encouraging the reduction in use of electricity and water, i.e. towels washed only when necessary; switch off lights, turn off taps, take a shower instead of a bath or the use of room key cards for turning on/off electrical appliances. The increasingly common practice in serviced accommodation in many countries across Europe, for example in Slovenia (Lebe and Zupan, 2012), is to invite guests not to change their towels daily, thus saving on energy, water and pollution. Drawing on other data from the study, approximately 50% of the serviced accommodation enterprises have adopted this practice yet as evident from Table 7.1 relatively few of the owners/managers who operate such a system considered this in response to the question on whether they take any actions to promote environmental awareness and/or environmentally friendly activities. As such, the interpretation of this finding is that the owners/managers see such an action more as a cost saving.

As regards the different categories of enterprises, it was found that attractions proportionally were the most forthcoming citing features such as practices that were promoted to encourage attention and care for the environment including litter bins, 'no litter' signs and educational interpretative material, mainly on the local flora/fauna. Indeed, one respondent who promotes the use of public transport noted that a bin for used tickets is placed by the door so not adding to litter, which evidences attention to small detail but significantly in the process draws attention both to litter and the use of public transport. In comparative terms, guest house operators are the least likely to promote any measures to encourage guests to be environmentally friendly. An alternative perspective on the promotion of EM practices is well conveyed in the following comment from one hotelier, 'Some environmental practices are perceived to detract from a guest's experience.' As the hotelier explained, there was a need for provision of individual toiletries in the bathrooms rather than large dispensers. By and large guests want to be pampered (or to pamper themselves, e.g. spa facilities and services) (see Chapter 3).

Do the Enterprises Encourage Guests to be Environmentally Friendly?

The participants in the study were invited to comment on whether they encouraged their guests to be 'environmentally friendly' in any way. Again few of those who responded 'Yes' (approximately 30%) mentioned guest towels whilst the most frequently cited was the promotion of recycling. Other means mentioned which are not encompassed in other chapters and merit attention are:

- 'We do not provide information on attractions which necessitate the use of a car.'
- 'We charge for gas and electricity consumption.' This comment was made in the context of self-catering. Implicit in the comment is that by charging for consumption, guests will be more aware of their use of energy and thus possibly seek to keep the cost down. Alternatively the owners want to ensure that such consumption does not impact on their operating cost margins.
- 'There are no all-inclusive public transport packages available here. However, bus timetables are available as well as information about the local attractions and the steamers on the lakes.'

There were also some opposite responses; witness the following:

- 'No: we believe the tourist authorities and National Park Authority are doing a good job of promoting environmental awareness.'

And, as one interviewee remarked (though in a different context) to the effect that:

- 'We do not put pressure on tourists about the impact of tourism.'

This raises the question: would tourists really be put off/offended by drawing their attention to potential negative impacts and ways of ameliorating them?

Information of a More General Nature Provided for Guests

Information is one of the keys to influencing patterns of behaviour – most clearly and simply illustrated by 'no smoking' signs in hospitality establishments. However, the latter is now regulation in many countries. A more direct and evidently successful example is as follows: In Venice, there are 13 million plastic water bottles discarded by tourists despite the quality of the local water supply and the fountains provided in the city. This is also a problem in others areas. The region of Cinque Terra, for example, launched a successful marketing campaign with branded reusable bottles and branded fountains in the area, which raised awareness amongst tourists and has reduced the volume of plastic bottles deposited as litter (Venice Tourist and Information Site, 2010). But in reality that is 'there' whilst elsewhere for most tourists it is behave as per usual. Just as a visitor from the UK who smokes will readily have a cigarette in a hospitality enterprise in another country if such activity is not banned. Even so, suggesting how to behave, be that through a code of conduct that could be as simple as 'take only photographs, leave only footprints' or some other method, may well influence behavioural patterns. Therefore, the survey included a broad list of possible material and invited respondents to indicate whether it is available to guests.

The findings were that accommodation enterprises particularly displayed information pamphlets that were readily available – the most common being those on attractions and the least being information on available walks in the area. There was little evidence on the part of the 2011 enterprises of environment related information which might be considered to be expected given their urban locality, possibly not seen to be relevant to the guest's experience but this was also found not to be the case for most of the enterprises involved in the Fringe Study. The one area of special note was that of information on the TCP (see Chapter 3) and the promotion of donating to this scheme (see Chapter 4), which was mentioned by 30% of the enterprises in the 2001 population. In general, every enterprise depends on the environment for its leisure-based custom irrespective of the reason for the visit. The very fact that these enterprises are in such a renowned landscape is sufficient in itself let alone that the majority of visitors are there because of its physical attractiveness. To demonstrate this point: it is well recognized

that environmental concerns have increased amongst the general populace and thus logic dictates also amongst tourists even if whilst they are tourists such concerns are 'left at home'. For example research carried out in 2002 by the Association of British Travel Agents showed that for 87% of respondents it was very important not to damage the environment. Hwang et al. (2005) in their study, based in a national park, make the point that involving visitors more through interpretation, education and so forth increases visitor satisfaction and also significantly increases their attachment in the sense of 'place' and potentially perhaps in the longer term and wider context – in a sense 'take home' (Ballantyne et al., 2010). Theoretically at least, this would encourage concern for maintaining the quality of that environment. Furthermore it is not as if the information provided on the TCP is in any way discouraging visitors; for example, as to where or where not to go with regard to conservation initiatives. As Raffaele (2003) found in his study of the town of Denham that is heavily dependent on tourists who are visiting mainly for the sole purpose of seeing and possibly feeding the dolphins at the shoreline. But at times there are too many visitors and despite the promotion of other attractions, e.g. Woomarel Banks, a World Heritage site, within the locality of Denham, many of them do not visit other areas nearby. Furthermore, Wurzinger and Johansson (2006) carried out a study into environmental concern among three groups of Swedish tourists. Based on the results of the research they suggested that there exists a relation between the extent of the focus on nature in the trip and the basic level of environmental concern. The higher level of natural aspects in holidays, the higher awareness of environmental protection among tourists. Why so comparatively few of the tourism enterprises in the LDNP did not (and still do not) promote this lauded initiative is a major concern and all the more so in the context of sustainability.

The point made in Chapter 6 on the awareness or rather lack of information on the availability of local produce and products was found to apply also to the range of literature, visitor information pamphlets on walking, cycling and the availability/use of public transport within and around the area identified by rural enterprises as not being available. The findings also established there were wide differences within any one category of enterprise and that no one category was consistently different from any of the others, further reinforcing the view that such awareness is not a function of the enterprise business but rather that of the owner/manager's interests and attitudes. It appears that these enterprises take little opportunity to inform, let alone advise, guests on environmentally friendly practices or indeed local produce and crafts and practices. This may be because so many of their customers are from within the UK but more likely this reflects a lack of consideration, especially for example in the LDNP which gains many international visitors. In contrast Mensah's (2009) study into the environmental performance of hotels in Ghana found the very opposite, with slightly more on average than 50% of the hotels providing guests with information and advice in both these areas. Possibly the reason for the difference is that the latter gain many foreign and diverse customers. Though Gaunt's (2004) study also found a comparatively better performance, with 42% of small tour operators in Scotland saying they seek to raise awareness of environmental issues amongst their clients; and, though to a lesser extent, Vernon et al. (2005). However, the enterprises do perform better than that found by Erdogan (2009) and are similar to Carlsen et al. (2001). The one exception between the categories and the only category to promote local products and produce was found to be the owners of self-catering properties; 82% indicated they provide information on where to shop for local produce and 75% on outlets for local crafts.

On the basis of these findings and, as noted, those of similar research, there appears to be little commitment on the part of tourism enterprises to doing this. Yes, one may argue that national and particularly MNCs involved in tourism are apparently doing far more as manifest in their promotional material and PR, perhaps none more evidently so than TUI. According to TUI, the company aims to encourage responsive actions in reducing energy and water consumption, e.g. packing lightly;

taking shorter showers when on holiday. Further: 'Taking care of the environment and learning about local cultures is now well established as part of Kids' Clubs activities in Thomson and First Choice resorts' (TUI, 2011, p. 2) – an approach which certainly supports the need to address the demand side and in this to educate tourists, thus consumers.

Overall the outcome of this aspect of the study rather indicates that the owners/managers for the most part do not think that they have a role in influencing their customers' environmental awareness and behaviour except when it directly involves their own operation. What is promoted appears to be more a measure of the attitudes and interests of the owners/managers and thus it is not surprising that relatively little is done given the limited attention to EM and CSR outside of energy consumption on the part of many of these enterprises. However, such speculation does raise the question of does it matter? In this instance, does it matter to the majority of visitors – are they interested?

Are They Interested?

In much the same way as with SSCM and more broadly under the umbrella of responsible tourism, tourism enterprises are encouraged through a range of tourism policy initiatives and professional agencies to influence their customers and, more widely, visitors by promoting EM practices and potentially thereby influencing their environmental behaviour. The key question here is – are they really interested?

In the course of the study, the owners/managers had many opportunities to offer their own views/comments on any of the areas within the survey and interviews. One of the most fruitful areas was that section designed to investigate their attitudes and perceptions (see Chapter 9). Within this area, it became apparent that many owners/managers did not consider that there was a clear demand for EMS accreditation etc., as illustrated here in two of the responses to the question, 'What factors may discourage you from adopting more environmentally friendly practices':

- '90% of tourists would not adjust their holiday arrangements for environmental issues.'
- 'Guests are not interested.'

Significantly, 87% of respondents 'agreed' to 'strongly agreed' that tourists are not interested in the impacts of tourism on the environment. Around the time of the first stage of the study, the findings of Fairweather et al.'s (2005) study rather supported this outcome that tourists are not that interested, and also by the outcomes of a survey of tourists in Scotland (Anderson et al., 2001) which found that of those surveyed, 67% could not say whether or not they had stayed in accredited green accommodation and 70% indicated that 'it did not matter' to them. However, 18% did say they researched potential accommodation to establish those with green policies prior to deciding where to actually stay. But no more than 7% considered this was important when it came to deciding their choice of accommodation, with location, facilities and price all ranking higher.

These findings merit further consideration and thus the discussion now moves to consider first, indication that tourists are interested, followed by contradictory indication and second, seeking to gain a better understanding to bring into contention a range of wider aspects.

Indications of Interest and Responsive Action

Over the period of the study there have been a number of articles suggesting that tourists are concerned about environmental matters and that this can influence their choice of tour operator or accommodation and potentially that they are prepared to pay a higher price. Such articles were especially noted in the early 2000s, the most cited of which is Tearfund's (2002) report, which evidently contributed to another cited study, namely Goodwin and Francis (2003) who commented that 45% of those surveyed were prepared to pay extra for preserving the local environment and a similar percentage prepared to pay an additional cost of between £5-£10; that is with all other things being equal. Also, those TOs with clear,

responsible tourism practices would gain business over those without. Albeit in the wider context of destinations, Kelly et al.'s (2007) study into the preferences of tourists regarding the introduction of additional fees for services found some support and, as they expressed it, a degree of tolerance, but noted that such tolerance declined as the scale of fee increases and where such fees are imposed this would not necessarily change behavioural patterns. An outcome similar to that reported by TUI, which undertook customer research and found that 96% of holidaymakers polled care about protecting the local environment and wildlife in the resorts they visit. A further 83% said they appreciate advice from a tour operator on how to make their holiday more environmentally and socially responsible when they are abroad and 73% want to be able to easily identify a 'greener holiday' (TUI, 2010). Further to these findings, a Lonely Planet survey of 24,500 consumers from 144 countries found that 93% of people said they want to take part in environmentally friendly travel in the future.

On choice of accommodation:

- Vaughn and Allen (2007) found that approximately half of the consumers they surveyed said that they take environmental issues into consideration when booking a holiday whilst 75% said that they believed that an enterprise with green credentials led to a better quality of service (similarly Han et al., 2010; Lee et al., 2010).
- The Market Metrix Hospitality index found that CSR programmes are attractive and were considered to be important to the more affluent customer (Anon., 2010, p. 2).

On paying a premium:

- According to a Trip Advisor poll 38% said that environmentally friendly tourism is a consideration when travelling and a similar percentage were prepared to pay more to stay in environmentally friendly hotels, the premium being identified to be between 5% and 10% (Dodds, 2008).
- According to the Market Metrix Hospitality index (Anon., 2010, p. 1) 'Guests who rank a hotel's green programme highly are willing to pay at least 7% more for their

room compared to other guests.' (see also Dodds, 2008).

- InterContinental Hotels argue that 40% of their priority club members select hotels on the basis of their environmental credentials (Anon., 2010, p. 3).
- Fairweather et al.'s (2005) study findings were that tourists may be prepared to pay a premium of between 3.4% and 7.2% (similarly Tukker et al., 2010).

To such findings it might be added that attitudes vary between different societies, for example Germans, Dutch and Scandinavians are generally more environmentally aware, are sympathetic towards 'environmentalism' and may be prepared to pay more for services which demonstrate related practices. Further to which there is a raft of reports from Mintel over the past decade on tourists and tourism which note that many, many consumers/tourists are very positive when asked about their attitudes to supporting destination environments, the local culture, EM practices and so forth but invariably such support is couched in terms of 'prepared to', 'are willing to' and 'prefer' rather than actually have done or do (see Leslie, 2012).

Contrary Indications

These indications that tourists actually do pay more for green accredited enterprises have been brought into question by a number of commentators, a recent example being Ottman and Terry in a green gauge report in the USA (Roberts and Hall, 2001, p. 21). Further, 67% of American travellers considered an increased price for accredited green accommodation to be a barrier (Dodds, 2008) and comparatively less affluent tourists do not support such an additional cost (Anon., 2010). Whilst it might be a lesser consideration by the more affluent, a key point here is that the more affluent a consumer is the more resources they consume. Nor is it a given that they will pay additional fees for environmental initiatives, as Nepal (2007) found from his research in that despite the tourists involved indicating a general level of satisfaction with their tour in Nepal's Annapurna region, this did not mean

that they would support the payment of an 'eco-fee'.

Studies into the influential factors in holiday planning invariably find that cost is the most important consideration in the holiday purchase (Sharpley, 2009; TUI, 2010; see also Lockyer, 2005); an outcome which appears generally applicable across all socio-economic groups (see Francis, 2008). This is further supported by the continued popularity of 'all inclusive' resorts and cruises, both of which enable the consumer to more quickly assess the cost of their holiday; to which one might add the growth in attention to 'last minute deals' and greater use of the Internet to seek out the best deals on price. Further questions also arise over the actual influence of eco-labels in visitor choice, as illustrated by McKenna et al.'s (2010) research into the influence of Blue Flag awards for beaches which identified that they are hardly of significance compared with factors of proximity, available activities and scenic value.

A particularly interesting observation, and all the more significant by its absence from many of the studies arguing that tourists will contribute to a particular scheme and/or want green tourism enterprises, is a lack of inclusion of a question based around 'what if the price of a destination/TO package to that destination increased?' On the basis of the foregoing comment then the expected answer would be that tourists would opt for a different albeit similar destination. This significance of cost is well portrayed in the outcry that arose over the imposition of a 'tourist tax' in the Balearic Islands, revenues from which were to be used to support conservation measures. Both tour operators offering package holidays to the islands and tourism enterprises within complained, arguing that this would cause a decline in demand. According to one report, tourist demand dropped by 20% following the introduction of the tax (Brown, 2003). The tax was promptly rescinded following national elections leading to a change in government. This case illustrates that both TOs and local tourism enterprises involved clearly do not consider that tourists are prepared to pay extra even when such marginal additional cost is, in part at least, presented as a means of supporting environmental initiatives. A further example of tourists not paying an extra cost on the basis of environmental impacts is that of carbon offsetting (see Chapter 8).

A logical step on from this is to raise the question of 'why do people go on holiday?' Certainly there are many reasons but common threads are; to escape, to get away for a few days and relax, to which could be added because it is expected (by peers) and in many societies it is taken as a given, very much a part of the annual cycle of activities. As Weaver (2005, p. 170) states 'individuals take vacations to escape their own problems and hardships temporarily'. Going on holiday is considered to be a positive satisfaction, contributing to a general sense of well-being; as Gilbert and Abdullah (2004, p. 118) argue 'people travel because they have been motivated by some felt needs, which are psychological in nature and can only be satisfied by tourism activity.' Perhaps it is more the case today in post-industrialized society that people 'travel to different sorts of places seeking different distractions because they are tired of soft living and always seek after something which eludes them' (Seneca c.BC4–AD65, cited in Leslie, 1987, p. 3). Combine these views with the perception that to holiday is a 'right' then it is difficult to understand why a tourist would be (and as some commentators suggest, should be) some sort of environmental anthropologist. As Krippendorf (1987, p. 42) so eloquently put it 'The tourist is his own advocate and not an international ambassador; he is not there to aid development or protect the environment.' Overall, one may well suggest that perhaps people do not care about their impact and see it as a right to go on holiday regardless.

It might be argued that such green consumerism manifests itself in the demand for ecotourism, that is ecotourism which adheres to the principles and criteria as laid down by the International Ecotourism Society and ideally accredited as such. This category of tourism may after all be as self-indulgent as any other category of tourism, which is 'about tourists spending their leisure time in a way that gives them the benefits they seek' (Swarbrooke and Horner, 2007, p. 208). Therefore by way of furthering discussion the attention turns to consider ecotourists. Holden and Sparrowhawk (2002) identified key traits

of ecotourists as attitude and education, noting that generally they are of comparatively higher education attainment and more affluent. They argue that in terms of maintaining the quality of the environment and the experience there is a need to give more consideration to the type of tourist attracted. To an extent this is true but there is an assumption in this that ecotourists are all similar in their attitudes and values and different from other tourists. But are they? For example, the profile of attendees at birding festivals (some of which are promoted as ecotourism) is very similar to that of ecotourists – comparatively higher educational attainment, above average income and evident pro-environmental concerns and attitudes (Lawton and Weaver, 2009). Ecotourism has been criticised for its negative impacts, especially in the context of more remote, more fragile environments which hardly reflects well on the participants, the ecotourists (for example, McLaren, 1998; Redclift, 2001; Honey, 2008). Duffy (2002 cited in Carrier and Macleod, 2005, p. 322) takes this a stage further by arguing that they '"pretend to rough it" for their own self-esteem and conscience' and that the majority of ecotourists do not consider the impacts of their trip. More recently, Sharpley (2006) argued that eco-tourists are not any more concerned about environment than the mainstream tourist. Certainly, as Zografos and Allcroft (2007) commented, environmental attitudes amongst ecotourists are found to be highly variable, which highlights that as always there are exceptions.

A simplistic illustration perhaps, but to put a perspective on the choice of environmental concern going away – getting a suntan – the increasing demand for sun-based holidays may be seen to conflict with concern over melanoma skin cancer which has been steadily rising in the UK (Anon., 2005). As Tiscali (2007) identifies, 67% of the British holidaymakers do not even think about the impact their trips could have on the environment; and tourists more generally (Bestard and Nadal, 2007). Enjoying the sun in the Maldives or Caribbean seems to be the most important and desirable aspect of holidays. Furthermore how else can one explain the continued popularity of sand, sun and sea holidays? If consumers/tourists were truly concerned over the impact of their holiday on the environment then basically they would not take one but rather stay at home.

The Wider Context

By far the major support for the view that tourists not only support environmental initiatives but also are prepared to pay an additional cost for such environmental actions, predominantly comes from visitor and consumer surveys. The key point of this is that what people say they do in surveys is often not manifest in practice, suggesting that people seek to respond appropriately, i.e. support what they perceive to be environmentally positive behaviour. Thus what they 'ought to do' rather than that which they actually do. There is little doubt that generally participants in consumer or tourist surveys will tend to say what they consider to be the 'right' response, in effect to agree with 'expected behaviour'. This is especially true when it comes to questions that involve no commitment to action, e.g. 'would you' rather than 'have you'. Additionally, there is also the factor that whilst a respondent might well like to do X, other criteria may often have a stronger influence. Hence, for example, the situation arises from consumer surveys on buying organic produce that when the data are extrapolated in terms of indicative sales, actual sales of organic food produce are far lower. An outcome that has been described in various ways; for example Weaver (2011) calls this 'veneer environmentalism' or the green values gap, whilst the WWF (2008), and perhaps more clearly, described it as the 'attitude behaviour gap'.

This is not to say that there is not a clear market for what consumers generally perceive as environmentally friendly goods. Indeed, the ethically active consumer market in developed countries has been assessed to be between 12% and 30% (OCA, 2006). But the size and strength of this market will vary and is not always, it appears, necessarily related to the state of the wider economy. A regular survey of public attitudes to quality of life and the environment found in 2002 that participation in pro-environmental behaviours was lower

than in 1996 (DEFRA, 2002). But there is no escaping from the fact that environmentalism support in any guise does rise during periods of affluence in any society and equally declines during recessionary times (Leslie, 2012), which may in part at least explain the outcome of a survey of small businesses that found that many consider that customers will not pay higher prices for environmentally friendly goods or services and indeed the number saying 'yes' had declined since 2007 (Greenbiz, 2009); a decline which might partly be attributed to the prevailing economic recession of the time. However, whilst consumers may evidence increased concern over the environment and awareness and actions, e.g. recycling – there is little evidence of this on the part of tourists. As Cotterill *et al.* (2002) argued 'green' behaviour at home does not indicate similar behaviour away – in other words there is no evidence of a relationship (see Whitmarsh and O'Neill, 2010; Leslie, 2012). For example, a survey of householders' environmental attitudes found that 80% of participants were not willing to reduce their holiday flights and indicated that they were far more likely to do positive actions in the home, e.g. reduce water consumption, walk rather than take the car, if a short walk (Energy Savings Trust, 2007). In general people will not give up or change a behavioural pattern unless it is easy or convenient to do so. Rarely will they go beyond the first few steps – for example, change to low energy light bulbs or recycle waste material (see Jackson *et al.*, 2009).

A further consideration regarding the environmental behaviour of people is that this generally varies according to such demographic factors as age. Darnton (2004) notes the general trend as that older people give higher priority to and have more positive attitudes, whilst 18–25 year olds are the most likely to say they have no time for environmental or social issues and teenagers evidence even less concern, less interest and find such generally 'boring' (similarly, DEFRA, 2002). The significance here is whether these differences between groups is a factor of age or of the society within which they grow up, leading to speculation that as people get older they become more environmentally concerned but alternatively will those currently less than 36 years old continue to evidence less concern than their current older contemporaries.

The question of whether tourists are interested in the environmental impact of their trips, be this of the mode of transportation, the tourism enterprises which seek to cater to them or the wider environment of the destination, brings into consideration whether they are that interested in their destination's wider environment, be this a rural location or a well developed and thus urbanized seaside resort. For example and in general, are they interested in the flora and fauna? According to Cotterill et al.'s (2002) research this does not rank that highly compared with other factors such as local culture and local products. Even then, it is argued, many tourists are not that interested in the local people and culture – as Atkins noted from his visits to Cornwall, Bahamas and Trinidad 'I also met a lot of holiday-makers who scoffed at the idea that they should feel obliged to pay attention to the people and places around them' (Atkins, 2010, p. 3). Further, just how far do the tourists in such locations go away from their cosseted touristic environments?

A weakness of many of the more cited studies is a lack of background on the research itself. It is easy to ignore the mere fact that as regards leisure tourists (excluding Visiting Friends and Relatives (VFR)) it is the actual attraction of the physical environment that mostly draws the tourist not, as recently attested by Bradley (2010), the green credentials of the TO or the accommodation provider. At best, these may be considerations after where to go and the cost. Furthermore, perceptions of the attractiveness of the destination are open to interpretation in that tourists may evidence little notice of change over time when returning to a popular destination, as Gulez (1994) reported on a survey into the perceptions of tourists visiting the same tourist resort, undertaken in 1977 and 1989. He found that the only significant difference was a drop by 5% of visitors considering the nature of the area was unspoiled. As with any resource, demand must be managed and in the sense that the Earth is not a free good, so too tourism. Development and globalization have speeded up communication and with it so too has the opportun-

ity for the more affluent to visit almost anywhere (Crowley, 1998). The 'haves' in this world are not prepared to 'go without'; well, perhaps not at least until the next person follows suit. Meanwhile the 'have nots' understandably want what the 'haves' have. It appears that achieving some balance between tourism consumerism and sustainability will be 'mission impossible' (Johns and Leslie, 2008) until there is some prolonged significant change. Consequently how, if in any way, are they altering their decision-making process and behavioural patterns to adapt to current impacts and help mitigate or reduce their long-term impacts (Johns and Leslie, 2008)?

All of which rather echoes Isaak's (1997, p. 80) observation that:

> Globalisation contracts time and space and stimulates a sense of placelessness and everything everywhere, resulting in widespread short-term material gratification regardless of the consequences for future generations.

This is so well illustrated by resorts that are hot spots for '18–30s' holidays, e.g. Faliraki on the island of Rhodes, Greece; Ayia Napa, Cyprus; or Magaluf, Majorca. Young people enjoying themselves away from the gaze of their family at home, who manifestly demonstrate that behavioural patterns do not change, only the circumstance to constrain or ease. As Jackson (2005) established, tourists tend to conform to their usual 'environmental' behaviour [whether environmentally friendly or not] while on holiday, i.e. being in a different environment tends to have little effect on behavioural patterns (Jackson, 2005). In the late 1980s, Sherman (1988) berated the influx of tourists and attendant problems caused in the context of government subsidy and promotion, questioning the costs and benefits. His diatribe resonates all too well with places such as Faliraki. In this context one can well understand Calder's (1999) anecdote when he cites the story of 'A dissatisfied, rowdy audience was faced by Joni Mitchell, who said "Hey Man! – You're all behaving like tourists!" – the crowd went quiet!' There is little to doubt that 'Tourism corrodes and weakens national identity' (Minhinnick, 1993, p. 36). Witness tourists on popular package holidays who when asked where they had been might well say 'I don't know, went by plane' (Sykes, 1995, p. 15); exaggerated perhaps, but many tourists evidenced little knowledge of the place, in this instance Mallorca, particularly outside of their tourist 'enclave'. Furthermore, a view which is furthered by Ritzer (2000, p. 77) on the subject of package tours, who argues that 'devotees of package tours are hard-pressed to tell their friends very much about the countries they have visited or the sights they saw.' In developed resorts they may well cause less environmental harm than niche market eco or adventure tourists. As Courtney (1993) opined:

> The package holidaymakers do no lasting damage, except possibly to themselves by over-indulging in beer, sex and ultraviolet rays. The prime function of the locals is to exploit the holidaymaker to the full – possibly it is they, the holidaymakers, who should be protected from locals. At least that is the right way round. Nor are the locals in resorts being corrupted by their visitors. They are far too busy taking those hard-earned savings off them – and looking forward to the off-season when they lead their own lives – to worry about such excesses.

He continues '… Allow the rich, as they have done for centuries, to buy their own exclusivity. But, above all, leave the package holiday to those to whom it is geared.' To which should be added that given the ongoing efforts of TOs, their CSR, SSCM and EM initiatives and so forth combined with those of the hotel companies involved, then these resorts are potentially if not actually more in tune with environmental actions and sustainability than many niche tourism products. Furthermore, they are supported in the process through comparatively better regulation and the necessary supporting infrastructure.

Undoubtedly most international holidays involve popular destinations facilitated by TOs, but also notably so in the case of Europe, by low cost airlines. The destinations available are very much a matter of supply thus suppliers' costs and therefore economies of scale are substantial factors and thus so too demand. In this sense many places are 'self-perpetuating'. Witness the long-term popularity of resorts along the northern coast of the Mediterranean Sea and the Caribbean isles. Conversely there are niche products as, for example, presented in the The

Ethical Travel Guide (Pattullo and Minelli, 2006). The latter brings to attention one final wider consideration, namely that of the 'new tourist' who is more discerning and seeking authentic experiences. The foregoing discussion rather brings this into question given the continuing and increasing popularity of resorts, all-inclusive holidays and cruises. Certainly there are some tourists seeking something which they perceive as more authentic but how far are they prepared to accept such authenticity? To illustrate: invariably 'the authentic' in tourism is discussed in the context of local culture but rarely if at all in terms of accommodation provision for example. Do tourists really want authentic accommodation presented according to the norms of the local populace with the correlating sanitary facilities? Arguably not, as Nepal's (2007) study into ecotourists and their accommodation facilities in Nepal's Annapurna region found. Whilst there were complaints that some accommodation operations were disappointing in that they were similar to those in more commercialized destinations, dissatisfaction was expressed over sanitation and cleanliness issues. Nepal argues that there is a need to address sanitation and hygiene issues. Would this be counter to the authenticity of the tourists' experience or is it more the reality that they expect that such facilities are basically the same as they are used to in their home environments?

Conclusion

Overall, these tourism enterprises in general do not promote environmental awareness and action and those operations which do tend to promote energy conservation. Some accommodation enterprises do seek to promote public transport to their guests and visitors, though in rural areas such access is not always easy and in some cases very difficult given a lack of services. Even then when at the destination, tourists will find problems in getting around in many localities, especially if less able and/or with young children. However, it is notable that the continuing popularity of cycling is apparent from the number of audited enterprises in rural localities that provide bicycle storage areas.

There is a general lack of information provided on the enterprises' green credentials, yet many provide a wide range of standard promotional material for visitors (presumably on the basis that they consider such information would be of interest to their customers). This leads to speculation that those EM practices they have implemented and indeed whether or not they have EMS accreditation is considered by the owners to be more of an internal matter; on costs, savings, etc. (allowing for possible promotional value on their website and brochures, with the exception of room cards and promoting to not change towels daily.) What is inescapable from the research is that the majority of enterprises practising EM, and though to a lesser extent CSR, were doing so irrespective of external policies and initiatives. Also that some of the practices of those operations which were part of a larger company were very much a function of internal policy.

In many ways these findings are not to be unexpected, as in reality the owners/managers are not in the business of environmental education; that is seeking to educate their customers by way of raising their awareness and influencing their behaviour. Even so, what might be considered surprising is that those enterprises which are most proactive in EM and CSR do not appear to consider promoting such activity more, given the higher profile that environmental concerns and green consumerism has gained over the last 20 years. This is well illustrated by the TCP, which is undoubtedly a successful visitor payback scheme, which aims to redress damage to the physical environment caused by visitors, e.g. wear and tear of trails. An environment that is quintessential to the very attractiveness which draws customers to these enterprises, it is evident from the findings that this scheme is not supported by many an enterprise and further many of those which do, did not mention it in response to open questions where such reference would have been expected. This leads to speculation that some owners/ managers join the scheme because other enterprises have done so, rather than because they are personally committed and thus actively support, and others who are not involved are just not interested, perhaps seeing it not relevant to their customers (i.e. their business)

and/or seeing it as something of a 'bother' explaining to customers the scheme and seeking their support, e.g. 'no time for that'. Certainly it is true that many visitors do not opt to donate, which itself opens up another debate and apart from any other considerations indicates that whilst some surveys may indicate that tourists are willing to pay, in reality many do not. Yet the way it is promoted very much meets such criteria for success as meeting the '... concepts of immediacy, transience and wider societal concerns' (England, 2010, p. 13); the 'message' being locally relevant, personal and shows how their support will be beneficial to the locality and wider community. However, the limited support by both the enterprises and the visitors supports Holden's (2009, p. 381) query of '... what evidence is there of a strong enough environmental ethic in the tourism market to influence demand?' All of which reflects the wider argument that 'environmental education of consumers and increasing environmental awareness does not stimulate environmentally responsible behaviour.' (Sasidharan et al., 2002, p. 172; see also Kelly et al., 2007). Even then, changing behaviour is 'likely to have only a modest effect.' (Cairncross, 1995, p. 177).

Tourism is an area of discretionary expenditure but increasingly appears to be expectation based – greatly influenced by peer pressure and marketing – not a 'need' but a 'want', as holidays are increasingly taken as the norm in the annual cycle of life. Such consumption:

> has to be recognised as an integral part of the same social system that accounts for the drive to work, itself part of the social need to relate to other people, and to have mediating materials for relating to them. (Douglas and Isherwood, 1978, p. 5)

Thus for a tourist to mitigate their conscience (if applicable) it is easier for them to think in terms of 'What difference will I make?' and thus to 'pass the buck' to someone else to take responsibility, instead of taking responsibility for their own actions. As such, one of the difficulties (if not a barrier) is the 'I will if you will' syndrome (see SCRT, 2006). This is equally applicable to the tourism enterprises and their owners/managers.

In conclusion, concern over impacts relating to tourism on the part of consumers/tourists appears strong in words but weak in terms of touristic actions, what they say is not matched by what they do. It is clear from the momentum built up that everyone will have to play their part and the pain suffered by individuals in making changes will vary depending upon their current lifestyle and the policies and strategies implemented by government and related agencies. Without their leadership, i.e. regulation, it would appear the majority of consumers will continue to say they are aware and supportive of initiatives designed to address negative impacts, CSR activity etc., while in practice they will carry on behaving the way they are today using a suitable excuse, if required, to assuage their consciences. The level of enjoyment may be so great that this outweighs the feeling of guilt over the impact of their decisions. Witness the ongoing rise in demand for 'doom tourism', i.e. visit places in the world before they are gone, e.g. Antarctica!

Further Reading

For a seminal discussion on consumerism – see Douglas and Isherwood, B. (1978) *The World of Goods: towards an anthropology of consumption*. Pelican, Harmondsworth, UK.

On the reactions of local communities to 'intrusive' tourism development – Boissevain, J. (ed.) (1996) *Coping with Tourists: European reactions to mass tourism*. Berghahn Books, Oxford, UK.

On interactions between tourists, community and destinations – see Abram, S., Waldren, J. and MacLeod, D.V.L. (eds) (1997) *Tourists and Tourism: Identifying with People and Places*. Berg, Oxford, UK.

References

Anderson, A., Donachie, E., Elsby, J. and Erskine, L. (2001) Is the service accommodation sector in Scotland 'Going Green'? Tourism Project, BA (Hons) Tourism Management, Glasgow Caledonian University, Glasgow, UK, May.

Anon. (1989) Who knows what consumers are thinking. *The Grocer* 18 November, p. 17.

Anon. (2005) Sunbathing 'more dangerous than terrorism or crime'. Travel Section, *The Daily Telegraph*. p. 4.

Anon. (2010) What do customers Care. *Green Hotelier* Issue 52.

Atkins, R. (2010) What's it like to live with tourists. Travel Section. *The Guardian* 20 April, p. 2.

Ballantyne, R., Packer, J. and Falk, J. (2010) Visitors' learning for environmental sustainability: testing short- and long-term impacts of wildlife tourism experiences using structural equation modelling. *Tourism Management* 32, 1243–1252.

Bestard, A.B. and Nadal, J.R. (2007) Modelling environmental attitudes toward tourism. *Tourism Management* 28, pp. 688–695.

Bradley, J. (2010) *Drive to cash in on surge in demand for 'green' Scots tourism* [online] Edinburgh: news. scotsman.com. Available at http://news.scotsman.com/contactus.aspx (accessed 11th March 2011).

Brown, T. (2003) Holiday Isles scrap 'ecotax'. *The Daily Telegraph*. 14 July, p. 12.

Cairncross, F. (1995) *Green, Inc.: a guide to business and the environment*. Earthscan, London.

Calder, S. (1999) Banana pancakes and itchy feet – a short history of back-packing. *High Life*, British Airways, London, December, pp. 40–45.

Carlsen, J., Getz, D. and Ali-Knight, J. (2001) The environmental attitudes and practices of family run businesses in the rural tourism and hospitality sectors. *Journal of Sustainable Tourism* 9 (4), 281–297.

Carrier, J.G. and Macleod, D.V.L. (2005) Bursting the bubble: the socio-cultural context of ecotourism, *Journal of the Royal Anthropological Institute* 11 (2), 315–334.

Cole, P. (1999) Tourism – Wales' Most Sustainable Industry?, Paper by Managing Director of Tourism, South and West Wales, 19 January.

Cotterill, S., Van der Duim, R., Ankersind, P. and Kelder, L. (2002) Measuring Sustainability of Tourism in M. Antonio Quepos and Texel: A Tourist Perspective. Paper presented at ATLAS Conference, Estoril, November.

Courtney, N. (1993) The Last gasp: in defence of the package tour, in Wish you were here! *New Internationalist* Special Edition No. 245, p. 31.

Crowley, K. (1998) 'Glocalisation' and Ecological Modernity: challenges for local environmental governance in Australia. *Local Environment* 3(1), 91–97.

CTB (1998) Providing for People with Disabilities. *The Regional Tourism Strategy for Cumbria*, Cumbria Tourist Board, Cumbria Para. 41.

Cummings, L.E. (1997) Waste minimisation supporting urban tourism sustainability: A mega-resort case study. *Journal of Sustainable Tourism* 5 (2), 93–108.

Darnton, A. (2004) *Driving public behaviours for sustainable lifestyles*. Report for DEFRA, London, May.

DEFRA (2002) *Survey of public attitudes to quality of life and to the environment 2001*. News Release, Department for Environment Food and Rural Affairs, London, 9 October.

Dodds R. (2008) *Assessing the Demand for Sustainable Tourism* [online] Montréal: The Quebec source for information on global trends in international tourism. Available from: http://tourismintelligence. ca/2008/04/04/assessing-the-demand-for-sustainable-tourism/ (accessed 11th March 2011).

Douglas, M. and Isherwood, B. (1978) *The World of Goods: towards an anthropology of consumption*. Pelican, Harmondsworth, UK.

Elkington, J. (1989) Why it pays to be green. *Financial Times,* 14 October, p. 7.

Energy Savings Trust (2007) *Green barometer: measuring environmental attitudes*. Energy Saving Trust, London.

England, R. (2010) Unraveling the psychology of recycling. *Resource* 56 November/December, pp. 11–13.

Environment Council (2000) Greening the Supply Chain: The Route to Environmental Improvement? Environment Council Conference, London, 11 May.

Erdogan, N. (2009) Turkey's tourism policy and environmental performance of tourism enterprises. In: Leslie, D. (ed.) *Tourism Enterprises and sustainable development: International perspectives on responses to the sustainability agenda*. Routledge, New York, pp. 194–208.

Fairweather, J.R., Maslin, C. and Simmons, D.G. (2005) Environmental values and responses to ecolabels among international visitors to New Zealand. *Journal of Sustainable Tourism* 13 (1), 82–98.

Francis, J. (2008) Comment. Telegraph Travel, *The Daily Telegraph* 14 June, p. 14.

Gaunt, S. (2004) An analysis of environmental awareness among tour operators in Scotland. Unpublished dissertation, BA (Hons) International Travel with Information Systems. Glasgow Caledonian University, Glasgow, UK.

Gilbert, D. and Abdullah, J. (2004) Holidaytaking and the sense of well-being. *Annals of Tourism Research* 31 (1), pp. 103–121.

Goodwin, H. and Francis, J. (2003) Ethical and responsible tourism – consumer trends in the U.K. *Journal of Vacation Marketing* 9 (3), 271–284.

Greenbiz (2009) *Most small Biz owners say customers won't pay more for Green*. Available at http://www. greenbiz.com/news/ (accessed 21 June 2009).

Gulez, S. (1994) Green Tourism: a case study. *Annals of Tourism Research* 21 (2), 413–415.

Gustin, M.E. and Weaver, P.A. (1996) Are hotels prepared for the envirin0oemtnal consumer? *Hospitality Research Journal* 20 (2), pp. 1–14.

Han, H.S., Hsu, L.T. and Lee, J.-S. (2009) Empirical investigation of the roles of attitudes toward green behaviours, overall image, gender, and age in hotel customers' eco-friendly decision-making process. *International Journal of Hospitality Management* 28 (4), pp. 519–528.

Holden, A. (2009) The environment-tourism nexus. *Annals of Tourism Research* 36 (3), 373–389.

Holden, A. and Sparrowhawk, J. (2002) Understanding the motivations of ecotourists: the case of trekkers in Annapurna, Nepal. *International Journal of Tourism Research* 4, pp. 435–446.

Honey, M. (2008) *Ecotourism and Sustainable Development: Who owns Paradise?* 2nd edn. Island Press, Washington, DC.

Hwang, S.-N., Lee, C. and Chen, H.-J. (2005) The relationship among tourists' involvement, place attachment and interpretation satisfaction in Taiwan's national parks. *Tourism Management* 26 (2), 143–156.

Infor (2008) *Performance Management Strategies: creating social and financial value by Going Green.* Alpharetta, Georgia. Info, February.

Isaak, R. (1997) Globalisation and Green Entrepreneurship. *Greener Management International* 18 Summer, pp. 80–90.

Jackson, B., Lee-Woolf, C., Higginson, F., Wallace, J. and Agathou, N. (2009) *Strategies for reducing the climate impacts of red meat/dairy consumption in the UK*. Report for the Worldwide Fund for Nature, Imperial College, London, March.

Jackson, T. (2005) *Motivating Sustainable Consumption – a review of evidence on consumer behaviour and behavioural change*. Centre for Environmental Strategy. University of Surrey, Surrey, UK.

Johns, C. and Leslie, D. (2008) Leisure Consumers of Air Miles – the unlikelihood of change. In: Leslie, D. (Guest Ed.) Leisure, Consumerism and Sustainable Development: 'Mission Impossible'. *Leisure Studies Newsletter* 80, pp. 35–38.

Kelly, J., Haider, W., Williams, P.W. and Englund, K. (2007) Stated preferences of tourists for eco-efficient destination planning options. *Tourism Management* 28, 377–390.

Krippendorf, J. (1987) *The Holidaymakers.* Heinemann, Oxford, UK.

Lawton, L.J. and Weaver, D.B. (2009) Normative and innovative resources management at birding festivals. *Tourism Management* 31 (3), 527–536.

Lebe, S.S. and Zupan, S. (2012) From eco-ignorance to eco-certificates: Environmental management in Slovene hotels. In: Leslie, D. (ed.) *Tourism Enterprises and the Sustainability Agenda across Europe.* New Directions in Tourism Analysis. Ashgate, Farnham, UK, pp. 135–150.

Lee, J.S., Hsu, L.-T.J., Han, H. and Kim, Y. (2010) Understanding how consumers view green hotels: How a hotel's green image can influence behavioural intentions. *Journal of Sustainable Tourism* 18 (7), 901–914.

Leidner, R. (2004) T*he European Tourism industry – a multi-sector with dynamic markets. Structures, developments and importance for Europe's economy.* European Commission, Enterprise DG (Unit D.3) Publications, Brussels.

Leslie, D. (1987) Of leisure, tourism and tourists. In: McDowell, D. and Leslie, D. (eds) *Planning for Tourism and Leisure.* University of Ulster, Jordanstown, UK, May, pp. 2–6.

Leslie, D. (1991) Leisure policy and practice revisited: How green is your party? In: Botterill, D. and Tomlinson, A. (eds) *Ideology, Leisure Policy, and Practice.* Brighton Leisure Studies Association, Spring.

Leslie, D. (2012) The consumers of tourism. In: Leslie, D. (2012) *Responsible Tourism: Concepts, Theory and Practice.* CAB International, Wallingford, UK, pp. 54–71.

Lim, N. (1996) To Take a Stand: The greening of tourism. *Business World* (Philippines), p. 4.

Lockyer, T. (2005) The perceived importance of price as one hotel selection dimension. *Tourism Management* 26 (4), 529–537.

Martin, A. (1998) Tourism, the environment and consumers. *The Environment Papers Series* 2 (2), 24–32.

Masau, P. and Prideaux, B. (2003) Sustainable tourism: a role for Kenya's hotel industry. *Current Issues in Tourism* 6 (3), 197–208.

McBoyle, G. (1996) Industrial tourism and greenness: the example of Scottish whisky distilleries. The *Environment Papers Series* 1 (2), 7–12.

McKenna, J., Williams, A.T. and Cooper, A.C. (2010) Blue Flag or red herring: do beach awards encourage the public to visit beaches? *Tourism Management* 32 (3), 576–588.

McLaren, D. (1998) *Rethinking Tourism and Ecotravel: The Paving of Paradise and What You can do to Stop it.* Kurarian Press, Connecticut.

Mensah, I. (2009) Environmental performance of tourism enterprise in Ghana: A case study of hotels in the Greater Accra Region (GAR). In: Leslie, D. (ed.) *Tourism Enterprises and Sustainable Development: International Perspectives on Responses to the Sustainability Agenda.* Advances in Tourism Series. Routledge, New York, pp. 139–156.

Millman, R. (1989) Pleasure seeking v the 'greening' of world tourism. *Tourism Management* 10 (4), 275–278.

Minhinnick, R. (1993) *A Postcard Home – Tourism in the Mid-nineties.* Gomer, Llandysul, Wales, UK.

Nepal, S.K. (2007) Ecotourists' importance and satisfaction ratings of accommodation-related amenities. *Anatolia* 18 (2), 255–276.

OCA (Office of Consumer Affairs) (2006) *Corporate Social Responsibility: An Implementation Guide for Canadian Business.* Industry Canada, Ottawa.

OECD (2011) *Greening Household Behaviour: The Role of the Public Policy.* Organisation for Economic and Cultural Development, Paris.

Paavola, J. (2001) Economics, ethics and green consumerism. In: Cohen, M.J. and Murphy, J. (eds) *Exploring Sustainable Consumption: Environmental Policy and the Social Sciences.* Pergamom, Amsterdam, pp. 79–96.

Patullo, P. and Minelli, O. (2006) *The Ethical Travel Guide: Your Passport to Exciting Alternative Holidays.* Earthscan, London.

Poon, A. (1994) The 'new tourism' revolution. *Tourism Management* 15 (2), 91–92.

Raffaele, P. (2003) Feeding frenzy at Shark Bay. *The Daily Telegraph. Weekend Magazine* (date unknown), pp. 42–47.

Redclift, M. (2001) 'Changing nature': The consumption of space and the construction of nature on 'the Mayan Riviera'. In: Cohen, M.J. and Murphy, J. (eds) *Exploring Sustainable Consumption: Environmental Policy and the Social Sciences.* Pergamon, Amsterdam, pp. 121–136.

Ritzer, G. (2000) *The McDonaldization of Society*. New Century Edition, Pine Forge Press, California.

Roberts, L. and Hall, D. (2001) *Rural Tourism and Recreation: Principles to Practice*. CAB International, Wallingford, UK.

Sasidharan, V., Sirakaya, E. and Kerstetter, D. (2002) Developing countries and tourism ecolabels. *Tourism Management* 23, pp. 161–174.

Scottish Office. (1995) *Research Findings No.6*. Environment Research Programme, Scottish Office, Edinburgh, UK.

SCRT (2006) *I will if you will: towards sustainable consumption*. Sustainable Consumer Round Table, London, May.

Sharpley, R. (2006) Ecotourism: A consumptive perspective. *Journal of Ecotourism* 5 (1–2), 7–22.

Sharpley, R. (2009) *Tourism, Development and the Environment: Beyond Sustainability*. Earthscan, London.

Sherman, A. (1988) Falling into a tourist trap. *The Times* (London) Monday 20 June, p. 20.

Silano, M. and Meredith, S. (1997) Environmental Management in UK Hotels: The role of employees as stakeholders. Paper presented at the CHME: Hospitality Research Conference. Oxford, UK, April.

Swarbrooke, J. and Horner, P. (2007) *Consumer Behaviour in Tourism*. Butterworth Heinemann, Oxford, UK.

Sykes, L. (1995) The holiday crowd. *Geographical* February, pp. 14–15.

Tearfund (2002) *A Call for Responsible Global Tourism*. Tearfund, London.

Tiscali (2007) *Forget the carbon footprint, we want our summer back*. Summer Lifestyle Report, Tiscali UK Ltd, London.

TUI (2010) *New Holidays Forever brand outlines Thomson and First Choice's five year sustainable tourism commitments*. Press Release, 29th June.

TUI (2011) *The Sustainable Development Report*. Available at: http://www.tuitravelplc.com in the 'latest news' section.

Tukker, A., Cohen, M.J., Huback, K. and Mont, O. (2010) The impact of household consumption and options for change. *Journal of Industrial Ecology* 14 (1), pp. 13–30.

Vaughn, T. and Allen, A. (2007) Green land. *Caterer & Hotelkeeper* 127 (4463) February, pp. 29–33.

Venice Tourist and Information Site (2010) *Venice Sinking Under 13 Million Plastic Bottles Per Year*. [online] Available at: <http://www.veniceinfosite.com/2010/11/help-rid-venice-of-13-million-plastic-bottles (accessed 12 February 2011).

Vernon, J., Essex, S., Pinder, D. and Curry, K. (2005) Collaborative policymaking: local sustainable projects. *Annals of Tourism Research* 32 (2), 325–345.

Watkins, S. (1994) Do Guests Want Green Hotels? *Lodging Hospitality*, April.

Weaver, A. (2005) Representation and obfuscation: Cruise travel and the mystification of production. *Tourism, Culture & Communication* vol. 5, pp. 165–176.

Weaver, D. (2011) Can sustainable tourism survive climate change? *Journal of Sustainable Tourism* 19 (1), 5–15.

Whitmarsh, L. and O'Neill, S. (2010) Green identity, green living? The role of pro-environmental self-identity in determining consistency across diverse pro-environmental behaviours. *Journal of Environmental Psychology* 30, pp. 305–314.

WTTC, WTO and Earth Council Report (1996) *Agenda 21 For the Travel and Tourism Industry: Towards Environmentally Sustainable Development*. World Travel and Tourism Council, Madrid.

Wurzinger, S. and Johansson, M. (2006) Environmental concern and knowledge of ecotourism among three groups of Swedish tourists. *Journal of Travel Research* 45, pp. 217–226.

WWF (2008) Weathercocks & Signposts: the environment movement at a crossroads. World Wide Fund for Nature. Available at: http://www.wwf.org.uk/filelibrary/pdf/weathercosts_report2.pdf (accessed 20 February 2011).

Zografos, C. and Allcroft, D. (2007) The environmental values of potential ecotourists: a segmentation study. *Journal of Sustainable Tourism* 15, pp. 44–65.

8 Access to the Destination and the Enterprise: The Transportation Factor

Introduction

The mode of transport used first to access the chosen destination area and then the tourism enterprise of choice accounts for on average approximately 70% of the energy consumption of tourists (Becken *et al.*, 2003), which undoubtedly is a major contentious issue in terms of sustainability and tourism. It is this travel element that makes tourism an unsustainable pattern of consumption irrespective of the seemingly ubiquitous use of terms such as 'sustainable tourism', which as Button (2012, p. 36) argued: 'although convenient billboards, and perhaps even practically necessary, run against the entire grain of the idea of sustainability.' Furthermore, tourism is inextricably linked to the causes of climate change (CC) through the consumption of fossil fuels, and related pollution, to transport tourists to and from and within their destinations. It is surprising therefore that the mode of transport, particularly air travel, has gained for so long so little opprobrium. Yet transport is one of the main areas of energy consumption (Maguire *et al.*, 2008), on average accounting for 40% per person of their GHG emissions (Bristow *et al.*, 2008). Furthermore, forecasts indicate that '20% of the growth in energy demand between now and 2030 is due to increasing demand for transportation worldwide' (IEA, 2006 cited in Becken and Hay, 2007, p. 697). Passenger traffic is estimated to grow by 180% by 2026

with international travel being the fastest growing sector (Macintosh and Wallace, 2009). This apparently is particularly applicable to the UK, which is second only to the USA for aircraft emissions (Hailes, 2007). It is not only the number of international arrivals, estimated at 940m in 2010, that are expected to grow but also domestic tourism, which has been estimated to be 10 times greater (WTO, 2013).

There is a broad consensus supporting the theory of CC being linked to GHG concentration in the atmosphere which is largely the result of human activities including the burning of fossil fuels (IPCC, 2013). Furthermore with the attention to CC throughout the media over the last few years, as well illustrated by Gore's 'An Inconvenient Truth', it is arguable that people know about CC through its representation and the discourse that surrounds it.

Aviation is a major contributory factor in this, though to what extent is not clear. Counsell (2010) states that aviation accounts for 2% of global emissions whilst the WTO estimated that tourism's contribution to CC was 5% in 2005 and will increase by 160% by 2035 (NHTV, 2010). Leisure-based travellers are considered to account for approximately 60% of all air travel so it is unequivocal that this is a major contributor to atmospheric pollution (Johns and Leslie, 2008); one which shows no signs of abating. That is, even allowing for recent reports noting that there were indications around the end of the 2000s that most businesses were seeking to reduce air travel in part due to issues of CC (WWF, 2011). However, given the economic recession over the period perhaps this is not surprising although it does indicate how recession can actually encourage businesses to take actions which can be interpreted as 'going green or greener'; as also argued by the European Environment Agency (EEA, 2011). As for tourists, demand and global expansion continue as:

- the popularity of destinations further afield increases, facilitated by easier access; well illustrated by developments providing access to remote areas, e.g. helicopter for skiing, hiking and mountaineering in locations only accessible by helicopter in depths of winter (see Hudson and Miller, 2005; Herremans, 2006) or cruises to the Arctic or arriving in previously little known areas such as Tasiilaq;
- the relative cost of short trips decreases and the range of choice becomes more readily available as demand increases;
- trips become more spontaneous, fuelled by last minute bargains; and
- mobile behaviour patterns increase, i.e. take in more destinations; more frequent but shorter duration trips – facilitated by low-cost airlines.

According to research conducted by Kuoni (2011), over the next 10 years tourists will become much more concerned about the impacts of their holidays. However, even though the research shows a 40% increase in focus on sustainability concerns, the number of respondents who claimed they will stop flying was 6%. Certainly not aiding the situation is that the majority of holiday brochures are silent on CC, failing to inform consumers sufficiently about this issue. While holidays and destinations are described in terms of warm climates and attractive features, no mention is made of the volume of CO_2 emissions produced per traveller. Options to mitigate the impact of travel, such as carbon offsetting, tend only to be evident when booking via the internet (Johns and Leslie, 2008). An alternative approach is that of 'Slow Tourism', the accent here being on local development, which in some ways is very similar to the advocacy of

'Slow Travel' which rather gained attention in the 1980s, e.g. Sanfter Tourismus in Germany and Tourisme Doux in France (see Holland and Holland, 2012). However, in general the main concerns over tourism and sustainability arise over air travel.

It may well be argued that there is little the operators can do, as Wheatcroft, (1991, p. 124) opined:

> The best the air transport and tourism industries can do is to gain as much publicity as possible for the genuine efforts to reduce environmental nuisances. They must do this because a greener image is essential to growth.

Even so, whilst sustainability might not be seen to be a primary concern to many operators what undoubtedly is, is their fuel consumption. Therefore irrespective of the environmental argument, they have a vested interest in reducing such costs and concomitantly their consumption of fossil fuels. Counsell (2010) says that steps are being taken to reduce these costs through improved fuel efficiency and the use of bio-fuel (ideally from waste). They are also being encouraged to address the GHG emissions of their operations through governmental intervention. The EU, for example, has been seeking to introduce emissions trading for aviation from 2012, but then that is a scheme within the EU. What impact will this have on carriers outside of the EU? The scheme has already met with substantial opposition from outside of the EU, and meanwhile emissions will continue to rise despite innovations (Macintosh and Wallace, 2009).

By far the majority of visitors to any location within a country are domestic. As such, most customers of the enterprises involved in the study are residents of the UK. Even so, both the LDNP and Scotland receive many overseas tourists, the majority of whom will travel to the UK by air flights and then onward to their destination which may be by coach, e.g. tour company, rail or car. In the absence of these tourism enterprises there would be few tourists in the area as it is their very presence on which the scale and value of tourism to any locality is so dependent. Thus the mode of transport is inescapably relevant.

As Somerville (1993), Director of Environment programme with British Airways, argued at a conference attended by representatives of many leading stakeholders in tourism, the rest of the industry did have some responsibility for the impact of aviation.

Transport was identified as a factor in SSCM (see Chapter 3) but hardly gains consideration in the context of CSR nor is it a factor in an EMS for business in general. But, as discussed in Chapter 7, it does gain attention in various EMS schemes designed for tourism enterprises and is a wider consideration in the context of promoting environmentally friendly behaviours. This is one aspect of tourism that has also gained the attention of the OECD (2002) which considered the impact of travel and potential to influence consumer decision making as regards transportation used and related energy consumption and emissions; evidently to no effect.

Whilst a tourism enterprise may be performing well when judged on the basis of its EP, how customers travel to the destination and thus the enterprise invariably gains little attention in such considerations. However, this aspect was considered in the study in two main ways. First, how visitors accessed the enterprise and second, whether the enterprises encouraged customers to travel by public transport as opposed to being car based. Before discussing the outcomes of this area of the investigation, the main modes of transportation in tourism are briefly discussed to highlight the major differences between these modes, primarily with regards to GHG emissions. Following on from the study's findings and given the significance of air travel as the mode of transport for international tourists and thus a factor in the arrival of many visitors at their ultimate destination such as the LDNP or the Highlands of Scotland, the discussion moves on to consider the wider context of international travel and initiatives developed to address GHG emissions.

Mode of Transport

Although the exponents of slow travel argue for using comparatively low fuel consuming transportation, taking a slower route to the final destination and enjoying the journey, for international tourists let alone domestic, this is not an option. By and large, people are not prepared to spend what they may consider unnecessary time in transit, whether this be an extra day in reaching their chosen holiday location or extra hours in reaching their short-break destination. The developments in airline travel make such 'delays' unnecessary and leave all the more holiday time to enjoy at the destination. This is well exemplified by enthusiastic skiers living in Glasgow who will take a low-cost carrier flight to a ski-resort in the French Alps for two days of skiing rather than driving up to a ski resort such as Anoch Mor in the highlands. If asked why, they will argue that overall the travel element involves little more time, is easier to access, the skiing is often better and expenses such as fees, accommodation, etc. are less and overall not necessarily any more expensive. A factor apparently rarely considered in this context is that of purpose of trip. Dolnicar et al. (2010) illustrate that the mode of transport choice is influenced by the requirement for a car at the destination given the activities involved at the destination and thus equipment, e.g. mountain biking or water-based sport such as scuba diving.

Which mode of transport for tourists is considered to have the lowest environmental impact is, as to be expected, a complex calculation. It is not just a matter of GHG emissions or the type of those emissions but also the infrastructure essential to the transport operation and can include a range of other factors such as does the transportation involved also include freight. Further illustrating the complexities is a study involving a detailed comparative analysis of which mode of transport (train, plane or car) is the most environmentally ethical and includes such issues as transporting animals, how well the company looks after employees and also which produces the lowest carbon emissions over the same trip per head of traveller (Anon., 2008). Not surprisingly coach travel was identified to be the best based on the chosen criteria, whilst ferries do not come out very well and furthermore, some ferry companies across the range of criteria were identified to perform less well when compared with some major

European air carriers. An alternative and simpler approach, which does serve as a base guideline, is demonstrated by Holland and Holland (2012) in their analysis of a comprehensive range of modes of transport based on emissions. A study by NHTV (2010) took this a stage further with the aim of benchmarking the carbon footprint of Dutch holiday takers. They established that transport accounts for the largest share of GHG, and including accommodation as a major component, the 'worst' performing holidays were those that involved air travel (second was car based). They noted that in the case of such holidays, whilst total emissions per head evidenced a decline over the period 2002–2008, the emissions for holidays overall have gone up, so too holidays involving air travel over the same period. Of the types of holidays analysed, they established that cruises by far have the highest average impact followed by long-haul flights.

It is in recognition of GHG emissions that 'slow travel' has gained some degree of attention. As Dickinson and Lumsden (2010) establish, the concept of 'slow travel' is based on the notion of opting for those modes of transportation that comparatively emit lower noxious emissions and also the idea of enjoying the journey. The aim is to encourage change in the choice of mode of transportation and the focus on particular forms of low-carbon transport. Thus the modes of transport integral to slow travel are the train, bus/coach, cycling and water-based transport. Very much pre-dating 'slow travel', yet similar in concept are Heath's (1993) proposed three options, namely:

- 'Do not travel'. To adopt the 'don't travel' mode, Heath suggests, is as much about rejecting modernism and globalization of place as it is about environmentalism.
- Travel in a way that has minimum impact, e.g. short journeys and then only travel to places which in some way(s) contribute to conservation.
- Failing either of the first two options, travel by 'low impact' transport – the pragmatic option.

But the type and format of the trips being promoted under this umbrella of slow travel are in many ways just another package holiday which holds appeal to various niche markets. They also note that whilst bus and coach travel is falling out of favour with tourists in post-industrial societies it is nevertheless the most important in global terms. However, what is particularly clear is that air travel is to be discouraged, which is also the mode of transportation that has gained most attention by way of pollution. Thus it is this mode which is first considered and gains the most attention followed, albeit briefly, by ship-based transport and that apparently essential vehicle to domestic tourism – the car.

Air Travel

A review of the development of air travel post the 1940s shows continued development and expansion fuelled by seemingly endless growth in leisure-based travel (see Somerville, 2012). This has been furthered by airline deregulations (first in the USA and then the UK/EU) and the emergence of low-cost airlines, which facilitate consumers to enjoy lifestyles now, including jetting off to choice European cities for hen and stag parties that they previously could or would not have done, due to the price and frequency of these services. The continued development of low-cost airlines, for example Easy Jet who accumulated 21,566 million passenger kilometres in 2004 alone (BBC News online, 2007), shows that despite the global issue of climate change and the contribution low-cost airlines make towards it, demand continues to grow. Further, a greater choice of direct flights from regional airports is helping fuel growth; BAA Scotland alone reported a 13.7% rise in passengers for international flights for February 2008 compared with the same month in 2007. Indeed, statistical evidence from the Civil Aviation Authority shows that the increasing numbers of passengers using UK airports shows no sign of slowing down but conversely, trends indicate substantial and continued growth. Largely contributing to such growth has and continues to be the success of low-cost airlines whose dramatic reworking of the traditional airline business model has brought substantial economic and social benefits to consumers with their rock bottom prices and convenient regional departure points along with a frequency of service never seen before. However, on the downside these short haul flights are more polluting than long haul given take-offs and landings are more frequent.

Indeed one can hardly see air travel declining in the absence of some substantial change for the foreseeable future. It is not only an integral element of tourism but also a factor in internationalization and globalization (see Button, 2012). Yet invariably the air flight element of so many holidays is all too often missing from discourses on the environmental impacts of tourism, most especially in the context of ecotourism or 'eco-chic' (see Buckley, 2012). Although not an example of ecotourism and more so of eco-chic, this is well illustrated in the case of the major tourist development of Per Aquum, a luxurious five star beach resort in Nungwi, Zanzibar, that claims to be carbon-neutral. How does it account for GHG emissions arising from the tourists' return trip? (see Pleumarom, 2007). However, in the light of such ongoing demand one might echo Wheatcroft's (1991) comment that there is little the airline companies can do. Certainly they can continue to seek to reduce fuel consumption through reducing the weight carried, alternative fuels such as bio-fuel and through technological advances. For example, TUI has removed nearly nine tons of excess weight from aircraft (TUI, 2011). They were also the first airline in the UK to use bio-fuels to fly a commercial aircraft (28 July 2011) though Virgin Airways partly fuelled an air flight from London to Singapore on bio-fuels in 2010. British Airways recently took delivery of their first Airbus, acclaimed to be state of the art in technology, fuel efficiency and noise, whilst TUI have introduced the new fuel efficient and more sustainable Boeing 787 Dreamliner into its fleet of aircraft. But research has shown that the potential for increased efficiency from aircraft technology and air traffic management will not be sufficient to compensate for the projected growth in the commercial aviation industry (Johns and Leslie, 2008; Somerville, 2012). This is further affirmed by the studies of MacIntosh and

Wallace (2009) who argued that demand would have to be restricted if emissions attributed to air travel at the time were to be stabilized by 2025. Basically the aviation sector is essential to today's globalized economy. As with other major polluting sectors there is little that can be expected other than the suppliers and operators taking all possible steps to reduce and ameliorate negative impacts such as GHGs. At the same time it should be recognized that the aviation industry holds many economic benefits, not the least of which is as a major employer (see Button, 2012).

A possible option would be internalizing the externalities of air travel (see Schipper, 2004) though this would raise an outcry amongst operators and quite likely by passengers given the impact on ticket prices. It would also likely have a disproportionate effect on ticket prices between carriers, i.e. low-cost carriers would increase prices disproportionally to the mainline operators, leading to additional complexities and debate.

Ferries and Cruising

The first area to consider more broadly is that of shipping in general, which in terms of addressing sustainability issues and especially pollution, notably through fuel usage, is way behind other transport sectors (Anon., 2008; and see Somerville, 2012). For example, according to Spanner (2011) 'One in every 30 tonnes of CO_2 generated by human activity today comes from a ship.', and is currently considered to account for 3% of global GHG, which is predicted to double by 2050 (Anon., 2013). The reference here to shipping also serves well to illustrate key differences in emissions. Ships, and therefore ferries and cruise liners, are major generators of sulphur emissions. This has been recognized and is being addressed by the Marine Pollution Convention of the International Maritime Organizations, which has certainly encouraged the use of alternative fuels such as Liquid Petroleum Gas and low sulphur fuels, though the latter are not as energy rich. However progress has been slow and hence it is not surprising to find that the EU has taken the initiative to introduce the EU Sulphur Directive, designed to reduce sulphur emissions, which has major implications for the shipping sector. The Directive requires short sea and ferry companies to use low sulphur fuel from 2015, and apart from the cost implications there are also potential domino effects, including the possibility of re-routing carriage to rail and road. Little apparent consideration has been given to such effects including the possibility of some companies, for instance cross channel ferries, not being able to meet the Directive's requirements (Terilowski, 2012).

Cruises are certainly different from the other modes of transport discussed in this section. They are a mode of transportation, taking people to places to observe, see and visit different destinations without their passengers needing to make any effort – ensconced as they are in their very own eco-bubble. Cruises are a sector of tourism that has grown quite dramatically over the last 5 years (see Holland and Holland, 2012); for example, 21m passengers in 2012 (BBC, 2013) and in the process raising many concerns over sustainability. Clearly there is the pollution aspect, not only air pollution but the sea, due to and contrary to international law, discharging wastes (BBC, 2013). There is also the impact of the cruise ships which invade areas hitherto hardly touched by humankind such as the polar regions; and for example, popular holidays to the Galapagos Islands via a luxury cruise which is hardly a benefit to the local communities even allowing for the substantial visitor levy for the National Park that was first noted in the early 1990s (Middleton and Hawkins, 1993).

Car

There is no question that the use of the car is the predominant mode of transport for domestic tourism in post-industrial societies. Further, this is also increasingly evident in developing economies and lesser developed countries as cars become more accessible. They provide the convenience of being able to transport the occupants to where they wish to go and when they wish, along with any luggage and paraphernalia considered necessary. Whilst stating the obvious, cars consume fuel, mainly petrol, and emit pollution. They require land for roadways and for parking. As the former become congested then the roadways are widened, facilitating more traffic and enabling people to go further in the same time period as before, thus contributing to further congestion 'downstream', as portrayed in Joni Mitchell's renowned song 'Yellow Taxi'.

Further exacerbating the situation at popular destinations is that this car-based movement is seasonal and often contained within a short period, increasing the pressure on the infrastructure and leading to problems for local municipalities to address in their transport planning approaches. Demand continues to grow fuelled by increasing car ownership and the growing number of active, retired persons. Increases in fuel prices in the UK witnessed over the last decade appear to have no significant impact beyond the very short term. Indeed, it seems that it is sudden hikes in the price of fuel at the pumps or a sudden lack of supplies that generates mass outcries in society – more so than anything else. As with planes and boats, technology continues to seek ways of reducing pollution, as does the use of alternative fuels, whilst tax breaks seek to encourage the adoption of the latter, e.g. the UK reduced car tax on cars with comparatively low emissions such as hybrid cars.

A potential option, one which many people would consider to be extreme, is to 'ban the car' as for example in the case of the Goyt Valley (UK), a renowned visitor destination overrun by car-borne visitors in the 1960s, but more so some destinations in Austria and Switzerland which have been actively promoting 'car-free', building on an integrated system using public transport, transfers and pedestrian access. Such cases very much illustrate the overriding importance of the appropriate infrastructure being in place.

The Enterprises and Access

The first area considered is whether the enterprises were 'easily accessible by public transport'? A particularly important question, given that at the end of the 1990s the LDNP was considered as being:

> completely devoid of a public transport system, and as a result, millions of visitors who come to enjoy the scenery are contributing to its demise. (Anon., 1999)

This is to a small degree rather overstating the case, but if cars are to be discouraged then there have to be suitable alternatives which mean mainly the provision of a public transport service fit for purpose. This is particularly important given that cars are often essential to the less able members, including elder citizens, of society. Furthermore, in the absence of alternatives to the car the question of 'sustainable mobility' arises and the social exclusion of those members of society who do not have access to cars and potentially, therefore, limited opportunities to venture into other areas. Both of these areas, i.e. accessibility for all and encouraging the use of public transport, were identified as key issues in rural areas (ETC and CA, 2000). The second area of the study's findings on access is that of whether the enterprises sought to encourage guests to arrive by alternative means to that of the car.

Access

As the data in Table 8.1 demonstrate, by far the majority of guests arrive by car, which compares closely with the general statistics for both England and Scotland that invariably cite a figure of approximately 90% for access by

Table 8.1. How do guests mainly arrive?

Means of transport	Indicative numbers (%)
Car	88
Train	4
Train or bus	6
Bicycle or walking	2

car, which is not dissimilar to other countries (see Martin-Cejas and Sanchez, 2010). However, the number of guests arriving by car was actually far lower in the case of the 2011 enterprises, which were far more accessible by public transport, especially via train, than their rural counterparts in the 2001 and 2006 populations. It might well be argued therefore that accessibility by public transport is hardly an issue to most visitors. However, and especially so in comparison with accommodation and hospitality outlets, the attractions of 2001 evidenced far better progress in facilitating access for less able persons.

About half the enterprises were not 'easily accessible by public transport' and those enterprises in the fringe study even less so. Farm-based BBs and inns were less likely to be 'easily accessible' (50%). Additional confirmation of accessibility by public transport was forthcoming from the audits which found that 80% of the enterprises were accessible by bus and 36% by train, the latter mainly in urban locations. Invariably of more importance to many visitors is convenience, not only in accessing the desired location, but also in terms of subsequent travel within and around the area. This is especially important to major market segments – families with young children, retired people and those less able physically – and reflects the findings of earlier studies (see LDNPA, 1998).

Further adding to the dominance of car use by visitors is the finding that providing car spaces is considered by accommodation operators, especially in the LDNP, to be an important factor – most of whom had spaces to meet their customer needs. The growth in the popularity of cycling was recognized to some degree on the part of rural enterprises through the provision of an area for their storage, which is used as a promotional feature, especially when such provision is under cover and secure. A number of these enterprises also promoted environmentally friendly activities such as walking and cycling (14%). The exemplar for supporting the use of public transport, which also reflects the mode of transport used by many of their customers, is The Youth Hostels Association. Because of the poor public transport service this organization introduced a shuttle between their operations around Windermere and Ambleside and the train station. This popular service reflects a favoured means of transport by many of their guests but does place additional costs on their operation. This practice and the noted support for cycling well illustrate some of the ideas of 'slow travel'. However, in the absence of a perceived good, reliable public transport system in rural areas, which also operates throughout the day, i.e. early morning to late evening, then visitors will all too often have little choice but to use a car.

Encourage use of public transport

The interviewees were invited to comment on whether they encouraged guests to arrive by public transport: 80% indicated 'yes' or 'sort of', e.g. 'we make visitors aware but do not promote'. Further inquiry identified that this usually meant indicating what public transport was available. However, 42% did indicate that they will and do collect guests as needed from local termini, e.g. bus/train station; one interviewee noting that this 'was a possibility for the future'. The enterprise offering a discount for arriving by public transport and those few also who promote using public transport and offer to pick up their guests from the local terminus were by far in the minority. The majority of attractions also did not seek to promote how to access the site by public transport. Interestingly one attraction which did promote the use of public transport has a bin for used bus tickets prominently positioned by the entrance. A number of interviewees in their responses reflected wider concerns about the availability of public transport, e.g.:

- 'The public transport system is unreliable and expensive.'
- 'Buses are infrequent.'
- 'What is needed is a good, reliable bus system.'

Transport matters gained four comments; i.e.:

- 'There is a lack of good, reliable and frequent public transport in the Lakes.'
- 'There is a lack of public transport to the remoter areas.'

- 'Lack of adequate and reasonably priced car parking – results in cars polluting the atmosphere in town centres whilst looking for parking for a longer period.'
- 'Lack of parking facilities.'

Of particular note here is the high proportion of owners/managers saying 'Yes', yet did not mention this in response to the open question discussed. This particular outcome indicates some inconsistency between responses to pre-coded questions and those responses to open-ended questions. But of more significance overall is that such inconsistencies in the data sets were rare and as such further supports the interpretation that how the owners/managers perceive their own actions is not always as others might describe them.

Due consideration should be given here to the EU Package Holiday Directive which has meant that any enterprise offering any combination of at least two out of the three elements – accommodation, transport, activity – are liable if a problem arises with any of the elements involved. This Directive therefore actively discourages the smaller independent accommodation operators seeking to offer transport inclusive packages. The inquiry into 'packages' also elicited a number of responses about the lack of 'packages' for visitors once in the area, e.g.:

> Packages are not provided as such. The guest house has a number of leaflets and information pamphlets for the customers on day trips on offer around the area. Bus timetables are provided and we have a drawer full of train timetables. We undertake as much of the 'legwork' as possible on behalf of the guests.

Undoubtedly the car will continue to be the main means of transport, for local people, as well as visitors.

Wider Considerations

The reality is that in the absence of some form of motorized transport there would be little tourism activity. This would be economically calamitous today for so many destinations throughout the globe and equally many

localities within the UK not the least of which would be the LDNP; as manifest very briefly by a shortage of petrol supplies due to strike action by suppliers (see Leslie, 2002).

Whilst currently there appears little to dissuade tourists from flying or driving, the options appear to be limited to how to reduce consumption of fossil fuels and introducing ways to ameliorate GHGs such as carbon offsetting and carbon trading. There are two main reasons for such reduction. The first is that fossil fuels are limited and declining supplies not only holds substantial implications for tourism, especially international, but also and of far more importance would be the impact on raising costs and the socio-economic effects of this. Just how extensive oil reserves are is not that clear and as the Vice-Chairman of Boeing plc said there is 'plenty of fossil fuel around' (Gorman, 2003, p. 35). Even so, it is a non-renewable resource, essential in today's world for all manner of products and one might argue the very fabric of society. The second reason is that of the pollution and contribution to CC.

Alternative fuels

The main option appears to be the use of alternative fuels such as hydrogen or bio-fuels. Hydrogen, the production of which is complicated and quite probably is not the answer in terms of air pollution, particularly with attention to water vapour emissions (Gorman, 2003; also see the Aviation Environmental Federation at www.aef.org.uk), nor is it likely to be introduced in the near future (Peeters et al., 2007). Bio-fuels are a proven alternative for some transportation including air flights but its production raises many issues. However, its production and use is gaining substantial political support and action. The EU has introduced the European Renewable Energy Directive which seeks to achieve a baseline of 10% of transport fuels to be from renewable sources and also the Fuel Quality Directive which aims for reduction of 6% by 2020 in GHG emissions from petrol and diesel fuels (Masero, 2009).

The production of bio-fuels, e.g. bio-ethanol, bio-diesel, is supported through government subsidies in many countries, which has catalysed a dramatic increase in production this century. Yet, according to a recent report, bio-fuels just cannot meet EU targets for reduced emissions by 2017 (ActionAid et al., 2011). Based on recent forecasts the rate of bio-fuel production by 2050 has been estimated at 13.6 million barrels per day (World Economic Forum, 2011). Even so, it has been forecast that liquid bio-fuels are unlikely to increase their share of energy demand above 3.5% of global transport energy by 2030 (FAO, 2008). Bio-fuel production has received much criticism, well encapsulated here by Johnson (2008, p. 24) who argued that subsidies for bio-fuels 'are the most inefficient way of producing power ever conceived.' Whilst it may hold advantages over fossil fuels in terms of GHGs, there are also many issues over production. Major concerns arise over the use of land which would have been previously used for agricultural crops. One suggestion as to the extent of land required is that if all transport in UK used these fuels then the whole of UK land production would need to be converted! (Anon., 2007). In this, factors to consider as explained by Grewock (2010) are:

1. In times of food surpluses this is fine but harvest failures will generate problems. How will the absence of food surpluses impact on other regions suffering from a scarcity of staple foods?

2. Changing from food production to bio-fuel crops supports the need for imports and thus more fuel consumption.

3. Bio-fuel production no doubt requires fertilizers and pesticides to enhance and maintain production over time.

4. In world terms is it moral for the 'rich' countries to subsidize production of biofuel crops thereby further adding to the imbalance between nations in access to and consumption of natural resources?

Additional to these factors, Johnson (2008) draws attention to:

• Growing crops for bio-fuel holds opportunity costs – loss of land for other productive uses.

- Increases cost of what would otherwise be produced; witness increase in grain prices in 2007 (Vidal, 2007; Porritt, 2007).
- Land change use can further release CO_2.
- Consumes energy in production.
- Palm oil is favoured for bio-diesel, the plantation development of which impacts on indigenous peoples, e.g. Indonesia. Young (2011) further supports this, adding that a report from Wetlands International on production of palm oil has led to deforestation in Malaysia.

Furthermore, it has been argued that the production and processing of material for bio-fuels actually generate more GHG than the use of fossil fuels (ActionAid et al., 2011). Perhaps more of a concern is changing crop production to bio-fuel crops in developing countries for which the benefit to such countries is lower given the absence of subsidies (see FAO, 2008). Second, the quest for production of bio-fuels may well ignore other potential uses yet to be discovered, e.g. bio-prospecting (see UNCED-UK/Novartes, 1999). In summation biofuel as a viable alternative to fossil fuel appears to be fraught with problems and is certainly no panacea as Lomborg (2013), all too cogently, argues.

Overall, there is little to doubt that fossil fuels are still likely to be a major source of energy for years to come. But, irrespective of this there are still substantive arguments for the need for alternative fuels and perhaps more importantly in the short-term the need to address the infrastructure used to distribute energy supplies such as electricity to points of consumption which, it is argued, account for more lost energy than is actually consumed (Anon., 2007).

Emissions trading

The European Emissions Trading Scheme, which aimed to include aviation by 2012, and the introduction and also legislation for a minimum tax on fossil fuel products are all part of the EU's Energy Policy driven by its commitments to reducing emissions (EEA, 2011). All of which has to be adopted by Member States, e.g. the UK introduced the Carbon Reduction Commitment in 2010, which is a mandatory carbon trading scheme applicable at the moment only to large organizations (i.e. based on power consumption of 12k megawatt/per hour). The inclusion of the airline sector in the carbon trading scheme might be expected to substantially increase ticket costs. However, according to Button (2012) it would not add significantly to the cost of air tickets. More generally such schemes can be effective in reducing the target emissions, exemplified by the well established sulphur trading in the USA (Hawkins, 2000). The indicators are that carbon trading will prove to be equally successful.

A further consideration is propounded by Watts (2006), that those companies which many people would consider major polluters, e.g. oil companies, have gained from the scheme in the UK and furthermore they have been able to sell carbon credits which reflects one of the arguments against 'polluter pays', i.e. I have paid for pollution thus my pollution is OK. Watts also notes that part of the problem is the differences between the approaches of European countries.

Carbon offsetting

Carbon offsetting is explained as 'the purchase of credits from GHG emissions reduction projects in one place to counter the emissions of greenhouse gas in another place.' (POST, 2007). But carbon offsetting is not without issues, particularly due to the different schemes and their integrity (see Widdicombe, 2008). Pleumarom (2007) cites the example of Lufthansa, who sought to introduce a carbon offsetting scheme and in the process considered that out of 13 schemes investigated half were unreliable. Pleumarom also cites examples of places where local people have lost their own land to tree planting under offset programmes.

The opportunity when presented to customers to 'carbon offset' their flight may also be considered an aspect of CSR and certainly as a positive PR action to be promoted. Starmer-Smith (2008) presents an interesting comparative analysis based on the criteria of carbon reduction, carbon offsetting, conservation schemes and responsible tourism between diverse tour companies drawn from a cross-section of leading tour operators which offer to their customers a carbon offsetting scheme. For example, leading companies such as Abercrombie and Kent in the luxury market, and in the adventure tour market he identifies Intrepid, Explore, Wild Frontiers, Exodus and the Adventure Company. In the cruise market, which is arguably the least green form of holiday package, he cites Royal Caribbean as the green market leader and for ski holidays Neilson (part of Thomas Cook plc) is considered to perform comparatively well. This comparative analysis is presented in Table 8.2.

As apparent from Table 8.2, the cruise sector is the poorest performer which reflects the earlier comment on cruising and associated pollution. In contrast, the luxury operators perform very well, perhaps furthering support for the argument that it is the affluent in any society who can afford to go green. The same argument could be applied to the example of adventure tours though some commentators would certainly argue their performance could be due more to the environmental concerns of their customers. However, the promotion of offsetting schemes has attracted concerns, as Polonsky et al. (2010) identify:

- There is no uniform, accepted standard for carbon offsets or carbon related claims.
- The scope of what is being claimed, i.e. what is covered? For example, consumers may not fully know whether the fuel allocation is a significant part of the carbon associated with the airline.
- A carbon offset can include firms' internal activities that reduce their carbon pro-

duction. This could potentially include updating equipment to newer infrastructure that is more environmentally friendly.
- The timing of any environment improvements. That is, does an offset purchased today relate to a reduction in carbon today or in the future?

Overall, they argue that 'there is a real risk that marketers may turn carbon offset claims into a meaningless promotional tool (i.e. greenwash).' (Polonsky et al., 2010). It is though not just a matter of the type of such schemes but also potential negative impacts of some schemes (see Holden, 2009) and further that a project might involve storing up the carbon, e.g. forestry (see Gossling et al., 2007, p. 241)

A survey (Anon., 2010) conducted at Stansted Airport reported that approximately half of those surveyed were aware of the opportunity to carbon offset their flights yet just 7% overall of the passengers had taken up the opportunity. An outcome that suggests some improvement on participation previously, e.g. Crystal Holidays, a major ski tour specialist, which has been offering its customers the opportunity for carbon offset since 2003 yet fewer than 2% of its customers agreed to pay it in the first two years (East, 2005). The finding is also remarkably similar to the figure of a few years earlier, i.e. less than 8% to date contributed to a carbon offsetting scheme (Starmer-Smith, 2008). This hardly supports the findings of other research, e.g. 57% of airline travellers were prepared to pay a premium for flights with lower carbon emissions (Global Travel Market, 2009) or that of Deloitte Development's (2007) research

Table 8.2. Carbon offsetting and leading tour companies in diverse markets. (Adapted from Starmer-Smith, 2008.)

Market sector – Company	Carbon reduction	Carbon offsetting	Conservation schemes	Responsible tourism
Luxury – Audley Travel	**	****	****	****
Adventure – Adventure Company	**	****	****	****
Cruising – Royal Caribbean	*	*	***	**
Skiing – Neilson	**	*	****	****

one year on that a third of holiday makers are willing to pay between 5% and 10% more for the usual ticket price. This shows a drop when compared with a survey of readers by *The Daily Telegraph* which found that 75% would be prepared to pay more for flights – notably 23% said 'no' (Anon., 2003), a difference which *might* be attributed to the prevailing economic recession of the time. It does however correlate with First Choice's surveys, which found that customers do not understand carbon offsetting and are not prepared to pay for it, albeit they established that the environment is an issue to many respondents but it is not considered that important when it comes to holidays; cost being the only common factor across all participants in the survey at 43% (TUI, 2010). On the same survey travellers were asked if they had taken fewer flights over the previous year due to concern over environmental issues, 9% responded 'yes' (Anon., 2010), which rather begs the question of how many flights they took annually. This correlates with the findings of other more general environmental awareness studies, and further that it is people with higher disposable incomes who can afford to be 'environmentally friendly' (see Chapter 7; Johns and Leslie, 2008). An example of which is that of the highly expensive resort of Soneva Fushi (room rates range from $1000 to $8000 per night) in the Maldives, which applies a 2% carbon tax on all guest accounts, with the monies raised funding projects such as the development of wind turbines in southern India (Lean, 2010). Similarly to the findings on environmental concerns and identified variances on the basis of age group, is that 18 to 24 year olds have been identified more than any other age group as showing little concern over their carbon footprint (Skidmore, 2008). Yet this age group is a major market segment with longevity which raises concerns as to whether their attitudes will change as they grow older and the societal implications if their attitudes do not change in the future towards pro-environmental behaviour.

Whilst the data from these surveys predominantly do not include details on the profile of the respondents, speculation suggests that the 9% who said they had taken fewer flights due to environmental concerns (Anon.,

2010), accounts for the majority, if not all, of those who paid to offset and as such further supports the view that it is the more affluent in societies that can afford to 'go green'. Also that attitudes towards greening do vary between societies (see OECD, 2002; Brouwer *et al.*, 2008) and thus the profile of respondents in any survey is a factor in the findings and thus something which merits not only attention when reporting on the findings but could also be a significant factor to the outcomes of any survey. A final point on the findings of that survey is that 3% of those surveyed indicated 'yes' in response to the question of whether they chose the airline in relation to how environmentally friendly the airline company was perceived to be (Anon., 2010). This might not be readily established on the basis of the information provided by carriers; however, prospective tourists can refer to the Carbon Friendly Flight Search, which provides information on the availability of comparatively lower carbon emissions flights. To what extent the claim that over half of all enquiries lead to the take up of options involving an average premium of 19% over low-cost/high emissions flights rather requires verification. However, the system does provide the opportunity to choose a lower GHG emission flight as opposed to paying (or not) a fee for carbon offsetting (Global Travel Market, 2009).

It is all too clear that there is a range of issues on carbon offsetting. To which should be added a key point that it is a 'polluter pays' payment rather than a shift to a pro-environmental behaviour. As it is, and at best, presented as an optional extra then, just as with so many voluntary payment schemes, the majority of consumers will opt not to pay. Allowing for these issues, if the offsets schemes were solely to involve planting trees in itself this would have a major impact on land uses involve many concerns not dissimilar to those relating to bio-fuels, for example 'an area the size of Ireland would need to be planted every year to offset the world's aircraft emissions.' (Hailes, 2007, p. 33). An alternative to carbon offsetting would be to introduce a carbon tax. Again, there would be complications not the least of which is that one reason found for not supporting a carbon tax are perceptions that it will make no difference (Brouwer *et al.*,

2008). A more direct approach would be a personal carbon tax allowance, but whilst potentially acceptable in general, would be opposed given its impact on car use and air travel (see Bristow et al., 2008). One other approach merits attention which involves establishing the 'ecological footprint' of international travellers. As discussed by Hunter and Shaw (2007), this is based on the application of the concept of ecological footprint (EF) to international travellers. First the EF of the trip is established and then the EF for the same period based at home is deducted to establish the net figure. For some trips, according to the destination and services and facilities and duration, this could lead to a lower EF value for the holiday. A particular advantage of the development of such an approach lies in providing for a much clearer analysis of the differences in terms of consumption between different types of holiday, destinations and mode of transport.

Conclusion

Access is a complex area and often seen in terms of less able persons but there are many people for whom accessibility to places may be a problem, e.g. older persons, parents with young children and the generally disadvantaged in society. This is a problem for the tourism enterprises in the context of sustainability especially in rural locations as there may well be little alternative to the use of car-based transportation. To some extent this might be overcome by accommodation enterprises offering to transfer their customers from nearby railway stations or bus terminals. However, their guests most likely will wish to explore the area and/or have equipment with them for outdoor activity as well as luggage. Thus such an option when presented is of little attraction. Whilst the majority of enterprises could be reasonably reached via public transport, particularly given the increased availability of buses witnessed over the last decade in some of the areas involved, there are still many enterprises, including approximately half of the attractions in the more rural locations, which are not so readily accessible by public transport. Furthermore the times of

availability, e.g. early morning, evening services, may often be very limited. Even then, in the case of families with young children or with elderly persons less sure of walking then again the car is the transport mode of choice.

However, as discussed, access is not solely concerned with the final destination but also involves the whole trip, thus the journey from home to the ultimate destination, which for one reason or another is considered too far to travel by overland transport so a flight is taken or the arrangements for the trip include air flights, e.g. package tour. In respect of the destination enterprises, there is little they can do or indeed might be expected to do about how visitors access their operation. Nevertheless they are part of tourism, of the visitors' 'round trip'. Thus access is relevant in terms of the mode(s) of transport used and associated pollution, including GHG emissions, CC issues and, more widely, sustainability. It is in terms of the latter that tourism in general is unsustainable given the transport element and consumption of non-renewable resources, i.e. fossil fuels. As such, it is argued that all enterprises should address this issue in whatever way they can, be it direct or indirect.

There is no doubt that consumers and therefore in general tourists are aware of climate change as presented through the media and in some of the ways it is being addressed, e.g. renewable energy, hybrid cars. However, it remains unclear how this information is noticed, interpreted and used by consumers when making choices; in particular what influence, if any, has it had on consumer choice when it comes to choosing the mode of transport for touristic activities? A situation that is not aided by descriptions of holidays and destinations in terms of attractive climates and features but which make no mention of the volume of CO_2 emissions produced per traveller whilst options to mitigate the impact of travel, such as carbon offsetting, tend only to be evident when booking via the internet.

As the foregoing discussion attests, by far the large majority of tourists evidence little actual support for any method proposed or initiated to address sustainability issues arising from their choice of mode of transport. Indeed there is little sign that in general they are in any way altering their decision-making process and behavioural patterns to adapt, to reduce their carbon footprint. As Scott (2011, p. 25) argued:

> There is little evidence that tourists are willing to voluntarily change travel patterns (e.g. travel less by air, substitute destinations) despite the majority stating concerns about climate change and awareness of GHG emissions generated by travel.

As such there is little evidence of progress since the UNCSD (1999, p. 7) stated that:

> public sensitivity to environmental problems on holiday/business trips has not increased and is no more of a deterrent to repeat travel than it was previously.

In effect whilst the majority recognize their contribution towards climate change it translates, at best, into minority action. A situation which well illustrates 'Giddens' Paradox' – essentially that many people now recognize the problem yet rather ignore it in their behaviour, arguably because it is tomorrow's problem (see Giddens, 2009).

Whilst demand appears to be insatiable and intractable, the main areas of opportunity to address GHG emissions appear to be in reducing fossil fuel consumption and the use of alternative fuels, i.e. renewable energy sources. In this, technological advances and measures to reduce loading factors will continue to make a contribution but the indicators are that what reductions may be achieved will be counteracted by increasing demand. Alternative fuels also have their place but, as discussed, the production, for example, of bio-ethanol and bio-diesel raises many issues that are not so readily resolved. An additional step is the introduction of carbon trading. Economists continue to stress their belief that trading carbon with a value that is appropriate to generate a market will result in reduced emissions, a concept being actively pursued through the introduction of air travel and shipping into the EU Emission Trading Scheme (Johns and Leslie, 2008). Even then, as Somerville (2012, p. 48) argued:

> If emissions of greenhouse gases (GHGs) are to be reduced to levels deemed acceptable by organizations such as the Intergovernmental Panel on Climate Change (IPCC) then aviation faces a particularly tough challenge; failure to

reach targets through technology, trading etc. could result in demand control, with access to flying rationed in some as yet undetermined way.

Once again this brings demand back into consideration. At the moment initiatives directed at consumers are primarily carbon offsetting and taxes such as the UK's Air Passenger Duty (APD). These are forms of 'the polluter pays', which in some ways address the issue of GHG emissions but as a symptom of travel rather than the cause of the problem, i.e. reducing demand. So far they evidence little if any shift towards pro-environmental behaviour. Indeed, attempts in the UK to make air travel taxation as environmentally effective as possible appear to have had little effect, as the UK is considered in some quarters to be the world's worst offender for personal air travel, with estimates projecting related emissions in the order of 1.6 tons per person of CO_2 every year (Johns and Leslie, 2008). A further consideration is that taxation on air flights or increased prices due to emissions control may well have little real impact that is unless, according to a report from Green Futures, it results in a minimum charge of £76 being added to ticket prices. Furthermore, whilst consumers appear to accept green taxes, to an extent they want to see transparency in the process and that the revenues gained are directed towards addressing CC, otherwise it is/will be seen as another 'stealth tax' on the part of government; as the APD is considered to be. However, how effective a tax would be is debatable though one could certainly argue that this will further disparities between the 'haves' and 'have nots' in society and between societies. Even allowing for that, governments would face a major challenge to personalize and incentivize policies and measures to change behaviour which would successfully balance emission reductions against the potential for failure at the ballot box. What would certainly help in this for consumers/ tourists would be the provision of clarity of information, incentives and the opportunity to make low carbon choices before they will change behaviour.

In the meantime, the choices open to the consumer in this area of discretionary behaviour are difficult to balance; on the one hand expecting life supporting services but at the same time feeling little guilt over the climate impact of continued use of low-cost air travel; particularly when the latter is chosen over other forms of transport because it is perceived as quicker, cheaper and more convenient, and relatively small additional charges are unlikely to reduce demand.

An alternative approach to taxation and/ or inviting passengers to pay a carbon offset fee or personal carbon allowances is that of the Green Alliance (2010) who suggested introducing a place tax rather than a passenger tax, their argument being that this would encourage greater use of capacity on flights and potentially therefore reduce the number of flights. An immediately obvious difficulty would be how would such a tax be decided fairly and without contravening 'free trade' agreements? Potentially a more equitable approach is that suggested by Button (2012) who argues for 'trade offs' – that is saving carbon emissions elsewhere, e.g. at home to counterbalance emissions attributable to a holiday. To take this to its logical conclusion – every person would be allocated a carbon consumption allowance. On the one hand this would generate a market for personal trading, i.e. carbon trading, second and the more significant how would it be equitably decided not only for the people in one country but also parity between countries and peoples? Would, for example, a resident of the USA be granted an allowance equivalent to say a resident of Ghana? Could such a scheme be introduced by one country, perhaps initially in the context of air travel? Whilst both suggestions merit debate, a further factor to consider in this is that of what would be the impact on ground transportation, the demand for which is also increasing along with the demand for cars, thus increasing the congestion they generate at popular destinations during the tourist season?

The apparently inherent problems associated with access in today's globalized economy are not going to be resolved easily nor in the near future. Until such time as something substantive arises to curb demand then tourists will continue to travel and in increasing numbers globally.

Further Reading

For a particularly comprehensive discussion on the 'pros and cons' of biofuel production see FAO (2008).

On the subject of 'slow travel' see Dickinson, J. and Lumsden, L. (2010) *Slow Travel and Tourism*. Earthscan, London; whilst Transport 2000 (2001) *Tourism without traffic*. Transport 2000, London (www.transport2000.com) provides many practical examples.

The Carbon Consultancy (www.thecarbonconsultancy.co.uk) specializes in the delivery of carbon data, carbon and sustainability management support and education to the travel and tourism industry. Its products and services are deployed by travel management companies, travel agents, events agencies and tour operators, to support carbon reduction and sustainable operation. The company supports and advises industry associations and is committed to supporting the industry to educate and catalyse its stakeholders to deliver a sustainable and lower carbon performance.

The Carbon Friendly Flight search tool can be viewed at: http://www.sustainabilityintelligence.co.uk/carbonresponsible/flymart.php.

For carbon offsetting: see Wright, M. (ed.) (2011) *Offset Positive*. Special publication. *Green Futures*, Forum for the Future.

References

ActionAid *et al.* (2011) *Jatropha Biofuels in Dakatcha, Kenya – The Climate Consequences*. ActionAid, BirdLife International, Nature Kenya and the Royal Society for the Protection of Birds, London.
Anon. (1999) Pollution and litter 'ruining tourist spots'. *The Daily Telegraph* 6 September, p. 7.
Anon. (2003) No more airports, please. Telegraph Travel *The Daily Telegraph* 26 June, p. 5.
Anon. (2007) How to be a green traveller. Features Special *The Daily Telegraph*, 17 May.

Anon. (2008) Trains, Planes and Automobiles. *Ethical Consumer* May/June, pp. 8–13.

Anon. (2010) Few air travellers offset carbon emissions, study finds. *The Guardian*. Available online at http://www.guardian.co.uk/business/2010/aug/30/carbon-emissions-offset-civil-aviation-authority (accessed on 12 March 2011).

Anon. (2013) Shipping industry is steering on to a green path. EcoReport. *The Sunday Telegraph* September, p. 7.

BBC News online (2007) Easy Jet 2006 annual figures. Available from: http://news.bbc.co.uk/1/hi/business/7102995.stm (accessed 22 November 2007).

BBC (2013) *Costing the Earth*. Radio 4, Broadcast 14 May. British Broadcasting Company, London.

Becken, S. and Hay, J.E. (2007) *Tourism and Climate Change, Risks and Opportunities*. DECC. The 2050 Pathway Analysis Report, 2010.

Becken, S., Simmons, D.G. and Frampton, C. (2003) Energy use associated with different travel choices. *Tourism Management* 24, 267–277.

Bristow, A.L., Zannin, A.M., Wardman, M. and Chintakayala, P.K. (2008) *Personal Carbon Trading preference to investigate behavioural response*. Royal Society of Arts, Manufactures and Commerce, London, November.

Brouwer, R., Brander, L. and van Beukering, P. (2008) 'A convenient truth': air travel and passenger's willingness to pay to offset their CO_2 emissions. *Climatic Change* 90, pp. 299–313.

Buckley, R. (2012) Environmental performance. In: Leslie, D. (ed.) *Responsible Tourism: Concepts, Theories and Practice*. CAB International, Wallingford, UK, pp. 82–89.

Button, K. (2012) Air transport in Europe and the environmental challenges to the tourist market. In: Leslie, D. (ed.) *Tourism Enterprises and the Sustainability Agenda across Europe*. New Directions in Tourism Analysis. Ashgate, Farnham, UK, pp. 35–50.

Counsell, J. (2010) Flying clean away. *Our Planet* September, pp. 22–23.

Deloitte Development (2007) *Deloitte 2007 Annual Holiday Survey*. Available at: http://public.deloitte.com/media/0001/US_2007_Holiday_green.pdf (accessed 9 March 2011).

Dickinson, J. and Lumsden, L. (2010) *Slow Travel and Tourism*. Earthscan, London.

Dolnicar, S., Laesser, C. and Matus, K. (2010) Short-haul city travel is truly environmentally sustainable. *Tourism Management* 31 (4), 505–512.

East, R.E. (2005) Air milestone: 'It is big and it is clever' Special Briefing *Green Futures* May/June, pp. xiv–xv.

EEA (2011) *Recession Contributes to Air Pollution Emissions Decrease in 2009*. Available at www.eea.europe.eu (accessed 27 July).

ETC and CA (2000) *Rural Tourism: Working for the Countryside: A consultation paper by the English Tourism Council and the Countryside Agency*. English Tourism Council, London, March.

FAO (2008) *Reviewing Biofuel Policies and Subsidies*. United Nations Food and Agricultural Organisation. Available at: http://www.fao.org/newsroom/en/news (accessed 18 December 2008).

Giddens, A. (2009) *The Politics of Climate Change*. Polity Press, Oxford, UK.

Global Travel Market (2009) *Flight Search Data*. Global Travel Market. 18 June. Available at www.globaltravelmarket.co.uk

Gorman, M. (2003) Flights of Fancy. *Green Futures* Jan/Feb, pp. 32–35.

Gossling, S., Broderick, J., Upham, P., Ceron, J.-P., Dubois, G., Peeters, P. and Strasdas, W. (2007) Voluntary carbon offsetting schemes for aviation: efficiency, credibility and sustainable tourism. *Journal of Sustainable Tourism* 15(3), 223–248.

Green Alliance (2010) *Making Aviation 'Pay its Way'*. Green Alliance, London.

Grewock, L. (2010) *Biofuels: creating or solving global problems*. Available at http://responsibletravelnews/blogspot.com/2010/06/biofuels-creating-or-solving-global-problems (accessed 12 March 2011).

Hailes, J. (2007) How to be a green traveller. *The Daily Telegraph* 17 May, p. 33.

Hawkins, R. (2000) The use of economic instruments and green taxes to complement an environmental regulatory regime. *Water, Air and Soil Pollution* 123, pp. 379–394.

Heath, G. (1993) Tourism and the understanding of environmental issues. In: Veal, A.J., Johnson, P. and Cushmand, P. (eds) *Leisure and Tourism: Social and Environmental Change*. Conference proceedings, World Leisure and Recreation Conference, Sydney Centre for Leisure and Tourism Studies, July.

Herremans, J.M. (2006) *Cases in sustainable tourism: An experiential approach to making decisions*. The Haworth Hospitality Press, Binghampton, New York.

Holden, A. (2009) The environment-tourism nexus. *Annals of Tourism Research* 36(3), 373–389.

Holland, R. and Holland, J. (2012) Non-aviation based tourism: A UK perspective. In: Leslie, D. (ed.) *Tourism Enterprises and the Sustainability Agenda across Europe*. New Directions in Tourism Analysis. Ashgate, Farnham, UK, pp. 51–70.

Hudson, S. and Miller, G.A. (2005) The responsible marketing of tourism: the case of Canadian Mountain Holidays. *Tourism Management* 26 (2), 133–142.

Hunter, C. and Shaw, J. (2007) The ecological footprint as a key indicator of sustainable tourism. *Tourism Management* 28 (1), 46–57.

IPCC (2013) *Fifth Assessment Report of the Intergovernmental Panel on Climate Change*. Cambridge University Press, Cambridge, UK and New York.

Johns, C. and Leslie, D. (2008) Leisure consumers of air miles – the unlikelihood of change. In: Leslie, D. (Guest Ed.) Leisure, Consumerism and Sustainable Development: 'Mission Impossible'. *Leisure Studies Newsletter* 80, pp. 35–39.

Johnson, P. (2008) Roasted on a gridiron for the sake of Green pseudo-conscience. *The Spectator* 23 August, p. 24.

Kuoni (2011) *Kuoni Holiday Report*. Available at http://www.kuoni.co.uk/en/services/about_kuoni/news/press_releases/holiday-report-2011/pages/holidayreport2011.aspx (accessed 17 March 2011).

Lean, G. (2010) Luxury with a conscience – at a price. *The Daily Telegraph*. October 9, p. 27.

Leslie, D. (2002) National parks and the tourism sector. *Countryside Recreation* 10 (3/4) Autumn/Winter, pp. 5–10.

LDNPA (1998) *Education Service: Tourism Factsheet*. Lake District National Park Authority, Kendal, UK.

Lomborg, B. (2013) Scandal of the wasteful biofuels. *The Daily Telegraph*. 17 December, p. 32.

Macintosh, A. and Wallace, L. (2009) International aviation emissions to 2025: can emissions be stabilised without restricting demand? *Energy Policy* 37, pp. 264–273.

Maguire, C., Curry, R. and McClenaghan, A. (2008) *Northern Ireland Visions – Footpaths to Sustainability*. Sustainability Resources Institute, Department of the Environment, London.

Martin-Cejas, R.R. and Sanchez, P.P. (2010) Ecological footprint analysis of road transport related to tourism activity: the case of Lanzarote Island. *Tourism Management* 31 (1), 98–103.

Masero, S. (2009) Why it pays to ACT NOW. *Sustainable Business* August/September, pp. 19–19.

Middleton, V. and Hawkins, R. (1993) Practical environmental policies in travel and tourism. Part 1: The hotel sector. *Travel and Tourism Analyst* Number 1, pp. 63–76.

NHTV (2010) *Travelling Large in 2008*. Centre for Sustainable Tourism and Transport, NHTV, Breda University of Applied Sciences, NRIT Research and NBTG-NIPO Research.

OECD (2002) *Household tourism travel: trends, environmental impacts and policy responses*. Environment Directorate, Organisation for Economic Co-operation and Development, Paris, April.

Peeters, P., Williams, V. and Gössling, S. (2007) Air transport greenhouse gas emissions. In: Peeters, P. (ed.) *Tourism and Climate Change Mitigation – Methods, Greenhouse Gas Reductions and Policies*. Breda Stichting NHTV Breda. pp. 29–50.

Pleumarom, A. (2007) Does tourism benefit the Third World? *Third World Resurgence*. 207-208 December, pp. 10–12.

Polonsky, M.J., Landreth, S. and Garma, R. (2010) The new greenwash? Potential marketing problems with carbon offsets. *International Journal of Business Studies* 18 (1), pp. 49–54.

Porritt, J. (2007) Fuelling the future. *Countryside Voice*. Campaign to Protect Rural England, Spring, p. 17.

POST (2007) *Voluntary carbon offsets*. POSTnote No.290 The Parliamentary Office of Science and Technology, London.

Schipper, Y. (2004) Environmental costs in European aviation. *Transport Policy* 11, pp. 141–154.

Scott, D. (2011) Why sustainable tourism must address climate change. *Journal of Sustainable Tourism* 19 (1), pp. 17–34.

Skidmore, J. (2008) Britons: more mean than green. Telegraph Travel, *The Daily Telegraph* 14 June, p. T4.

Somerville, H. (1993) *How the airline industry can manage its environmental impacts*. Paper presented at Conference on Sustainable Tourism, Marriott Hotel, London, May 11–12.

Somerville, H. (2012) International transport and climate change: taking responsibility seriously. In: Leslie, D. (ed.) *Responsible Tourism: Concepts, Theory and Practice*. CAB International, Wallingford, UK, pp. 43–51.

Spanner, H. (2011) Sea change. *Green Futures* 79, January, pp. 26–30.

Starmer-Smith, C. (2008) How green is your travel company? Travel Section *The Daily Telegraph*, 12 January, pp. 1–4.

Terilowski, S. (2012) Green seas? The EU Sulphur Directive. *Focus – Logistics & Transport* 14 (8), August.

TUI (2010) *New Holidays Forever brand outlines Thomson and First Choice's five year sustainable tourism commitments*. Press Release, 29th June.

TUI (2011) *Sustainable Development Report 2010.* TUI Travel Plc. Available at http://www.tuitravelplc.com (accessed 20 July 2011).

UNCED-UK/Novartes (1999) *Bio-prospecting and benefits sharing.* Report by UNED-UK and Novartes, London.

UNCSD (1999) *Does the customer care?* United Nations Commission on Sustainable Development.

Vidal, J. (2007) Global food crisis looms as climate change and fuel shortages bite. *The Guardian*, London, 3 November, p. 7.

Watts, R. (2006) Carbon trading leaves a nasty smell. *The Sunday Telegraph* July 2, B6.

Wheatcroft, S. (1991) Airlines, tourism and the environment. *Tourism Management* 12, 119–124.

Widdicombe, H. (2008) Pay as you go: the carbon offset game. *Resource* 41 May-June, pp 4–5.

World Economic Forum (2011) *Policies and Collaborative Partnership for Sustainable Aviation.* Available at www.weforum.org/reports/policies-and-collaborative-partnership-sustainable-aviation?fo=1 (accessed 30 May 2011).

WTO (2013) *Tourism Highlights.* World Tourism Organisation, Madrid.

WWF (2011) *Moving on: Why Flying Less Means More for Business.* World Wide Fund for Nature, London.

Young, T. (2011) Malaysian palm oil destroying forests. *The Guardian*. 2 February, p. 8.

9 Enterprise Owners/Managers – Awareness, Perceptions and Attitudes

Introduction

The introduction of EM and CSR practices and the adoption of an EMS by an enterprise are substantially influenced by company policy, as noted in earlier discussions. However, this applies to very few tourism operations due to the high proportion of small and micro privately owned businesses, which dominate supply. Thus, and as this study attests, for the large majority of tourism enterprises it is owners who are the driving force when it comes to sustainability initiatives and the operation of the enterprises. Therefore the perceptions and attitudes of the owners of these businesses are key factors to the introduction of EMS, coupled with their level of awareness and knowledge of such practices, all of which influence environmental behaviour (for example, see DEFRA, 2009).

The focus of this chapter therefore is on the owners/managers of these enterprises and the areas explored, largely, though not exclusively during the interviews. The first area to be discussed is their awareness of a number of what, in terms of simplicity, are considered as green initiatives and their involvement in such initiatives. Attention then turns to their perceptions of the greening of enterprise, followed by what they perceive to be the influence of external factors to achieving progress towards more enterprises 'going green'. Discussion then moves to addressing the outcomes of enquiries into their attitudes

regarding a range of factors considered influential to EM practices and enhancing their EP overall, and culminating with what they consider to be most important in terms of managing the business.

The aim of this facet of the study is to help develop a better understanding of the owners/managers involved in the study and thus why some enterprises are far more proactive in terms of greening and sustainability than many others.

Awareness of 'Green' Measures

The awareness of the enterprise owners/managers of EM practices in general and more specifically of EMSs given the absence of media attention to such matters may be attributable to membership of one or more of the agencies and professional organizations involved in tourism (see Chapter 2). Such knowledge could also be gained from other practitioners and through attending seminars promoting an EMS. However, few interviewees had attended seminars on 'greening'; of those who had, 6% cited a seminar staged by the CTB or VS whilst 12% indicated 'other' seminars. A number of reasons were offered as to why such seminars had not been attended, e.g. no time, cost. This finding further helps to explain the general levels of lack of awareness and also is rather indicative of a lack of interest. The latter is reinforced by the reasons given by

Area Tourist Boards in Scotland for stopping hosting seminars on greening and the GTBS in rural areas, which were that these were not cost effective and that there was a lack of demand and interest in the subject (Anderson *et al.*, 2001; Erdogan and Baris, 2006). This situation rather reflects Levett's (1993, p. 263) view that 'The businesses and managers who most need environmental advice and information are precisely those who are least likely to go out of their way to get it'.

As identified in Chapter 4, knowledge of an EMS is not a prerequisite to introducing EM practices, though it can be a key indicator of the likely involvement in such schemes (see Tzschentke *et al.*, 2004). However, an EMS presents greater scope for the incorporation of such practices into businesses and presents the opportunity for accreditation which can then be used in promotion. Thus, the study aimed to establish the owners'/managers' knowledge of a number of the more commonly cited systems, and related initiatives, in the professional press (the findings are presented in Table 9.1). Respondents were also invited to identify any measures which they thought should have been included, which led to just one other initiative being noted thus affirming the comprehensiveness of the range presented to them in the survey. As Table 9.1 shows, the levels of awareness among respondents across the range of initiatives are generally low which is supported by the findings of a range of other studies (Slee *et al.*, 1999; Vernon *et al.*, 2003; Hillary, 2004; Gaunt, 2004; Erdogan and

Baris, 2006). Interestingly the EA's (2005) research suggested that awareness levels of EM practices and related measures were increasing, which is very questionable on the basis of these findings. However, far higher levels of awareness were found by Bohdanowicz (2006) in her study into large hotels in Sweden and Poland, though the latter comparatively less so than the Swedish hotelier, which was attributed to the importance given to the environment by the Swedish Government. Also Scanlon's (2007) research into EM practices in major hotels and resort properties in the USA, whilst finding much to applaud, also noted that many of the managers involved in the study lacked awareness of what can be achieved to the benefit of the business. A key factor, though, in drawing comparisons between these different findings is that the latter studies involved major operations and not small/micro business. Even so, it is evidently not the case that large operations are necessarily any more aware or comparatively more proactive.

The most recognized measures were that of the TCP and GTBS. To an extent, the level of awareness of the Green Audit Kit in 2001 might be considered surprisingly low, given this has been promoted by the CTB since 1995. In contrast, Hobson and Essex's study (2001) found that 39% of their sample was aware of the Green Audit Kit. This difference might be explained by the fact that this 'Kit' was developed in the area of their study and, as such, reinforces the point of the need for

Table 9.1. Awareness of selected 'green' measures.

		Aware (%)		
		Audits		Audits
Initiative	2001	2001	2006	2011
BS 7750	18	20	23	16
Ecolabelling	18	14	15	16
ISO14001	10	12	17	16
The Green Audit Kit	8	12	4	11
Green Globe	8	14	6	4
British Airways Environment Awards	8	18	7	4
TCP (LDNP)	30	36	n/a	n/a
Green Business Scheme (includes GTBS)	6	12	27	14
IHEI	3	2	4	6

schemes to 'connect' with local enterprise owners/managers if they are to be effective. This finding is equally applicable across Europe (see Bendell and Font, 2004; Halme and Fadeeva, 2001).

Not surprisingly, perhaps, given their participation in interview stages the audited enterprises of 2001 collectively evidence a higher level of awareness of most initiatives compared with the data from the main survey. However, the reverse appears to be the case for 2011 compared with 2006. On the basis of the latter, it might be argued that awareness has decreased. But the higher levels of 2006 in part will have been boosted by the number of attractions in the sample that consistently demonstrated comparatively greater knowledge of these measures. It should also be remembered that the data for 2011 come from enterprises that were directly invited to participate rather than volunteered as in the case of the 2001 audits. Therefore the 2011 findings may well be a more accurate reflection of the tourism sector as a whole. The difference in awareness of the GTBS between 2006 and 2011 is all the more remarkable given that VS was promoting this scheme in the 1990s and for much of the 2000s, thus the expectation that members of this Tourist Board (approx. 60% in the 2006 sample) would at least be aware of the GTBS.

Further exploration of the data did not find a definitive correlation between membership of any organization and awareness, with the exception of the GTBS. This outcome reflects similar studies; for example Sloan *et al.*'s (2004) research into German hoteliers' attitudes toward EM (the hotels in this study were in the category of 3 to 5 stars, medium size) though not that of Carlsen *et al.* (2001) who did find a correlation between membership of a conservation group and EM. This finding supports Clarke (2004) who argued that many national trade associations are not promoting the need to address environmental performance and Mastny (2002) who suggested that many efforts to promote green initiatives fail to reach the small operators. It was also established that relatively few owners/ managers were aware of more than a few of these measures. No substantive variances on the basis of other profiling factors, for example

length of career in the sector, were found with two exceptions. First, in the case of the LDNP there was a clear bias to awareness on the part of newer entrants. Second, in the case of the serviced accommodation category the majority of respondents who indicated that they were aware of any of the measures were also members of the Institute of Hospitality. However their levels of awareness across the range was comparatively lower than that of other categories in 2001 and in 2006, i.e. the attractions category consistently showed a higher level of awareness across all the measures; similarly though less so the self-catering property owners, with the inns category also showing slightly better awareness.

To be aware of these initiatives does not mean participation/adoption (see Chapter 8) and thus their involvement in any of these systems was subsequently explored.

Involvement

Awareness of the measures noted in Table 9.1 and also of 'green' initiatives does not automatically mean that the appropriate responsive action will be taken, as their involvement in a number of such initiatives demonstrates (see Table 9.2). Involvement in some of these, and related, initiatives is discussed in some depth in Chapter 5 and in relation to locally based projects in Chapter 4, and thus only a brief note on these findings is presented here. However given the attention in this chapter specifically to the owners'/ managers' views there are a number of points on the involvement of owners/managers in the GTBS that merit attention here as they relate to perceptions and interest. Tzschentke *et al.* (2004) found from their study into tourism SMEs in Scotland that key criteria were lifestyle choices and personal ethics (similarly Carter *et al.*, 2004) – in other words intrinsic factors. However, identifying such factors in owners did not automatically indicate that they would have taken up the GTBS and equally so the absence of such did not mean no participation as they found that alternatively the reason for obtaining accreditation was that of close attention to the effective and efficient management of resources (similar to Blanco

Table 9.2. Involvement in selected 'green' and related initiatives.

Initiative	Involved – Yes (%)			
	2001	Audits 2001	2006	Audits 2011
Made in Cumbria/Made in Scotland	7	12	4	1
Business Environment Network	2	2	2	6
Green Business Scheme	2	2	11	16
A Tourism Forum[a]	n/a	n/a	14	10
TCP (LDNP)/Participate in a Conservation Scheme (Scotland)	12	18	16	6
IHEI	1	1	2	1

[a]Participation in a 'Tourism Forum' was not included in the LDNP stage of the study.

et al., 2009). In contrast, Blackstock *et al.*'s (2008) study involving tourism enterprises in the Cairngorms National Park found a lack of interest in EMSs despite the promotion of this scheme. Similarly Erdogan and Baris's (2006) study, involving mainly 3 to 4 star, 40-bedroom hotels in Ankara, found most managers lacked interest in such matters, whilst Hillary's (2004) study based on empirical research and drawing on an extensive range of research articles all based on SMEs in the general business sector found that the great majority were not convinced of any real need for such systems.

The most notable difference across the findings presented in Table 9.2 is the comparative levels of involvement in a green business scheme between the enterprises in Scotland, especially those urban based, and the LDNP data sets. The owners'/managers' involvement in these green initiatives is very limited amongst the 2011 population. The majority of those involved in a green business scheme (three of which were Green Glasgow, the Carbon Trust and Hospitable Climates) not accounted for by participation in the GTBS are all enterprises that are part of a regional/ national organization. This finding further affirms that what the multinational and national companies are doing as regards EMSs and CSR is not representative of tourism supply as a whole (see EA, 2005). The limited participation in more general environment initiatives reinforces the internal focus of EM on operational practices and costs.

Further analysis of the data found no substantive correlation between membership of a professional or a green organization and involvement – in effect participation is not a definite indicator of environmental values (see Barr *et al.*, 2010). An important factor to emerge is that comparatively recent owners are more likely to be environmentally aware, and when compared with long term owners more responsive and supportive of environmental initiatives, a finding very similar to Barrow and Burnett's (1990) study. A further correlation identified is that owners/ managers in rural areas are more likely to be involved in a tourism or local community forum and conversely a business forum rather than those in an urban area, e.g. Chamber of Commerce. Also 24% of the 2011 enterprises were involved in local projects or community schemes (mainly relating to licensing practices and/or 'neighbour watch', though two projects in some way related to a conservation scheme) thus indicating some degree of further involvement with the local community.

These findings on awareness and involvement reflect the discussions in Chapters 4 and 5 and are similar to those of other studies that gave consideration to awareness of and involvement in sustainability initiatives not only undertaken in the UK (see Revell and Blackburn, 2004; Dewhurst and Thomas, 2003) but also across Europe (see Donovan and McElligott, 2000; Warnken *et al.*, 2005; Vernon *et al.*, 2003; Erdogan and Tosun, 2009; Kucerova, 2012). Overall, given that comparatively few interviewees were members of any other tourism, community or environmental forum this is a clear indication of both the limited involvements in professional organizations and of their 'green' credentials.

On this basis it can be speculated that the majority of owners/managers are not interested in the environment per se yet this appears to be contradicted by the findings presented later in Table 9.6.

Perceptions

To gain further insights into the way the owners/managers perceived the greening of enterprises, the interviewees were presented with a range of statements relating to the EP of tourism enterprises derived from both the research literature and outcomes from the initial survey. They were invited to rate each statement on the basis of 1 = 'strongly disagree' to 5 = 'strongly agree'. The statements and results are presented in Table 9.3 in rank order of bias to 'agree' based on the mean responses from the 2011 data.

The data presented in Table 9.3 suggest that for the most part the owners/managers are fairly ambivalent in their perceptions. Also there is no substantive difference between the outcomes of 2001 compared with those of 2011, rather indicating that little progress has been made by way of changing perceptions over the intervening years and especially so when it to comes to any changes in their understanding of and responses to sustainability issues as they relate to their businesses. The data presented here also suggest that they do not see the benefits such as cost savings, that is beyond first steps, marketing and PR advantages as advocated by, for example, government agencies, professional organizations, nor do the data appear to support the promulgation of such benefits in the academic literature (see Chapter 4). However, the findings of four of the statements merit further consideration:

1. 'First steps'. The high bias to 'strongly agree' affirms that it is the easy steps which are likely to be taken but owners/managers will not necessarily go further than this, such as introducing an EMS programme like the GTBS (as also found by Lawton and Weaver, 2009; Preigo et al., 2011). Yet the majority appear to be rather ambivalent in their perceptions as to whether the introduction of further EM practices would or would not lead to further cost savings, which rather supports the argument that once these initial steps have been introduced there is limited effort to going further, e.g. to seek EMS certification (see Chapter 5; also Lawton and Weaver, 2009; Freezer and Font, 2010).
2. 'Customers are primarily concerned with price'. The high level of agreement with this

Table 9.3. The greening of tourism enterprise.

Statement	Mean[a]	
	2001	2011
The 'first steps' practices, e.g. reducing heating costs and waste all save on costs.	4.34	4.36
By and large, the deciding factor for potential customers is the price of the accommodation.	3.90	4.10
Anyone can introduce some environmentally friendly practices and claim to be green.	3.80	3.56
Apart from a few notable examples, little progress has been made over the last 5 years.	3.26	3.18
Operators should support local producers, even if the products cost a little more.	3.78	3.14
Guests are not really concerned about the environment.	2.82	3.14
Compared with five years ago, owners/managers have a better understanding of how to maintain financial performance while improving environmental and social performance.	3.02	2.95
Commitment to 'greening' the business is being used to gain competitive advantage.	2.34	2.59
Environmental problems are threatening the future of the local tourism industry.	2.84	2.52
Once the 'first steps' have been taken, there are few – if any – cost savings.	2.80	2.47

[a]Mean based on: 1 = strongly disagree to 5 = strongly agree.

statement supports similar findings and discussion in Chapter 8 that the primary determinant in tourists' choice of accommodation is price, all other factors being equal, i.e. similar services. This outcome also correlates with other indicators as noted in the discussion on attitudes (see page 156).

3. 'Anyone can claim to be green'. The bias towards agreement that enterprises may claim to be 'green' whilst adopting limited EM activity rather supports the sceptical view that the promotion of green credentials may be seen as a 'greenwash'. The criticism here reflects Hudson and Miller's (2005) point that the active promotion of environmental management practices can and does raise the profile of the business which then gains the interest of groups which seek to establish the honesty of such promotional messages. Even so, the Greenbiz (2009) survey found that businesses promoting green credentials were doing so for the perceived PR benefit and competitive advantage and, as Preigo et al. (2011) suggest, is less reflective of demand.

4. 'Support for local producers'. The greater support for purchasing local produce identified in the 2001 audits compared with 2011 correlates with a similar difference in such support identified between these two research populations in support for local products and produce identified in Chapter 7. This supports the traditional paradigm of 'go green, save money' and implies attention to the adoption of EM practices that save on cost and not necessarily those practices that may increase costs, e.g. purchase of local products and produce (Carter et al., 2004).

To further this aspect of the study into the perceptions of the owners/managers towards addressing sustainability issues in their operational practices the interviewees were presented with a range of potentially influential factors that could stimulate more attention to the EP of tourism enterprises. They were invited to indicate how significant a role they would predict each of these factors will play in advancing progress over the next 5 years and to grade their consideration of each factor on the basis of '1 = minor influence' to '5 = major influence'. The findings, based on the mean response, are presented in Table 9.4.

Evidently, as the data in Table 9.4 show, all the factors listed could have some influence, though none are considered very significant with the exception of government policy, which implies the introduction of some form of regulation. Possibly reflecting more the reality of demand is that green consumerism is seen to be no more influential than the majority of the other factors. Overall these findings suggest that by far the majority of the interviewees did not foresee any real change to the current situation.

This outcome rather brings into question arguments that 'greening' the enterprise will give a competitive advantage and perceptions that customers generally are interested and thus this will influence their choice, for example, of accommodation, albeit it is recognized that it can influence some customers (Masau and Prideaux, 2003; Leidner, 2004; Fairweather et al., 2005). This is perhaps surprising given the regularity with which consumers indicate their concern for the

Table 9.4. Influence of external factors on progress towards improving environmental performance.

Question	Mean[a]
Government policy to adopt environmentally friendly practices	3.58
Green Consumerism	2.98
Legislation requiring environmental audits	2.92
Economic instruments, e.g. taxes	2.86
Growing competition between green products	2.78
Voluntary agreements and industry-led initiatives	2.78
Business customers requesting environmental policy statements	2.62
International/national role models	2.48
Voluntary environmental reporting	2.44

[a]Mean based on: 1 = minor influence to 5 = major influence

environment (EC, 2003). Also, and in combination with other data, it was identified that the least likely influence would be international and national role models (similarly Gaunt, 2004), albeit role models are advocated as potential significant influencers on both environmental behaviour (DEFRA, 2009) and voluntary environmental reporting which rather suggest this is a peripheral issue. Yet it is partly due to these factors that major hotel companies and leisure groups are adopting EMS, albeit primarily due to corporate influence (Chan *et al.*, 2005). This further affirms the need for localized, locally owned initiatives in the case of the many small/micro enterprises involved in tourism.

The Impact of Tourism and Related Aspects

The final area investigated into the perceptions of the owners/managers was that of the impact of tourism and related aspects to 'going green' to provide further insights into their understanding of a range of pertinent issues, and therefore to help gain a better understanding of their actions as regards EM, CSR and overall, their EP. All participants in the study were invited to grade a number of statements, as presented in Table 9.5, on the basis '1 = strongly disagree' to '5 = strongly agree'. These same statements, appropriately adjusted for the different context, were presented to A & C producers involved in the first stage of the study. These data are included in Table 9.5 by way of providing a contrast to the responses of the owners/managers of the tourism enterprises. Before considering the data in this table it might be of value to bear in mind, especially as most of the respondents are also local residents, the following influential factor on perceptions of impacts noted by Bestard and Nadal (2006). They found that the perceptions of residents of the Balearic Islands on the impact of visitors on the environment and also on the environmental impact of tourism varied in that the higher the density of accommodation, the less tourism is seen to be of negative impact and the more favourable attitudes were towards tourism. These results in part at least were attributed to economic benefits associated with tourism development.

There is little change across the decade in the mean responses to the statements presented, the main exception being that of an increase in agreement that claiming to be 'green' is more of a marketing ploy and, to a lesser extent, that the 2011 enterprises are more in agreement that tourism's impact is less than that of the manufacturing sector. Is this bias due to their urban location? Perhaps

Table 9.5. Perceptions of the sector's impact and related aspects.

	Mean[a]				
Question	2001	Audits 2001	2006	Audits 2011	A & C 2001
The sector[b] has an impact on the environment.	3.77	4.02	3.90	3.96	4.07
The sector's[b] impact on the environment is significantly less than the manufacturing sector.	3.58	3.54	3.50	3.81	3.27
Operators who claim to be 'green' are using it as a marketing ploy.	3.11	3.06	3.40	3.67	3.47
Most owners/managers do not have time to worry about the environment.	3.13	2.92	3.20	3.11	2.67
Customers are not interested in whether an operation is environmentally friendly.	2.42	2.56	2.51	2.37	2.93
It is not possible to be profitable and be environmentally friendly.	2.00	2.06	3.00	2.19	2.20

[a]Mean: based on scale of 1 = 'Strongly disagree' – 5 = 'Strongly agree'
[b]The appropriate category of supply was stated in each of the surveys specifically tailored to that category.

not, given Gaunt (2004) found that most small TOs in Scotland considered that they had little impact on the environment and even less so when asked to consider their own business operations.

The inclusion of the equivalent findings for the A & C producers makes for an interesting comparison with the tourism enterprises, in that they agree more that tourism has an impact and are the least likely to agree that such impact is lesser than the manufacturing sector though not dissimilar to the audited enterprises of 2001. Also of particular note is the general bias to dis-agreement that it is not possible to be profitable whilst being environmentally friendly. This rather suggests that costs in such matters are not *very* significant. However, this would be misleading given that cost was identified by many of the owners/managers as a barrier to progress. As regards the other statements, there again appears to be a large degree of ambivalence. Partly contrary to this is the finding for 2011 that 20% of the enterprises seek to attract custom through 'green' messages. Indeed, the Caravan and Camping site category was found to be *the* category which most disagreed with this statement.

Evidently many of the owners/managers consider tourism to have a lower environmental impact than the manufacturing sector, which is similar to Bohdanowicz (2006). This echoes Barrow and Burnett (1990) that SMEs in general do not consider they generate pollution and that a third of their sample considered environmental issues have no effect on their business hence an unwillingness to put an EMS in place. Also Berry and Ladkin's (1997) study which found that many owners/managers considered that tourism was not damaging the environment and argued that it is the big industries that have the negative impacts. In combination this supports Holden's (2009, p. 380) claim that 'environmental policy has to date had relatively little effect on the workings of the tourism market'.

In general, those enterprises agreeing with 'customers not being interested' were also identified as giving little or no attention to promoting 'green' practices (similar to Revell and Blackburn, 2004). However, there is a

slight bias to disagreeing which is supported by discussion in Chapter 8 and reflects the findings of other studies. For example, Fairweather *et al.* (2005), Masau and Prideaux (2003) and the EA's (2007) survey of SMEs, all show that there is some degree of customer interest in green accredited accommodation, particularly on the part of international visitors. Note, however, that the former research was not based on small/micro enterprises. In contrast, Craig and Leslie's (1997) study into EM and tourism enterprises in Glasgow found that the managers did not really consider customer demand as a factor, similarly Hobson and Essex (2001), Hillary (2004) and Scanlon (2007). This ambivalence towards customer interest correlates with responses to other enquiries and, overall, indicates limited support for the introduction of EM practices, a finding which reflects a survey of business SMEs in general undertaken by Greenbiz (2009) which found that the majority of small businesses do not consider customers will pay a premium for 'green products' and furthermore that the number of businesses that do think they will pay a premium had declined since 2007, a trend that is supported by the findings of this study. It seems all too true that:

> The idea that consumers will pay a premium for 'green' products and services was always reliant upon a favourable economic climate and ignored the increasing evidence that consumers were looking for companies to deliver goods and services whilst 'taking care of the environment'. (Anon., 2006)

Further analysis of the data established that the restaurant category was found to be the one most in agreement with 'marketing ploy'; restaurateurs had no time to worry about the environment and thought that customers were not interested, which rather concurs with Revell and Blackburn (2004) whose study included restaurants, finding that they gave little attention to environmental issues and did not consider that introducing EM practices would influence customer demand. The SC property owners were the ones who most disagreed with the statement that it is not possible to be profitable and be environmentally friendly. The inns category was found to agree more than the others with the view that tourism impacts on the environment less than the manufacturing sector.

support for 'greening', which in itself is not necessarily a behavioural trait (Frey and George, 2009).

Attitudes

The interviews involved further and more direct exploration of the owners'/managers' attitudes involving three sets of questions that were put directly to the interviewees. These sought to explore first their attitudes to the enterprise's environment, second a range of factors considered influential to EM practices, which was also included in the general surveys of 2001 and 2006, and finally, what they thought to be most important in managing their businesses. Albeit the opportunity was presented to comment on these questions during the interviews, very few of the interviewees offered additional comment and then no degree of similarity was evident except for a small number of owners involved in 2001 who mentioned that there were too many cars and/or visitors. Before presenting these findings it should be borne in mind that attitudes are not always reliable predictors of behaviour; 'people are happy to say they believe it is important to act in an environmental friendly way but are often less happy actually to do so' (Cooper et al., 2010, p. 17) as, for example, in the number of tourists who indicate support for paying an additional cost for an environmental initiative and the number who actually then pay such a cost when it is voluntary (see Chapters 5 and 8). It is also noted that attitudes are a key factor but the attitude to management practices (e.g. not changing approach in the way the resources of the business are managed) may well outweigh attitudes to other aspects, e.g.

The enterprise's environment

As presented in Table 9.6, the interviewees were asked a number of questions relating to their interest in the impact of their business and that of tourism on their environment and whether they were committed to reducing such impacts. The high level of interest shown in 2001 and, though comparatively less, in 2011 contrasts with the findings of Carlsen et al. (2001), Revell and Blackburn (2004) and Erdogan and Tosun (2009) but does bear some similarity with that of Leidner's (2004) study. The contrast between expression of interest and commitment to reducing is remarkable and to some degree bears witness to Barrow and Burnett's (1990) research which found an unwillingness to put 'green policies' in place. In effect '... expressing concern over environmental problems ..., but unwilling to make difficult or inconvenient lifestyle changes that cumulatively could ameliorate these problems.' (Lawton and Weaver, 2009, p. 2); a simple indicator of such commitment to reducing negative impacts is whether the owners/managers use diesel fuelled or hybrid cars. The finding across the whole study was that less than 70% of the owners/managers have vehicles that use diesel fuel and few had a hybrid car.

These findings also contradict the notion or potential expectation, based on the findings of general surveys into environmental behaviours, that far more owners/managers would have said 'Yes' – that they were committed. This finding, that they are not that

Table 9.6. Indicative attitudes of owners/managers towards the enterprise's environment.

Factor	Yes (%)	
	2001	2011
Is the owner/manager interested in the impact on the environment of the business?	98	77
Is the owner/manager interested in the impact on the environment of tourism in the local area?	92	70
Is the owner/manager committed to reducing negative impacts?	58	32

committed is similar to Chan and Hawkins (2011) and is manifest in the limited adoption of EM practices on the part of the majority of enterprises. Evidently interest does not translate into commitment which is a general finding of many surveys into environmental behaviours. It might be expected that interest would be high given their involvement, especially if taken in consideration with the view that:

> Since tourism relies on the preservation and controlled development of any given destination, hotels, along with other local tourism partners, are intrinsically 'responsible' for maintaining and protecting the environment (Anon., 2003, p. 4).

Furthermore, one might expect high levels of interest in both the impacts of their business and that of local tourism for two reasons. First, it would be considered as 'the correct' response. Second is the fact that they participated in the interviews. However, whilst this applies to the 2001 set in that they volunteered this does not apply to the 2011 set, which certainly may account in part for the substantive difference between 2001 and 2011. A third consideration to account for this difference is that of the different locations, i.e. LDNP and city/urban. Those interviewees who indicated a commitment to reducing negative environmental impacts were more likely to disagree with the suggestion that owners/managers over the last 5 years have developed a better understanding of how to manage profitability whilst also addressing their environmental performance.

Overall the findings suggest greater interest amongst the majority of owners/managers, which is counter to the argument that:

> Conventional wisdom has it that small local business will have the greatest regard for the community environment but there is scant evidence to justify that. The opposite seems probable. (EIU, 1993, p. 96)

Furthermore, the levels of interest indicated compared with actual commitment raises an interesting question, namely how one interprets two other outcomes of the 2011 audits. First, that 53% of the owners/managers said that the principle and practices involved in EMS and CSR, as identified within the survey and interviews, should be more widely adopted. Second, that 62% indicated that they support the introduction of an accredited environmental award scheme. These data suggest EM practices would have been more widely adopted and there would be a greater number with EMS accreditation than the relatively small numbers found. A potential explanation for this discrepancy between support and action is that there are differences between what people say or agree to support and what they actually do themselves. Second, that awareness and attitudes are also influential factors on choice and in decision-making and thus the limited awareness shown in Table 9.1 may be far more significant than on initial consideration.

Influences on the introduction of EM practices

To investigate what has or would influence the introduction of EM practices, all the participant enterprises were presented with a range of factors considered potentially influential and asked to rate them on a scale of '1 = least important' to '5 = most important'. The results are presented in rank order based on the mean figures for the 2011 data set (see Table 9.7). The first point of note is that the audited enterprises of 2001 evidence no significant variance with the main research population for 2001, which serves to further affirm that those who participated in the audits were not substantially different in their attitudes and practices to many of the other enterprises.

Whilst the factors and data presented in Table 9.7 each have their own merits, it is not necessary to discuss here all of them but rather those considered comparatively more significant to this context.

Cost savings

Cost savings are ranked as the most important factor in 2011 and rather similarly in 2006 and 2001, which is an outcome also of Garay and Font (2012). The data also show cost savings have followed an upward trajectory over the timeframe which may reflect the wider

Table 9.7. Factors potentially influential to the introduction of EM practices.

| | | Mean[a] | | |
| | | Audits | | Audits |
Factor	2001	2001	2006	2011
Cost savings	3.74	3.88	4.23	4.55
Customer care	3.96	3.94	4.34	4.06
Quality management	3.11	3.30	3.85	3.97
Competitors' actions	2.04	2.14	2.71	3.89
Industry standards	2.52	2.44	3.13	3.88
Health and safety	3.65	3.48	4.29	3.83
Potential legislation	2.57	2.62	3.19	3.81
Public relations	3.06	2.96	3.83	3.74
Care for the environment	3.77	3.76	4.23	3.64
Customer demand	3.60	3.74	3.96	3.57
Personal beliefs	3.47	3.64	3.81	3.54

[a]Mean based on 1 = least important to 5 = most important.

economic recession over the later part of the study, but the similar ranking of 2006 brings such speculation into question.

This outcome further indicates that owners/managers are more internally focused on their operations. Saving on costs also helps explain why many owners/managers cite cost as a barrier to further progress in the adoption of EM practices and EMS accreditation (IH, 2007; Baird, 2010). A counterpoint to this is that 'Companies worried about the cost of greening their operations should perhaps be worrying about the cost of not doing so instead' (Simms, 2006, p. 24). This is a view recognized by the N/MNCs in the hotel sector; for example Bohdanowicz (2006) found that the main reason for introducing EM practices in hotels in Sweden and Poland was cost savings (also see Sloan et al., 2004).

Customer care and quality management

These two areas, highly ranked in importance of influence, further support the introspective nature of the owners/managers in regard to the management of their enterprise.

Competitors' actions

It appears that the owners/managers in rural settings do not consider that competitors are likely to be much of an influence which leads to

speculation that for the most part they do not see their competitors doing much in the way of addressing their environmental performance as to become a threat albeit many commentators advocate the marketing benefits to be achieved through such actions (see Carter et al., 2004; Chapters 4 and 5). However, the 2011 enterprises clearly see competitors' actions as being more important, an outcome which is certainly bolstered by a combination of enterprises in cities and the higher number of company operations within the sample.

Potential legislation

That legislation is ranked seventh in terms of the list of influential factors is probably understated given that many hoteliers have been found to be unaware of current environmental legislation (that is outside of main health and safety aspects), e.g. waste disposal regulations (Radwan et al., 2010). Further, the higher importance attributed to this factor over the three stages of the study could be indicative that enterprises may consider government intervention has become more of a possibility now than 15 years ago.

Customer demand

A conundrum with the high level of importance attributed to this factor is that it could be seen to contradict other findings relating to customers. However, the point here is not on customer demand per se but whether the owners/managers consider there is a demand for 'going green'. Whilst they evidently rate it of some importance it is clearly considered of lesser importance than most of the other factors as its ranking, i.e. tenth, demonstrates. This comparatively low level of importance attached to customer demand being influential evidences little change over the years, despite the findings of other surveys such as Mintel (see Chapter 8; Leslie, 2012). This also correlates with other studies such as Fairweather et al. (2005) who, based on an extensive survey of tourists in New Zealand, found that less than 20% could recall any accommodation mentioning some form of EMS accreditation and that approximately 90% had not heard of tourism ecolabels; see also Preigo et al. (2011). Furthermore, these findings show little support for an outcome of Barnett's (2004) study into Green Globe 21, that 67% of managers thought that customer demand for EMS certification was increasing; nor for the purported market demand for 'green hotels' (or so accredited eco-labelled) (see Infor, 2008; Leslie, 2011). However, Baird (2010) concluded from her study into GTBS members in Scotland that 77% had joined the scheme because of the promoted benefits, i.e. increase in customer demand. But 52% said that it had subsequently made no difference, though 4% considered it had helped towards gaining over a 10% increase in the business.

What are the Key Factors in the Management of the Enterprise?

Each interviewee was presented with a range of factors considered key to the management of an enterprise and asked to grade each factor in terms of importance on the basis of 1 = not at all important to 5 = very important. The results in rank order of attributed importance based on the mean response of 2011 are presented in Table 9.8. What is immediately apparent is the marked difference between the two factors relating to environmental performance and the other management functions. Clearly profitability and financial performance are considered to be of primary importance amongst the 2011 population. In contrast the LDNP audit enterprises considered customer complaints the most important. This difference between these two sets of enterprises may well be explained by the higher proportion of managers in 2011 that are answerable to their stakeholders. Interestingly Sloan et al.'s (2004) study, which involved managers, found that the majority indicated they do not consider improving profitability to be more important than concern for the environment. However, the high ranking of profitability and budget achievement indicates an internal management focus and cost centred approach, which is rather contradictory to Drucker's (1955, p. 3) argument that 'profit is not the explanation, cause or rationale of business behaviour and growth decisions but the test of their validity.'

This outcome undoubtedly also contradicts suppositions (for example, see Wanhill, 1997)

Table 9.8. Relative importance of key management factors.

Factor	Mean[a]	
	2001	2011
Maintenance/improvement of profitability	4.46	4.56
Achievement of budget	4.26	4.47
Addressing customer complaints	4.80	4.37
Staff retention	3.04	4.14
Environmental reporting	2.22	2.38
Achieving environmental targets	2.42	2.36

[a]Based on Likert scale: 1 = not at all important to 5 = very important.

that because many of these owners may be in the business due to motivations such as lifestyle and quality of life (see Chapter 2), that they are in some ways more likely to manage their business on the basis of consideration for environmental concerns and sustainability issues appears to be ill-founded. But the importance given to these factors does lend itself to one of the pillars of sustainability in that staying in business and thus being a net contributor to the economy and local community (as an employer) is a primary responsibility of any business. The data also evidence little variance in such findings over the last decade with the exception of staff retention. The latter's increased significance may well be due to the economic climate, with managers recognizing that on the one hand it is more cost effective to retain quality staff but on the other being able to retain staff in a recession may also be an influence on their decision here. Conversely, it is harder to obtain staff in the LDNP thus one might have expected the 2001 figure to be higher. Staff retention is clearly more important to the urban enterprises than those in the LDNP. This is perhaps not surprising given that there are wider and more opportunities for employment in urban areas.

As regards staff retention, most studies into EMS and more so CSR find that involving staff in the development of these activities invariably has positive outcomes in terms of staff morale and retention (see Bohdanowicz and Zientara, 2008; Chan, 2011; Ioannides and Petridou, 2012). This is evidently not recognized or realized by the majority of enterprises! Not surprising perhaps when one considers that 23% of the managers do not think staff are concerned over such matters and a further 37% 'don't know'. Perhaps they are not, but it is interesting to note that a survey on wiredgov (Anon., 2009) found that only 5% of the workforce of organizations noted that they were more environment conscious at work than at home and overall there was a remarkable degree of 'eco-apathy'; as illustrated by the findings of a study that 48% of staff noted that they had no interest in environment matters or their employer's policy on environmental matters at work (Anon., 2009). Additional to this is that of Mokower

(2009) who found that being environmentally friendly was ranked below jobs, protecting employees and improving the quality of products. In effect being a good employer was ranked higher than being environmentally responsible.

The little importance given to environmental reporting and environmental targets reflects that, in general, owners/managers do not see possible wider business benefits, e.g. reputation, marketing, and in this are similar to the findings of Pratt's (2011) study. Further support for this view is that the 'hospitality sector is looking for evidence that investment in sustainability makes business sense' (Anon., 2010, p. 1).

Barriers to Progress

The participants in all three stages were asked: Are there any factors which you can think of which discourage introducing more environmentally friendly practices? Analysis of the responses to this question leads to identifying the following main factors achieving some degree of consensus from each research population. Further, the factors noted are those which gained similar levels of comparative consistency across the three stages. The common factors so identified were awareness/ knowledge/information, resource constraints and attitudes. An outcome that bears witness to the fact that these discouraging factors, in effect barriers, have changed little over time. However, it is not the case that these factors apply to all the owners/managers involved in the study nor that they are all equally applicable but rather, and to varying degrees, they apply to the majority. For example, a need for more information was noted by 20% of the owners/ managers in the 2011 audits and 32% in the 2001 audits, which suggests far greater awareness of potential practices than that found in the EA's (2007) general survey wherein 50% of respondents suggested they considered there to be a lack of information. However, given the findings noted in Table 9.1, the low levels of awareness of a range of practices/initiatives suggests that many more owners/managers lack knowledge in such matters thus indicating the need for information.

Information

As previously noted, the need for information gained the highest degree of consensus in both 2001 (32%), with a further 24% noting that such improvement should be practical, and 2011 (20%) to which might be added the 8% of interviewees who mentioned a 'lack of knowledge'. This remarkable consistency over the study's timeframe suggests it is not a matter of a lack of information but rather more a case of lack of knowledge and thus interest and consideration of greening and sustainability issues as they relate to their own enterprise. Also, some level of misunderstanding of what is actually involved, perhaps perceiving that EM practice, especially when considered in the context of an EMS for business per se or a scheme such as the GTBS, is more complex than it is really. A secondary point made within the context of suggestions of a lack of information was the need for more practical measures. A lack of exemplars was also noted as not being helpful. A key point here is that the exemplars should be local and promoted at the local level. Interestingly some of the owners/managers also noted that they would like to see information on the perceptions of customers towards EMSs and EP more generally and in some cases noting in the process that there was a lack of market research into up-to-date visitor opinions and attitudes. Comments which correlate with the earlier finding that many owners/managers considered there was a lack of visitor interest in the EP of tourism enterprises. In itself this is a particularly interesting observation given that the opportunity was presented, prior to finalizing the research programme, to CTB to undertake such research amongst visitors to the area during the extensive fieldwork at no cost; an opportunity they declined. Within this context it was also noted that there was a lack of availability of accurate information on local products and produce. A speculation on this point is whether it would have arisen if this area of enquiry had not been included in the surveys and audits.

A follow-up inquiry involved asking the interviewees to indicate who they thought should be responsible for providing such information. The general consensus was that it should come from government – at local and national level. However, no one made reference to readily accessible information sources and guidance such as the Business Environmental Training Initiative Plus or to the Environment Agency's 'NetRegs' or any other sources of information. However, in the 2001 interviews 10% did comment that such information on many of the aspects covered in the interviews was readily available. It should also be remembered that during the 1990s the greening of tourism enterprise was being extensively promoted through government tourism policy by the Tourist Boards, with particular promotion of the GTBS in Scotland. Furthermore during the mid-late 1990s 'Local Agenda 21' planning was being undertaken by many local authorities, during the process of which information based on the slogan of 'think local, act local' was very much in evidence, including basic EM practices (see Leslie and Hughes, 1997). Thus in combination with the promotion of energy and water-saving measures and recycling it is arguably difficult on face value to understand why the need for information should have gained so many comments. Certainly this indicates a lack of interest and commitment to greening. A factor that is further affirmed by the 34% of interviewees who do not consider that the practices identified within the audits should be more widely adopted.

Resources

The resources factor encompasses costs and also includes time and effort; for example, the perceptions of owners/managers as to the time (14%) and effort (e.g. 'too busy'; 'disruption to everyday running of the business'; 'the inconvenience'), required to consider and then introduce EM and CSR practices. Time and effort were particularly noted by Craig and Leslie (1997) and Revell and Blackburn (2004). However the noting of costs accounts for the majority of those owners/managers (28%) and this is not surprising given the importance placed on cost savings (Table 9.7) and profitability (Table 9.8) and further manifest in attitudes to 'buying local' (Chapter 6; see Craig and Leslie, 1997).

Some of the interviewees who noted costs mentioned other areas such as the costs involved in establishing an EMS such as that required by the GTBS or in the purchase of 'green products' or new, more energy efficient equipment and fittings. But it would also be true to say that in many cases it is more a matter of perception as to costs, which suggests some degree of a lack of knowledge and understanding of what is involved (Lin and Hemmington, 1997; Baird 2010); similarly Sloan et al.'s (2004) study into the adoption of an EMS which found that some participants considered that they were complicated and would require training, which indicates a lack of expertise, as noted by Smith and Reynolds (1999). However this is hardly true of those schemes promoted in tourism.

A key consideration in this is that neither EM nor CSR necessarily increases costs albeit there may be some initial costs involved in establishing best practice, though, as often argued, these will then be offset by subsequent savings and increased demand. Even allowing for the latter, introducing EM and CSR practices does not necessarily mean raised costs nor do any costs actually incurred need to be passed on to customers (see Anon., 2010). A caveat here though is if an EMS, such as the GTBS, is established based on perceptions of increased customer demand then what assurance has the enterprise of continuity of such demand (Baird, 2010)? A consideration that reinforces the view that if EMS accreditation is sought on the basis of cost savings and as such is extrinsic not an intrinsic behavioural change in the absence of evident additional demand, then what is the likelihood of the enterprise maintaining its accreditation. Even so, the costs involved in gaining EMS accreditation in one form or another are inescapable, which does act as a barrier, as noted in Baird's (2010) study into members of the GTBS, who noted that participants did see membership as a recurrent expense and also noted that some of the information the scheme requires the business to gather makes no contribution to the profitability of the business, is time consuming to collect and then does nothing for business efficiency which acted as a further discouraging factor.

These are the key factors that many of the owners/managers to varying degrees consider as to why more enterprises have not adopted EM practices throughout the management and operations of their enterprises, including building on interrelationships with local enterprises. Factors that have also been identified in other studies related to the EP of tourism enterprises (see Berry and Ladkin, 1997; Craig and Leslie, 1997; Kirk, 1998; Leslie, 2001; Vernon et al., 2003; Barnett, 2004; Blackstock et al., 2008; Chan, 2009). Furthermore and from the preceding discussion in the case of larger operations, the attitudes and involvement of senior management will also be key (see Atkinson, 1993). These barriers to progress are similar to those found in more general studies of SMEs in business (see Revell and Blackburn, 2004; and in particular Hillary, 2004). Hillary's empirical research also draws on an extensive range of research studies. Notably, many of these factors can be related to consumer behaviour and in such a context are also considered barriers to positive environmental behaviours amongst consumers in general (see Carter et al., 2004; DEFRA, 2009; Chapter 8).

Other factors

Whilst these factors account for by far the majority of comments, some other areas did gain a degree of commonality, which are as important given the low number of comments. For example a small number of participants noted a lack of visitor interest; as one manager remarked: 'there is a lack of pressure/demand'. Grading schemes were also perceived as something of a barrier to EM practices by some accommodation operators in the LDNP. Take individual toiletries in guest rooms, viewed as wasteful packaging, yet encouraged by the Tourist Board grading schemes and as one owner opined: 'They are very concerned about the grading of guest houses rather than the environmental impact.' A few respondents noted that their local authority was not very helpful and in one case remarked that the: 'Local council is rebuffing environmentally friendly schemes in favour of tourism.' However, other factors gaining some consensus were location specific and in this were mainly from the LDNP group apart from issues such as traffic and/or accessibility, raising awareness and monitoring demand. The only one to gain any substantive consensus was a need to address the traffic and transportation problems in and around the LDNP. A final point of interest on the responses to this enquiry was the suggestion by some respondents that 'green' organizations such as Friends of the Earth, Greenpeace and the Friends of the Lake District have little or no regard for the local community. One respondent expressed the opinion that 'The Fiends [sic] of the Lake District' have a 'secret agenda' and do nothing for 'genuine' projects.

Following on from the question on possible barriers, the audited enterprises were invited to suggest ways through which the EP of enterprises could be furthered. The response was limited with just two suggestions gaining some commonality, namely advertising (24%), that is of EM practices, and that people (referring to other owners/managers) need to be pushed (16%).

Do they support Environmental Award Schemes

The final area of enquiry was to ask if the owners/managers interviewed would support an Environmental Performance Award scheme which can be introduced to a tourism enterprise. Rather surprisingly perhaps the majority (62%) of respondents were in favour of such a scheme. Of the 26% who did not support the introduction of such a scheme there was no clear consensus amongst the reasons cited against such an Award. However, the following points illustrate the negative responses:-

- 'People do not understand the grading system never mind an environmental scheme.'
- 'Guests don't seem bothered.'
- 'Cost.'

Other reasons cited against such an award:

- 'More red tape and nothing would get done.'

- 'Grading for CTB – "jobs for the boys". In the last 12 years no one has asked for grading – it is the Government who want such schemes.'
- 'Disagree with system at present – no control. Can't change people's attitudes.'
- 'Do not want to jump on the bandwagon.'

Interestingly, the only comment noted in favour of such a scheme (beyond indicating 'yes') emphasizes the importance of viewing environmental management as a long-term consideration as opposed to a tool with which to generate additional income.

Conclusion

This chapter has focused on the owners/ managers and the findings of the enquiries into their awareness and involvement in green initiatives and their perceptions and attitudes towards a range of factors and initiatives relating to the EP of their enterprises. In effect, these are the underlying factors which help towards gaining a better understanding of their responses to the sustainability agenda and how these translate into the management and operational practices of the enterprise.

Comparative analysis of the data from the audit stages of 2001 and 2011 and, where appropriate, the data of 2006, reveals little real difference between the findings of the three research populations across the period of the research. The main outcomes are as follows:

1. Awareness of an initiative or EM practice is not an indicator of participation, as manifest in the limited involvement of the enterprises in directly supporting local initiatives or in the adoption of EM practices beyond the first steps such as seeking to reduce energy costs. This lack of awareness, which has been recognized by the European Union (EU, 2004), brings into question the efficacy of government led efforts, especially where such effort is neither localized nor takes account of the practical realities of the enterprises involved (Thomas, 2000; Leslie, 2005; Vernon et al., 2005).

2. Most owners and, though less so, managers tend to agree that their category of enterprise does have an impact on the environment but substantially fewer of these owners/managers indicated that they were committed to reducing such impacts. One interpretation of this is that they do not consider that their enterprise actually contributes to such impacts. Notwithstanding that these enterprises gain substantially from the very quality of their surroundings, whether in rural or urban locations, they do not appear to recognize this in terms of their own actions in relation to this environment. In essence, the argument is that they all have a responsibility which is clearly not considered or recognized by the individual owner or manager.

3. Cost savings are considered a major influential factor in encouraging the introduction of EM practices though apparently rather more so only in terms of first steps. This appears at odds with the finding that most enterprises tended to disagree that it is not possible to be profitable and be environmentally friendly. Furthermore, the possibility that they might be influenced in their actions by competitors, industry standards or role models were all rated comparatively of little significance. This reinforces the point that the promotion of best practice as portrayed, for example, in policy documents is of little value. As such, owners/managers seem rather insular in their actions as if what others may do does not affect their operations.

4. Environmental factors were identified as being of little importance compared with improving profitability and achieving budgets and addressing customer complaints, which were all considered to be important/very important. Yet, as noted in preceding chapters, it is invariably argued that going green holds economic benefits for the enterprises involved (see Pratt, 2011). However, the large majority of owners/managers showed little interest and evidently remain to be convinced of the need to address their EP.

5. The audits established that enterprises were generally ambivalent in their views on the impact of a range of factors over the next 5 years which could influence the introduction of environmentally friendly practices. The one exception was government policy to adopt such measures. The implication is that it is only the introduction of regulations that will generate substantive change in their management and operational practices. A key point here is that whilst the introduction of regulations will influence responsive action, it hardly led to a change in attitude or behaviour; rather it is just another criterion that they have to meet.

6. The substantially low interest in addressing environmental matters as implied by these findings correlates with indicative attitudes that most owners/managers do not consider customers are really interested. There is no real conviction on the part of most of the enterprises that they – the customers – are interested in the EP of the enterprise, and thus no real demand for 'going green'. As such, it is argued that green consumerism is hardly transferring into tourism demand, which means that if left to market forces, as Holden (2009, p. 273) argues 'it is the environmental ethics of the market that will be deterministic to the balance of the tourism-environment relationship.' Little change is likely in the foreseeable future. Rather, as Josephides (2001) argued, ethics are of little interest to customers and as Cairncross (1995, p. 177) opined, changing consumer behaviour, and thus tourists' behaviour, is 'likely to have only a modest effect.' Evidently little has changed over the last 20 years beyond such a 'modest effect'.

The results across all the categories of enterprise are similar, evidencing a degree of cynicism and a large amount of ambivalence. In comparative terms, the exception is the CC category, which demonstrated greater concern for the environment and an orientation to positive action. To varying degrees these findings are not unexpected and consistently compare over the period of study with the outcomes of other studies which gave attention to these areas (Leslie, 1998; McCready, 2000; Hillary, 2000; Hobson and Essex, 2001; Revell and Blackburn, 2004; Blackstock et al., 2008; Erdogan, 2009; Baird, 2010).

Further analysis of the data found few substantial variances between the owner-managed enterprises, by far the large majority, and those enterprises with a manager. This might be considered surprising given that it could be expected that the managers would be more aware of EM and related practices and, on the basis of commentary in the tourism/hospitality professional press, the perceived benefits. Even if they were so aware, that does not necessarily mean they would take the action(s) beyond the first steps, i.e. cost saving measures. The influence of employed managers on company policy could be quite limited especially when compared with owner-managers. Also, and rather affirmed by the 2011 data, managers are judged on the basis of attaining defined performance indicators and not, as such, addressing the EP of their operation and wider aspects of sustainability. As preceding chapters attest (e.g. Chapters 3 to 5), the introduction of EMS and CSR activities are for the most part in the case of N/MNC a function of corporate governance. Even then, and allowing for such companies, it is not the case that the larger operations are necessarily comparatively more responsive to greening or sustainability issues (see Bohdanowicz, 2006; Erdogan and Baris, 2006; Mensah, 2009).

Accepting that an EMS brings benefits, including reduced costs to an enterprise, then logic dictates that all enterprises would have introduced such a system. However, it is clear that these owners and for the most part managers do not to any substantial degree see that such benefits are to be achieved by adopting and integrating environmental policies into the wider operations framework of their enterprise. This outcome is consistent with other research into the EP of SMEs whether in tourism or business more generally. This has been the case for well over 20 years; witness Hodgson (1995) 'Despite the obvious benefits to participating … engaging small companies in environmental improvement activities is extremely difficult.' and as argued in the early 1990s, there are myriad enterprises that lack the knowledge and/or desire and/or resources to go green (EIU, 1993). One explanation for this is that:

> companies do not make such improvements whenever they offer a financial payback, or even when it is a very quick payback. But only when it is the quickest and surest payback out of all the essential, optional projects competing for attention - and then, only when

the core business can spare any management attention or investment capacity to progress them (Levett, 2001, p. 4).

These findings bring into question the efficacy of national policies, which is hardly surprising as the majority of the owners/managers evidence limited knowledge of many initiatives and green practices as advocated in the context of tourism policy and sustainability more widely. Even when they are aware, some degree of confusion may arise as tourism policies invariably contain mixed messages in that on the one hand they espouse attention to sustainability (invariably translated as 'sustainable tourism') whilst on the other hand advocating the promotion and development of tourism, with the latter invariably given preference. Witness the EU's tourism policy and related initiatives (Leslie, 2011) and the Davos Declaration (see www.unwto.org) that despite its good intentions it is rather more an agenda for tourism business to continue to expand and develop. To a large extent this bias to economic growth over social and environmental issues explains why policies are so often ineffective, lacking in implementation (for example, see Lin and Hemmington, 1997; Dodds and Butler, 2010). As Ioannides (2008) argued, such top-down approaches to policy and planning just do not work for all areas and especially so in the context of tourism. Essentially, promotion and action must be manifest and championed at the local level (Levett, 2001). This reinforces the need for the 'message' to be locally relevant, personal and therefore to show how doing such and such an action is beneficial to the person and/or their community, e.g. a local tax reduced, improved amenities. Thus the need to think more in terms of '… concepts of immediacy, transience and wider societal concerns' (England, 2010, p. 13) in order to achieve more participation and further for such positive environmental actions to become the norm.

In the meantime, the wider scale adoption of EM practices is likely to arise only when enterprises are forced through legislation to do so, a view that appears to correlate with the attitudes of the owners/managers who gave a high ranking to government policy as a major influential factor in the adoption of EM practices. In combination with the importance they attached to government regulation, this seems to be for many owners/managers more a case of 'passing the buck'. In effect, they see no reason to change their operational practices and for them to do so rather demands that someone else takes on the responsibility for taking action to progress the greening of tourism enterprise. In effect, they appear to expect that it is up to others to take (enforce) action rather than take responsibility themselves (see SCRT, 2006). The down side of the introduction of such regulation is the probability of minimal compliance (see Preigo et al., 2011), which certainly in the case of some enterprises and more so N/MNCs may well be less than their current practices when taken all together. However regulation would not change attitudes or commitment and as such might well be considered a retrograde step, which is the basis of arguments propounded by leading role players in tourism.

Undoubtedly there is a clear need for change in perceptions and attitudes towards EP which have evidently hardly changed to any notable degree over the last 20 years. However it is inescapable that what is really needed is a fundamental change in business attitudes to growth and the values of the owners/managers of these tourism enterprises if progress in the adoption of EM and CSR activity is to be truly achieved.

Further Reading

Climate Change and Tourism: responding to global Challenges. UNWTO, UNEP and World Meteorological Organisation (2008); see in particular Chapter 3: Impacts and Adaptation at Tourism Destinations (for potential impacts and implications of climate change on destinations).

References

Anderson, A., Donachie, E., Elsby, J. and Erskine, L. (2001) Is the serviced accommodation sector in Scotland 'going green'? Hosted Project, BA (Hons) Tourism Management, Glasgow Caledonian University, Glasgow, UK.

Anon. (2003) 'Social Responsibility' new industry buzzword. *Hotels* March, IH&RA, p. 4.

Anon. (2006) *Wave goodbye to green premiums.* Travelmole.

Anon. (2009) *Environment Faces Major Threat from 'Eco-apathy' of UK Office Workers.* wiredgov. Available at net/wg/wg-content-1.nsf/vLookupIndustryNewsByD/21? (accessed 27 July 2010).

Anon. (2010) What do customers care. *Green Hotelier* Issue 52.

Atkinson, R. (1993) Tour operators' contribution to sustainable tourism. Paper presented to Developing Sustainable Tourism, Conference, London Marriott Hotel, May.

Baird, J.H. (2010) Green tourism accreditation: The impacts of the Green Tourism Business Scheme (GTBS) on Scotland's Tourism Sector. Unpublished Dissertation, BA (Hons) Tourism and International Travel Management, Glasgow Caledonian University, Glasgow, UK.

Barnett, S. (2004) Perceptions, understanding and awareness of Green Globe 21: the New Zealand Experience. Paper presented at the State of the Art Conference II, Glasgow, July.

Barr, S., Shaw, G., Coles, T. and Prillwitz, J. (2010) 'A holiday is a holiday': practicing sustainability, home and way. *Journal of Transport Geography* 18, pp. 474–481.

Barrow, C. and Burnett, A. (1990) *How Green are Small Companies?* Cranfield School of Management, Cranfield, UK, October.

Bendell, J. and Font, X. (2004) Which tourism rules? Green Standards and GATS. *Annals of Tourism Research* 30 (1), 139–156.

Berry, S. and Ladkin, A. (1997) Sustainable tourism: A regional perspective. *Tourism Management* 19 (7), 433–440.

Bestard, A.B. and Nadal, J.R. (2006) Modelling environmental attitudes toward tourism. *Tourism Management* 28 (3), 688–695.

Blackstock, K.L., White, V., McCrum, G., Scott, A. and Hunter, C. (2008) Measuring responsibility: an appraisal of a Scottish National Park's Sustainable Tourism Indicators. *Journal of Sustainable Tourism* 16 (3), 276–297.

Blanco, E., Rey-Maquieira, J. and Lozano, J. (2009) Economic incentives for tourism firms to undertake voluntary environmental management. *Tourism Management* 30 (1), 112–122.

Bohdanowicz, P. (2006) Environmental awareness and initiatives in the Swedish and Polish hotel industries – survey results. *International Journal of Hospitality Management* 25 (4), 662–682.

Bohdanowicz, P. and Zientara, P. (2008) Hotel companies' contribution to improving the quality of life of local communities and the well-being of their employees. *Tourism and Hospitality Research* 9 (2), 147–158.

Cairncross, F. (1995) *Green, Inc.: a guide to business and the environment.* Earthscan, London.

Carlsen, J., Getz, D. and Ali-Knight, J. (2001) The environmental attitudes and practices of family business in the rural tourism and hospitality sectors. *Journal of Sustainable Tourism* 9 (4), 281–297.

Carter, R.W., Whiley, D. and Knight, C. (2004) Improving environmental performance in the tourism accommodation sector. *Journal of Ecotourism* 3 (1), 46–68.

Chan, E.S.W. (2011) Implementing environmental management systems in small and medium sized hotels. *Journal of Hospitality and Tourism Research* 35 (1), 3–23.

Chan, E.S.W. and Hawkins, R. (2011) Application of EMSs in a hotel context: a case study. *Tourism Management* 31 (2), 405–418.

Chan, W.W. (2009) Environmental measures for hotel's environmental management systems ISO 140001. *International Journal of Contemporary Hospitality Management* 21 (5), 542–560.

Chan, W.W., Wong, K.K.F. and Lo, J.Y. (2005) Partial analysis of the environmental costs generated by hotels in Hong Kong. *International Journal of Hospitality Management* 24, pp. 517–531.

Clarke, J. (2004) Trade associations: an appropriate channel for developing sustainable practice in SMEs. *Journal of Sustainable Tourism* 12 (3), 194–208.

Cooper, C., Muhern, G. and Colley, A. (2010) Sustainability, the environment and climate change. *Academy of Social Sciences and The British Psychological Society Report.* No.3, London/Leicester, UK.

Craig, C. and Leslie, D. (1997) Environmental initiatives: awareness and action on the part of the business sector in tourism – a case study of Glasgow. Paper presented at the Environment Matters Conference, Marriott Hotel, Glasgow, UK, April/May.

DEFRA (2009) *Public Attitudes and Behaviours towards the Environment.* Tracker Survey. Department of Environment, Food and Rural Affairs, London.

Dewhurst, H. and Thomas, R. (2003) Encouraging sustainable business practices in a non-regulatory environment: a case study of small tourism firms in a UK National Park. *Journal of Sustainable Tourism* 11 (5), 383–403.

Dodds, R. and Butler, R. (2010) Barriers to implementing sustainable tourism policy in mass tourism destinations. *Tourismos* 5 (1), 35–53.

Donovan, T. and McElligott, B. (2000) Environmental management in the Irish Hotel sector – policy and practice. In: Robinson, M., Swarbrooke, J., Evans, N., Long, P. and Sharpley, R. (eds) *Environmental Management and Pathways to Sustainable Tourism.* Business Education, Sunderland, UK, pp. 55–80.

Drucker, P.F. (1955) *The Practice of Management.* Heinemann, London.

EA (2005) *NetRegs.* Environment Agency, London.

EA (2007) *Business and industry – more small businesses taking environmental actions.* Environment Agency, London.

EC (2003) *Using natural and cultural heritage to develop sustainable tourism.* Director-General Enterprise – Tourism Unit, Commission of the European Communities, Brussels.

EIU (1993) *Travel and Tourism Analyst.* Economic Intelligence Unit, London, Number 1.

England, R. (2010) Unravelling the psychology of recycling. *Resource* 56 November/December 4, 11–13.

Erdogan, N. (2009) Turkey's tourism policy and environmental performance of tourism enterprises. In: Leslie, D. (ed.) *Tourism Enterprises and Sustainable Development: International Perspectives on Responses to the Sustainability Agenda.* Routledge, New York, pp. 194–208.

Erdogan, N. and Baris, E. (2006) Environmental protection programs and conservation practices of hotels in Ankara, Turkey. *Tourism Management* 28 (2), 604–614.

Erdogan, N. and Tosun, C. (2009) Environmental performance of tourism accommodations in the protected areas: Case of Goreme Historical National Park. *International Journal of Hospitality Management* 28, pp. 406–414.

EU (2004) *Strategy for Integrating the Environment into Industry.* Available at europe.eu.int/scadplus/leg/en/lvb/l28093.htm (accessed 5 November 2004).

Fairweather, J.R., Maslin, C. and Simmons, D.G. (2005) Environmental values and responses to ecolabels among international visitors to New Zealand. *Journal of Sustainable Tourism* 13 (1), pp. 82–98.

Freezer, J. and Font, X. (2010) Marketing Sustainability for Small Leisure and Tourism Firms. *Countryside Recreation* 18 (1), 9–11.

Frey, N. and George, R. (2009) Responsible tourism management: the missing link between business owners' attitudes and behaviour in the Cape Town tourism industry. *Tourism Management* 31 (5), 621–628.

Garay, L. and Font, X. (2012) Doing good to do well? Corporate social responsibility reasons, practices and impacts in small and medium accommodation enterprises. *Journal of Hospitality Management* 31, 329–337.

Gaunt, S. (2004) An analysis of environmental awareness among tour operators in Scotland. Unpublished Dissertation, BA (Hons) International Travel with Information Systems. Glasgow Caledonian University, Glasgow, UK.

Greenbiz (2009) *Most Small Biz Owners Say Customers Won't Pay for Green.* Available at http://www.greenbiz.com/news (accessed 21 June 2009).

Halme, M. and Fadeeva, Z. (2001) Networking toward sustainability – value added? Findings from tourism networks. In: Green, K., Groenewegen, P. and Hofman, P. (eds) *Ahead of the Curve: Cases of Innovation in Environmental Management.* Kluwer, Dordrecht, the Netherlands, pp. 143–163.

Hillary, R. (ed.) (2000) *Small and Medium-Sized Enterprises and the Environment.* Greenleaf, Sheffield, UK.

Hillary, R. (2004) Environmental management systems and the smaller enterprise. *Journal of Cleaner Production* 12, 561–569.

Hobson, K. and Essex, S. (2001) Sustainable tourism: A view from accommodation businesses. *The Service Industries Journal* 21 (4), 133–146.

Hodgson, S.B. (1995) SMEs and environmental management: The European experience. *Eco-Management and Auditing* 2, pp. 85–89.

Holden, A. (2009) The environment-tourism nexus – influence of market ethics. *Annals of Tourism* 36 (3), 373–389.

Hudson, S. and Miller, G.A. (2005) The responsible marketing of tourism: the case of Canadian Mountain Holidays. *Tourism Management* 26 (2), 133–142.

IH (2007) *Envirowise and Institute of Hospitality 'green' survey.* Institute of Hospitality, London.

Infor (2008) *Performance Management Strategies: Creating Social and Financial Value by Going Green.* Infor, Alpharetta, Georgia. February.

Ioannides, D. (2008) Hypothesising the shifting mosaic of attitudes through time: a dynamic framework for sustainable tourism development on a 'Mediterranean island'. In: McCool, S.F. and Moisey, R.N. (eds) *Tourism, Recreation and Sustainability – Linking Culture & the Environment,* 2nd edn. CAB International, Wallingford, UK, pp. 51–75.

Ioannides, D. and Petridou, E. (2012) Tourism workers and the equity dimension of sustainability. In: Leslie, D. (ed.) *Tourism Enterprises and the Sustainability Agenda across Europe.* New Directions in Tourism Analysis. Ashgate, Farnham, UK, pp. 187–204.

Josephides, N. (2001) Ethics don't interest clients. *Travel Trade Gazette* 4 February, p. 2.

Kirk, D. (1998) Attitudes to environmental management held by a group of hotel managers in Edinburgh. *Hospitality Management* 17, pp. 33–47.

Kucerova, J. (2012) Environmental management and accommodation facilities in Slovakia. In: Leslie, D. (ed.) *Tourism Enterprises and the Sustainability Agenda across Europe.* New Directions in Tourism Analysis. Ashgate, Farnham, UK, pp. 121–134.

Lawton, L.J. and Weaver, D.B. (2009) Normative and innovative resources management at birding festivals. *Tourism Management* 31 (4), 527–536.

Leidner, R. (2004) *The European Tourism Industry – a Multi Sector with Dynamic Markets. Structures, Developments and Importance for Europe's Economy.* European Commission, Enterprise DG (Unit D.3) Publication, Brussels.

Leslie, D. (1998) Perspectives on Agenda 21 and tourism. *The Environment Papers Series* 1 (3), pp. 3–4.

Leslie, D. (2001) Serviced accommodation, environmental performance and benchmarks. *Journal of Quality Assurance in Hospitality & Tourism* 2 (3), 127–147.

Leslie, D. (2005) Rural tourism businesses and environmental management systems. In: Hall, D., Kirkpatrick, I. and Mitchell, M. (eds) *Rural Tourism – Issues and Impacts.* Aspects of Tourism Series 26, Channel View, Clevedon, London, pp. 228–249.

Leslie, D. (2011) The European Union, sustainable tourism policy and rural Europe. In: Macleod, D.V.L. and Gillespie, S.A. (eds) *Sustainable Tourism in Rural Europe: Approaches to Development.* Routledge, New York, pp. 43–60.

Leslie, D. (2012) The consumers of tourism. In: Leslie, D. (ed.) *Responsible Tourism: Concepts, Theory and Practice*. CAB International, Wallingford, UK, pp. 54–71.

Leslie, D. and Hughes, H. (1997) Agenda 21, local authorities and tourism in the UK. *International Journal of Managing Leisure* 2 (3), pp. 143–154.

Levett, R. (1993) Business, the environment and local government. In: Welford, R. and Starkey, R. (eds) *The Earthscan Reader in Business and the Environment*. Earthscan, London, pp. 251–268.

Levett, R. (2001) Sustainable development and capitalism. *Renewal* 9 2/3, pp. 1–9.

Lin, Y.-H. and Hemmington, N. (1997) The impact of environmental policy on the tourism industry in Taiwan. *Progress in Tourism and Hospitality Research* 3 (1), 35–46.

Masau, P. and Prideaux, B. (2003) Sustainable tourism: a role for Kenya's hotel industry. *Current Issues in Tourism* 6 (3), pp. 197–208.

Mastny, L. (2002) *Redirecting International Tourism in State of the World*. World Watch Institute. Earthscan, London, pp. 101–124.

McCready, L. (2000) Local Agenda 21 and Tourism Planning in Northern Ireland. BA (Hons) Tourism Management Dissertation, unpublished, Glasgow Caledonian University, Glasgow, UK.

Mensah, I. (2009) Environmental performance of tourism enterprises in Ghana: A case study of hotels in the Greater Accra Region (GAR). In: Leslie, D. (ed.) *Tourism Enterprises and Sustainable Development – International Perspectives on Responses to the Sustainability Agenda*. Routledge Advances in Tourism Series, Routledge, New York, pp. 139–156.

Mokower, J. (2009) *Green consumers and the recession. Is it really different this time?* Greenbiz.com (accessed 9 November).

Pratt, L. (2011) *Tourism: Investing in energy and resources efficiency*. United Nations Environment Programme, Kenya.

Preigo, M.J.B., Najera, J.J. and Font, X. (2011) Environmental management decision-making in certified hotels. *Journal of Sustainable Tourism* 19 (3), 361–381.

Radwan, H.R.I., Jones, E. and Minoli, D. (2010) Managing solid waste in small hotels. *Journal of Sustainable Tourism* 18 (2), 175–190.

Revell, A. and Blackburn, R. (2004) *UK SMEs and their response to environmental issues*. Small Business Research Centre, Kingston University, March.

Scanlon, N. (2007) An analysis and assessment of environmental operating practices in hotel and resort properties. *Hospitality Management* 26, 711–723.

SCRT (2006) *I will if you will: Towards sustainable consumption*. Sustainable Consumption Round Table, London, May.

Simms, J. (2006) A green light for change. *Director* November, p. 24.

Slee, B., Hunter, C. and Liversedge, A. (1999) Tourism and sustainability in Ross and Cromarty. *The Environment Papers Series* 2 (1), pp. 15–28.

Sloan, P., Legrand, W. and Chen, J.S. (2004) Factors influencing German hoteliers attitudes toward environmental management. *Advances in Hospitality and Leisure* 1, pp. 179–188.

Smith, A. and Reynolds, K. (1999) *Large Organisation Supports of Redevelopment of Supplier's Environmental Management Systems: ADAPT Project*. Environment Council, London.

Thomas, R. (2000) Small firms in the tourism industry: Some conceptual issues. *International Journal of Tourism Research* 2, pp. 345–353.

Tzschentke, N.A., Kirk, D. and Lynch, P.A. (2004) Reasons for going green in serviced accommodation establishments. *International Journal of Contemporary Hospitality Management* 16 (2), pp. 116–124.

Vernon, J., Essex, S., Pinder, D. and Curry, K. (2003) The 'greening' of tourism micro business: Outcomes of group investigations in south-east Cornwall. *Business Strategy and the Environment* 12 (1), 49–69.

Vernon, J., Essex, S., Pinder, D. and Curry, K. (2005) Collaborative policymaking: local sustainable projects. *Annals of Tourism Research* 32 (2), 325–345.

Wanhill, S. (1997) Peripheral area tourism: a European perspective. *Progress in Tourism and Hospitality Research* 3 (1), 47–70.

Warnken, J., Bradley, M. and Guilding, C. (2005) Eco-resorts vs. mainstream accommodation providers: an investigation of the viability of benchmarking environmental performance. *Tourism Management* 26, pp. 367–379.

10 Conclusion

The last 50 years have witnessed extensive commentary and initiatives on the state of the environment; from agriculture to rainforests and the recognition of unsustainable consumption and of the processes supporting it. For example, between 1950 and 2005 oil consumption increased eightfold, natural gas 14-fold, whilst resource extraction at some 60 billion tons is 50% higher than in 1980 (UNEP, 2010). This period has also witnessed the emergence of sustainable development (SD) and then global warming, along with a correlating rise of the green agenda and a plethora of international, intra and national government policies and initiatives. Consumption has increased inexorably and so too tourism, domestically and globally, fuelled by easing constraints in the west and the growing economies of countries such as Brazil, China and India (see EEA, 2013).

The three key areas of human activity giving rise to most negative environmental impacts and thus issues of sustainability in industrialized countries are mobility (car, air transport including holidays), food and housing, which collectively account for 70–80% of those impacts (Tukker *et al.*, 2010a). These are all applicable to tourism enterprises, which are also often the home of the owners. The key element in this is the interrelationship between the three pillars of sustainability – social/economic/environmental. However, it is perhaps clearer to consider the environment rather in terms of the biosphere, whether within a locality or globally, as opposed to the way it may often be interpreted in the context of tourism, namely as relating to the physical environment of tourist destinations. In this wider sense it becomes clear as to how environmental policies are not just about the physical but '... they are about sustainability, justice and redistribution' (Keil and Desfor, 2003, p. 28). Implicit in the advocacy of SD is the concept of limits (see Roderick, 2011), primarily of natural capital and inherently therefore access to such key resources which are in decline. This means, given the current status quo, increasing inequity between nations and between peoples, depending on their access to and consumption of those resources. As, for example, illustrated by Munasinghe (2010, p. 4):

> 1.2 billion people in top 20th percentile of the world's population by income consume almost 85% of global output, or 60 times more than the poorest 20th percentile.

The top 20th percentile also accounts for 75% of global emissions. A situation that certainly has been aided by major improvements in the more efficient use of resources.

This increased efficiency has further fuelled demand albeit in the process such efficiencies contributed to mitigating increased pollution in the 20th century. Therefore it can be interpreted from much that has been written that sustainable development and tourism are primarily about reducing consumption of principally non-renewable resources – hence the 'greening' of tourism enterprise. The objective of 'greener' tourism enterprises demands that they operate in more sustainable ways, and in the process developing and building on more extensive links with other sectors of the local economy and with the local community more generally. Thus tourism is not some singular activity that is separate from the locality but rather is entwined with all facets of that locality, the community and society more widely. The extent of these inter-relationships may all too often not be realized. To a large extent this echoes the major thrust of ecological modernization, which is being advocated by governments, notably so in the case of the EU. Basically ecological modern-ization is the greening of capitalism, which has merit in terms of sustainability and progress. However the degree to which the processes involved gain parity with more short-term management functions such as competitive-ness, marketability and development is highly questionable (see Keil and Desfor, 2003); all the more so given the priority to the economic dimension in national tourism policies wherein the social and environmental facets of sustainability are generally found somewhere down the list of action fields (see ECORYS, 2009; Leslie, 2011).

The responses of governments to this agenda as shown in tourism policies, and also by leading stake-holders representing private sector interests, have been mainly in the guise, in one form or another, of sustainable tourism or ecotourism. These are somewhat erroneously considered to be new forms of tourism but for the most part they are variations on the theme of greening. As De Lacy and Lipman (2010) argued 'we use eco, sustainable and responsible tourism as buzzwords rather than fundamental business shifts'. That is a shift on the part of tourism enterprises to maximize reduction of resource consumption, to reducing their ecological footprint and as such it matters little what terminology is used (see Farsari et al., 2007). In this quest for improved sustainability every enterprise therefore has a responsibility to address this objective. However, this responsibility is not solely about their consumption of non-renewable resources. Enterprises have a wider

responsibility which brings into contention ethics in terms of fair share, equity in dealings with others and in the benefits arising from touristic activity and thus is also a social responsibility. They are dependent to varying degrees on their environment and thus the quality of both the physical and cultural environs.

Therefore sustainability, and in this context environmental management, is not just about such resources but how those resources may be sustained in the most appropriate and equitable way in terms of the needs of the community. Furthermore it is not just sustainability issues that are gaining in importance. Environmental management and performance are of rising importance as, for example, utility costs increase and impact on business performance as well as the availability of resources such as clean fresh water which, as noted in Chapter 5, is becoming an issue in many regions popular with tourists. These issues are not solely related to business and will not be resolved through technology alone. Dependence on technology is literally a technical fix and unlikely to be of benefit to most tourism enterprises. However, it is recognized that it is more suited to major role players, N/MNCs with the requisite capital for investment but even then achieving actual net benefit is a matter of debate. Beyond the short term, regulation also holds limited prospects of achieving substantial and sustained progress. Rather what is needed is to address consumption patterns and, in the first instance, unsustainable patterns of consumption such as tourism (see Cohen and Murphy, 2002). Therefore it is inescapable that addressing the sustainability of the development of tourism enterprises and their responsiveness to the sustainability agenda also involves addressing demand and in this the motivations of tourists, which makes for an even more complex situation.

In total, the foregoing discussion establishes the basis of the arguments as to why owners/managers of tourism enterprises should be addressing the environmental performance of their operations, which is well encapsulated in the concept of responsible tourism. This is not a form of tourism as, for example, sustainable tourism but rather a paradigm for behaviour that involves the values and attitudes of all involved in tourism, in that every stakeholder has a responsibility for their actions and the impacts thereof. Thus enterprises and the community need to be more efficient, e.g. to consume less energy, to generate less waste. As well as conserving natural resources and reducing waste they should also promote awareness of visitors of the natural and cultural heritage within their respective locales. As such there is a demand for not treating enterprises and operations in terms of their products/services alone but in the wider context of their external environment. An approach which reflects much greater awareness of the interconnectedness of the economic, physical and social dimensions of the environment, thus sustainability rather than just the physical or natural, e.g. pollution and damage. Given the need for all sectors of the community to become involved there is substantial potential to address these linkages and seek ways to regenerate them. Linkages can serve to accentuate the importance of the environment to the community and thereby encourage more responsive action on the part of the community towards conservation. But this will require the development of supportive networks, co-operation and communication.

To what extent the majority of tourism enterprises have/are addressing this is little known, primarily due to a lack of research into tourism enterprise outside of N/MNC companies and comparatively large hotel operations. Thomas *et al.* (2011), from their review of tourism research publications, identify the very limited extent to which tourism enterprises have been studied. Furthermore, as Buckley (2007, p. 70) noted 'Remarkably little has been published about the actual practices of commercial tourism corporations and operators in reducing their environmental impacts' and even less on matters such as motivations, benefits and costs and most notably an absence of any longitudinal studies. Further accounting for this lack is an increased accent on research methodologies over the last decade, including statistical analyses, also whatever issue happens to be 'flavour of the month' and, of no little significance, the availability of funding. This situation is not

helped by the possibility that 'Academic tourism journals, and their referees, seem to look down on such submissions as too descriptive.' (Buckley, 2007, p. 70). Academic articles may also suffer from a lack of practical application, written more to impress their peers than inform business (see Weaver, 2007). In some instances research also evidences a lack of understanding of small firms, in part due to no experience of working in small firms, which is also discernible in the plethora of research papers and the rhetoric of so many a Chief Executive of a National or Regional Tourist Organization. This is not surprising given that such organizations are not part of the actual business sectors they seek to influence.

Basically commentators fail to consider these small/micro, mainly owner-managed enterprises in tourism other than as some sort of standard business that fits with general business studies, in other words N/MNC companies. What research there is, as demonstrated throughout the preceding pages, tends to be one-off studies with few researchers showing consistency in their research in this field and even fewer longitudinal studies. As such this study has not only sought to address some of these weaknesses but also, given the longitudinal nature, seeks to present a valuable contribution in this field.

The Enterprises and Key Outcomes

The findings, as discussed in these chapters, indicate some degree of progress in the adoption of EM practices and, albeit to a lesser extent, wider aspects pertaining to the EP of the enterprise, for example, activities within the scope of social responsibility (e.g. CSR). The one activity that does stand out in terms of progress since the 1990s is that of recycling and this is largely attributed to EU Directives on waste, promotion of recycling and subsequent actions and facilitating infrastructure on the part of local authorities. Except for recycling, the most common EM practice identified was reducing energy consumption, encouraged by the onset of the economic recession in 2008, and which logic dictates will increase as energy supply costs rise, exacerbated by government intervention and responses to climate change issues. As noted throughout the chapters, these findings are supported by and/or reflect a variety of other, often singular, research studies, not only in the UK and across Europe but more widely as they relate to the owners/managers of these small/micro tourism enterprises that numerically account for between 80–90% of the supply side of tourism.

In general, these outcomes apply to all the categories of tourism enterprise involved though with some differences and occasional variances with possibly most progress manifest in the hotel category and TOs. In these categories it is predominantly N/MNCs that demonstrate accredited EMSs and CSR activity, which might be considered more driven by wider factors relating to stakeholders and politics than any intrinsic concerns over sustainability issues (see Buckley, 2007; Weaver 2007). CSR, as such, is more an 'add on' to the business – a positive extra – but not a substantial change in practice as required by sustainability (see Henderson, 2007). Furthermore, N/MNCs in the hospitality sector are considered to be behind many other sectors in terms of progress, albeit some newer 'brands' are placing sustainability more centrally (Anon., 2009). In contrast to the study's enterprises these N/MNC companies can achieve substantial cost savings through resource efficiencies, e.g. energy consumption, and purchasing through economies of scale, though this is not necessarily compatible with SSCM nor support for local suppliers. Also, given their diversity of operations and services, at one and the same time they are also major consumers of resources. However, a plus point is that once EMS and CSR practices are introduced they will be applied throughout the company's operations. In contrast to these N/MNCs and across the whole spectrum of supply, many of the small owner-managed enterprises are performing better overall in terms of their EP. Even so, the findings indicate a lack of commitment to EM and wider aspects such as CSR and SSCM, and in building support and developing linkages with other enterprises and the local/regional economy.

The emphasis, in the majority of cases, is on maximizing financial returns based on current operational practices, which in many instances are long-standing. However, it is inescapable that more can and should be being done by these enterprises in terms of resource efficiency at the very least and in this without necessarily incurring net additional cost. The support for other small/micro enterprises such as those involved in producing local produce, foods and products is no better. This might be surprising given visitor interest and support for local produce/products and all the more so given the arguments promoting this, which are not just about local/regional economics and communities but also global issues such as food processing, carbon footprints, water consumption and food security. These are all facets of sustainability. Reference to these matters brings into contention the concept of environmental space. As Wright (2002) explains, this basically is how much land area is required by any person to sustain wellbeing. In the case of the UK the actual environmental space required to meet consumer demand is more than the size of the UK given the imports of, for example, coffee, tea, fruit and vegetables and beef. Tourism activity is undoubtedly a contributor to such an unsustainable situation. This all further reinforces support for promoting local products and produce.

Drawing on the attitudes of the owners/managers there are two main factors considered the most influential to change in their approach in the management of their enterprises. First more information on these matters, though given the extent of information available this leads to speculation that for the most part this is a rather spurious reason for a lack of action. The second factor is clear leadership from government, which suggests more a case of 'passing the buck' than an invitation to government to take action. Both these factors were very much a part of Local Agenda 21 planning by local authorities in the 1990s/2000s, yet evidently gained little recognition on the part of most of the owners/managers of these enterprises. The majority of these owners/managers were also found to be unaware of many initiatives, for example, as promoted by Regional Tourist Boards and in the professional press. This is neither unexpected nor surprising as it could well be asked 'Why should they be aware?' – especially for the majority of owner managers that are not in the business with the sole intent of 'making money' even though they are attentive to their profit margins.

There is also a dysfunction between awareness and action, i.e. knowing of a practice does not mean it will be adopted even when such practice will save on costs in the longer term. More likely because their motivations for being in the business are often personal (see Chapter 2) they do not consider they have a wider role and/or are not interested in considering the wider context – their place in the community and local economy. This view is supported by other findings such as the low levels of membership of professional tourism associations and from the attitudinal questions which evidence a degree of cynicism and a large amount of ambivalence to 'green' ideas, environmental impacts and related initiatives (see Chapter 9). It is thus the values and attitudes of the owners of these enterprises, coupled with their knowledge and understanding of environmental issues and related practices, which are seen as the key influences that lead to addressing environmental performance and therefore the related practices.

However, it is evident from the outcomes that there is substantial scope for enhancing this role and developing the environmental performance – the sustainability – of tourism enterprises and particularly those activities which come within the scope of social responsibility. That individual environmental awareness and practice is limited indicates that there is clearly no collective commitment to cultural and social sustainability. This also appears to apply in varying measures to any aspect of EM/CSR practice as well illustrated in the discussion on local produce and products (see Chapter 6). Thus there is:

> ... a requirement for more creative planning in order to maximise the cross-sectoral economic links that can be achieved in the development of tourism. This demands a more comprehensive approach (Leslie, 2002, p. 9).

This is exemplified herein in the attention given to purchasing local produce and products. As such, developing much stronger linkages with other more localized sectors and promoting greater production and utilization of local produce and products will contribute to the sustainability of the local economy with more opportunities for employment.

This is not to say that there are not many tourism enterprises that are notably active in both EM practices and CSR activity, albeit not formally accredited or necessarily recognized as such, but these are in the minority. The owners involved in these cases often hold intrinsic values that not only steer their own environmental behaviour but also lead them to apply such pro-environmental behaviours in their businesses operations. As Carter et al. (2004, p. 65) argue, EP improvement is largely dependent 'on the presence of an environmental ethic in influential staff' which, for most tourism enterprises means the owner. In larger companies this could be the presence of 'sustainable leaders' – key players in positions of influence in the organization who are seen as having a more personal relationship with the organization and its culture and work conditions (see Casserley and Critchley, 2010). For the large majority, however, there is a clear need for more direct promotion and encouragement that takes into consideration major influential factors on their behaviour that manifestly underpin those factors, as identified by the owners/managers, that are discouraging progress.

Discouraging Factors in the Quest for Progress

Based on this longitudinal study, and the findings of related studies over the time frame, there is a clear consistency in factors considered to discourage progress. Primarily these are encompassed within two areas. First, interest and this is underpinned by behavioural aspects, i.e. knowledge, values and attitudes and in the entailed sense of responsibility, social norms and habits. The second area is that of resource constraints, which mainly concerns costs. A further factor that should also be recognized (and one which demonstrably emerges from the findings) is that in the main owners/managers do not consider for the most part that there is clear visitor demand for 'going green'.

Interest

There is a lack of interest, inertia and ambivalence on the part of many owners/managers towards EM and CSR practice and more broadly sustainability as it applies to their enterprise. In combination this largely accounts for a second factor – that of limited awareness and understanding – which is partly attributed on their part to limited information. Over the time frame of this study this is difficult to assess given the scope of coverage of environmental issues by professional organizations, albeit limited and rarely 'headlined', and in the media and increasingly readily accessible via the Internet. Yet this appears at best to gain limited attention. However, as the findings suggest, given the limited interest many of these owners/managers are unlikely to go out of their way to obtain information. But it should also be remembered that many practices are plain common sense, application of thrift and good housekeeping. Even so, to influence them through information campaigns and to promote their awareness of these practices thus changing their attitudes and habits (e.g. usual operational practices), will probably only have a marginal effect in isolation (see Tukker et al., 2010b). This may well already have been achieved. As manifest in these findings, cultural/social factors, and indeed habit, as well as opportunity to undertake a desired action, are all the more significant (see Lindholdt, 1998; Levett, 2001; DEFRA, 2009; Southerton et al., 2011; IEEP, 2011). Basically, what is required is a shift from extrinsic to intrinsic values.

Even so, if such information is presented in context, related to the enterprises, the locality and the community, and is practical and encouraging then it is more likely to have a positive effect; as in the example of the New Forest (see page 182). But there needs to be a willingness to act combined with local support and organization to succeed. This is not a practice often witnessed in the delivery of tourism policy, or environmental policy, which in general is neither localized nor takes account of the practical realities of the enterprises involved; as well portrayed in tourism policy promotion documents and through tourism organizations and the professional press, let

alone the academic press. Indeed, such material is unlikely to be present in these small/micro tourism enterprises. Perhaps the promotional line in supporting pro-environmental action 'X' is misjudged when it is based on a 'win, win' scenario, as it is so often. Alternatively, as Han et al. (2011) advocated, the message promoting the value of an accredited EMS system should be more about the positive dimensions such as healthy food, local produce and CSR activity, rather than the EMS accreditation. Overall, the need is to communicate effectively to the target audience, explain simply and clearly how such practices apply to them and then involve them in taking the desired action forward. Potentially helping to overcome barriers to such measures would be more collective actions within communities, e.g. initiatives such as 'Village in Bloom' which does generate participation and a collective pride in their own locality (see Cooper et al., 2010).

That more progress has not been made serves to reinforce the view that the availability of information is not in itself sufficient or effective to assume awareness and to engender positive action as the even lower levels of involvement in a range of initiatives/activities demonstrated. At best this will only happen through increased awareness of the 'why', 'what' and 'how' involved in addressing environmental performance and a requisite for such 'messages' to be presented in the most effective way. This reinforces the fact that what works in situation A is not necessarily transferable to situation B in that, for example, the key role-players will be different, so too commitment and who is the champion? Such factors bring into question the effectiveness, past and present, of approaches to the dissemination of information. In actuality this seems to be more about the activities of the agencies involved. In effect actions are taken to justify their existence, demonstrate their worth rather than any actual consideration of their effectiveness; to be seen to be 'doing something' rather than addressing the actual responses of the enterprises.

To be effective the need in each locale is for an organization to take forward 'the message' which is then promoted through local leadership – a 'champion' in an influential position. Furthermore, appropriate encouragement will be required in order to overcome a primary difficulty (if not a barrier), which is 'why should I do this – no one else is.' Further, relevant exemplars drawn from within the area are a necessity, illustrating the advantages of the pertinent systems and practices that will have to be identified, presented effectively and with facilitating mechanisms to be of any real effect. Even so this will lead to only a small increase in the number of enterprises taking the desired action. Doubtlessly for the majority of owners/managers engaged in the operation of the plethora of small/micro independent tourism enterprises, taking further 'green' steps will only be accomplished in the short term through regulation.

Resource constraints

These mainly involve issues of perception, whether this is in terms of costs of introducing EM and CSR practices, the additional comparative purchasing cost of local produce/products or investing in new equipment, e.g. energy saving measures. This rather brings to attention Revell and Blackburn's (2004, p. 51) proposal of 'encouraging firms to view their environmental obligations as a legitimate business expense, rather than consistently a win-win game.' Such an approach combined with 'the commensurate level of legislative compulsion for change in business practices, the behaviour of owner-managers would be more likely to change towards more environmentally sustainable practices.' However, resource constraints also encompass the oft-cited factor of lack of time, e.g. the time required in undertaking one or more of the following actions – to investigate what could be done, to establish the necessary action, to implement new practices. These aspects are considered by some owners to discourage action but given the size of their enterprises, i.e. small/micro, then in reality the time involved is hardly onerous. In contrast, for large companies, especially those involving group operations, these factors may be of little significance because the organization can share the requisite knowledge and experience throughout the company and, as appropriate,

gain eco-label accreditation. In the case of accreditation there are certainly costs involved in following due process to gain this and then for annual renewal. The argument that such an eco-label will generate additional business obviously holds influence for many tourism enterprises that decide to take up such a scheme, but what happens when the renewal time comes up and the owner/manager can see no extra business as a result?

Visitor demand

As discussed in Chapter 9, the owners/managers generally consider there is little real evidence of demand for greening, of EMS accreditation or CSR activity on the part of visitors, which is further supported by the findings of Chapter 7. That there are some visitors who are influenced by such factors is undoubtedly true but this will have always been the case. What is evidently not happening is a substantial increase in the number of such visitors despite the development of green consumerism. Given the EP activities of some N/MNCs it might be argued that their attention to EMS and CSR is indicative of such demand but this would be to ignore the fact that they have a diverse range of stakeholders to satisfy. Secondly they may well be in partnership with other N/MNCs not involved in the tourism sector which are particularly attentive to SSCM in their operations. Further, such argument finds favour in the view that the EP activity of these N/MNCs may be seen to be generally little more than cosmetic and even where more is done they do not bear witness to 'fundamental change in the underlying assumptions that inform the actions of the typical tourism corporation' (Weaver, 2007, p. 65).

When it comes down to choice of destination, the likelihood that visitors, for the most part, would be swayed in their choice of holiday or other tourism product/service by eco-labels and/or CSR actions is somewhat unrealistic (see Devinney et al., 2012). Albeit that this may be contrary to much that has been written implying or claiming the opposite (see Grobois, 2012; Chapters 7 and 8). Even then, these outcomes reflect arguments articulated some 20 years ago that consumer pressure will not lead to substantive development in enterprises addressing their environmental performance (for example, see Cairncross, 1995). A 'simple' illustration of this is Devinney *et al.*'s (2012) argument that it was Gore's widely disseminated book 'An Inconvenient Truth' that had the major influence on government actions in response to global warming not consumer pressure.

A Key Weakness

Overall, and despite international agreements, policies and initiatives all with good intentions, these findings are not unexpected, effectively questioning the efficacy of government tourism policies and demonstrating that the policies presented by the leading bodies involved are often little more than rhetoric, often lacking in details and action regarding the broader context of sustainable development (see Farsari *et al.*, 2007). This is not surprising given that such organizations are not part of the actual business sectors they seek to influence (to which one might add – and who do not 'practice what they preach'). This factor not only brings into question their value, approaches to dissemination and imple-mentation, but also poses the very question, just who are such policies designed to serve? Furthermore, such policies, especially national tourism policy, whilst promoting sustainable development as applied to tourism (most often under the title of sustainable tourism) invariably contain mixed messages with the promotion of economic activity being to the fore. Evidently there is substantial scope for enhancing the role and contribution of tourism enterprises through developing their environmental performance. As Mastny (2002, p. 120) argued:

> ... while many industry efforts embrace a shift toward environmental sustainability, they are less willing to incorporate social and cultural needs, including addressing labour and employment issues, protecting cultures, and maximizing linkages with local economies and communities.

To achieve this requires change. As Mowforth and Munt (2009, p. xi) argue 'progress in

promoting more locally rooted, more equitable, and environmentally responsive forms of tourism ... has been painfully slow.' Overall, it may well be argued that today there is little real change if at all beyond that enforced by regulations (see Casserley and Critchley, 2010).

Why are not more enterprises taking the appropriate responsive action? Partly because of an absence of responsibility in the context of greening on the part of many enterprises whether individual or organization. A further factor is that in essence:

> although sustainable development is high in the policy agenda, the principles of sustainability are not yet widely understood or taken for granted in day to day activities (ECORYS, 2009, p. ix).

There is a need for change on the part of the owners/managers, to take responsibility and thus accountability for the wider impacts of their own actions which rather demands change in attitudes and values, with more consideration for the wider context and the longer term. Factors which are all influenced by their own culture and social norms and not easily changed.

Nevertheless, in the longer term, rather than the introduction of incentives and regulation, substantial change in the way the environmental performance of tourism enter-prises is seen and addressed is needed. Post-industrial societies are still using far too much energy and creating far too much waste. These damaging trends cannot be reversed by timid measures at the margin (Osborn, 2000). Governments must be bolder with their power to move the economy in more sustainable directions. More problematic in the short term is how to encourage the myriad of tourism enterprises to put environmental issues, and the adoption of 'environmentally friendly' management practices, to the forefront of their business operations and strategic decisions. In the short term this suggests a need for government intervention, which appears to correlate with the perceptions of owners/managers in suggesting that govern-ment action is most likely to be the most influential factor to achieving further progress. This could be interpreted as a willingness to accept government intervention and a degree of collective responsibility. In a sense that policy and strict regulation may guarantee that everyone 'plays by the rules' thus aiming to overcome the 'I will if they will' syndrome.

The Issue of Regulation

In the short-term there is little escaping from introducing regulation. However, the intro-duction of direct regulation to achieve progress in tourism enterprises further developing and adopting measures in response to this sustainability agenda is unlikely given today's global economy, disparities between nations and the political influences and power of international business. This is particularly applicable to international agreements and protocols on world trade – witness the recent meeting of the World Trade Organization in Bali (December, 2013), the outcomes of which have been applauded by post-industrial nations for supporting more open markets. In effect international trade agreements can conflict with governments seeking to introduce environmental regulations (for example, in the case of tourism, see Pleumarom, 2012). As Mason (1999, p. 226) expressed, 'strategic motives, both within and between states, often override consideration of social and ecological problems.'; and furthermore he noted that a key weakness by the turn of the century was that the World Trade Organization appeared to be unable to integrate environmental considerations within trading rules, and this has changed little since. In the case of tourism, this continues to raise concerns over internationally agreed environment protocols, for example on issues relating to the cruise sector and pollution in Polar regions.

In contrast, Cairncross (1995) argued that regulating industry is not the best way forward to achieve environmental improvements in industry. As her book demonstrates, and so too that of Elkington and Burke (1987), there were many companies performing well in this area, and more so since, in the absence of regulation. This is undoubtedly true as many, but by no means the majority, of the tourism enterprises in the study attest. Further supporting such argument is that if regulation through legislation is introduced this could lead to minimal compliance and bring into contention costs and arguments over what could be seen as unfair competition and/or barriers to trade on the part of N/MNCs in tourism. This is not to say that policy instruments, ranging from legislation to user fees and eco-labels to taxes, e.g. a tourist tax, do not have their place. Indeed, some form of regulation could be introduced, for example regulations that directly target resource consumption and other green taxes. This is already evident in many areas; for example in the UK – landfill tax, petrol 'green' tax, a tax on energy usage and the introduction of carbon trading. But the adoption of such economic instruments as taxes and charges is variable in effect (see Osborn, 2000; Logar, 2009). Further, whilst green taxes draw attention to ecological aspects of products, they are rather insular and have little effect on other choices of the consumer or on their environmental behaviour per se.

The EP of tourism per se is not solely about the enterprises involved but also the key facet of transportation and the tourists – the consumers of tourism. As such the role of travel and thus transportation must not be overlooked. Transportation, as discussed in Chapter 8, is recognized as a major polluter, a contributory factor to global warming. Yet despite over two decades of such rhetoric, today there are more cars and ever greater demand for air travel. The demand for these modes of transport, perceived as quicker, cheaper and, especially in the case of car ownership, more convenient both inter-nationally and domestically, is further fuelled by the rapidly developing economies of countries across the globe. In terms of sustainability it is the Achilles heel of tourism.

The Achilles Heel of Tourism

How this element of tourism is addressed is a conundrum. The approach to date so far appears based on encouraging quieter, more fuel-efficient planes, carbon trading and taxes; for example, the UK Advance Passenger Duty – reputedly a green tax. This tax, although adding a substantial cost to ticket prices, has evidently had little impact on demand. Also there are voluntary initiatives such as carbon offsetting. Possibly internalizing the externalities of air travel could be a step forward but such a step, even if possible, is unlikely to be viable given the conflicts that would arise, for example between low-cost carriers and standard airlines, arguments over barriers to trade and the impact of this on demand, as well as issues of equity and access. If introduced by all carriers across the globe it might not lead to more than a small increase in ticket cost. However unlikely this is, such international agreement would then have little impact on demand and potentially act as a break on further progress in research, for example into improving fuel efficiency, noise and alternative fuels. Even so this is simply addressing the symptoms rather than the causes. In this regard the findings also reflect businesses more generally (see Ethical Corporation, 2010) and are similar to related studies into consumer behaviour (see Jackson, 2005) and the environmental performance of households (Pepper and Nigbur, 2005). As has been argued:

> Although sustainable development is high in the policy agenda, the principles of sustainability are not yet widely understood or taken for granted in day to day activities (ECORYS, 2009, p. ix).

Overall, these issues are not solely related to tourism enterprise or business more generally and will not be resolved through technology nor perhaps regulation in the longer term. Rather the need is to address consumption (see Cohen and Murphy, 2002). Primarily it is consumer demand and the unsustainable patterns of consumption which have generated the stresses on the environment, in its widest sense, catalysing so much debate and reaction.

For the most part these enterprises are family owned and managed. The owners of these small/micro enterprises are also members of the community and society more widely and in this context equally they are consumers. This brings to the fore a key question – namely: Why should they behave in ways differently from most consumers when it comes to issues of sustainability and their own environmental behaviours?

Consumers of Tourism and Consumerism

Tourism is an area of behaviour that is discretionary, a by-product of affluence (see Galbraith, 1985). It is expectation based and for most people a 'want' not a 'need'. In affluent society today it is very much taken as the norm in the yearly cycle of life, whether in the form of leisure trips, short breaks or holidays. To mitigate their conscience (if applicable) over their all too conspicuous consumption of tourism and related impacts it is easier to think in terms of 'what difference will I make?' and to 'pass the buck' to someone else to take responsibility, which invariably means government. If real progress is to be made towards sustainable development then these attitudes and behavioural aspects must change. As the conclusions to the EU's 'Strategy for Integrating the Environment into Industry' argued, there is a need to: '… encourage changes in the behaviour of consumers …' (EU, 2004). There is little evidence of this today especially where change has not been driven by legislation/regulation.

If tourism and thus tourism enterprises are to develop and progress their responses and actions to the sustainability agenda in ways more compatible with the objectives of sustainability then so too must the processes that underpin it. If this is to be achieved the norms, values and attitudes of the enterprise owners, managers and tourists (and thus they, as consumers) need to change. But this is hardly likely to happen as 'Increasingly, it seems, the institutions of consumer society encourage individualism and competition and discourage social behaviours' (Jackson, 2008, p. 56). It is not surprising therefore that, as Hultsman (1995) heralded in the mid-1990s, people in post-industrial societies, especially young people, have or are losing a sense of connection with the natural world and with it a sense of place, which is becoming ever more manifest in post-industrial, post-modern, societies.

The what, how and why of consumerism is complex and thus all the harder to influence in any particular direction other than to consume more. Certainly in part this is because some consumer goods and services hold a symbolic identity; they are positional goods conveying status and place in society and can hold a sense of well-being (see Jackson and Michaelis, 2003; Jackson, 2009; Tukker *et al.*, 2010b). In this, 'the holiday' today is not seen as a luxury but considered a necessity, a social requirement and also a right and for some, if not many, people it is seen to hold status – a positional good. Contrarily Johnston (2006, p. 253) argues that 'we must abstain from "consumer" holidays and search out opportunities for *real connections* [author's emphasis] and purpose.' Though this may be true, this rather suggests that there are alternative holiday options, possibly rather in the style of low key eco-tourism, which bring their own problems (see Chapters 3 and 4). Even so Johnston does highlight the intrusiveness of tourism and the plight of indigenous peoples and their cultural heritage in many developing tourist destinations, which conflicts with the aims of CSR and, all the more so, responsible tourism. A further point on holidaying is the suggestion, by The Future Laboratory (2010), that by 2030 all holidays will have to take into account sustainability issues and notably that it will be the mass market that is key to sustainable travel. Their view of 'tomorrow's holidays' appears to be very much based on assumptions that technological advances, e.g. computer-based systems, in hospitality operations will drive down energy consumption. But then computer systems are not as 'green' as many persons appear to consider. To which one might add Lindholdt's (1998, p. 6) argument that 'More and more students of literature and culture are coming to acknowledge the negative consequences of technology on people and the environment.' Undoubtedly the point here is true today but it appears to gain little consideration whilst the use and invasiveness of information technology systems appears to inexorably increase.

Irrespective of consumers'/tourists' concern over climate change, and sustainability issues more broadly, that they are not manifested in responsive, positive action is evident from a plethora of surveys; the majority of consumers say they are aware and supportive of change in response to these global issues while in practice they will carry on behaving in much the same way. Perhaps at times using a suitable excuse founded in the confusion that surrounds the subject and/or are 'becoming resilient to environmental warnings' (England, 2010, p. 12). Also of influence is that the level of enjoyment may be so great that this outweighs any feeling of guilt (if at all considered) over the impact of their decisions. Indeed, it appears that in the main they pay little attention to 'green credentials', especially when considered a necessity, e.g the short-break or holiday. Witness the rise in demand for 'doom tourism', i.e. visiting places in the world before they are gone, e.g. Antarctica. Tell people that a particular animal is under threat, for example from global warming or deforestation, and subsequently demand for holidays to see/view that animal has escalated. Furthermore, as with other popular consumer goods, demand is increasing in developing and emerging economies around the world.

This demand is fuelling the development of new and emerging destinations wherein there is more than likely a lack of government policy on planning and, in particular, control on such developments. As Saarinen *et al.* (2009) identified, there is often a failing to recognize and appreciate that tourism takes place and develops in destinations within the context of prevailing government policy and thus whichever way a destination develops largely rests in the purvey of the government. Governments rarely seek to limit economic activity such that it can be contained within the boundaries of initial development and thus more in tune with locality or community, leading to the social and environmental considerations being balanced with economic aspects rather than the economic given prominence (see Pearce, 1995; Butler, 2007). Thus when a new tourism destination becomes popular, subsequent development may lead to problems of over-development and exceed capacity limits (see Butler, 1994; Johnston, 2003 and 2006). How readily do/would enterprises support limitations, for example on the scale of development or on the numbers of visitors – certainly not all (see Bennett, 2006). David Bellamy in his address at the annual Tourism and Conservation Partnership Conference in 2000 at the Langdale Hotel (LDNP) clearly made the point that visitor numbers in the LDNP were probably at the maximum in terms of the capacity of the area to sustain without increasing environmental degradation. He suggested that there should now be a period of not promoting the area. However, these comments were basically ignored by the audience, mainly practitioners and representatives of local authorities and tourism organizations, and in reports on the conference. This echoes the point made in the mid 1980s that:

> The market for tourism is not in a position to guarantee a path of development which in the long run is in its own interests (Brugger et al., 1984, p. 615 cited in Butler, 1994, p. 35).

Butler (1994, p. 35) further argues that 'Nor, one might add, is it in a position to guarantee a level or magnitude of development in anyone's best interest.'

In summation this echo's Hardin's (1969) 'Tragedy of the commons' irrespective, by and large, of the EMS/CSR actions of many N/MNC, as Weaver (2007, p. 65 – author's emphasis) argued:

> one often hears of a corporation's commitment to 'smart *growth*' or 'sustainable *development*', but almost never of any decision to actually *curtail* growth or *cancel* a development in favour of ecological or social considerations.

In effect, there is a quest for short-term gain which is hardly compatible with the responsibility implicit in EMS and CSR actions. A further and not inconsiderable point is the way destinations may develop given the involvement of MNCs, which is also contrary to sustainability. To varying degrees, the development of tourist destinations tends to reflect the culture of the dominant tourist market segment (see Nash, 1989). This is nowhere more manifest than in luxury eco-tours. But there is a darker and unsustainable aspect to this in tourism which reflects Harvey's (1996, p. 185 cited in Adams, 2001, p. 285) critique of society that:

> Not only do the rich occupy privileged niches in the habitat while the poor tend to work and live in the more toxic or hazardous zones, but the very design of the transformed ecosystem is redolent of its social relations.

This is manifestly also applicable to tourism development, perhaps more so. However, such a critique does not address the demand side and as long as suppliers continue to see opportunities in the market then so development will continue. That is until such time as tourists demand changes and this is unlikely in the absence of changes in behavioural attitudes and actions on the part of consumers per se.

Certainly consumers can be influenced through regulation (see Jackson, 2008) and, in the very short-term, by events such as food scares but often only briefly unless legislation is introduced, for example, no smoking policies or speed limits on roads. But such regulation has limited influence on attitudes and values even though over time their effect could become greater. This is well illustrated in today's attitudes towards slavery, working conditions and clean air, all of which have been changed for the better through legislation. The key point is that none of these outcomes were achieved through voluntary measures on the part of the owners/managers involved in the 'offending' enterprise.

It has been argued for over 20 years now that market forces 'are not likely to produce a substantial and sustainable reaction to the consumption of finite resources in the short term' (Leslie, 1994, p. 31) nor perhaps more than a small effect on progress towards more sustainable consumption in the future (Cohen and Murphy, 2002). Hence the need for a sustained, focused, coordinated policy to promote and further sustainable production and consumption. Such a step holds substantial implications for consumerism, especially in the high-consumption based economies of post-industrial societies and would 'run up against the entrenched ethos of a consumer society seemingly oblivious to social and ecological costs.' (Mason, 1999, p. 233–234). This may well explain why so little progress has been made in this field in the first 15 years of the 21st century, which is also in no small way due to the limited understanding of 'the influence of policy measures to achieve progress to more sustainable consumption and production' (Tukker et al., 2010a, p. 2). Evidently there is still much work to be done on how to realize change, nowhere more so than in tourism as Holden (2009, p. 384) so well encapsulates:

> In a system that encourages individuality, consumption and freedom of choice, symbolized by the right to travel for recreational purposes, a move towards what may be regarded as a more ascetic lifestyle will pose a major challenge.

The Wider Context

In the wider context, one explanation as to why progress is lacking is the absence of a well-defined, clearly focused policy with a targeted strategy to address these matters. Certainly there are a plethora of policies developed and driven by a cornucopia of government organizations and related agencies but this is in itself also a problem. In the absence of the requisite policy, planning and control there is little to be expected in the way of substantive change in tourism enterprises addressing their EP. As Giddens (2009) well makes the point, the need is for integrated policies to address sustainability with all areas involved thus, for example, including energy and water security and food and therefore the incorporation of environmental policies (Davies, 2009). Furthermore such policies need to be forward looking and require comprehensive and detailed planning. In the absence of this 'and acceptance of what is involved, one is likely to see only continued and often inappropriate development' (Butler, 2007, p. 22) which in this context could be taken as energy and water guzzling eco-chic or ultra-tourism developments (see Leslie, 2012).

To further progress and move forward there is a need for the evolvement of policy pertaining to development to be at least at the regional and maybe more so at the local level – if any real degree of integration across policy, planning and development is to be achieved. But, as exemplified in the case of Clark's (1993) study of Malta's sustainable tourism planning, their lack of success was attributed to a lack of commitment, limited attention to planning (especially forward), inter-departmental conflicts over resources, a lack of co-ordination and a lack of control. Also due care needs to be exercised in such planning as

what has worked well in terms of sustainability in one area may well not automatically work elsewhere (see Teo, 2000; Keil and Desfor, 2003); as illustrated in the two examples discussed in this section. The need is for change away from what may all too often be a re-working of past policy/plans wherein too often process appears more important than outcome, i.e. what is actually achieved rather than any inherent change, and the building of partnerships and recognition of such (Butler, 2007), with an accent on community involvement and planning albeit this requisite is difficult to achieve effectively (see Leslie, 2005; Collins and Ison, 2009).

This is well exemplified in the New Forest District Council's tourism and visitor management strategy 'Our Future Together' (CA, 2001), which gave rise to the acronym VICE – visitor, industry, community, environment. The strategy included the formulation of the equivalent of the GTBS 'Little Acorns'. A bottom up approach was adopted commencing with meetings with local stakeholders and the community. But its success was in no small part due to strong leadership, a local champion, coupled with a clear strategy involving regular visitor research, setting and regularly checking standards of supply, maintaining throughout a close working relationship with all the participants and regular reviews and feedback. This approach is in some ways similar to 'Integrated quality management' of destinations which aims to increase economic activity, employment opportunities and overall the quality of life, thus explicitly involving local people and tourism business (see Denman, 2000). The integration of this approach into an overall and comprehensive policy can lead to addressing with some degree of success problems arising from tourism development. This is demonstrated in the case of Whistler, Canada. As discussed by Williams and Ponsford (2009), the local authority's 'sustainability focused' plans, embedded in their planning framework and processes, involved all stakeholders, leading to a comprehensive sustainable plan including consideration up as well as downstream and a vision for 2020.

In both cases the key factor is the recognition of the differences between policy instruments and building stake-holding through the process in order to address the issues and to achieve the objectives. They also bear witness to the faults endemic in many a 'sustainable tourism policy' – a lack of detail and action (see Farsari *et al.*, 2007). Furthermore, these two examples illustrate the need in each locale for an organization to take forward 'the message'. In effect, a 'champion', respected by the 'tourism community', promoting and supporting a locally based and accredited system if it is to be effective. This system needs to be flexible to accommodate the different categories of, and variances between, tourism enterprises and thus greater cooperation between the organizations involved and the provision of 'hands-on tools for integrating environmental and social concerns in day-to-day business, and establish economic conditions that reward such efforts.' (Von Geibler and Kuhndt, 2002, p. 63).

Until such integration is achieved the reality is that the performance of tourism enterprises in response to sustainability will continue to be very much primarily the outcome of the intrinsic values of their owners. Hence there is all too little to signify further development and progress in addressing and responding proactively to the widening issues of sustainability until all involved accept they have a responsibility for the impacts of their actions on the environment.

Further Reading

For a range of critical insights on politics, policy and tourism see Pleumarom, A. (2012) *The Politics of Tourism, Poverty Reduction and Sustainable Development*. Third World Network, Penang, Malaysia.

For an analysis of global consumption and development see Hone, D and Schmitz, S. (2004) *Facts and Trends to 2050: Energy and Climate Change*. World Business Council on Sustainable Development. Switzerland, August. For further reading on sustainable production and consumption see Tukker, A., Cohen, M.J. Huback, K. and Mout, O. (2010) Sustainable Consumption and Production. Special Edition. *Journal of Industrial Ecology* 14 (1), 1–3.

Recommended for further reading on business practices as well as consumers is Devinney, T.M., Anger, P. and Eckhart, G.M. (2012) *The Myth of the Ethical Consumer*. Cambridge University Press, Cambridge, UK.

References

Adams, W.M. (2001) *Green Development: Environment and Sustainability in the Third World.* 2nd edn. Routledge, Oxford, UK.

Anon. (2009) *Environment Faces Major Threat from 'Eco-apathy' of UK Office Workers.* wiredgov. Available at net/wg/wg-content-1.nsf/vLookupIndustryNewsByD/21? (accessed 27 July 2010).

Bennett, L. (2006) Duty Free? *Resource* July/August, pp. 20–22.

Buckley, R. (2007) Is mass tourism serious about sustainability? *Tourism Recreation Research* 32(3), 70–72.

Butler, R. (1994) Alternative tourism: The thin end of the wedge. In: Smith, V.L. and Eadington, W.R. (eds) (199) *Tourism Alternatives: Potentials and Problems in the Development of Tourism.* Wiley, Chicester, UK, pp. 31–46.

Butler, R. (2007) Destinations – development and redevelopment or visioning and revisioning? In: Smith. M and Onderwater, L. (eds) *Destinations Revisited. Perspectives on Development and Managing Tourist Areas.* ATLAS, Arnhem, the Netherlands, pp. 17–24.

CA (2001) *Sustainable Tourism Management in the New Forest.* The Countryside Agency, Cheltenham, UK.

Cairncross, F. (1995) *Green, Inc.: a guide to business and the environment.* Earthscan, London.

Carter, R.W., Whiley, D. and Knight, C. (2004) Improving environmental performance in the tourism accommodation sector. *Ecotourism* 3 (1), 46–68.

Casserley, T. and Critchley, B. (2010) Personal philosophy. *People Management.* 12 August, pp. 20–24.

Clark, B. (1993) Strategies for sustainable tourism: the proposed Malta demonstration project. Paper presented to Developing Sustainable Tourism, Conference, London Marriott Hotel, May.

Cohen, M.J. and Murphy, J. (eds) (2002) *Exploring Sustainable Consumption: Environmental Policy and the Social Sciences.* Elsevier, Oxford, UK.

Collins, K. and Ison, R. (2009) Jumping of Arnstien's Ladder: Social learning and new policy paradigm for climate change adaptation. *Environmental Policy and Governance* 19, pp. 358–373.

Cooper, C., Muhern, G. and Colley, A. (2010) *Sustainability, the environment and climate change.* Academy of Social Sciences and The British Psychological Society. No 3. London/Leicester, UK.

Davies, A.R. (2009) Does sustainability count? Environmental policy, sustainable development and the governance of grassroots sustainability enterprises in Ireland. *Sustainable Development* 17, pp. 174–182.

DEFRA (2009) *Public Attitudes and Behaviours towards The Environment.* Tracker Survey. Department for Environment Food and Rural Affairs, London, 9 October.

De Lacy, T. and Lipman, G. (2010) Moving to carbon clean destinations. In: Schott, C. (ed.) *Tourism and the implications of climate change: Issues and* actions. Emerald Group, Bingley, UK, pp. 299–312.

Denman, R. (2000) Integrated quality management of rural tourist destinations. In: Barratt, E. (ed.) *Breaking New Ground in Sustainable Tourism.* Cardiff University, Countryside Recreation Network. June, pp. 5–16.

Devinney, T.M., Anger, P. and Eckhart, G.M. (2012) *The Myth of the Ethical Consumer.* Cambridge University Press, Cambridge, UK.

ECORYS (2009) *Study on the competitiveness of the EU tourism industry – with specific focus on the accommodation and tour operators travel agent industries.* Final Report, Directorate-General Enterprise and Industry, European Commission, Brussels.

EEA (2013) *Global Megatrends.* European Environment Agency, Copenhagen, Denmark.

Elkington, J. and Burke, T. (1987) *The Green Capitalists: Industry's search for environmental excellence.* Victor Gollancz, London.

England, R. (2010) Unravelling the psychology of recycling. *Resource* 56 (4), 11–13 November/December.

Ethical Corporation (2010) Social and economic impacts: measurement, evaluation and reporting. *Ethical Corporation.* September.

EU (2004) *Strategy for Integrating the Environment into Industry.* Available at europe.eu.int/scadplus/leg/en/lvb/128093.htm (accessed 5 November 2004).

Farsari. Y., Butler, R. and Prastacos, P. (2007) Sustainable tourism policy for Mediterranean destination: issues and interrelationships. *International Journal of Tourism Policy* 1 (1), 58–78.

Galbraith, K. (1985) *The Affluent Society.* 4th edn. Andre Deutsch, London.

Giddens, A. (2009) *The Politics of Climate Change.* Polity Press, Oxford, UK.

Grobois, D. (2013) Measurement of corporate social performance in tourism. In: Holden, A. and Fennell, D. (2013) *Handbook of Tourism and Environment.* Routledge, New York, pp. 556–566.

Han, H., Hsu, L.-T.J., Lee, J.-S. and Sheu, C. (2011) Are lodging customers ready to go green? An examination of attitudes, demographics, and eco-friendly intentions. *International Journal of Hospitality Management* 30 (2), pp. 345–355.

Hardin, G. (1969) The tragedy of the commons. *Science* 162, pp. 1243–1248.

Henderson, J.C. (2007) Corporate social responsibility and tourism: Hotel companies in Phuket, Thailand, after the Indian Ocean tsunami. *Hospitality Management* 26, pp. 228–239.

Holden, A. (2009) The environment-tourism nexus. *Annals of Tourism Research* 36 (3), 373–389.

Hultsman, J. (1995) Just tourism: an ethical framework. *Annals of Tourism Research* 22 (3), 553–567.

Hunter, C. and Shaw, J. (2007) The ecological footprint as a key indicator of sustainable tourism. *Tourism Management* 28, 46–57.

IEEP (2011) EU natural resources policy: signposts on the roadmap to sustainability. *Directions in European Environmental Policy.* Institute for European Environmental Policy 2 May.

Jackson, T. (2005) *Motivating Sustainable Consumption – a review of evidence on consumer behaviour and behavioural change.* Centre for Environmental Strategy. University of Surrey, Surrey, UK.

Jackson, T. (2008) The challenge of sustainable lifestyles. In: *State of the World 2008.* Innovations for a Sustainable Economy. World Watch Institute, pp. 45–60.

Jackson, T. (2009) *Prosperity Without Growth: The transition to a sustainable economy.* Sustainable Development Commission. London, March.

Jackson, T. and Michaelis, L. (2003) *Policies for Sustainable Consumption.* Sustainable Development Commission. London, October.

Johnston, A.M. (2003) Self-determination: exercising indigenous rights in Tourism. In: Timothy, D.J. and Dowling, R.K. (2003) *Tourism in Destination Communities.* CAB International, Wallingford, UK, pp. 115–134.

Johnston, A.M. (2006) *Is the Sacred Song for Sale? Tourism and Indigenous Peoples.* Earthscan, London.

Keil, R. and Desfor, G. (2003) Ecological modernisation in Los Angeles and Toronto. *Local Environment* 8 (1), 27–44.

Leslie, D. (1994) Sustainable tourism or developing sustainable approaches to lifestyle? *Journal of Leisure and Recreation* 36 (3), 26–33.

Leslie, D. (2002) The influence of UK government agencies on the 'greening' of tourism. *Tourism Today* No. 2 Summer, pp. 95–110.

Leslie, D. (2005) Effective community involvement in the development and sustainability of cultural tourism: an exploration in the case of new Lanark. In: Sigala, M. and Leslie, D. (eds) *International Cultural Tourism: Management, Implications and Cases.* Butterworth-Heinemann, Oxford, UK, pp. 122–136.

Leslie, D. (2011) The European Union, sustainable tourism policy and rural Europe. In: Macleod, D.V.L. and Gillespie, S.A. (eds) *Sustainable Tourism in Rural Europe: Approaches to Development.* Routledge, London, pp. 43–60.

Leslie, D. (ed.) (2012) *Responsible Tourism: Concepts, Theory and Practice.* CAB International, Wallingford, UK.

Leslie, D. and Hughes, G. (1997) Local authorities and tourism in the UK. *International Journal of Managing Leisure* 2 (3), 143–154.

Levett, R. (2001) Sustainable development and capitalism. *Renewal* 9 2/3, pp. 1–9.

Lindholdt, L. (1998) Writing from a sense of place. *Journal of Environmental Education,* pp. 4–10.

Logar, I. (2009) Sustainable tourism management in Crikvenica, Croatia: an assessment of policy instruments. *Tourism Management* 31 (1), pp. 125–135.

Mason, M. (1999) *Environmental Democracy.* Earthscan, London.

Mastny, L. (2002) *Redirecting International Tourism in State of the World.* World Watch Institute. Earthscan, London, pp. 101–124.

Mowforth, M. and Munt, I. (2009) *Tourism and Sustainability: Development, Globalization and New Tourism in the Third World.* 3rd edn. Routledge, London.

Munasinghe, M. (2010) Can sustainable consumers and products save the planet? *Journal of Industrial Ecology* 14 (1), pp. 4–6.

Nash, D. (1989) Tourism as a form of imperialism. In: Smith, V.L. (ed.) *Hosts and Guests: The Anthropology of Tourism.* University of Pennsylvania Press, Philadelphia, Pennsylvania, pp. 37–54.

Osborn, D. (2000) *Economic Instruments 'not too difficult!'* UK Round Table on Sustainable Development, Department of Energy, Transport and the Regions, April, (press release).

Pearce, D.W. (1995) *Blueprint 4. Capturing global environmental value.* Earthscan, London.

Pepper, M. and Nigbur, D. (2005) The psychology of recycling. *Resource* 25, pp. 31–33, July-August.

Pleumarom, A. (2012) *The Politics of Tourism, Poverty Reduction and Sustainable Development.* Third World Network, Penang, Malaysia.

Revell, A. and Blackburn, R. (2004) *UK SMEs and their response to environmental issues.* Small Business Research Centre, Kingston University, London, March.

Roderick, P. (2011) *The Feasibility of Environmental Limits Legislation.* A discussion paper. World Wide Fund for Nature, London.

Saarinen, J., Becker, F. Manwa, H. and Wilson, D. (eds) (2009) *Sustainable Tourism in Southern Africa: Local Commentates and Natural Resources in Transitions.* Channel View, Clevedon, UK.

Southerton, D., McMeekin, A. and Evans, S.D. (2011) *International Review of Behaviourism Change: Initiating Climate Change Behaviours.* Research programme, Scottish Government Social Research, Edinburgh, UK.

Teo, P. (2000) Striking a balance for sustainable tourism: implications of the discourse on globalisation. *Journal of Sustainable Tourism* 10 (6), 459–474.

The Future Laboratory (2010) *Thomson Holidays: Sustainable Holiday Futures.* Report for Thomson Holidays, The Future Laboratory, London.

Thomas, T., Shaw, G. and Page, S.J. (2011) Understanding small firms in tourism: A perspective on research trends and challenges. *Tourism Management* 32 (5), 963–976.

Tukker, A., Cohen, M.J. Huback, K. and Mout, O. (2010a) Editorial: Sustainable Consumption and Production. Special Edition. *Journal of Industrial Ecology* 14 (1), 1–3.

Tukker, A., Cohen, M.J., Huback, K. and Mont, O. (2010b) The impact of household consumption and options for change. Special Edition *Journal of Industrial Ecology* 14 (1), 13–30.

UNEP (2010) *Task Force on Sustainable Lifestyles.* Futerra Sustainability Communications/United Nations Environment Programme, Kenya.

Von Geibler, J. and Kuhndt, M. (2002) *Helping small and not so small businesses improve their triple bottom line performance.* UNEP Industry and Environment, July-December, pp. 63–66.

Weaver, D. (2007) Towards sustainable mass tourism: paradigm shift or paradigm nudge? *Tourism Recreation Research* 32 (3), 65–69.

Williams, P.W. and Ponsford, I.F. (2009) Confronting tourism's environmental paradox: Transitioning for sustainable tourism. *Futures* 41, 396–404.

Wright, M. (2002) Sustainable stufflust. *Green Futures* July/August, pp. 22–26.

Index